The Odyssey of Homer by Homer

Translated by Alexander Pope

Alexander Pope was born on May 21st, 1688 in London into a Catholic family.

His education was affected by the recent Test Acts, upholding the status of the Church of England and banning Catholics from teaching. In effect this meant his formal education was over by the age of 12 and Pope was to now immerse himself in classical literature and languages and to, in effect, educate himself.

From this age too he also suffered from numerous health problems including a type of tuberculosis (Pott's disease) which resulted in a stunted, deformed body. Only to grow to a height of 4' 6", with a severe hunchback and complicated further by respiratory difficulties, high fevers, inflamed eyes and abdominal pain all of which served to further isolate him, initially, from society.

However his talent was evident to all. Best known for his satirical verse, his translations of Homer and the use of the heroic couplet, he is the second-most frequently quoted writer in The Oxford Dictionary of Quotations, after Shakespeare.

With the publication of Pastorals in 1709 followed by An Essay on Criticism (1711) and his most famous work The Rape of the Lock (1712; revised and enlarged in 1714) Pope became not only famous but wealthy.

His translations of the Iliad and the Odyssey further enhanced both reputation and purse. His engagement to produce an opulent new edition of Shakespeare met with a mixed reception. Pope attempted to "regularise" Shakespeare's metre and rewrote some of his verse and cut 1500 lines, that Pope considered to be beneath the Bard's standard, to mere footnotes.

Alexander Pope died on May 30th, 1744 at his villa at Twickenham (where he created his famous grotto and gardens) and was buried in the nave of the nearby Church of England Church of St Mary the Virgin.

Over the years and centuries since his death Pope's work has been in and out of favour but with this distance he is now truly recognised as one of England's greatest poets.

Index of Contents

INTRODUCTION

Scepticism is as much the result of knowledge, as knowledge is of scepticism. To be content with what we at present know, is, for the most part, to shut our ears against conviction; since, from the very gradual character of our education, we must continually forget, and emancipate ourselves from, knowledge previously acquired; we must set aside old notions and embrace fresh ones; and, as we learn, we must be daily unlearning something which it has cost us no small labour and anxiety to acquire.

And this difficulty attaches itself more closely to an age in which progress has gained a strong ascendency over prejudice, and in which persons and things are, day by day, finding their real level, in lieu of their conventional value. The same principles which have swept away traditional abuses, and which are making rapid havoc among the revenues of sinecurists, and stripping the thin, tawdry veil from attractive superstitions, are working as actively in literature as in society. The credulity of one writer, or the partiality of another, finds as powerful a touchstone and as wholesome a chastisement in the healthy scepticism of a temperate class of antagonists, as the dreams of conservatism, or the impostures of pluralist sinecures in the Church. History and tradition, whether of ancient or comparatively recent times, are subjected to very different handling from that which the indulgence or credulity of former ages could allow. Mere statements are jealously watched, and the motives of the writer form as important an ingredient in the analysis or his history, as the facts he records. Probability is a powerful and troublesome test; and it is by this troublesome standard that a large portion of historical evidence is sifted. Consistency is no less pertinacious and exacting in its demands. In brief, to write a history, we must know more than mere facts. Human nature, viewed under an introduction of extended experience, is the best help to the criticism of human history. Historical characters can only be estimated by the standard which human experience, whether actual or traditionary, has furnished. To form correct views of individuals we must regard them as forming parts of a great whole—we must measure them by their relation to the mass of beings by whom they are surrounded; and, in contemplating the incidents in their lives or condition which tradition has handed down to us, we must rather consider the general bearing of the whole narrative, than the respective probability of its details.

It is unfortunate for us, that, of some of the greatest men, we know least, and talk most. Homer, Socrates, and Shakespere have, perhaps, contributed more to the intellectual enlightenment of mankind than any other three writers who could be named, and yet the history of all three has given rise to a boundless ocean of discussion, which has left us little save the option of choosing which theory or theories we will follow. The personality of Shakespere is, perhaps, the only thing in which critics will allow us to believe without controversy; but upon everything else, even down to the authorship of plays, there is more or less of doubt and uncertainty. Of Socrates we know as little as the contradictions of Plato and Xenophon will allow us to know. He was one of the dramatis personae in two dramas as unlike in principles as in style. He appears as the enunciator of opinions as different in their tone as those of the writers who have handed them down. When we have read Plato or Xenophon, we think we know something of Socrates; when we have fairly read and examined both, we feel convinced that we are something worse than ignorant.

It has been an easy, and a popular expedient of late years, to deny the personal or real existence of men and things whose life and condition were too much for our belief. This system—which has often comforted the religious sceptic, and substituted the consolations of Strauss for those of the New Testament has been of incalculable value to the historical theorists of the last and present centuries. To question the existence of Alexander the Great, would be a more excusable act, than to believe in that of Romulus. To deny a fact related in Herodotus, because it is inconsistent with a theory developed from an Assyrian inscription which no two scholars read in the same way, is more pardonable, than to believe in the good-natured old king whom the elegant pen of Florian has idealized—Numa Pompilius.

Scepticism has attained its culminating point with respect to Homer, and the state of our Homeric knowledge may be described as a free permission to believe any theory, provided we throw overboard all written tradition, concerning the author or authors of the Iliad and Odyssey. What few authorities exist on the subject, are summarily dismissed, although the arguments appear to run in a circle. "This cannot be true, because it is not true; and that is not true, because it cannot be true." Such seems to be the style, in which testimony upon testimony, statement upon statement, is consigned to denial and oblivion.

It is, however, unfortunate that the professed biographies of Homer are partly forgeries, partly freaks of ingenuity and imagination, in which truth is the requisite most wanting. Before taking a brief review of the Homeric theory in its present conditions, some notice must be taken of the treatise on the Life of Homer which has been attributed to Herodotus.

According to this document, the city of Cumae in AEolia was, at an early period, the seat of frequent immigrations from various parts of Greece. Among the immigrants was Menapolus, the son of Ithagenes. Although poor, he married, and the result of the union was a girl named Critheis. The girl was left an orphan at an early age, under the guardianship of Cleanax, of Argos. It is to the indiscretion of this maiden that we "are indebted for so much happiness." Homer was the first fruit of her juvenile frailty, and received the name of Melesigenes from having been born near the river Meles in Boeotia, whither Critheis had been transported in order to save her reputation.

"At this time," continues our narrative, "there lived at Smyrna a man named Phemius, a teacher of literature and music, who, not being married, engaged Critheis to manage his household, and spin the flax he received as the price of his scholastic labours. So satisfactory was her performance of this task, and so modest her conduct, that he made proposals of marriage, declaring himself, as a further inducement, willing to adopt her son, who, he asserted, would become a clever man, if he were carefully brought up."

They were married; careful cultivation ripened the talents which nature had bestowed, and Melesigenes soon surpassed his schoolfellows in every attainment, and, when older, rivalled his preceptor in wisdom. Phemius died, leaving him sole heir to his property, and his mother soon followed. Melesigenes carried on his adopted father's school with great success, exciting the admiration not only of the inhabitants of Smyrna, but also of the strangers whom the trade carried on there, especially in the exportation of corn, attracted to that city. Among these visitors, one Mentes, from Leucadia, the modern Santa Maura, who evinced a knowledge and intelligence rarely found in those times, persuaded Melesigenes to close his school, and accompany him on his travels. He promised not only to pay his expenses, but to furnish him with a further stipend, urging, that, "While he was yet young, it was fitting that he should see with his own eyes the countries and cities which might hereafter be the subjects of his discourses." Melesigenes consented, and set out with his patron, "examining all the curiosities of the countries they visited, and informing himself of everything by interrogating those whom he met." We may also suppose, that he wrote memoirs of all that he deemed worthy of preservation. Having set sail from Tyrrhenia and Iberia, they reached Ithaca. Here Melesigenes, who had already suffered in his eyes, became much worse; and Mentes, who was about to leave for Leucadia, left him to the medical superintendence of a friend of his, named Mentor, the son of Alcinor. Under his hospitable and intelligent host, Melesigenes rapidly became acquainted with the legends respecting Ulysses, which afterwards formed the subject of the Odyssey. The inhabitants of Ithaca assert, that it was here that Melesigenes became blind, but the Colophonians make their city the seat of that misfortune. He then returned to Smyrna, where he applied himself to the study of poetry.

But poverty soon drove him to Cumae. Having passed over the Hermaean plain, he arrived at Neon Teichos, the New Wall, a colony of Cumae. Here his misfortunes and poetical talent gained him the friendship of one Tychias, an armourer. "And up to my time," continues the author, "the inhabitants showed the place where he used to sit when giving a recitation of his verses; and they greatly honoured the spot. Here also a poplar grew, which they said had sprung up ever since Melesigenes arrived."

But poverty still drove him on, and he went by way of Larissa, as being the most convenient road. Here, the Cumans say, he composed an epitaph on Gordius, king of Phrygia, which has however, and with greater probability, been attributed to Cleobulus of Lindus.

Arrived at Cumae, he frequented the conversaziones of the old men, and delighted all by the charms of his poetry. Encouraged by this favourable reception, he declared that, if they would allow him a public maintenance, he would render their city most gloriously renowned. They avowed their willingness to support him in the measure he proposed, and procured him an audience in the council. Having made the speech, with the purport of which our author has forgotten to acquaint us, he retired, and left them to debate respecting the answer to be given to his proposal.

The greater part of the assembly seemed favourable to the poet's demand, but one man "observed that if they were to feed Homers, they would be encumbered with a multitude of useless people." "From this circumstance," says the writer, "Melesigenes acquired the name of Homer, for the Cumans call blind men Homers." With a love of economy, which shows how similar the world has always been in its treatment of literary men, the pension was denied, and the poet vented his disappointment in a wish that Cumae might never produce a poet capable of giving it renown and glory.

At Phocaea Homer was destined to experience another literary distress. One Thestorides, who aimed at the reputation of poetical genius, kept Homer in his own house, and allowed him a pittance, on condition of the verses of the poet passing in his name. Having collected sufficient poetry to be profitable, Thestorides, like some would-be literary publishers, neglected the man whose brains he had sucked, and left him. At his departure, Homer is said to have observed: "O Thestorides, of the many things hidden from the knowledge of man, nothing is more unintelligible than the human heart."

Homer continued his career of difficulty and distress, until some Chian merchants, struck by the similarity of the verses they heard him recite, acquainted him with the fact that Thestorides was pursuing a profitable livelihood by the recital of the very same poems. This at once determined him to set out for Chios. No vessel happened then to be setting sail thither, but he found one ready to start for Erythrae, a town of Ionia, which faces that island, and he prevailed upon the seamen to allow him to accompany them. Having embarked, he invoked a favourable wind, and prayed that he might be able to expose the imposture of Thestorides, who, by his breach of hospitality, had drawn down the wrath of Jove the Hospitable.

At Erythrae, Homer fortunately met with a person who had known him in Phocaea, by whose assistance he at length, after some difficulty, reached the little hamlet of Pithys. Here he met with an adventure, which we will continue in the words of our author. "Having set out from Pithys, Homer went on, attracted by the cries of some goats that were pasturing. The dogs barked on his approach, and he cried out. Glaucus (for that was the name of the goat-herd) heard his voice, ran up quickly, called off his dogs, and drove them away from Homer. For some time he stood wondering how a blind man should have reached such a place alone, and what could be his design in coming. He then went up to him and inquired who he was, and how he had come to desolate places and untrodden spots, and of what he stood in need. Homer, by recounting to him the whole history of his misfortunes, moved him with compassion; and he took him and led him to his cot, and, having lit a fire, bade him sup.

"The dogs, instead of eating, kept barking at the stranger, according to their usual habit. Whereupon Homer addressed Glaucus thus: O Glaucus, my friend, prythee attend to my behest. First give the dogs their supper at the doors of the hut: for so it is better, since, whilst they watch, nor thief nor wild beast will approach the fold.

"Glaucus was pleased with the advice and marvelled at its author. Having finished supper, they banqueted afresh on conversation, Homer narrating his wanderings, and telling of the cities he had visited.

"At length they retired to rest; but on the following morning, Glaucus resolved to go to his master, and acquaint him with his meeting with Homer. Having left the goats in charge of a fellow-servant, he left Homer at home, promising to return quickly. Having arrived at Bolissus, a place near the farm, and finding his mate, he told him the whole story respecting Homer and his journey. He paid little attention to what he said, and blamed Glaucus for his stupidity in taking in and feeding maimed and enfeebled persons. However, he bade him bring the stranger to him.

"Glaucus told Homer what had taken place, and bade him follow him, assuring him that good fortune would be the result. Conversation soon showed that the stranger was a man of much cleverness and general knowledge, and the Chian persuaded him to remain, and to undertake the charge of his children."

Besides the satisfaction of driving the impostor Thestorides from the island, Homer enjoyed considerable success as a teacher. In the town of Chios he established a school, where he taught the precepts of poetry. "To this day," says Chandler, "the most curious remain is that which has been named, without reason, the School of Homer. It is on the coast, at some distance from the city, northward, and appears to have been an open temple of Cybele, formed on the top of a rock. The shape is oval, and in the centre is the image of the goddess, the head and an arm wanting. She is represented, as usual, sitting. The chair has a lion carved on each side, and on the back. The area is bounded by a low rim, or seat, and about five yards over. The whole is hewn out of the mountain, is rude, indistinct, and probably of the most remote antiquity."

So successful was this school, that Homer realised a considerable fortune. He married, and had two daughters, one of whom died single, the other married a Chian.

The following passage betrays the same tendency to connect the personages of the poems with the history of the poet, which has already been mentioned:—

"In his poetical compositions Homer displays great gratitude towards Mentor of Ithaca, in the Odyssey, whose name he has inserted in his poem as the companion of Ulysses, in return for the care taken of him when afflicted with blindness. He also testifies his gratitude to Phemius, who had given him both sustenance and instruction."

His celebrity continued to increase, and many persons advised him to visit Greece whither his reputation had now extended. Having, it is said, made some additions to his poems calculated to please the vanity of the Athenians, of whose city he had hitherto made no mention, he set out for Samos. Here, being recognized by a Samian, who had met with him in Chios, he was handsomely received, and invited to join in celebrating the Apaturian festival. He recited some verses, which gave great satisfaction, and by singing the Eiresione at the New Moon festivals, he earned a subsistence, visiting the houses of the rich, with whose children he was very popular.

In the spring he sailed for Athens, and arrived at the island of Ios, now Ino, where he fell extremely ill, and died. It is said that his death arose from vexation, at not having been able to unravel an enigma proposed by some fishermen's children.

Such is, in brief, the substance of the earliest life of Homer we possess, and so broad are the evidences of its historical worthlessness, that it is scarcely necessary to point them out in detail. Let us now consider some of the opinions to which a persevering, patient, and learned—but by no means consistent—series of investigations has led. In doing so, I profess to bring forward statements, not to vouch for their reasonableness or probability.

"Homer appeared. The history of this poet and his works is lost in doubtful obscurity, as is the history of many of the first minds who have done honour to humanity, because they rose amidst darkness. The majestic stream of his song, blessing and fertilizing, flows like the Nile, through many lands and nations; and, like the sources of the Nile, its fountains will ever remain concealed."

Such are the words in which one of the most judicious German critics has eloquently described the uncertainty in which the whole of the Homeric question is involved. With no less truth and feeling he proceeds:—

"It seems here of chief importance to expect no more than the nature of things makes possible. If the period of tradition in history is the region of twilight, we should not expect in it perfect light. The creations of genius always seem like miracles, because they are, for the most part, created far out of the reach of observation. If we were in possession of all the historical testimonies, we never could wholly explain the origin of the Iliad and the Odyssey; for their origin, in all essential points, must have remained the secret of the poet."

From this criticism, which shows as much insight into the depths of human nature as into the minute wire-drawings of scholastic investigation, let us pass on to the main question at issue. Was Homer an individual? or were the Iliad and Odyssey the result of an ingenious arrangement of fragments by earlier poets?

Well has Landor remarked: "Some tell us there were twenty Homers; some deny that there was ever one. It were idle and foolish to shake the contents of a vase, in order to let them settle at last. We are perpetually labouring to destroy our delights, our composure, our devotion to superior power. Of all the animals on earth we least know what is good for us. My opinion is, that what is best for us is our admiration of good. No man living venerates Homer more than I do."

But, greatly as we admire the generous enthusiasm which rests contented with the poetry on which its best impulses had been nurtured and fostered, without seeking to destroy the vividness of first impressions by minute analysis, our editorial office compels us to give some attention to the doubts and difficulties with which the Homeric question is beset, and to entreat our reader, for a brief period, to prefer his judgment to his imagination, and to condescend to dry details. Before, however, entering into particulars respecting the question of this unity of the Homeric poems, (at least of the Iliad,) I must express my sympathy with the sentiments expressed in the following remarks:—

"We cannot but think the universal admiration of its unity by the better, the poetic age of Greece, almost conclusive testimony to its original composition. It was not till the age of the grammarians that its primitive integrity was called in question; nor is it injustice to assert, that the minute and analytical spirit of a grammarian is not the best qualification for the profound feeling, the comprehensive conception of an harmonious whole. The most exquisite anatomist may be no judge of the symmetry of the human frame; and we would take the opinion of Chantrey or Westmacott on the proportions and general beauty of a form, rather than that of Mr. Brodie or Sir Astley Cooper.

"There is some truth, though some malicious exaggeration, in the lines of Pope:—

"'The critic eye—that microscope of wit—
Sees hairs and pores, examines bit by bit;
How parts relate to parts, or they to whole.
The body's harmony, the beaming soul,
Are things which Kuster, Burmann, Wasse, shall see,
When man's whole frame is obvious to a flea.'"

Long was the time which elapsed before any one dreamt of questioning the unity of the authorship of the Homeric poems. The grave and cautious Thucydides quoted without hesitation the Hymn to Apollo, the authenticity of which has been already disclaimed by modern critics. Longinus, in an oft-quoted passage, merely expressed an opinion touching the comparative inferiority of the Odyssey to the Iliad; and, among a mass of ancient authors, whose very names it would be tedious to detail, no suspicion of the personal non-existence of Homer ever arose. So far, the voice of antiquity seems to be in favour of our early ideas on the subject: let us now see what are the discoveries to which more modern investigations lay claim.

At the end of the seventeenth century, doubts had begun to awaken on the subject, and we find Bentley remarking that "Homer wrote a sequel of songs and rhapsodies, to be sung by himself, for small comings and good cheer, at festivals and other days of merriment. These loose songs were not collected together, in the form of an epic poem, till about Peisistratus' time, about five hundred years after."

Two French writers—Hedelin and Perrault—avowed a similar scepticism on the subject; but it is in the "Scienza Nuova" of Battista Vico, that we first meet with the germ of the theory, subsequently defended by Wolf with so much learning and acuteness. Indeed, it is with the Wolfian theory that we have chiefly to deal, and with the following bold hypothesis, which we will detail in the words of Grote:—

"Half a century ago, the acute and valuable Prolegomena of F. A. Wolf, turning to account the Venetian Scholia, which had then been recently published, first opened philosophical discussion as to the history of the Homeric text. A considerable part of that dissertation (though by no means the whole) is employed in vindicating the position, previously announced by Bentley, amongst others, that the separate constituent portions of the Iliad and Odyssey had not been cemented together into any compact body and unchangeable order, until the days of Peisistratus, in the sixth century before Christ. As a step towards that conclusion, Wolf maintained that no written copies of either poem could be shown to have existed during the earlier times, to which their composition is referred; and that without writing, neither the perfect symmetry of so complicated a work could have been originally conceived by any poet, nor, if realized by him, transmitted with assurance to posterity. The absence of easy and convenient writing, such as must be indispensably supposed for long manuscripts, among the early Greeks, was thus one of the points in Wolf's case against the primitive integrity of the Iliad and Odyssey. By Nitzsch, and other leading opponents of Wolf, the connection of the one with the other seems to have been accepted as he originally put it; and it has been considered incumbent on those who defended the ancient aggregate character of the Iliad and Odyssey, to maintain that they were written poems from the beginning.

"To me it appears, that the architectonic functions ascribed by Wolf to Peisistratus and his associates, in reference to the Homeric poems, are nowise admissible. But much would undoubtedly be gained towards that view of the question, if it could be shown, that, in order to controvert it, we were driven to the necessity of admitting long written poems, in the ninth century before the Christian aera. Few things, in my opinion, can be more improbable; and Mr. Payne Knight, opposed as he is to the Wolfian hypothesis, admits this no less than Wolf himself. The traces of writing in Greece, even in the seventh century before the Christian aera, are exceedingly trifling. We have no remaining inscription earlier than the fortieth Olympiad, and the early inscriptions are rude and unskilfully executed; nor can we even assure ourselves whether Archilochus, Simonides of Amorgus, Kallinus Tyrtaeus, Xanthus, and the other early elegiac and lyric poets, committed their compositions to writing, or at what time the practice of doing so became familiar. The first positive ground which authorizes us to presume the existence of a manuscript of Homer, is in the famous ordinance of Solon, with regard to the rhapsodies at the Panathenaea: but for what length of time previously manuscripts had existed, we are unable to say.

"Those who maintain the Homeric poems to have been written from the beginning, rest their case, not upon positive proofs, nor yet upon the existing habits of society with regard to poetry—for they admit generally that the Iliad and Odyssey were not read, but recited and heard,—but upon the supposed necessity that there must have been manuscripts to ensure the preservation of the poems—the unassisted memory of reciters being neither sufficient nor trustworthy. But here we only escape a smaller difficulty by running into a greater; for the existence of trained bards, gifted with extraordinary memory, is far less astonishing than that of long manuscripts, in an age essentially non-reading and non-writing, and when even suitable instruments and materials for the process are not obvious. Moreover, there is a strong positive reason for believing that the bard was under no necessity of refreshing his memory by consulting a manuscript; for if such had been the fact, blindness would have been a disqualification for the profession, which we know that it was not, as well from the example of Demodokus, in the Odyssey, as from that of the blind bard of Chios, in the Hymn to the Delian Apollo, whom Thucydides, as well as the general tenor of Grecian legend, identifies with Homer himself. The author of that hymn, be he who he may, could never have described a blind man as attaining the utmost perfection in his art, if he had been conscious that the memory of the bard was only maintained by constant reference to the manuscript in his chest."

The loss of the digamma, that crux of critics, that quicksand upon which even the acumen of Bentley was shipwrecked, seems to prove beyond a doubt, that the pronunciation of the Greek language had undergone a considerable change. Now it is certainly difficult to suppose that the Homeric poems could have suffered by this change, had written copies been preserved. If Chaucer's poetry, for instance, had not been written, it could only have come down to us in a softened form, more like the effeminate version of Dryden, than the rough, quaint, noble original. "At what period," continues Grote, "these poems, or indeed any other Greek poems, first began to be written, must be matter of conjecture, though there is ground for assurance that it was before the time of Solon. If, in the absence of evidence, we may venture upon naming any more determinate period, the question at once suggests itself, What were the purposes which, in that state of society, a manuscript at its first commencement must have been intended to answer? For whom was a written Iliad necessary? Not for the rhapsodes; for with them it was not only planted in the memory, but also interwoven with the feelings, and conceived in conjunction with all those flexions and intonations of voice, pauses, and other oral artifices which were required for emphatic delivery, and which the naked manuscript could never reproduce. Not for the general public—they were accustomed to receive it with its rhapsodic delivery, and with its accompaniments of a solemn and crowded festival. The only persons for whom the written Iliad would be suitable would be a select few; studious and curious men; a class of readers capable of analyzing the complicated emotions which they had experienced as hearers in the crowd, and who would, on perusing the written words, realize in their imaginations a sensible portion of the impression communicated by the reciter. Incredible as the statement may seem in an age like the present, there is in all early societies, and there was in early Greece, a time when no such reading class existed. If we could discover at what time such a class first began to be formed, we should be able to make a guess at the time when the old epic poems were first committed to writing. Now the period which may with the greatest probability be fixed upon as having first witnessed the formation even of the narrowest reading class in Greece, is the middle of the seventh century before the Christian aera (B.C. 660 to B.C. 630), the age of Terpander, Kallinus, Archilochus, Simenides of Amorgus, &c. I ground this supposition on the change then operated in the character and tendencies of Grecian poetry and music—the elegiac and the iambic measures having been introduced as rivals to the primitive hexameter, and poetical compositions having been transferred from the epical past to the affairs of present and real life. Such a change was important at a time when poetry was the only known mode of publication (to use a modern phrase not altogether suitable, yet the nearest approaching to the sense). It argued a new way of looking at the old epical treasures of the people, as well as a thirst for new poetical effect; and the men who stood forward in it may well be considered as desirous to study, and competent to criticize, from their own individual point of view, the written words of the Homeric rhapsodies, just as we are told that Kallinus both noticed and eulogized the Thebais as the production of Homer. There seems, therefore, ground for conjecturing that (for the use of this newly-formed and important, but very narrow class), manuscripts of the Homeric poems and other old epics,—the Thebais and the Cypria, as well as the Iliad and the Odyssey,—began to be compiled towards the middle of the seventh century B.C. I; and the opening of Egypt to Grecian commerce, which took place about the same period, would furnish increased facilities for obtaining the requisite papyrus to write upon. A reading class, when once formed, would doubtless slowly increase, and the number of manuscripts along with it: so that before the time of Solon, fifty years afterwards, both readers and manuscripts, though still comparatively few, might have attained a certain recognized authority, and formed a tribunal of reference against the carelessness of individual rhapsodies."

But even Peisistratus has not been suffered to remain in possession of the credit, and we cannot help feeling the force of the following observations:—

"There are several incidental circumstances which, in our opinion, throw some suspicion over the whole history of the Peisistratid compilation, at least over the theory that the Iliad was cast into its present stately and harmonious form by the directions of the Athenian ruler. If the great poets, who flourished at the bright period of Grecian song, of which, alas! we have inherited little more than the fame, and the faint echo; if Stesichorus, Anacreon, and Simonides were employed in the noble task of compiling the Iliad and Odyssey, so much must have been done to arrange, to connect, to harmonize, that it is almost incredible that stronger marks of Athenian manufacture should not remain. Whatever occasional anomalies may be detected, anomalies which no doubt arise out of our own ignorance of the language of the Homeric age; however the irregular use of the digamma may have perplexed our Bentleys, to whom the name of Helen is said to have caused as much disquiet and distress as the fair one herself among the heroes of her age; however Mr. Knight may have failed in reducing the Homeric language to its primitive form; however, finally, the Attic dialect may not have assumed all its more marked and distinguishing characteristics:—still it is difficult to suppose that the language, particularly in the joinings and transitions, and connecting parts, should not more clearly betray the incongruity between the more ancient and modern forms of expression. It is not quite in character with such a period to imitate an antique style, in order to piece out an imperfect poem in the character of the original, as Sir Walter Scott has done in his continuation of Sir Tristram.

"If, however, not even such faint and indistinct traces of Athenian compilation are discoverable in the language of the poems, the total absence of Athenian national feeling is perhaps no less worthy of observation. In later, and it may fairly be suspected in earlier times, the Athenians were more than ordinarily jealous of the fame of their ancestors. But, amid all the traditions of the glories of early Greece embodied in the Iliad, the Athenians play a most subordinate and insignificant part. Even the few passages which relate to their ancestors, Mr. Knight suspects to be interpolations. It is possible, indeed, that in its leading outline, the Iliad may be true to historic fact; that in the great maritime expedition of western Greece against the rival and half-kindred empire of the Laomedontiadae, the chieftain of Thessaly, from his valour and the number of his forces, may have been the most important ally of the Peloponnesian sovereign: the pre-eminent value of the ancient poetry on the Trojan war may thus have forced the national feeling of the Athenians to yield to their taste. The songs which spoke of their own great ancestor were, no doubt, of far inferior sublimity and popularity, or, at first sight, a Theseid would have been much more likely to have emanated from an Athenian synod of compilers of ancient song, than an Achilleid or an Odysseid. Could France have given birth to a Tasso, Tancred would have been the hero of the Jerusalem. If, however, the Homeric ballads, as they are sometimes called, which related the wrath of Achilles, with all its direful consequences, were so far superior to the rest of the poetic cycle, as to admit no rivalry,—it is still surprising, that throughout the whole poem the callida junctura should never betray the workmanship of an Athenian hand; and that the national spirit of a race, who have at a later period not inaptly been compared to our self-admiring neighbours, the French, should submit with lofty self-denial to the almost total exclusion of their own ancestors—or, at least, to the questionable dignity of only having produced a leader tolerably skilled in the military tactics of his age."

To return to the Wolfian theory. While it is to be confessed, that Wolf's objections to the primitive integrity of the Iliad and Odyssey have never been wholly got over, we cannot help discovering that they have failed to enlighten us as to any substantial point, and that the difficulties with which the whole subject is beset, are rather augmented than otherwise, if we admit his hypothesis. Nor is Lachmann's modification of his theory any better. He divides the first twenty-two books of the Iliad into sixteen different songs, and treats as ridiculous the belief that their amalgamation into one regular poem belongs to a period earlier than the age of Peisistratus. This as Grote observes, "ex-plains the gaps and contradictions in the narrative, but it explains nothing else." Moreover, we find no contradictions warranting this belief, and the so-called sixteen poets concur in getting rid of the following leading men in the first battle after the secession of Achilles: Elphenor, chief of the Euboeans; Tlepolemus, of the Rhodians; Pandarus, of the Lycians; Odins, of the Halizonians: Pirous and Acamas, of the Thracians. None of these heroes again make their appearance, and we can but agree with Colonel Mure, that "it seems strange that any number of independent poets should have so harmoniously dispensed with the services of all six in the sequel." The discrepancy, by which Pylaemenes, who is represented as dead in the fifth book, weeps at his son's funeral in the thirteenth, can only be regarded as the result of an interpolation.

Grote, although not very distinct in stating his own opinions on the subject, has done much to clearly show the incongruity of the Wolfian theory, and of Lachmann's modifications, with the character of Peisistratus. But he has also shown, and we think with equal success, that the two questions relative to the primitive unity of these poems, or, supposing that impossible, the unison of these parts by Peisistratus, and not before his time, are essentially distinct. In short, "a man may believe the Iliad to have been put together out of pre-existing songs, without recognising the age of Peisistratus as the period of its first compilation." The friends or literary /employes/ of Peisistratus must have found an Iliad that was already ancient, and the silence of the Alexandrine critics respecting the Peisistratic "recension," goes far to prove, that, among the numerous manuscripts they examined, this was either wanting, or thought unworthy of attention.

"Moreover," he continues, "the whole tenor of the poems themselves confirms what is here remarked. There is nothing, either in the Iliad or Odyssey, which savours of modernism, applying that term to the age of Peisistratus—nothing which brings to our view the alterations brought about by two centuries, in the Greek language, the coined money, the habits of writing and reading, the despotisms and republican governments, the close military array, the improved construction of ships, the Amphiktyonic convocations, the mutual frequentation of religious festivals, the Oriental and Egyptian veins of religion, &c., familiar to the latter epoch. These alterations Onomakritus, and the other literary friends of Peisistratus, could hardly have failed to notice, even without design, had they then, for the first time, undertaken the task of piecing together many self-existent epics into one large aggregate. Everything in the two great Homeric poems, both in substance and in language, belongs to an age two or three centuries earlier than Peisistratus. Indeed, even the interpolations (or those passages which, on the best grounds, are pronounced to be such) betray no trace of the sixth century before Christ, and may well have been heard by Archilochus and Kallinus—in some cases even by Arktinus and Hesiod—as genuine Homeric matter. As far as the evidences on the case, as well internal as external, enable us to judge, we seem warranted in believing that the Iliad and Odyssey were recited substantially as they now stand (always allowing for partial divergences of text and interpolations) in 776 B.C., our first trustworthy mark of Grecian time; and this ancient date, let it be added, as it is the best-authenticated fact, so it is also the most important attribute of the Homeric poems, considered in reference to Grecian history; for they thus afford us an insight into the anti-historical character of the Greeks, enabling us to trace the subsequent forward march of the nation, and to seize instructive contrasts between their former and their later condition."

On the whole, I am inclined to believe, that the labours of Peisistratus were wholly of an editorial character, although I must confess that I can lay down nothing respecting the extent of his labours. At the same time, so far from believing that the composition or primary arrangement of these poems, in their present form, was the work of Peisistratus, I am rather persuaded that the fine taste and elegant, mind of that Athenian would lead him to preserve an ancient and traditional order of the poems, rather than to patch and reconstruct them according to a fanciful hypothesis. I will not repeat the many discussions respecting whether the poems were written or not, or whether the art of writing was known in the time of their reputed author. Suffice it to say, that the more we read, the less satisfied we are upon either subject.

I cannot, however, help thinking, that the story which attributes the preservation of these poems to Lycurgus, is little else than a version of the same story as that of Peisistratus, while its historical probability must be measured by that of many others relating to the Spartan Confucius.

I will conclude this sketch of the Homeric theories with an attempt, made by an ingenious friend, to unite them into something like consistency. It is as follows:—

"No doubt the common soldiers of that age had, like the common sailors of some fifty years ago, some one qualified to 'discourse in excellent music' among them. Many of these, like those of the negroes in the United States, were extemporaneous, and allusive to events passing around them. But what was passing around them? The grand events of a spirit-stirring war; occurrences likely to impress themselves, as the mystical legends of former times had done, upon their memory; besides which, a retentive memory was deemed a virtue of the first water, and was cultivated accordingly in those ancient times. Ballads at first, and down to the beginning of the war with Troy, were merely recitations, with an intonation. Then followed a species of recitative, probably with an intoned burden. Tune next followed, as it aided the memory considerably.

"It was at this period, about four hundred years after the war, that a poet flourished of the name of Melesigenes, or Moeonides, but most probably the former. He saw that these ballads might be made of great utility to his purpose of writing a poem on the social position of Hellas, and, as a collection, he published these lays connecting them by a tale of his own. This poem now exists, under the title of the 'Odyssea.' The author, however, did not affix his own name to the poem, which, in fact, was, great part of it, remodelled from the archaic dialect of Crete, in which tongue the ballads were found by him. He therefore called it the poem of Homeros, or the Collector; but this is rather a proof of his modesty and talent, than of his mere drudging arrangement of other people's ideas; for, as Grote has finely observed, arguing for the unity of authorship, 'a great poet might have re-cast pre-existing separate songs into one comprehensive whole; but no mere arrangers or compilers would be competent to do so.'

"While employed on the wild legend of Odysseus, he met with a ballad, recording the quarrel of Achilles and Agamemnon. His noble mind seized the hint that there presented itself, and the Achilleis grew under his hand. Unity of design, however, caused him to publish the poem under the same pseudonyme as his former work; and the disjointed lays of the ancient bards were joined together, like those relating to the Cid, into a chronicle history, named the Iliad. Melesigenes knew that the poem was destined to be a lasting one, and so it has proved; but, first, the poems were destined to undergo many vicissitudes and corruptions, by the people who took to singing them in the streets, assemblies, and agoras. However, Solon first, and then Peisistratus, and afterwards Aristoteles and others, revised the poems, and restored the works of Melesigenes Homeros to their original integrity in a great measure."

Having thus given some general notion of the strange theories which have developed themselves respecting this most interesting subject, I must still express my conviction as to the unity of the authorship of the Homeric poems. To deny that many corruptions and interpolations disfigure them, and that the intrusive hand of the poetasters may here and there have inflicted a wound more serious than the negligence of the copyist, would be an absurd and captious assumption; but it is to a higher criticism that we must appeal, if we would either understand or enjoy these poems. In maintaining the authenticity and personality of their one author, be he Homer or Melesigenes, /quocunque nomine vocari eum jus fasque sit/, I feel conscious that, while the whole weight of historical evidence is against the hypothesis which would assign these great works to a plurality of authors, the most powerful internal evidence, and that which springs from the deepest and most immediate impulse of the soul, also speaks eloquently to the contrary.

The minutiae of verbal criticism I am far from seeking to despise. Indeed, considering the character of some of my own books, such an attempt would be gross inconsistency. But, while I appreciate its importance in a philological view, I am inclined to set little store on its aesthetic value, especially in poetry. Three parts of the emendations made upon poets are mere alterations, some of which, had they been suggested to the author by his Maecenas or Africanus, he would probably have adopted. Moreover, those who are most exact in laying down rules of verbal criticism and interpretation, are often least competent to carry out their own precepts. Grammarians are not poets by profession, but may be so per accidens. I do not at this moment remember two emendations on Homer, calculated to substantially improve the poetry of a passage, although a mass of remarks, from Herodotus down to Loewe, have given us the history of a thousand minute points, without which our Greek knowledge would be gloomy and jejune.

But it is not on words only that grammarians, mere grammarians, will exercise their elaborate and often tiresome ingenuity. Binding down an heroic or dramatic poet to the block upon which they have previously dissected his words and sentences, they proceed to use the axe and the pruning knife by wholesale; and, inconsistent in everything but their wish to make out a case of unlawful affiliation, they cut out book after book, passage after passage, till the author is reduced to a collection of fragments, or till those who fancied they possessed the works of some great man, find that they have been put off with a vile counterfeit got up at second hand. If we compare the theories of Knight, Wolf, Lachmann; and others, we shall feel better satisfied of the utter uncertainty of criticism than of the apocryphal position of Homer. One rejects what another considers the turning-point of his theory. One cuts a supposed knot by expunging what another would explain by omitting something else.

Nor is this morbid species of sagacity by any means to be looked upon as a literary novelty. Justus Lipsius, a scholar of no ordinary skill, seems to revel in the imaginary discovery, that the tragedies attributed to Seneca are by four different authors. Now, I will venture to assert, that these tragedies are so uniform, not only in their borrowed phraseology—a phraseology with which writers like Boethius and Saxo Grammaticus were more charmed than ourselves—in their freedom from real poetry, and last, but not least, in an ultra-refined and consistent abandonment of good taste, that few writers of the present day would question the capabilities of the same gentleman, be he Seneca or not, to produce not only these, but a great many more equally bad. With equal sagacity, Father Hardouin astonished the world with the startling announcement that the AEneid of Virgil, and the satires of Horace, were literary deceptions. Now, without wishing to say one word of disrespect against the industry and learning—nay, the refined acuteness—which scholars like Wolf have bestowed upon this subject, I must express my fears, that many of our modern Homeric theories will become matter for the surprise and entertainment, rather than the instruction, of posterity. Nor can I help thinking that the literary history of more recent times will account for many points of difficulty in the transmission of the Iliad and Odyssey to a period so remote from that of their first creation.

I have already expressed my belief that the labours of Peisistratus were of a purely editorial character; and there seems no more reason why corrupt and imperfect editions of Homer may not have been abroad in his day, than that the poems of Valerius Flaccus and Tibullus should have given so much trouble to Poggio, Scaliger, and others. But, after all, the main fault in all the Homeric theories is, that they demand too great a sacrifice of those feelings to which poetry most powerfully appeals, and which are its most fitting judges. The ingenuity which has sought to rob us of the name and existence of Homer, does too much violence to that inward emotion, which makes our whole soul yearn with love and admiration for the blind bard of Chios. To believe the author of the Iliad a mere compiler, is to degrade the powers of human invention; to elevate analytical judgment at the expense of the most ennobling impulses of the soul; and to forget the ocean in the contemplation of a polypus. There is a catholicity, so to speak, in the very name of Homer. Our faith in the author of the Iliad may be a mistaken one, but as yet nobody has taught us a better.

While, however, I look upon the belief in Homer as one that has nature herself for its mainspring; while I can join with old Ennius in believing in Homer as the ghost, who, like some patron saint, hovers round the bed of the poet, and even bestows rare gifts from that wealth of imagination which a host of imitators could not exhaust,—still I am far from wishing to deny that the author of these great poems found a rich fund of tradition, a well-stocked mythical storehouse, from whence he might derive both subject and embellishment. But it is one thing to use existing romances in the embellishment of a poem, another to patch up the poem itself from such materials. What consistency of style and execution can be hoped for from such an attempt? or, rather, what bad taste and tedium will not be the infallible result?

A blending of popular legends, and a free use of the songs of other bards, are features perfectly consistent with poetical originality. In fact, the most original writer is still drawing upon outward impressions—nay, even his own thoughts are a kind of secondary agents which support and feed the impulses of imagination. But unless there be some grand pervading principle—some invisible, yet most distinctly stamped archetypus of the great whole, a poem like the Iliad can never come to the birth. Traditions the most picturesque, episodes the most pathetic, local associations teeming with the thoughts of gods and great men, may crowd in one mighty vision, or reveal themselves in more substantial forms to the mind of the poet; but, except the power to create a grand whole, to which these shall be but as details and embellishments, be present, we shall have nought but a scrap-book, a parterre filled with flowers and weeds strangling each other in their wild redundancy; we shall have a cento of rags and tatters, which will require little acuteness to detect.

Sensible as I am of the difficulty of disproving a negative, and aware as I must be of the weighty grounds there are for opposing my belief, it still seems to me that the Homeric question is one that is reserved for a higher criticism than it has often obtained. We are not by nature intended to know all things; still less, to compass the powers by which the greatest blessings of life have been placed at our disposal. Were faith no virtue, then we might indeed wonder why God willed our ignorance on any matter. But we are too well taught the contrary lesson; and it seems as though our faith should be especially tried, touching the men and the events which have wrought most influence upon the condition of humanity. And there is a kind of sacredness attached to the memory of the great and the good, which seems to bid us repulse the scepticism which would allegorize their existence into a pleasing apologue, and measure the giants of intellect by an homaeopathic dynameter.

Long and habitual reading of Homer appears to familiarize our thoughts even to his incongruities; or rather, if we read in a right spirit and with a heartfelt appreciation, we are too much dazzled, too deeply wrapped in admiration of the whole, to dwell upon the minute spots which mere analysis can discover. In reading an heroic poem, we must transform ourselves into heroes of the time being, we must in imagination must fight over the same battles, woo the same loves, burn with the same sense of injury, as an Achilles or a Hector. And if we can but attain this degree of enthusiasm (and less enthusiasm will scarcely suffice for the reading of Homer), we shall feel that the poems of Homer are not only the work of one writer, but of the greatest writer that ever touched the hearts of men by the power of song.

And it was this supposed unity of authorship which gave these poems their powerful influence over the minds of the men of old. Heeren, who is evidently little disposed in favour of modern theories, finely observes:—

"It was Homer who formed the character of the Greek nation. No poet has ever, as a poet, exercised a similar influence over his countrymen. Prophets, lawgivers, and sages have formed the character of other nations; it was reserved to a poet to form that of the Greeks. This is a feature in their character which was not wholly erased even in the period of their degeneracy. When lawgivers and sages appeared in Greece, the work of the poet had already been accomplished; and they paid homage to his superior genius. He held up before his nation the mirror in which they were to behold the world of gods and heroes, no less than of feeble mortals, and to behold them reflected with purity and truth. His poems are founded on the first feeling of human nature; on the love of children, wife, and country; on that passion which outweighs all others, the love of glory. His songs were poured forth from a breast which sympathized with all the feelings of man; and therefore they enter, and will continue to enter, every breast which cherishes the same sympathies. If it is granted to his immortal spirit, from another heaven than any of which he dreamed on earth, to look down on his race, to see the nations from the fields of Asia, to the forests of Hercynia, performing pilgrimages to the fountain which his magic wand caused to flow; if it is permitted to him to view the vast assemblage of grand, of elevated, of glorious productions, which had been called into being by means of his songs; wherever his immortal spirit may reside, this alone would suffice to complete his happiness."

Can we contemplate that ancient monument, on which the "Apotheosis of Homer" is depictured, and not feel how much of pleasing association, how much that appeals most forcibly and most distinctly to our minds, is lost by the admittance of any theory but our old tradition? The more we read, and the more we think—think as becomes the readers of Homer,—the more rooted becomes the conviction that the Father of Poetry gave us this rich inheritance, whole and entire. Whatever were the means of its preservation, let us rather be thankful for the treasury of taste and eloquence thus laid open to our use, than seek to make it a mere centre around which to drive a series of theories, whose wildness is only equalled by their inconsistency with each other.

As the hymns, and some other poems usually ascribed to Homer, are not included in Pope's translation, I will content myself with a brief account of the Battle of the Frogs and Mice, from the pen of a writer who has done it full justice:—

"This poem," says Coleridge, "is a short mock-heroic of ancient date. The text varies in different editions, and is obviously disturbed and corrupt to a great degree; it is commonly said to have been a juvenile essay of Homer's genius; others have attributed it to the same Pigrees mentioned above, and whose reputation for humour seems to have invited the appropriation of any piece of ancient wit, the author of which was uncertain; so little did the Greeks, before the age of the Ptolemies, know or care about that department of criticism employed in determining the genuineness of ancient writings. As to this little poem being a youthful prolusion of Homer, it seems sufficient to say that from the beginning to the end, it is a plain and palpable parody, not only of the general spirit, but of numerous passages of the Iliad itself; and, even if no such intention to parody were discernible in it, the objection would still remain, that to suppose a work of mere burlesque to be the primary effort of poetry in a simple age, seems to reverse that order in the development of national taste, which the history of every other people in Europe, and of many in Asia, has almost ascertained to be a law of the human mind; it is in a state of society much more refined and permanent than that described in the Iliad, that any popularity would attend such a ridicule of war and the gods as is contained in this poem; and the fact of there having existed three other poems of the same kind attributed, for aught we can see, with as much reason to Homer, is a strong inducement to believe that none of them were of the Homeric age. Knight infers from the usage of the word /deltoz/, 'writing tablet,' instead of /diphthera/, 'skin,' which, according to Herod 5, 58, was the material employed by the Asiatic Greeks for that purpose, that this poem was another offspring of Attic ingenuity; and generally that the familiar mention of the cock (v. 191) is a strong argument against so ancient a date for its composition."

Having thus given a brief account of the poems comprised in Pope's design, I will now proceed to make a few remarks on his translation, and on my own purpose in the present edition.

Pope was not a Grecian. His whole education had been irregular, and his earliest acquaintance with the poet was through the version of Ogilby. It is not too much to say that his whole work bears the impress of a disposition to be satisfied with the general sense, rather than to dive deeply into the minute and delicate features of language. Hence his whole work is to be looked upon rather as an elegant paraphrase than a translation. There are, to be sure, certain conventional anecdotes, which prove that Pope consulted various friends, whose classical attainments were sounder than his own, during the undertaking; but it is probable that these examinations were the result rather of the contradictory versions already existing, than of a desire to make a perfect transcript of the original. And in those days, what is called literal translation was less cultivated than at present. If something like the general sense could be decorated with the easy gracefulness of a practised poet; if the charms of metrical cadence and a pleasing fluency could be made consistent with a fair interpretation of the poet's meaning, his words were less jealously sought for, and those who could read so good a poem as Pope's Iliad had fair reason to be satisfied.

It would be absurd, therefore, to test Pope's translation by our own advancing knowledge of the original text. We must be content to look at it as a most delightful work in itself,—a work which is as much a part of English literature as Homer himself is of Greek. We must not be torn from our kindly associations with the old Iliad, that once was our most cherished companion, or our most looked-for prize, merely because Buttmann, Loewe, and Liddell have made us so much more accurate as to /amphikipellon/ being an adjective, and not a substantive. Far be it from us to defend the faults of Pope, especially when we think of Chapman's fine, bold, rough old English;—far be it from us to hold up his translation as what a translation of Homer might be. But we can still dismiss Pope's Iliad to the hands of our readers, with the consciousness that they must have read a very great number of books before they have read its fellow.

THEODORE ALOIS BUCKLEY.
Christ Church

THE ODYSSEY OF HOMER

BOOK I

ARGUMENT

MINERVA'S DESCENT TO ITHACA

The poem opens within forty eight days of the arrival of Ulysses in his dominions. He had now remained seven years in the Island of Calypso, when the gods assembled in council, proposed the method of his departure from thence and his return to his native country. For this purpose it is concluded to send Mercury to Calypso, and Pallas immediately descends to Ithaca. She holds a conference with Telemachus, in the shape of Mantes, king of Taphians; in which she advises him to take a journey in quest of his father Ulysses, to Pylos and Sparta, where Nestor and Menelaus yet reigned; then, after having visibly displayed her divinity, disappears. The suitors of Penelope make great entertainments, and riot in her palace till night. Phemius sings to them the return of the Grecians, till Penelope puts a stop to the song. Some words arise between the suitors and Telemachus, who summons the council to meet the day following.

The man for wisdom's various arts renown'd,
Long exercised in woes, O Muse! resound;
Who, when his arms had wrought the destined fall
Of sacred Troy, and razed her heaven-built wall,
Wandering from clime to clime, observant stray'd,
Their manners noted, and their states survey'd,
On stormy seas unnumber'd toils he bore,
Safe with his friends to gain his natal shore:
Vain toils! their impious folly dared to prey
On herds devoted to the god of day;

The god vindictive doom'd them never more
(Ah, men unbless'd!) to touch that natal shore.
Oh, snatch some portion of these acts from fate,
Celestial Muse! and to our world relate.

Now at their native realms the Greeks arrived;
All who the wars of ten long years survived;
And 'scaped the perils of the gulfy main.
Ulysses, sole of all the victor train,
An exile from his dear paternal coast,
Deplored his absent queen and empire lost.
Calypso in her caves constrain'd his stay,
With sweet, reluctant, amorous delay;
In vain-for now the circling years disclose
The day predestined to reward his woes.
At length his Ithaca is given by fate,
Where yet new labours his arrival wait;
At length their rage the hostile powers restrain,
All but the ruthless monarch of the main.
But now the god, remote, a heavenly guest,
In AEthiopia graced the genial feast
(A race divided, whom with sloping rays
The rising and descending sun surveys);
There on the world's extremest verge revered
With hecatombs and prayer in pomp preferr'd,
Distant he lay: while in the bright abodes
Of high Olympus, Jove convened the gods:
The assembly thus the sire supreme address'd,
AEgysthus' fate revolving in his breast,
Whom young Orestes to the dreary coast
Of Pluto sent, a blood-polluted ghost.

"Perverse mankind! whose wills, created free,
Charge all their woes on absolute degree;
All to the dooming gods their guilt translate,
And follies are miscall'd the crimes of fate.
When to his lust AEgysthus gave the rein,
Did fate, or we, the adulterous act constrain?
Did fate, or we, when great Atrides died,
Urge the bold traitor to the regicide?
Hermes I sent, while yet his soul remain'd
Sincere from royal blood, and faith profaned;
To warn the wretch, that young Orestes, grown
To manly years, should re-assert the throne.
Yet, impotent of mind, and uncontroll'd,
He plunged into the gulf which Heaven foretold."

Here paused the god; and pensive thus replies

Minerva, graceful with her azure eyes:

"O thou! from whom the whole creation springs,
The source of power on earth derived to kings!
His death was equal to the direful deed;
So may the man of blood be doomed to bleed!
But grief and rage alternate wound my breast
For brave Ulysses, still by fate oppress'd.
Amidst an isle, around whose rocky shore
The forests murmur, and the surges roar,
The blameless hero from his wish'd-for home
A goddess guards in her enchanted dome;
(Atlas her sire, to whose far-piercing eye
The wonders of the deep expanded lie;
The eternal columns which on earth he rears
End in the starry vault, and prop the spheres).
By his fair daughter is the chief confined,
Who soothes to dear delight his anxious mind;
Successless all her soft caresses prove,
To banish from his breast his country's love;
To see the smoke from his loved palace rise,
While the dear isle in distant prospect lies,
With what contentment could he close his eyes!
And will Omnipotence neglect to save
The suffering virtue of the wise and brave?
Must he, whose altars on the Phrygian shore
With frequent rites, and pure, avow'd thy power,
Be doom'd the worst of human ills to prove,
Unbless'd, abandon'd to the wrath of Jove?"

"Daughter! what words have pass'd thy lips unweigh'd!
(Replied the Thunderer to the martial maid;)
Deem not unjustly by my doom oppress'd,
Of human race the wisest and the best.
Neptune, by prayer repentant rarely won,
Afflicts the chief, to avenge his giant son,
Whose visual orb Ulysses robb'd of light;
Great Polypheme, of more than mortal might?
Him young Thousa bore (the bright increase
Of Phorcys, dreaded in the sounds and seas);
Whom Neptune eyed with bloom of beauty bless'd,
And in his cave the yielding nymph compress'd
For this the god constrains the Greek to roam,
A hopeless exile from his native home,
From death alone exempt—but cease to mourn;
Let all combine to achieve his wish'd return;
Neptune atoned, his wrath shall now refrain,
Or thwart the synod of the gods in vain."

"Father and king adored!" Minerva cried,
"Since all who in the Olympian bower reside
Now make the wandering Greek their public care,
Let Hermes to the Atlantic isle repair;
Bid him, arrived in bright Calypso's court,
The sanction of the assembled powers report:
That wise Ulysses to his native land
Must speed, obedient to their high command.
Meantime Telemachus, the blooming heir
Of sea-girt Ithaca, demands my care;
'Tis mine to form his green, unpractised years
In sage debates; surrounded with his peers,
To save the state, and timely to restrain
The bold intrusion of the suitor-train;
Who crowd his palace, and with lawless power
His herds and flocks in feastful rites devour.
To distant Sparta, and the spacious waste
Of Sandy Pyle, the royal youth shall haste.
There, warm with filial love, the cause inquire
That from his realm retards his god-like sire;
Delivering early to the voice of fame
The promise of a green immortal name."

She said: the sandals of celestial mould,
Fledged with ambrosial plumes, and rich with gold,
Surround her feet: with these sublime she sails
The aerial space, and mounts the winged gales;
O'er earth and ocean wide prepared to soar,
Her dreaded arm a beamy javelin bore,
Ponderous and vast: which, when her fury burns,
Proud tyrants humbles, and whole hosts o'erturns.
From high Olympus prone her flight she bends,
And in the realms of Ithaca descends,
Her lineaments divine, the grave disguise
Of Mentes' form conceal'd from human eyes
(Mentes, the monarch of the Taphian land);
A glittering spear waved awful in her hand.
There in the portal placed, the heaven-born maid
Enormous riot and misrule survey'd.
On hides of beeves, before the palace gate
(Sad spoils of luxury), the suitors sate.
With rival art, and ardour in their mien,
At chess they vie, to captivate the queen;
Divining of their loves. Attending nigh,
A menial train the flowing bowl supply.
Others, apart, the spacious hall prepare,
And form the costly feast with busy care.

There young Telemachus, his bloomy face
Glowing celestial sweet, with godlike grace
Amid the circle shines: but hope and fear
(Painful vicissitude!) his bosom tear.
Now, imaged in his mind, he sees restored
In peace and joy the people's rightful lord;
The proud oppressors fly the vengeful sword.
While his fond soul these fancied triumphs swell'd,
The stranger guest the royal youth beheld;
Grieved that a visitant so long should wait
Unmark'd, unhonour'd, at a monarch's gate;
Instant he flew with hospitable haste,
And the new friend with courteous air embraced.
"Stranger, whoe'er thou art, securely rest,
Affianced in my faith, a ready guest;
Approach the dome, the social banquet share,
And then the purpose of thy soul declare."

Thus affable and mild, the prince precedes,
And to the dome the unknown celestial leads.
The spear receiving from the hand, he placed
Against a column, fair with sculpture graced;
Where seemly ranged in peaceful order stood
Ulysses' arms now long disused to blood.
He led the goddess to the sovereign seat,
Her feet supported with a stool of state
(A purple carpet spread the pavement wide);
Then drew his seat, familiar, to her side;
Far from the suitor-train, a brutal crowd,
With insolence, and wine, elate and loud:
Where the free guest, unnoted, might relate,
If haply conscious, of his father's fate.
The golden ewer a maid obsequious brings,
Replenish'd from the cool, translucent springs;
With copious water the bright vase supplies
A silver laver of capacious size;
They wash. The tables in fair order spread,
They heap the glittering canisters with bread:
Viands of various kinds allure the taste,
Of choicest sort and savour, rich repast!
Delicious wines the attending herald brought;
The gold gave lustre to the purple draught.
Lured with the vapour of the fragrant feast,
In rush'd the suitors with voracious haste;
Marshall'd in order due, to each a sewer
Presents, to bathe his hands, a radiant ewer.
Luxurious then they feast. Observant round
Gay stripling youths the brimming goblets crown'd.

The rage of hunger quell'd, they all advance
And form to measured airs the mazy dance;
To Phemius was consign'd the chorded lyre,
Whose hand reluctant touch'd the warbling wire;
Phemius, whose voice divine could sweetest sing
High strains responsive to the vocal string.

Meanwhile, in whispers to his heavenly guest
His indignation thus the prince express'd:

"Indulge my rising grief, whilst these (my friend)
With song and dance the pompous revel end.
Light is the dance, and doubly sweet the lays,
When for the dear delight another pays.
His treasured stores those cormarants consume,
Whose bones, defrauded of a regal tomb
And common turf, lie naked on the plain,
Or doom'd to welter in the whelming main.
Should he return, that troop so blithe and bold,
With purple robes inwrought, and stiff with gold,
Precipitant in fear would wing their flight,
And curse their cumbrous pride's unwieldy weight.
But ah, I dreaml-the appointed hour is fled.
And hope, too long with vain delusion fed,
Deaf to the rumour of fallacious fame,
Gives to the roll of death his glorious name!
With venial freedom let me now demand
Thy name, thy lineage, and paternal land;
Sincere from whence began thy course, recite,
And to what ship I owe the friendly freight?
Now first to me this visit dost thou deign,
Or number'd in my father's social train?
All who deserved his choice he made his own,
And, curious much to know, he far was known."

"My birth I boast (the blue-eyed virgin cries)
From great Anchialus, renown'd and wise;
Mentes my name; I rule the Taphian race,
Whose bounds the deep circumfluent waves embrace;
A duteous people, and industrious isle,
To naval arts inured, and stormy toil.
Freighted with iron from my native land,
I steer my voyage to the Brutian strand
To gain by commerce, for the labour'd mass,
A just proportion of refulgent brass.
Far from your capital my ship resides
At Reitorus, and secure at anchor rides;
Where waving groves on airy Neign grow,

Supremely tall and shade the deeps below.
Thence to revisit your imperial dome,
An old hereditary guest I come;
Your father's friend. Laertes can relate
Our faith unspotted, and its early date;
Who, press'd with heart-corroding grief and years,
To the gay court a rural shed pretors,
Where, sole of all his train, a matron sage
Supports with homely fond his drooping age,
With feeble steps from marshalling his vines
Returning sad, when toilsome day declines.

"With friendly speed, induced by erring fame,
To hail Ulysses' safe return I came;
But still the frown of some celestial power
With envious joy retards the blissful hour.
Let not your soul be sunk in sad despair;
He lives, he breathes this heavenly vital air,
Among a savage race, whose shelfy bounds
With ceaseless roar the foaming deep surrounds.
The thoughts which roll within my ravish'd breast,
To me, no seer, the inspiring gods suggest;
Nor skill'd nor studious, with prophetic eye
To judge the winged omens of the sky.
Yet hear this certain speech, nor deem it vain;
Though adamantine bonds the chief restrain,
The dire restraint his wisdom will defeat,
And soon restore him to his regal seat.
But generous youth! sincere and free declare,
Are you, of manly growth, his royal heir?
For sure Ulysses in your look appears,
The same his features, if the same his years.
Such was that face, on which I dwelt with joy
Ere Greece assembled stemm'd the tides to Troy;
But, parting then for that detested shore,
Our eyes, unhappy? never greeted more."

"To prove a genuine birth (the prince replies)
On female truth assenting faith relies.
Thus manifest of right, I build my claim
Sure-founded on a fair maternal fame,
Ulysses' son: but happier he, whom fate
Hath placed beneath the storms which toss the great!
Happier the son, whose hoary sire is bless'd
With humble affluence, and domestic rest!
Happier than I, to future empire born,
But doom'd a father's wretch'd fate to mourn!"

To whom, with aspect mild, the guest divine:
"Oh true descendant of a sceptred line!
The gods a glorious fate from anguish free
To chaste Penelope's increase decree.
But say, yon jovial troops so gaily dress'd,
Is this a bridal or a friendly feast?
Or from their deed I rightlier may divine,
Unseemly flown with insolence and wine?
Unwelcome revellers, whose lawless joy
Pains the sage ear, and hurts the sober eye."

"Magnificence of old (the prince replied)
Beneath our roof with virtue could reside;
Unblamed abundance crowned the royal board,
What time this dome revered her prudent lord;
Who now (so Heaven decrees) is doom'd to mourn,
Bitter constraint, erroneous and forlorn.
Better the chief, on Ilion's hostile plain,
Had fall'n surrounded with his warlike train;
Or safe return'd, the race of glory pass'd,
New to his friends' embrace, and breathed his last!
Then grateful Greece with streaming eyes would raise,
Historic marbles to record his praise;
His praise, eternal on the faithful stone,
Had with transmissive honour graced his son.
Now snatch'd by harpies to the dreary coast.
Sunk is the hero, and his glory lost;
Vanish'd at once! unheard of, and unknown!
And I his heir in misery alone.
Nor for a dear lost father only flow
The filial tears, but woe succeeds to woe
To tempt the spouseless queen with amorous wiles
Resort the nobles from the neighbouring isles;
From Samos, circled with the Ionian main,
Dulichium, and Zacynthas' sylvan reign;
Ev'n with presumptuous hope her bed to ascend,
The lords of Ithaca their right pretend.
She seems attentive to their pleaded vows,
Her heart detesting what her ear allows.
They, vain expectants of the bridal hour,
My stores in riotous expense devour.
In feast and dance the mirthful months employ,
And meditate my doom to crown their joy."

With tender pity touch'd, the goddess cried:
"Soon may kind Heaven a sure relief provide,
Soon may your sire discharge the vengeance due,
And all your wrongs the proud oppressors rue!

Oh! in that portal should the chief appear,
Each hand tremendous with a brazen spear,
In radiant panoply his limbs incased
(For so of old my fathers court he graced,
When social mirth unbent his serious soul,
O'er the full banquet, and the sprightly bowl);
He then from Ephyre, the fair domain
Of Ilus, sprung from Jason's royal strain,
Measured a length of seas, a toilsome length, in vain.
For, voyaging to learn the direful art
To taint with deadly drugs the barbed dart;
Observant of the gods, and sternly just,
Ilus refused to impart the baneful trust;
With friendlier zeal my father's soul was fired,
The drugs he knew, and gave the boon desired.
Appear'd he now with such heroic port,
As then conspicuous at the Taphian court;
Soon should you boasters cease their haughty strife,
Or each atone his guilty love with life.
But of his wish'd return the care resign,
Be future vengeance to the powers divine.
My sentence hear: with stern distaste avow'd,
To their own districts drive the suitor-crowd;
When next the morning warms the purple east,
Convoke the peerage, and the gods attest;
The sorrows of your inmost soul relate;
And form sure plans to save the sinking state.
Should second love a pleasing flame inspire,
And the chaste queen connubial rights require;
Dismiss'd with honour, let her hence repair
To great Icarius, whose paternal care
Will guide her passion, and reward her choice
With wealthy dower, and bridal gifts of price.
Then let this dictate of my love prevail:
Instant, to foreign realms prepare to sail,
To learn your father's fortunes; Fame may prove,
Or omen'd voice (the messenger of Jove),
Propitious to the search. Direct your toil
Through the wide ocean first to sandy Pyle;
Of Nestor, hoary sage, his doom demand:
Thence speed your voyage to the Spartan strand;
For young Atrides to the Achaian coast
Arrived the last of all the victor host.
If yet Ulysses views the light, forbear,
Till the fleet hours restore the circling year.
But if his soul hath wing'd the destined flight,
Inhabitant of deep disastrous night;
Homeward with pious speed repass the main,

To the pale shade funereal rites ordain,
Plant the fair column o'er the vacant grave,
A hero's honours let the hero have.
With decent grief the royal dead deplored,
For the chaste queen select an equal lord.
Then let revenge your daring mind employ,
By fraud or force the suitor train destroy,
And starting into manhood, scorn the boy.
Hast thou not heard how young Orestes, fired
With great revenge, immortal praise acquired?
His virgin-sword AEgysthus' veins imbrued;
The murderer fell, and blood atoned for blood.
O greatly bless'd with every blooming grace!
With equal steps the paths of glory trace;
Join to that royal youth's your rival name,
And shine eternal in the sphere of fame.
But my associates now my stay deplore,
Impatient on the hoarse-resounding shore.
Thou, heedful of advice, secure proceed;
My praise the precept is, be thine the deed.

"The counsel of my friend (the youth rejoin'd)
Imprints conviction on my grateful mind.
So fathers speak (persuasive speech and mild)
Their sage experience to the favourite child.
But, since to part, for sweet refection due,
The genial viands let my train renew;
And the rich pledge of plighted faith receive,
Worthy the air of Ithaca to give."

"Defer the promised boon (the goddess cries,
Celestial azure brightening in her eyes),
And let me now regain the Reithrian port;
From Temese return'd, your royal court
I shall revisit, and that pledge receive;
And gifts, memorial of our friendship, leave."

Abrupt, with eagle-speed she cut the sky;
Instant invisible to mortal eye.
Then first he recognized the ethereal guest;
Wonder and joy alternate fire his breast;
Heroic thoughts, infused, his heart dilate;
Revolving much his father's doubtful fate.
At length, composed, he join'd the suitor-throng;
Hush'd in attention to the warbled song.
His tender theme the charming lyrist chose.
Minerva's anger, and the dreadful woes
Which voyaging from Troy the victors bore,

While storms vindictive intercept the store.
The shrilling airs the vaulted roof rebounds,
Reflecting to the queen the silver sounds.
With grief renew'd the weeping fair descends;
Their sovereign's step a virgin train attends:
A veil, of richest texture wrought, she wears,
And silent to the joyous hall repairs.
There from the portal, with her mild command,
Thus gently checks the minstrel's tuneful hand:

"Phemius! let acts of gods, and heroes old,
What ancient bards in hall and bower have told,
Attemper'd to the lyre, your voice employ;
Such the pleased ear will drink with silent joy.
But, oh! forbear that dear disastrous name,
To sorrow sacred, and secure of fame;
My bleeding bosom sickens at the sound,
And every piercing note inflicts a wound."

"Why, dearest object of my duteous love,
(Replied the prince,) will you the bard reprove?
Oft, Jove's ethereal rays (resistless fire)
The chanters soul and raptured song inspire
Instinct divine? nor blame severe his choice,
Warbling the Grecian woes with heart and voice;
For novel lays attract our ravish'd ears;
But old, the mind with inattention hears:
Patient permit the sadly pleasing strain;
Familiar now with grief, your tears refrain,
And in the public woe forget your own;
You weep not for a perish'd lord alone.
What Greeks new wandering in the Stygian gloom,
Wish your Ulysses shared an equal doom!
Your widow'd hours, apart, with female toil
And various labours of the loom beguile;
There rule, from palace-cares remote and free;
That care to man belongs, and most to me."

Mature beyond his years, the queen admires
His sage reply, and with her train retires.
Then swelling sorrows burst their former bounds,
With echoing grief afresh the dome resounds;
Till Pallas, piteous of her plaintive cries,
In slumber closed her silver-streaming eyes.

Meantime, rekindled at the royal charms,
Tumultuous love each beating bosom warms;
Intemperate rage a wordy war began;

But bold Telemachus assumed the man.
"Instant (he cried) your female discord end,
Ye deedless boasters! and the song attend;
Obey that sweet compulsion, nor profane
With dissonance the smooth melodious strain.
Pacific now prolong the jovial feast;
But when the dawn reveals the rosy east,
I, to the peers assembled, shall propose
The firm resolve, I here in few disclose;
No longer live the cankers of my court;
All to your several states with speed resort;
Waste in wild riot what your land allows,
There ply the early feast, and late carouse.
But if, to honour lost, 'tis still decreed
For you my bowl shall flow, my flock shall bleed;
Judge and revenge my right, impartial Jove!
By him and all the immortal thrones above
(A sacred oath), each proud oppressor slain,
Shall with inglorious gore this marble stain."

Awed by the prince, thus haughty, bold, and young,
Rage gnaw'd the lip, and wonder chain'd the tongue.
Silence at length the gay Antinous broke,
Constrain'd a smile, and thus ambiguous spoke:
"What god to your untutor'd youth affords
This headlong torrent of amazing words?
May Jove delay thy reign, and cumber late
So bright a genius with the toils of state!"

"Those toils (Telemachus serene replies)
Have charms, with all their weight, t'allure the wise.
Fast by the throne obsequious fame resides,
And wealth incessant rolls her golden tides.
Nor let Antinous rage, if strong desire
Of wealth and fame a youthful bosom fire:
Elect by Jove, his delegate of sway,
With joyous pride the summons I'd obey.
Whene'er Ulysses roams the realm of night,
Should factious power dispute my lineal right,
Some other Greeks a fairer claim may plead;
To your pretence their title would precede.
At least, the sceptre lost, I still should reign
Sole o'er my vassals, and domestic train."

To this Eurymachus: "To Heaven alone
Refer the choice to fill the vacant throne.
Your patrimonial stores in peace possess;
Undoubted, all your filial claim confess:

Your private right should impious power invade,
The peers of Ithaca would arm in aid.
But say, that stranger guest who late withdrew,
What and from whence? his name and lineage shew.
His grave demeanour and majestic grace
Speak him descended of non vulgar race:
Did he some loan of ancient right require,
Or came forerunner of your sceptr'd sire?"

"Oh son of Polybus!" the prince replies,
"No more my sire will glad these longing eyes;
The queen's fond hope inventive rumour cheers,
Or vain diviners' dreams divert her fears.
That stranger-guest the Taphian realm obeys,
A realm defended with encircling seas.
Mentes, an ever-honour'd name, of old
High in Ulysses' social list enroll'd."

Thus he, though conscious of the ethereal guest,
Answer'd evasive of the sly request.
Meantime the lyre rejoins the sprightly lay;
Love-dittied airs, and dance, conclude the day
But when the star of eve with golden light
Adorn'd the matron brow of sable night,
The mirthful train dispersing quit the court,
And to their several domes to rest resort.
A towering structure to the palace join'd;
To this his steps the thoughtful prince inclined:
In his pavilion there, to sleep repairs;
The lighted torch, the sage Euryclea bears
(Daughter of Ops, the just Pisenor's son,
For twenty beeves by great Laertes won;
In rosy prime with charms attractive graced,
Honour'd by him, a gentle lord and chaste,
With dear esteem: too wise, with jealous strife
To taint the joys of sweet connubial life.
Sole with Telemachus her service ends,
A child she nursed him, and a man attends).
Whilst to his couch himself the prince address'd,
The duteous dame received the purple vest;
The purple vest with decent care disposed,
The silver ring she pull'd, the door reclosed,
The bolt, obedient to the silken cord,
To the strong staple's inmost depth restored,
Secured the valves. There, wrapped in silent shade,
Pensive, the rules the goddess gave he weigh'd;
Stretch'd on the downy fleece, no rest he knows,
And in his raptured soul the vision glows.

BOOK II

THE COUNCIL OF ITHACA

Telemachus in the assembly of the lords of Ithaca complains of the injustice done him by the suitors, and insists upon their departure from his palace; appealing to the princes, and exciting the people to declare against them. The suitors endeavour to justify their stay, at least till he shall send the queen to the court of Icarius her father; which he refuses. There appears a prodigy of two eagles in the sky, which an augur expounds to the ruin of the suitors. Telemachus the demands a vessel to carry him to Pylos and Sparta, there to inquire of his father's fortunes. Pallas, in the shape of Mentor (an ancient friend of Ulysses), helps him to a ship, assists him in preparing necessaries for the voyage, and embarks with him that night; which concludes the second day from the opening of the poem. The scene continues in the palace of Ulysses, in Ithaca.

Now reddening from the dawn, the morning ray
Glow'd in the front of heaven, and gave the day
The youthful hero, with returning light,
Rose anxious from the inquietudes of night.
A royal robe he wore with graceful pride,
A two-edged falchion threaten'd by his side,
Embroider'd sandals glitter'd as he trod,
And forth he moved, majestic as a god.
Then by his heralds, restless of delay,
To council calls the peers: the peers obey.
Soon as in solemn form the assembly sate,
From his high dome himself descends in state.
Bright in his hand a ponderous javelin shined;
Two dogs, a faithful guard, attend behind;
Pallas with grace divine his form improves,
And gazing crowds admire him as he moves,

His father's throne he fill'd; while distant stood
The hoary peers, and aged wisdom bow'd.

'Twas silence all. At last AEgyptius spoke;
AEgyptius, by his age and sorrow broke;
A length of days his soul with prudence crown'd,
A length of days had bent him to the ground.
His eldest hope in arms to Ilion came,
By great Ulysses taught the path to fame;
But (hapless youth) the hideous Cyclops tore
His quivering limbs, and quaff'd his spouting gore.
Three sons remain'd; to climb with haughty fires

The royal bed, Eurynomus aspires;
The rest with duteous love his griefs assuage,
And ease the sire of half the cares of age.
Yet still his Antiphus he loves, he mourns,
And, as he stood, he spoke and wept by turns,

"Since great Ulysses sought the Phrygian plains,
Within these walls inglorious silence reigns.
Say then, ye peers! by whose commands we meet?
Why here once more in solemn council sit?
Ye young, ye old, the weighty cause disclose:
Arrives some message of invading foes?
Or say, does high necessity of state
Inspire some patriot, and demand debate?
The present synod speaks its author wise;
Assist him, Jove, thou regent of the skies!"

He spoke. Telemachus with transport glows,
Embraced the omen, and majestic rose
(His royal hand the imperial sceptre sway'd);
Then thus, addressing to AEgyptius, said:

"Reverend old man! lo here confess'd he stands
By whom ye meet; my grief your care demands.
No story I unfold of public woes,
Nor bear advices of impending foes:
Peace the blest land, and joys incessant crown:
Of all this happy realm, I grieve alone.
For my lost sire continual sorrows spring,
The great, the good; your father and your king.
Yet more; our house from its foundation bows,
Our foes are powerful, and your sons the foes;
Hither, unwelcome to the queen, they come;
Why seek they not the rich Icarian dome?
If she must wed, from other hands require
The dowry: is Telemachus her sire?
Yet through my court the noise of revel rings,
And waste the wise frugality of kings.
Scarce all my herds their luxury suffice;
Scarce all my wine their midnight hours supplies.
Safe in my youth, in riot still they grow,
Nor in the helpless orphan dread a foe.
But come it will, the time when manhood grants
More powerful advocates than vain complaints.
Approach that hour! insufferable wrong
Cries to the gods, and vengeance sleeps too long.
Rise then, ye peers! with virtuous anger rise;
Your fame revere, but most the avenging skies.

By all the deathless powers that reign above,
By righteous Themis and by thundering Jove
(Themis, who gives to councils, or denies
Success; and humbles, or confirms the wise),
Rise in my aid! suffice the tears that flow
For my lost sire, nor add new woe to woe.
If e'er he bore the sword to strengthen ill,
Or, having power to wrong, betray'd the will,
On me, on me your kindled wrath assuage,
And bid the voice of lawless riot rage.
If ruin to your royal race ye doom,
Be you the spoilers, and our wealth consume.
Then might we hope redress from juster laws,
And raise all Ithaca to aid our cause:
But while your sons commit the unpunish'd wrong,
You make the arm of violence too strong."

While thus he spoke, with rage and grief he frown'd,
And dash'd the imperial sceptre to the ground.
The big round tear hung trembling in his eye:
The synod grieved, and gave a pitying sigh,
Then silent sate—at length Antinous burns
With haughty rage, and sternly thus returns:

"O insolence of youth! whose tongue affords
Such railing eloquence, and war of words.
Studious thy country's worthies to defame,
Thy erring voice displays thy mother's shame.
Elusive of the bridal day, she gives
Fond hopes to all, and all with hopes deceives.
Did not the sun, through heaven's wide azure roll'd,
For three long years the royal fraud behold?
While she, laborious in delusion, spread
The spacious loom, and mix'd the various thread:
Where as to life the wondrous figures rise,
Thus spoke the inventive queen, with artful sighs:

"Though cold in death Ulysses breathes no more,
Cease yet awhile to urge the bridal hour:
Cease, till to great Laertes I bequeath
A task of grief, his ornaments of death.
Lest when the Fates his royal ashes claim,
The Grecian matrons taint my spotless fame;
When he, whom living mighty realms obey'd,
Shall want in death a shroud to grace his shade.'

"Thus she: at once the generous train complies,
Nor fraud mistrusts in virtue's fair disguise.

The work she plied; but, studious of delay,
By night reversed the labours of the day.
While thrice the sun his annual journey made,
The conscious lamp the midnight fraud survey'd;
Unheard, unseen, three years her arts prevail;
The fourth her maid unfolds the amazing tale.
We saw, as unperceived we took our stand,
The backward labours of her faithless hand.
Then urged, she perfects her illustrious toils;
A wondrous monument of female wiles!

"But you, O peers! and thou, O prince! give ear
(I speak aloud, that every Greek may hear):
Dismiss the queen; and if her sire approves
Let him espouse her to the peer she loves:
Bid instant to prepare the bridal train,
Nor let a race of princes wait in vain.
Though with a grace divine her soul is blest,
And all Minerva breathes within her breast,
In wondrous arts than woman more renown'd,
And more than woman with deep wisdom crown'd;
Though Tyro nor Mycene match her name,
Not great Alemena (the proud boasts of fame);
Yet thus by heaven adorn'd, by heaven's decree
She shines with fatal excellence, to thee:
With thee, the bowl we drain, indulge the feast,
Till righteous heaven reclaim her stubborn breast.
What though from pole to pole resounds her name!
The son's destruction waits the mother's fame:
For, till she leaves thy court, it is decreed,
Thy bowl to empty and thy flock to bleed."

While yet he speaks, Telemachus replies:
"Ev'n nature starts, and what ye ask denies.
Thus, shall I thus repay a mother's cares,
Who gave me life, and nursed my infant years!
While sad on foreign shores Ulysses treads.
Or glides a ghost with unapparent shades;
How to Icarius in the bridal hour
Shall I, by waste undone, refund the dower?
How from my father should I vengeance dread!
How would my mother curse my hated head!
And while In wrath to vengeful fiends she cries,
How from their hell would vengeful fiends arise!
Abhorr'd by all, accursed my name would grow,
The earth's disgrace, and human-kind my foe.
If this displease, why urge ye here your stay?
Haste from the court, ye spoilers, haste away:

Waste in wild riot what your land allows,
There ply the early feast, and late carouse.
But if to honour lost, 'tis still decreed
For you my howl shall flow, my flocks shall bleed;
Judge, and assert my right, impartial Jove!
By him, and all the immortal host above
(A sacred oath), if heaven the power supply,
Vengeance I vow, and for your wrongs ye die."

With that, two eagles from a mountain's height
By Jove's command direct their rapid flight;
Swift they descend, with wing to wing conjoin'd,
Stretch their broad plumes, and float upon the wind.
Above the assembled peers they wheel on high,
And clang their wings, and hovering beat the sky;
With ardent eyes the rival train they threat,
And shrieking loud denounce approaching fate.
They cuff, they tear; their cheeks and neck they rend,
And from their plumes huge drops of blood descend;
Then sailing o'er the domes and towers, they fly,
Full toward the east, and mount into the sky.

The wondering rivals gaze, with cares oppress'd,
And chilling horrors freeze in every breast,
Till big with knowledge of approaching woes,
The prince of augurs, Halitherses, rose:
Prescient he view'd the aerial tracks, and drew
A sure presage from every wing that flew.

"Ye sons (he cried) of Ithaca, give ear;
Hear all! but chiefly you, O rivals! hear.
Destruction sure o'er all your heads impends
Ulysses comes, and death his steps attends.
Nor to the great alone is death decreed;
We and our guilty Ithaca must bleed.
Why cease we then the wrath of heaven to stay?
Be humbled all, and lead, ye great! the way.
For lo? my words no fancied woes relate;
I speak from science and the voice of fate.

"When great Ulysses sought the Phrygian shores
To shake with war proud Ilion's lofty towers,
Deeds then undone me faithful tongue foretold:
Heaven seal'd my words, and you those deeds behold.
I see (I cried) his woes, a countless train;
I see his friends o'erwhelm'd beneath the main;
How twice ten years from shore to shore he roams:
Now twice ten years are past, and now he comes!"

To whom Eurymachus—"Fly, dotard fly,
With thy wise dreams, and fables of the sky.
Go prophesy at home, thy sons advise:
Here thou art sage in vain—I better read the skies
Unnumber'd birds glide through the aerial way;
Vagrants of air, and unforeboding stray.
Cold in the tomb, or in the deeps below,
Ulysses lies; oh wert thou laid as low!
Then would that busy head no broils suggest,
For fire to rage Telemachus' breast,
From him some bribe thy venal tongue requires,
And interest, not the god, thy voice inspires.
His guideless youth, if thy experienced age
Mislead fallacious into idle rage,
Vengeance deserved thy malice shall repress.
And but augment the wrongs thou would'st redress,
Telemachus may bid the queen repair
To great Icarius, whose paternal care
Will guide her passion, and reward her choice
With wealthy dower, and bridal gifts of price.
Till she retires, determined we remain,
And both the prince and augur threat in vain:
His pride of words, and thy wild dream of fate,
Move not the brave, or only move their hate,
Threat on, O prince! elude the bridal day.
Threat on, till all thy stores in waste decay.
True, Greece affords a train of lovely dames,
In wealth and beauty worthy of our flames:
But never from this nobler suit we cease;
For wealth and beauty less than virtue please."

To whom the youth: "Since then in vain I tell
My numerous woes, in silence let them dwell.
But Heaven, and all the Greeks, have heard my wrongs;
To Heaven, and all the Greeks, redress belongs;
Yet this I ask (nor be it ask'd in vain),
A bark to waft me o'er the rolling main,
The realms of Pyle and Sparta to explore,
And seek my royal sire from shore to shore;
If, or to fame his doubtful fate be known,
Or to be learn'd from oracles alone,
If yet he lives, with patience I forbear,
Till the fleet hours restore the circling year;
But if already wandering in the train
Of empty shades, I measure back the main,
Plant the fair column o'er the mighty dead,
And yield his consort to the nuptial bed."

He ceased; and while abash'd the peers attend,
Mentor arose, Ulysses' faithful friend:
(When fierce in arms he sought the scenes of war,
"My friend (he cried), my palace be thy care;
Years roll'd on years my godlike sire decay,
Guard thou his age, and his behests obey.")
Stern as he rose, he cast his eyes around,
That flash'd with rage; and as spoke, he frown'd,

"O never, never more let king be just,
Be mild in power, or faithful to his trust!
Let tyrants govern with an iron rod,
Oppress, destroy, and be the scourge of God;
Since he who like a father held his reign,
So soon forgot, was just and mild in vain!
True, while my friend is grieved, his griefs I share;
Yet now the rivals are my smallest care:
They for the mighty mischiefs they devise,
Ere long shall pay—their forfeit lives the price.
But against you, ye Greeks! ye coward train!
Gods! how my soul is moved with just disdain!
Dumb ye all stand, and not one tongue affords
His injured prince the little aid of words."

While yet he spoke, Leocritus rejoined:
"O pride of words, and arrogance of mind!
Would'st thou to rise in arms the Greeks advise?
Join all your powers? in arms, ye Greeks, arise!
Yet would your powers in vain our strength oppose.
The valiant few o'ermatch a host of foes.
Should great Ulysses stern appear in arms,
While the bowl circles and the banquet warms;
Though to his breast his spouse with transport flies,
Torn from her breast, that hour, Ulysses dies.
But hence retreating to your domes repair.
To arm the vessel, Mentor! be thy care,
And Halitherses! thine: be each his friend;
Ye loved the father: go, the son attend.
But yet, I trust, the boaster means to stay
Safe in the court, nor tempt the watery way."

Then, with a rushing sound the assembly bend
Diverse their steps: the rival rout ascend
The royal dome; while sad the prince explores
The neighbouring main, and sorrowing treads the shores.
There, as the waters o'er his hands he shed,
The royal suppliant to Minerva pray'd:

"O goddess! who descending from the skies
Vouchsafed thy presence to my wondering eyes,
By whose commands the raging deeps I trace,
And seek my sire through storms and rolling seas!
Hear from thy heavens above, O warrior maid!
Descend once more, propitious to my aid.
Without thy presence, vain is thy command:
Greece, and the rival train, thy voice withstand."

Indulgent to his prayer, the goddess took
Sage Mentor's form, and thus like Mentor spoke:

"O prince, in early youth divinely wise,
Born, the Ulysses of thy age to rise
If to the son the father's worth descends,
O'er the wide wave success thy ways attends
To tread the walks of death he stood prepared;
And what he greatly thought, he nobly dared.
Were not wise sons descendant of the wise,
And did not heroes from brave heroes rise,
Vain were my hopes: few sons attain the praise
Of their great sires, and most their sires disgrace.
But since thy veins paternal virtue fires,
And all Penelope thy soul inspires,
Go, and succeed: the rivals' aims despise;
For never, never wicked man was wise.
Blind they rejoice, though now, ev'n now they fall;
Death hastes amain: one hour o'erwhelms them all!
And lo, with speed we plough the watery way;
My power shall guard thee, and my hand convey:
The winged vessel studious I prepare,
Through seas and realms companion of thy care.
Thou to the court ascend: and to the shores
(When night advances) bear the naval stores;
Bread, that decaying man with strength supplies,
And generous wine, which thoughtful sorrow flies.
Meanwhile the mariners, by my command,
Shall speed aboard, a valiant chosen band.
Wide o'er the bay, by vessel vessel rides;
The best I choose to waft then o'er the tides."

She spoke: to his high dome the prince returns,
And, as he moves, with royal anguish mourns.
'Twas riot all, among the lawless train;
Boar bled by boar, and goat by goat lay slain.
Arrived, his hand the gay Antinous press'd,
And thus deriding, with a smile address'd:

"Grieve not, O daring prince! that noble heart;
Ill suits gay youth the stern heroic part.
Indulge the genial hour, unbend thy soul,
Leave thought to age, and drain the flowing bowl.
Studious to ease thy grief, our care provides
The bark, to waft thee o'er the swelling tides."

"Is this (returns the prince) for mirth a time?
When lawless gluttons riot, mirth's a crime;
The luscious wines, dishonour'd, lose their taste;
The song is noise, and impious is the feast.
Suffice it to have spent with swift decay
The wealth of kings, and made my youth a prey.
But now the wise instructions of the sage,
And manly thoughts inspired by manly age,
Teach me to seek redress for all my woe,
Here, or in Pyle—in Pyle, or here, your foe.
Deny your vessels, ye deny in vain:
A private voyager I pass the main.
Free breathe the winds, and free the billows flow;
And where on earth I live, I live your foe."

He spoke and frown'd, nor longer deign'd to stay,
Sternly his hand withdrew, and strode away.

Meantime, o'er all the dome, they quaff, they feast,
Derisive taunts were spread from guest to guest,
And each in jovial mood his mate address'd:

"Tremble ye not, O friends, and coward fly,
Doom'd by the stern Telemachus to die?
To Pyle or Sparta to demand supplies,
Big with revenge, the mighty warrior flies;
Or comes from Ephyre with poisons fraught,
And kills us all in one tremendous draught!"

"Or who can say (his gamesome mate replies)
But, while the danger of the deeps he tries
He, like his sire, may sink deprived of breath,
And punish us unkindly by his death?
What mighty labours would he then create,
To seize his treasures, and divide his state,
The royal palace to the queen convey,
Or him she blesses in the bridal day!"

Meantime the lofty rooms the prince surveys,
Where lay the treasures of the Ithacian race:

Here ruddy brass and gold refulgent blazed;
There polished chests embroider'd vestures graced;
Here jars of oil breathed forth a rich perfume;
There casks of wine in rows adorn'd the dome
(Pure flavorous wine, by gods in bounty given
And worthy to exalt the feasts of heaven).
Untouch'd they stood, till, his long labours o'er,
The great Ulysses reach'd his native shore.
A double strength of bars secured the gates;
Fast by the door the wise Euryclea waits;
Euryclea, who great Ops! thy lineage shared,
And watch'd all night, all day, a faithful guard.

To whom the prince: "O thou whose guardian care
Nursed the most wretched king that breathes the air;
Untouch'd and sacred may these vessels stand,
Till great Ulysses views his native land.
But by thy care twelve urns of wine be fill'd;
Next these in worth, and firm these urns be seal'd;
And twice ten measures of the choicest flour
Prepared, are yet descends the evening hour.
For when the favouring shades of night arise,
And peaceful slumbers close my mother's eyes,
Me from our coast shall spreading sails convey,
To seek Ulysses through the watery way."

While yet he spoke, she fill'd the walls with cries,
And tears ran trickling from her aged eyes.
"O whither, whither flies my son (she cried)
To realms; that rocks and roaring seas divide?
In foreign lands thy father's days decay'd.
And foreign lands contain the mighty dead.
The watery way ill-fated if thou try,
All, all must perish, and by fraud you die!
Then stay, my, child! storms beat, and rolls the main,
Oh, beat those storms, and roll the seas in vain!"

"Far hence (replied the prince) thy fears be driven:
Heaven calls me forth; these counsels are of Heaven.
But, by the powers that hate the perjured, swear,
To keep my voyage from the royal ear,
Nor uncompell'd the dangerous truth betray,
Till twice six times descends the lamp of day,
Lest the sad tale a mother's life impair,
And grief destroy what time awhile would spare."

Thus he. The matron with uplifted eyes
Attests the all-seeing sovereign of the skies.

Then studious she prepares the choicest flour,
The strength of wheat and wines an ample store.
While to the rival train the prince returns,
The martial goddess with impatience burns;
Like thee, Telemachus, in voice and size,
With speed divine from street to street she flies,
She bids the mariners prepared to stand,
When night descends, embodied on the strand.
Then to Noemon swift she runs, she flies,
And asks a bark: the chief a bark supplies.

And now, declining with his sloping wheels,
Down sunk the sun behind the western hills
The goddess shoved the vessel from the shores,
And stow'd within its womb the naval stores,
Full in the openings of the spacious main
It rides; and now descends the sailor-train,

Next, to the court, impatient of delay.
With rapid step the goddess urged her way;
There every eye with slumberous chains she bound,
And dash'd the flowing goblet to the ground.
Drowsy they rose, with heavy fumes oppress'd,
Reel'd from the palace, and retired to rest.
Then thus, in Mentor's reverend form array'd,
Spoke to Telemachus the martial maid.
"Lo! on the seas, prepared the vessel stands,
The impatient mariner thy speed demands."
Swift as she spoke, with rapid pace she leads;
The footsteps of the deity he treads.
Swift to the shore they move along the strand;
The ready vessel rides, the sailors ready stand.

He bids them bring their stores; the attending train
Load the tall bark, and launch into the main,
The prince and goddess to the stern ascend;
To the strong stroke at once the rowers bend.
Full from the west she bids fresh breezes blow;
The sable billows foam and roar below.
The chief his orders gives; the obedient band
With due observance wait the chief's command;
With speed the mast they rear, with speed unbind
The spacious sheet, and stretch it to the wind.
High o'er the roaring waves the spreading sails
Bow the tall mast, and swell before the gales;
The crooked keel the parting surge divides,
And to the stern retreating roll the tides.
And now they ship their oars, and crown with wine

The holy goblet to the powers divine:
Imploring all the gods that reign above,
But chief the blue-eyed progeny of Jove.

Thus all the night they stem the liquid way,
And end their voyage with the morning ray.

BOOK III

ARGUMENT

THE INTERVIEW OF TELEMACHUS AND NESTOR

Telemachus, guided by Pallas in the shape of Mentor, arrives in the morning at Pylos, where Nestor and his sons are sacrificing on the sea-shore to Neptune. Telemachus declares the occasion of his coming: and Nestor relates what passed in their return from Troy, how their fleets were separated, and he never since heard of Ulysses. They discourse concerning the death of Agamemnon, the revenge of Orestes, and the injuries of the suitors. Nestor advises him to go to Sparta, and inquire further of Menelaus. The sacrifice ending with the night, Minerva vanishes from them in the form of an eagle: Telemachus is lodged in the palace. The next morning they sacrifice a bullock to Minerva; and Telemachus proceeds on his journey to Sparta, attended by Pisistratus.

The scene lies on the sea-shore of Pylos.

The sacred sun, above the waters raised,
Through heaven's eternal brazen portals blazed;
And wide o'er earth diffused his cheering ray,
To gods and men to give the golden day.
Now on the coast of Pyle the vessel falls,
Before old Neleus' venerable walls.
There suppliant to the monarch of the flood,
At nine green theatres the Pylians stood,
Each held five hundred (a deputed train),
At each, nine oxen on the sand lay slain.
They taste the entrails, and the altars load
With smoking thighs, an offering to the god.
Full for the port the Ithacensians stand,
And furl their sails, and issue on the land.
Telemachus already press'd the shore;
Not first, the power of wisdom march'd before,
And ere the sacrificing throng he join'd,
Admonish'd thus his well-attending mind:

"Proceed, my son! this youthful shame expel;
An honest business never blush to tell.
To learn what fates thy wretched sire detain,

We pass'd the wide immeasurable main.
Meet then the senior far renown'd for sense
With reverend awe, but decent confidence:
Urge him with truth to frame his fair replies;
And sure he will; for wisdom never lies."

"Oh tell me, Mentor! tell me, faithful guide
(The youth with prudent modesty replied),
How shall I meet, or how accost the sage,
Unskill'd in speech, nor yet mature of age?
Awful th'approach, and hard the task appears,
To question wisely men of riper years."

To whom the martial goddess thus rejoin'd:
"Search, for some thoughts, thy own suggesting mind;
And others, dictated by heavenly power,
Shall rise spontaneous in the needful hour.
For nought unprosperous shall thy ways attend,
Born with good omens, and with heaven thy friend."

She spoke, and led the way with swiftest speed;
As swift, the youth pursued the way she led;
and join'd the band before the sacred fire,
Where sate, encompass'd with his sons, the sire.
The youth of Pylos, some on pointed wood
Transfix'd the fragments, some prepared the food:
In friendly throngs they gather to embrace
Their unknown guests, and at the banquet place,
Pisistratus was first to grasp their hands,
And spread soft hides upon the yellow sands;
Along the shore the illustrious pair he led,
Where Nestor sate with the youthful Thrasymed,
To each a portion of the feast he bore,
And held the golden goblet foaming o'er;
Then first approaching to the elder guest,
The latent goddess in these words address'd:
"Whoe'er thou art, from fortune brings to keep
These rites of Neptune, monarch of the deep,
Thee first it fits, O stranger! to prepare
The due libation and the solemn prayer;
Then give thy friend to shed the sacred wine;
Though much thy younger, and his years like mine,
He too, I deem, implores the power divine;
For all mankind alike require their grace,
All born to want; a miserable race!"
He spake, and to her hand preferr'd the bowl;
A secret pleasure touch'd Athena's soul,
To see the preference due to sacred age

Regarded ever by the just and sage.
Of Ocean's king she then implores the grace.
"O thou! whose arms this ample globe embrace,
Fulfil our wish, and let thy glory shine
On Nestor first, and Nestor's royal line;
Next grant the Pylian states their just desires,
Pleased with their hecatomb's ascending fires;
Last, deign Telemachus and me to bless,
And crown our voyage with desired success."

Thus she: and having paid the rite divine,
Gave to Ulysses' son the rosy wine.
Suppliant he pray'd. And now the victims dress'd
They draw, divide, and celebrate the feast.
The banquet done, the narrative old man,
Thus mild, the pleasing conference began:

"Now gentle guests! the genial banquet o'er,
It fits to ask ye, what your native shore,
And whence your race? on what adventure say,
Thus far you wander through the watery way?
Relate if business, or the thirst of gain,
Engage your journey o'er the pathless main
Where savage pirates seek through seas unknown
The lives of others, venturous of their own."

Urged by the precepts by the goddess given,
And fill'd with confidence infused from Heaven,
The youth, whom Pallas destined to be wise
And famed among the sons of men, replies:
"Inquir'st thou, father! from what coast we came?
(Oh grace and glory of the Grecian name!)
From where high Ithaca o'erlooks the floods,
Brown with o'er-arching shades and pendent woods
Us to these shores our filial duty draws,
A private sorrow, not a public cause.
My sire I seek, where'er the voice of fame
Has told the glories of his noble name,
The great Ulysses; famed from shore to shore
For valour much, for hardy suffering more.
Long time with thee before proud Ilion's wall
In arms he fought; with thee beheld her fall.
Of all the chiefs, this hero's fate alone
Has Jove reserved, unheard of, and unknown;
Whether in fields by hostile fury slain,
Or sunk by tempests in the gulfy main?
Of this to learn, oppress'd with tender fears,
Lo, at thy knee his suppliant son appears.

If or thy certain eye, or curious ear,
Have learnt his fate, the whole dark story clear
And, oh! whate'er Heaven destined to betide,
Let neither flattery soothe, nor pity hide.
Prepared I stand: he was but born to try
The lot of man; to suffer, and to die.
Oh then, if ever through the ten years' war
The wise, the good Ulysses claim'd thy care;
If e'er he join'd thy council, or thy sword,
True in his deed, and constant to his word;
Far as thy mind through backward time can see
Search all thy stores of faithful memory:
'Tis sacred truth I ask, and ask of thee."

To him experienced Nestor thus rejoin'd:
"O friend! what sorrows dost thou bring to mind!
Shall I the long, laborious scene review,
And open all the wounds of Greece anew?
What toils by sea! where dark in quest of prey
Dauntless we roved; Achilles led the way;
What toils by land! where mix'd in fatal fight
Such numbers fell, such heroes sunk to night;
There Ajax great, Achilles there the brave,
There wise Patroclus, fill an early grave:
There, too, my son—ah, once my best delight
Once swift of foot, and terrible in fight;
In whom stern courage with soft virtue join'd
A faultless body and a blameless mind;
Antilochus—What more can I relate?
How trace the tedious series of our fate?
Not added years on years my task could close,
The long historian of my country's woes;
Back to thy native islands might'st thou sail,
And leave half-heard the melancholy tale.
Nine painful years on that detested shore;
What stratagems we form'd, what toils we bore!
Still labouring on, till scarce at last we found
Great Jove propitious, and our conquest crown'd.
Far o'er the rest thy mighty father shined,
In wit, in prudence, and in force of mind.
Art thou the son of that illustrious sire?
With joy I grasp thee, and with love admire.
So like your voices, and your words so wise,
Who finds thee younger must consult his eyes.
Thy sire and I were one; nor varied aught
In public sentence, or in private thought;
Alike to council or the assembly came,
With equal souls, and sentiments the same.

But when (by wisdom won) proud Ilion burn'd,
And in their slips the conquering Greeks return'd,
'Twas God's high will the victors to divide,
And turn the event, confounding human pride;
Some be destroy'd, some scatter'd as the dust
(Not all were prudent, and not all were just).
Then Discord, sent by Pallas from above,
Stern daughter of the great avenger Jove,
The brother-kings inspired with fell debate;
Who call'd to council all the Achaian state,
But call'd untimely (not the sacred rite
Observed, nor heedful of the setting light,
Nor herald sword the session to proclaim),
Sour with debauch, a reeling tribe the came.
To these the cause of meeting they explain,
And Menelaus moves to cross the main;
Not so the king of men: be will'd to stay,
The sacred rites and hecatombs to pay,
And calm Minerva's wrath. Oh blind to fate!
The gods not lightly change their love, or hate.
With ireful taunts each other they oppose,
Till in loud tumult all the Greeks arose.
Now different counsels every breast divide,
Each burns with rancour to the adverse side;
The unquiet night strange projects entertain'd
(So Jove, that urged us to our fate, ordain'd).
We with the rising morn our ships unmoor'd,
And brought our captives and our stores aboard;
But half the people with respect obey'd
The king of men, and at his bidding stay'd.
Now on the wings of winds our course we keep
(For God had smooth'd the waters of the deep);
For Tenedos we spread our eager oars,
There land, and pay due victims to the powers;
To bless our safe return, we join in prayer;
But angry Jove dispersed our vows in air,
And raised new discord. Then (so Heaven decreed)
Ulysses first and Neator disagreed!
Wise as he was, by various counsels away'd,
He there, though late, to please the monarch, stay'd.
But I, determined, stem the foamy floods,
Warn'd of the coming fury of the gods.
With us, Tydides fear'd, and urged his haste:
And Menelads came, but came the last,
He join'd our vessels in the Lesbian bay,
While yet we doubted of our watery way;
If to the right to urge the pilot's toil
(The safer road), beside the Psyrian isle;

Or the straight course to rocky Chios plough,
And anchor under Mimas' shaggy brow?
We sought direction of the power divine:
The god propitious gave the guiding sign;
Through the mid seas he bid our navy steer,
And in Euboea shun the woes we fear.
The whistling winds already waked the sky;
Before the whistling winds the vessels fly,
With rapid swiftness cut the liquid way,
And reach Gerestus at the point of day.
There hecacombs of bulls, to Neptune slain,
High-flaming please the monarch of the main.
The fourth day shone, when all their labours o'er,
Tydides' vessels touched the wish'd-for shore.
But I to Pylos scud before the gales,
The god still breathing on my swelling sails;
Separate from all, I safely landed here;
Their fates or fortunes never reach'd my ear.
Yet what I learn'd, attend; as here I sat,
And ask'd each voyager each hero's fate;
Curious to know, and willing to relate.

"Safe reach'd the Myrmidons their native land,
Beneath Achilles' warlike son's command.
Those, whom the heir of great Apollo's art,
Brave Philoctetes, taught to wing the dart;
And those whom Idomen from Ilion's plain
Had led, securely cross'd the dreadful main
How Agamemnon touch'd his Argive coast,
And how his life by fraud and force he lost,
And how the murderer, paid his forfeit breath;
What lands so distant from that scene of death
But trembling heard the fame? and heard, admire.
How well the son appeased his slaughter'd sire!
Ev'n to the unhappy, that unjustly bleed,
Heaven gives posterity, to avenge the deed.
So fell Aegysthus; and mayest thou, my friend,
(On whom the virtues of thy sire descend,)
Make future times thy equal act adore,
And be what brave Orestes was before!"

The prudent youth replied: "O thou the grace
And lasting glory of the Grecian race!
Just was the vengeance, and to latest days
Shall long posterity resound the praise.
Some god this arm with equal prowess bless!
And the proud suitors shall its force confess;
Injurious men! who while my soul is sore

Of fresh affronts, are meditating more.
But Heaven denies this honour to my hand,
Nor shall my father repossess the land;
The father's fortune never to return,
And the sad son's to softer and to mourn!"
Thus he; and Nestor took the word: "My son,
Is it then true, as distant rumours run,
That crowds of rivals for thy mother's charms
Thy palace fill with insults and alarms?
Say, is the fault, through tame submission, thine?
Or leagued against thee, do thy people join,
Moved by some oracle, or voice divine?
And yet who knows, but ripening lies in fate
An hour of vengeance for the afflicted state;
When great Ulysses shall suppress these harms,
Ulysses singly, or all Greece in arms.
But if Athena, war's triumphant maid,
The happy son will as the father aid,
(Whose fame and safety was her constant care
In every danger and in every war:
Never on man did heavenly favour shine
With rays so strong, distinguish'd and divine,
As those with which Minerva mark'd thy sire)
So might she love thee, so thy soul inspire!
Soon should their hopes in humble dust be laid,
And long oblivion of the bridal bed."

"Ah! no such hope (the prince with sighs replies)
Can touch my breast; that blessing Heaven denies.
Ev'n by celestial favour were it given,
Fortune or fate would cross the will of Heaven."

"What words are these, and what imprudence thine?
(Thus interposed the martial maid divine)
Forgetful youth! but know, the Power above
With ease can save each object of his love;
Wide as his will, extends his boundless grace;
Nor lost in time nor circumscribed by place.
Happier his lot, who, many sorrows' pass'd,
Long labouring gains his natal shore at last;
Than who, too speedy, hastes to end his life
By some stern ruffian, or adulterous wife.
Death only is the lot which none can miss,
And all is possible to Heaven but this.
The best, the dearest favourite of the sky,
Must taste that cup, for man is born to die."

Thus check'd, replied Ulysses' prudent heir:

"Mentor, no more—the mournful thought forbear;
For he no more must draw his country's breath,
Already snatch'd by fate, and the black doom of death!
Pass we to other subjects; and engage
On themes remote the venerable sage
(Who thrice has seen the perishable kind
Of men decay, and through three ages shined
Like gods majestic, and like gods in mind);
For much he knows, and just conclusions draws,
From various precedents, and various laws.
O son of Neleus! awful Nestor, tell
How he, the mighty Agamemnon, fell;
By what strange fraud Aegysthus wrought, relate
(By force he could not) such a hero's fate?
Live Menelaus not in Greece? or where
Was then the martial brother's pious care?
Condemn'd perhaps some foreign short to tread;
Or sure Aegysthus had not dared the deed."
To whom the full of days: Illustrious youth,
Attend (though partly thou hast guess'd) the truth.
For had the martial Menelaus found
The ruffian breathing yet on Argive ground;
Nor earth had bid his carcase from the skies,
Nor Grecian virgins shriek'd his obsequies,
But fowls obscene dismember'd his remains,
And dogs had torn him on the naked plains.
While us the works of bloody Mars employ'd,
The wanton youth inglorious peace enjoy'd:
He stretch'd at ease in Argos' calm recess
(Whose stately steeds luxuriant pastures bless),
With flattery's insinuating art
Soothed the frail queen, and poison'd all her heard.
At first, with the worthy shame and decent pride,
The royal dame his lawless suit denied.
For virtue's image yet possess'd her mind.
Taught by a master of the tuneful kind;
Atrides, parting for the Trojan war,
Consign'd the youthful consort to his care.
True to his charge, the bard preserved her long
In honour's limits; such the power of song.
But when the gods these objects of their hate
Dragg'd to the destruction by the links of fate;
The bard they banish'd from his native soil,
And left all helpless in a desert isle;
There he, the sweetest of the sacred train,
Sung dying to the rocks, but sung in vain.
Then virtue was no more; her guard away,
She fell, to lust a voluntary prey.

Even to the temple stalk'd the adulterous spouse,
With impious thanks, and mockery of the vows,
With images, with garments, and with gold;
And odorous fumes from loaded altars roll'd.
"Meantime from flaming Troy we cut the way
With Menelaus, through the curling sea.
But when to Sunium's sacred point we came,
Crown'd with the temple of the Athenian dame;
Atride's pilot, Phrontes, there expired
(Phrontes, of all the songs of men admired
To steer the bounding bark with steady toil,
When the storm thickens, and the billows boil);
While yet he exercised the steerman's art,
Apollo touch'd him with his gentle dart;
Even with the rudder in his hand, he fell.
To pay whole honours to the shades of hell,
We check'd our haste, by pious office bound,
And laid our old companion in the ground.
And now the rites discharged, our course we keep
Far on the gloomy bosom of the deep:
Soon as Malae's misty tops arise,
Sudden the Thunderer blackens all the skies,
And the winds whistle, and the surges roll
Mountains on mountains, and obscure the pole.
The tempest scatters, and divides our fleet;
Part, the storm urges on the coast of Crete,
Where winding round the rich Cydonian plain,
The streams of Jardan issue to the main.
There stands a rock, high, eminent and steep,
Whose shaggy brow o'erhangs the shady deep,
And views Gortyna on the western side;
On this rough Auster drove the impetuous tide:
With broken force the billows roll'd away,
And heaved the fleet into the neighb'ring bay.
Thus saved from death, the gain'd the Phaestan shores,
With shatter'd vessels and disabled oars;
But five tall barks the winds and water toss'd,
Far from their fellows, on the Aegyptian coast.
There wander'd Menelaus through foreign shores
Amassing gold, and gathering naval stores;
While cursed Aegysthus the detested deed
By fraud fulfilled, and his great brother bled.
Seven years, the traitor rich Mycenae sway'd,
And his stern rule the groaning land obey'd;
The eighth, from Athens to his realm restored,
Orestes brandish'd the avenging sword,
Slew the dire pair, and gave to funeral flame
The vile assassin and adulterous dame.

That day, ere yet the bloody triumphs cease,
Return'd Atrides to the coast of Greece,
And safe to Argos port his navy brought,
With gifts of price and ponderous treasure fraught.
Hence warn'd, my son, beware! nor idly stand
Too long a stranger to thy native land;
Lest heedless absence wear thy wealth away,
While lawless feasters in thy palace away;
Perhaps may seize thy realm, and share the spoil;
And though return, with disappointed toil,
From thy vain journey, to a rifled isle.
However, my friend, indulge one labour more,
And seek Atrides on the Spartan shore.
He, wandering long a wider circle made,
And many-languaged nations has survey'd:
And measured tracks unknown to other ships,
Amid the monstrous wonders of the deeps,
(A length of ocean and unbounded sky.
Which scarce the sea-fowl in a year o'erfly);
Go then; to Sparta take the watery way,
Thy ship and sailors but for orders stay;
Or, if my land then choose thy course to bend,
My steeds, my chariots, and my songs, attend;
Thee to Atrides they shall safe convey,
Guides of thy road, companions of thy way.
Urge him with truth to frame his wise replies,
And sure he will; for Menelaus is wise."
Thus while he speaks the ruddy sun descends,
And twilight grey her evening shade extends.
Then thus the blue-eyed maid: "O full of days!
Wise are thy words, and just are all thy ways.
Now immolate the tongues, and mix the wine,
Sacred to Neptune and the powers divine,
The lamp of day is quench'd beneath the deep,
And soft approach the balmy hours of sleep;
Nor fits it to prolong the heavenly feast,
Timeless, indecent, but retire to rest."

So spake Jove's daughter, the celestial maid,
The sober train attended and obey'd.
The sacred heralds on their hands around
Pour'd the full urns; the youths the goblets crown'd;
From bowl to bowl the homely beverage flows;
While to the final sacrifice they rose.
The tongues they cast upon the fragrant flame,
And pour, above, the consecrated stream.
And now, their thirst by copious draughts allay'd,
The youthful hero and the Athenian maid

Propose departure from the finish'd rite,
And in their hollow bark to pass the night;
But this hospitable sage denied,
"Forbid it, Jove! and all the gods! (he cried),
Thus from my walls and the much-loved son to send
Of such a hero, and of such a friend!
Me, as some needy peasant, would ye leave,
Whom Heaven denies the blessing to relieve?
Me would ye leave, who boast imperial sway,
When beds of royal state invite your stay?
No—long as life this mortal shall inspire,
Or as my children imitate their sire.
Here shall the wandering stranger find his home,
And hospitable rites adorn the dome."

"Well hast thou spoke (the blue-eyed maid replies),
Beloved old man! benevolent as wise.
Be the kind dictates of thy heart obey'd,
And let thy words Telemachus persuade:
He to thy palace shall thy steps pursue;
I to the ship, to give the orders due,
Prescribe directions and confirm the crew.
For I alone sustain their naval cares,
Who boast experience from these silver hairs;
All youths the rest, whom to this journey move
Like years, like tempers, and their prince's love
There in the vessel shall I pass the night;
And, soon as morning paints the fields of light,
I go to challenge from the Caucons bold
A debt, contracted in the days of old,
But this, thy guest, received with friendly care
Let thy strong coursers swift to Sparta bear;
Prepare thy chariot at the dawn of day,
And be thy son companion of his way."

Then, turning with the word, Minerva flies,
And soars an eagle through the liquid skies.
Vision divine! the throng'd spectators gaze
In holy wonder fix'd, and still amaze.
But chief the reverend sage admired; he took
The hand of young Telemachus, and spoke:
"Oh, happy youth! and favoured of the skies,
Distinguished care of guardian deities!
Whose early years for future worth engage,
No vulgar manhood, no ignoble age.
For lo! none other of the course above,
Then she, the daughter of almighty Jove,
Pallas herself, the war-triumphant maid;

Confess'd is thine, as once thy fathers aid.
So guide me, goddess! so propitious shine
On me, my consort, and my royal line!
A yearling bullock to thy name shall smoke,
Untamed, unconscious of the galling yoke,
With ample forehead, and yet tender horns,
Whose budding honours ductile gold adorns."

Submissive thus the hoary sire preferr'd
His holy vow: the favouring goddess heard.
Then, slowly rising, o'er the sandy space
Precedes the father, follow'd by his race,
(A long procession) timely marching home
In comely order to the regal dome.
There when arrived, on thrones around him placed,
His sons and grandsons the wide circle graced.
To these the hospitable sage, in sign
Of social welcome, mix'd the racy wine
(Late from the mellowing cask restored to light,
By ten long years refined, and rosy bright).
To Pallas high the foaming bowl he crown'd,
And sprinkled large libations on the ground.
Each drinks a full oblivion of his cares,
And to the gifts of balmy sleep repairs.
Deep in a rich alcove the prince was laid,
And slept beneath the pompous colonnade;
Fast by his side Pisistratus was spread
(In age his equal) on a splendid bed:
But in an inner court, securely closed,
The reverend Nestor and his queen reposed.

When now Aurora, daughter of the dawn,
With rosy lustre purpled o'er the lawn,
The old man early rose, walk'd forth, and sate
On polish'd stone before his palace gate;
With unguents smooth the lucid marble shone,
Where ancient Neleus sate, a rustic throne;
But he descending to the infernal shade,
Sage Nestor fill'd it, and the sceptre sway'd.
His sons around him mild obeisance pay,
And duteous take the orders of the day.
First Eehephron and Stratius quit their bed;
Then Perseus, Aretus, and Thrasymed;
The last Pisistratus arose from rest:
They came, and near him placed the stranger-guest.
To these the senior thus declared his will:
"My sons! the dictates of your sire fulfil.
To Pallas, first of gods, prepare the feast,

Who graced our rites, a more than mortal guest
Let one, despatchful, bid some swain to lead
A well-fed bullock from the grassy mead;
One seek the harbour where the vessels moor,
And bring thy friends, Telemachus! ashore
(Leave only two the galley to attend);
Another Laerceus must we send,
Artist devine, whose skilful hands infold
The victim's horn with circumfusile gold.
The rest may here the pious duty share,
And bid the handmaids for the feast prepare,
The seats to range, the fragrant wood to bring,
And limpid waters from the living spring."

He said, and busy each his care bestow'd;
Already at the gates the bullock low'd,
Already came the Ithacensian crew,
The dexterous smith the tools already drew;
His ponderous hammer and his anvil sound,
And the strong tongs to turn the metal round.
Nor was Minerva absent from the rite,
She view'd her honours, and enjoyed the sight,
With reverend hand the king presents the gold,
Which round the intorted horns the gilder roll'd.
So wrought as Pallas might with pride behold.
Young Aretus from forth his bride bower
Brought the full laver, o'er their hands to pour,
And canisters of consecrated flour.
Stratius and Echephron the victim led;
The axe was held by warlike Thrasymed,
In act to strike; before him Perseus stood,
The vase extending to receive the blood.
The king himself initiates to the power:
Scatters with quivering hand the sacred flour,
And the stream sprinkles; from the curling brows
The hair collected in the fire he throws.
Soon as due vows on every part were paid,
And sacred wheat upon the victim laid,
Strong Thrasymed discharged the speeding blow
Full on his neck, and cut the nerves in two.
Down sunk the heavy beast; the females round
Maids, wives, and matrons, mix a shrilling sound.
Nor scorned the queen the holy choir to join
(The first born she, of old Clymenus' line:
In youth by Nestor loved, of spotless fame.
And loved in age, Eurydice her name).
From earth they rear him, struggling now with death;
And Nestor's youngest stops the vents of breath.

The soul for ever flies; on all sides round
Streams the black blood, and smokes upon the ground
The beast they then divide and disunite
The ribs and limbs, observant of the rite:
On these, in double cauls involved with art,
The choicest morsels lay from every part.
The sacred sage before his altar stands,
Turns the burnt offering with his holy hands,
And pours the wine, and bids the flames aspire;
The youth with instruments surround the fire.
The thighs now sacrificed, and entrails dress'd,
The assistants part, transfix, and broil the rest
While these officious tend the rites divine,
The last fair branch of the Nestorean line,
Sweet Polycaste, took the pleasing toil
To bathe the prince, and pour the fragrant oil.
O'er his fair limbs a flowery vest he throw,
And issued, like a god, to mortal view.
His former seat beside the king he found
(His people's father with his peers around);
All placed at ease the holy banquet join,
And in the dazzling goblet laughs the wine.

The rage of thirst and hunger now suppress'd,
The monarch turns him to his royal guest;
And for the promised journey bids prepare
The smooth hair'd horses, and the rapid car.
Observant of his word, tire word scarce spoke,
The sons obey, and join them to the yoke.
Then bread and wine a ready handmaid brings,
And presents, such as suit the state of kings.
The glittering seat Telemachus ascends;
His faithful guide Pisistratus attends;
With hasty hand the ruling reins he drew;
He lash'd the coursers, and the coursers flew.
Beneath the bounding yoke alike they hold
Their equal pace, and smoked along the field.
The towers of Pylos sink, its views decay,
Fields after fields fly back, till close of day;
Then sunk the sun, and darken'd all the way.

To Pherae now, Diocleus' stately seat
(Of Alpheus' race), the weary youths retreat.
His house affords the hospitable rite,
And pleased they sleep (the blessing of the night).
But when Aurora, daughter of the dawn,
With rosy lustre purpled o'er the lawn,
Again they mount, their journey to renew,

And from the sounding portico they flew.
Along the waving fields their way they hold
The fields receding as their chariot roll'd;
Then slowly sunk the ruddy globe of light,
And o'er the shaded landscape rush'd the night.

BOOK IV

ARGUMENT

THE CONFERENCE WITH MENELAUS

Telemachus with Pisistratus arriving at Sparta, is hospitably received by Menelaus to whom he relates
the cause of his coming, and learns from him many particulars of what befell the Greeks since the
destruction of Troy. He dwells more at large upon the prophecies of Proteus to him in his return; from
which he acquaints Telemachus that Ulysses is detained in the island of Calypso.

In the meantime the suitors consult to destroy Telemachus on the voyage home. Penelope is apprised of
this; but comforted in a dream by Pallas, in the shape of her sister Iphthima.

And now proud Sparta with their wheels resounds,
Sparta whose walls a range of hills surrounds;
At the fair dome the rapid labour ends;
Where sate Atrides 'midst his bridal friends,
With double vows invoking Hymen's power,
To bless his son's and daughter's nuptial hour.

That day, to great Achilles son resign'd,
Hermione, the fairest of her kind,
Was sent to crown the long-protracted joy,
Espoused before the final doom of Troy;
With steeds and gilded cars, a gorgeous train
Attend the nymphs to Phthia's distant reign.
Meanwhile at home, to Megapentha's bed
The virgin choir Alector's daughter led.
Brave Megapenthas From a stolen amour
To great Atrides' age his handmaid bore;
To Helen's bed the gods alone assign
Hermione, to extend the regal line;
On whom a radiant pomp oh Graces wait,
Resembling Venus in attractive state.

While this gay friendly troop the king surround,
With festival and mirth the roofs resound;
A bard amid the joyous circle sings
High airs attemper'd to the vocal strings;

Whilst warbling to the varied strain, advance
Two sprightly youths to form the bounding dance,
'Twas then, that issuing through the palace gate,
The splendid car roll'd slow in regal state:
On the bright eminence young Nestor shone,
And fast beside him great Ulysses' son;
Grave Eteoneous saw the pomp appear,
And speeding, thus address'd the royal ear;

"Two youths approach, whose semblant features prove
Their blood devolving from the source of Jove
Is due reception deign'd, or must they bend
Their doubtful course to seek a distant friend?"

"Insensate! (with a sigh the king replies,)
Too long, misjudging, have I thought thee wise
But sure relentless folly steals thy breast,
Obdurate to reject the stranger-guest;
To those dear hospitable rites a foe,
Which in my wanderings oft relieved my woe;
Fed by the bounty of another's board,
Till pitying Jove my native realm restored—
Straight be the coursers from the car released,
Conduct the youths to grace the genial feast."

The seneschal, rebuked, in haste withdrew;
With equal haste a menial train pursue:
Part led the coursers, from the car enlarged,
Each to a crib with choicest grain surcharged;
Part in a portico, profusely graced
With rich magnificence, the chariot placed;
Then to the dome the friendly pair invite,
Who eye the dazzling roofs with vast delight;
Resplendent as the blaze of summer noon,
Or the pale radiance of the midnight moon.
From room to room their eager view they bend
Thence to the bath, a beauteous pile, descend;
Where a bright damsel train attends the guests
With liquid odours, and embroider'd vests.
Refresh'd, they wait them to the bower of state,
Where, circled with his pears, Atrides sate;
Throned next the king, a fair attendant brings
The purest product of the crystal springs;
High on a massy vase of silver mould,
The burnish'd laver flames with solid gold,
In solid gold the purple vintage flows,
And on the board a second banquet rose.
When thus the king, with hospitable port;

"Accept this welcome to the Spartan court:
The waste of nature let the feast repair,
Then your high lineage and your names declare;
Say from what sceptred ancestry ye claim,
Recorded eminent in deathless fame,
For vulgar parents cannot stamp their race
With signatures of such majestic grace."

Ceasing, benevolent he straight assigns
The royal portion of the choicest chines
To each accepted friend; with grateful haste
They share the honours of the rich repast.
Sufficed, soft whispering thus to Nestor's son,
His head reclined, young Ithacus begun:

"View'st thou unmoved, O ever-honour'd most!
These prodigies of art, and wondrous cost!
Above, beneath, around the palace shines
The sunless treasure of exhausted mines;
The spoils of elephants the roofs inlay,
And studded amber darts the golden ray;
Such, and not nobler, in the realms above
My wonder dictates is the dome of Jove."

The monarch took the word, and grave replied:
"Presumptuous are the vaunts, and vain the pride
Of man, who dares in pomp with Jove contest,
Unchanged, immortal, and supremely blest!
With all my affluence, when my woes are weigh'd,
Envy will own the purchase dearly paid.
For eight slow-circling years, by tempests toss'd,
From Cypress to the far Phoenician coast
(Sidon the capital), I stretch'd my toil
Through regions fatten'd with the flows of Nile.
Next Aethiopia's utmost bound explore,
And the parch'd borders of the Arabian shore;
Then warp my voyage on the southern gales,
O'er the warm Lybian wave to spread my sails;
That happy clime, where each revolving year
The teeming ewes a triple offspring bear;
And two fair crescents of translucent horn
The brows of all their young increase adorn:
The shepherd swains, with sure abundance blest,
On the fat flock and rural dainties feast;
Nor want of herbage makes the dairy fail,
But every season fills the foaming pail.
Whilst, heaping unwash'd wealth, I distant roam,
The best of brothers, at his natal home,

By the dire fury of a traitress wife,
Ends the sad evening of a stormy life;
Whence, with incessant grief my soul annoy'd,
These riches are possess'd, but not enjoy'd!
My wars, the copious theme of every tongue,
To you your fathers have recorded long.
How favouring Heaven repaid my glorious toils
With a sack'd palace, and barbaric spoils.
Oh! had the gods so large a boon denied
And life, the just equivalent supplied
To those brave warriors, who, with glory fired
Far from their country, in my cause expired!
Still in short intervals of pleasing woe.
Regardful of the friendly dues I owe,
I to the glorious dead, for ever dear!
Indulge the tribute of a grateful tear.
But oh! Ulysses—deeper than the rest
That sad idea wounds my anxious breast!
My heart bleeds fresh with agonizing pain;
The bowl and tasteful viands tempt in vain;
Nor sleep's soft power can close my streaming eyes,
When imaged to my soul his sorrows rise.
No peril in my cause he ceased to prove,
His labours equall'd only by my love:
And both alike to bitter fortune born,
For him to suffer, and for me to mourn!
Whether he wanders on some friendly coast,
Or glides in Stygian gloom a pensive ghost,
No fame reveals; but, doubtful of his doom,
His good old sire with sorrow to the tomb
Declines his trembling steps; untimely care
Withers the blooming vigour of his heir;
And the chaste partner of his bed and throne
Wastes all her widow'd hours in tender moan."

While thus pathetic to the prince he spoke,
From the brave youth the streaming passion broke;
Studious to veil the grief, in vain repress'd,
His face he shrouded with his purple vest.
The conscious monarch pierced the coy disguise,
And view'd his filial love with vast surprise:
Dubious to press the tender theme, or wait
To hear the youth inquire his father's fate.
In this suspense bright Helen graced the room;
Before her breathed a gale of rich perfume.
So moves, adorn'd with each attractive grace,
The silver shafted goddess of the chase!
The seat of majesty Adraste brings,

With art illustrious, for the pomp of kings;
To spread the pall (beneath the regal chair)
Of softest wool, is bright Alcippe's care.
A silver canister, divinely wrought,
In her soft hands the beauteous Phylo brought;
To Sparta's queen of old the radiant vase
Alcandra gave, a pledge of royal grace;
For Polybus her lord (whose sovereign sway
The wealthy tribes of Pharian Thebes obey),
When to that court Atrides came, caress'd
With vast munificence the imperial guest:
Two lavers from the richest ore refined,
With silver tripods, the kind host assign'd;
And bounteous from the royal treasure told
Ten equal talents of refulgent gold.
Alcandra, consort of his high command,
A golden distaff gave to Helen's hand;
And that rich vase, with living sculpture wrought,
Which heap'd with wool the beauteous Phylo brought
The silken fleece, impurpled for the loom,
Rivall'd the hyacinth in vernal bloom.
The sovereign seat then Jove born Helen press'd,
And pleasing thus her sceptred lord address'd:

"Who grace our palace now, that friendly pair,
Speak they their lineage, or their names declare?
Uncertain of the truth, yet uncontroll'd,
Hear me the bodings of my breast unfold.
With wonder wrapp'd on yonder check I trace
The feature of the Ulyssean race:
Diffused o'er each resembling line appear,
In just similitude, the grace and air
Of young Telemachus! the lovely boy,
Who bless'd Ulysses with a father's joy,
What time the Greeks combined their social arms,
To avenge the stain of my ill-fated charms!"

"Just is thy thought, (the king assenting cries,)
Methinks Ulysses strikes my wondering eyes;
Full shines the father in the filial frame,
His port, his features, and his shape the same;
Such quick regards his sparkling eyes bestow;
Such wavy ringlets o'er his shoulders flow
And when he heard the long disastrous store
Of cares, which in my cause Ulysses bore;
Dismay'd, heart-wounded with paternal woes,
Above restraint the tide of sorrow rose;
Cautious to let the gushing grief appear,

His purple garment veil'd the falling tear."

"See there confess'd (Pisistratus replies)
The genuine worth of Ithacus the wise!
Of that heroic sire the youth is sprung,
But modest awe hath chain'd his timorous tongue.
Thy voice, O king! with pleased attention heard,
Is like the dictates of a god revered.
With him, at Nestor's high command, I came,
Whose age I honour with a parent's name.
By adverse destiny constrained to sue
For counsel and redress, he sues to you
Whatever ill the friendless orphan bears,
Bereaved of parents in his infant years,
Still must the wrong'd Telemachus sustain,
If, hopeful of your aid, he hopes in vain;
Affianced in your friendly power alone,
The youth would vindicate the vacant throne."

"Is Sparta blest, and these desiring eyes
View my friend's son? (the king exalting cries;)
Son of my friend, by glorious toils approved,
Whose sword was sacred to the man he loved;
Mirror of constant faith, revered and mourn'd—
When Troy was ruin'd, had the chief return'd,
No Greek an equal space had ere possess'd,
Of dear affection, in my grateful breast.
I, to confirm the mutual joys we shared,
For his abode a capital prepared;
Argos, the seat of sovereign rule, I chose;
Fair in the plan the future palace rose,
Where my Ulysses and his race might reign,
And portion to his tribes the wide domain,
To them my vassals had resign'd a soil,
With teeming plenty to reward their toil.
There with commutual zeal we both had strove
In acts of dear benevolence and love:
Brothers in peace, not rivals in command,
And death alone dissolved the friendly band!
Some envious power the blissful scene destroys;
Vanish'd are all the visionary joys;
The soul of friendship to my hope is lost,
Fated to wander from his natal coast!"

He ceased; a gush of grief began to rise:
Fast streams a tide from beauteous Helen's eyes;
Fast for the sire the filial sorrows flow;
The weeping monarch swells the mighty woe;

Thy cheeks, Pisistratus, the tears bedew,
While pictured so thy mind appear'd in view,
Thy martial brother; on the Phrygian plain
Extended pale, by swarthy Memnon slain!
But silence soon the son of Nestor broke,
And melting with fraternal pity, spoke:

"Frequent, O king, was Nestor wont to raise
And charm attention with thy copious praise;
To crowd thy various gifts, the sage assign'd
The glory of a firm capacious mind;
With that superior attribute control
This unavailing impotence of soul,
Let not your roof with echoing grief resound,
Now for the feast the friendly bowl is crown'd;
But when, from dewy shade emerging bright,
Aurora streaks the sky with orient light,
Let each deplore his dead; the rites of woe
Are all, alas! the living can bestow;
O'er the congenial dust enjoin'd to shear
The graceful curl, and drop the tender tear.
Then, mingling in the mournful pomp with you,
I'll pay my brother's ghost a warrior's due,
And mourn the brave Antilochus, a name
Not unrecorded in the rolls of fame;
With strength and speed superior form'd, in fight
To face the foe, or intercept his flight;
Too early snatch'd by fate ere known to me!
I boast a witness of his worth in thee."

"Young and mature! (the monarch thus rejoins,)
In thee renew'd the soul of Nestor shines;
Form'd by the care of that consummate sage,
In early bloom an oracle of age.
Whene'er his influence Jove vouchsafes to shower,
To bless the natal and the nuptial hour;
From the great sire transmissive to the race,
The boon devolving gives distinguish'd grace.
Such, happy Nestor! was thy glorious doom,
Around thee, full of years, thy offspring bloom.
Expert of arms, and prudent in debate;
The gifts of Heaven to guard thy hoary state.
But now let each becalm his troubled breast,
Wash, and partake serene the friendly feast.
To move thy suit, Telemachus, delay,
Till heaven's revolving lamp restores the day."

He said, Asphalion swift the laver brings;

Alternate, all partake the grateful springs;
Then from the rites of purity repair,
And with keen gust the savoury viands share.
Meantime, with genial joy to warm the soul,
Bright Helen mix'd a mirth inspiring bowl;
Temper'd with drugs of sovereign use, to assuage
The boiling bosom of tumultuous rage;
To clear the cloudy front of wrinkled Care,
And dry the tearful sluices of Despair;
Charm'd with that virtuous draught, the exalted mind
All sense of woe delivers to the wind.
Though on the blazing pile his parent lay.
Or a loved brother groan'd his life away.
Or darling son, oppress'd by ruffian force,
Fell breathless at his feet, a mangled corse;
From morn to eve, impassive and serene,
The man entranced would view the dreadful scene
These drugs, so friendly to the joys of life.
Bright Helen learn'd from Thone's imperial wife;
Who sway'd the sceptre, where prolific Nile
With various simples clothes the fatten'd soil.
With wholesome herbage mix'd, the direful bane
Of vegetable venom taints the plain;
From Paeon sprung, their patron-god imparts
To all the Pharian race his healing arts.
The beverage now prepared to inspire the feast,
The circle thus the beauteous queen addressed:

"Throned in omnipotence, supremest Jove
Tempers the fates of human race above;
By the firm sanction of his sovereign will,
Alternate are decreed our good and ill.
To feastful mirth be this white hour assign'd.
And sweet discourse, the banquet of the mind
Myself, assisting in the social joy,
Will tell Ulysses' bold exploit in Troy,
Sole witness of the deed I now declare
Speak you (who saw) his wonders in the war.

"Seam'd o'er with wounds, which his own sabre gave,
In the vile habit of a village slave,
The foe deceived, he pass'd the tented plain,
In Troy to mingle with the hostile train.
In this attire secure from searching eyes,
Till happily piercing through the dark disguise,
The chief I challenged; he, whose practised wit
Knew all the serpent mazes of deceit,
Eludes my search; but when his form I view'd

Fresh from the bath, with fragrant oils renew'd,
His limbs in military purple dress'd,
Each brightening grace the genuine Greek confess'd.
A previous pledge of sacred faith obtain'd,
Till he the lines and Argive fleet regain'd,
To keep his stay conceal'd; the chief declared
The plans of war against the town prepared.
Exploring then the secrets of the state,
He learn'd what best might urge the Dardan fate;
And, safe returning to the Grecian host,
Sent many a shade to Pluto's dreary coast.
Loud grief resounded through the towers of Troy,
But my pleased bosom glow'd with secret joy:
For then, with dire remorse and conscious shame
I view'd the effects of that disastrous flame.
Which, kindled by the imperious queen of love,
Constrain'd me from my native realm to rove:
And oft in bitterness of soul deplored
My absent daughter and my dearer lord;
Admired among the first of human race,
For every gift of mind and manly grace."

"Right well (replied the king) your speech displays
The matchless merit of the chief you praise:
Heroes in various climes myself have found,
For martial deeds and depth of thought renown'd;
But Ithacus, unrivall'd in his claim,
May boast a title to the loudest fame:
In battle calm he guides the rapid storm,
Wise to resolve, and patient to perform.
What wondrous conduct in the chief appear'd,
When the vast fabric of the steed we rear'd!
Some demon, anxious for the Trojan doom,
Urged you with great Deiphobus to come,
To explore the fraud; with guile opposed to guile.
Slow-pacing thrice around the insidious pile,
Each noted leader's name you thrice invoke,
Your accent varying as their spouses spoke!
The pleasing sounds each latent warrior warm'd,
But most Tydides' and coy heart alarm'd:
To quit the steed we both impatient press
Threatening to answer from the dark recess.
Unmoved the mind of Ithacus remain'd;
And the vain ardours of our love restrain'd;
But Anticlus, unable to control,
Spoke loud the language of his yearning soul:
Ulysses straight, with indignation fired
(For so the common care of Greece required),

Firm to his lips his forceful hands applied,
Till on his tongue the fluttering murmurs died.
Meantime Minerva, from the fraudful horse,
Back to the court of Priam bent your course."

"Inclement fate! (Telemachus replies,)
Frail is the boasted attribute of wise:
The leader mingling with the vulgar host,
Is in the common mass of matter lost!
But now let sleep the painful waste repair
Of sad reflection and corroding care."
He ceased; the menial fair that round her wait,
At Helen's beck prepare the room of state;
Beneath an ample portico they spread
The downy fleece to form the slumberous bed;
And o'er soft palls of purple grain unfold
Rich tapestry, stiff with interwoven gold:
Then, through the illumined dome, to balmy rest
The obsequious herald guides each princely guest;
While to his regal bower the king ascends,
And beauteous Helen on her lord attends.
Soon as the morn, in orient purple dress'd,
Unbarr'd the portal of the roseate east,
The monarch rose; magnificent to view,
The imperial mantle o'er his vest he threw;
The glittering zone athwart his shoulders cast,
A starry falchion low-depending graced;
Clasp'd on his feet the embroidered sandals shine;
And forth he moves, majestic and divine,
Instant to young Telemachus he press'd;
And thus benevolent his speech addressed:

"Say, royal youth, sincere of soul report
Whit cause hath led you to the Spartan court?
Do public or domestic care constrain
This toilsome voyage o'er the surgy main?"

"O highly-flavour'd delegate of Jove!
(Replies the prince) inflamed with filial love,
And anxious hope, to hear my parent's doom,
A suppliant to your royal court I come:
Our sovereign seat a lewd usurping race
With lawless riot and misrule disgrace;
To pamper'd insolence devoted fall
Prime of the flock, and choicest of the stall:
For wild ambition wings their bold desire,
And all to mount the imperial bed aspire.
But prostrate I implore, O king! relate

The mournful series of my father's fate:
Each known disaster of the man disclose,
Born by his mother to a world of woes!
Recite them; nor in erring pity fear
To wound with storied grief the filial ear.
If e'er Ulysses, to reclaim your right,
Avow'd his zeal in council or in fight,
If Phrygian camps the friendly toils attest,
To the sire's merit give the son's request."

Deep from his inmost soul Atrides sigh'd,
And thus, indignant, to the prince replied:
"Heavens! would a soft, inglorious, dastard train
An absent hero's nuptial joys profane!
So with her young, amid the woodland shades,
A timorous hind the lion's court invades,
Leaves in the fatal lair the tender fawns,
Climbs the green cliff, or feeds the flowery lawns:
Meantime return'd, with dire remorseless sway,
The monarch-savage rends the trembling prey.
With equal fury, and with equal fame,
Ulysses soon shall reassert his claim.
O Jove supreme, whom gods and men revere!
And thou! to whom 'tis given to gild the sphere!
With power congenial join'd, propitious aid
The chief adopted by the martial maid!
Such to our wish the warrior soon restore,
As when contending on the Lesbian shore
His prowess Philomelidies confess'd,
And loud-acclaiming Greeks the victor bless'd;
Then soon the invaders of his bed and throne
Their love presumptuous shall with life atone.
With patient ear, O royal youth, attend
The storied labour of thy father's friend:
Fruitful of deeds, the copious tale is long,
But truth severe shall dictate to my tongue:
Learn what I heard the sea-born seer relate,
Whose eye can pierce the dark recess of fate.

"Long on the Egyptian coast by calms confined,
Heaven to my fleet refused a prosperous wind;
No vows had we preferr'd, nor victims slain!
For this the gods each favouring gale restrain
Jealous, to see their high behests obey'd;
Severe, if men the eternal rights evade.
High o'er a gulfy sea, the Pharian isle
Fronts the deep roar of disemboguing Nile:
Her distance from the shore, the course begun

At dawn, and ending with the setting sun,
A galley measures; when the stiffer gales
Rise on the poop, and fully stretch the sails.
There, anchor'd vessels safe in harbour lie,
Whilst limpid springs the failing cask supply.

"And now the twentieth sun, descending, laves
His glowing axle in the western waves:
Still with expanded sails we court in vain
Propitious winds to waft us o'er the main;
And the pale mariner at once deplores
His drooping vigour and exhausted stores.
When lo! a bright cerulean form appears,
Proteus her sire divine. With pity press'd,
Me sole the daughter of the deep address'd;
What time, with hunger pined, my absent mates
Roam the wide isle in search of rural cates,
Bait the barb'd steel, and from the fishy flood
Appease the afflictive fierce desire of food."

"'Whoe'er thou art (the azure goddess cries)
Thy conduct ill-deserves the praise of wise:
Is death thy choice, or misery thy boast,
That here inglorious, on a barren coast,
Thy brave associates droop, a meagre train,
With famine pale, and ask thy care in vain?'
"Struck with the loud reproach, I straight reply:
'Whate'er thy title in thy native sky,
A goddess sure! for more than moral grace
Speaks thee descendant of ethereal race;
Deem not that here of choice my fleet remains;
Some heavenly power averse my stay constrains:
O, piteous of my fate, vouchsafe to show
(For what's sequester'd from celestial view?)
What power becalms the innavigable seas?
What guilt provokes him, and what vows appease?'

"I ceased, when affable the goddess cried:
'Observe, and in the truths I speak confide;
The oracular seer frequents the Pharian coast,
From whose high bed my birth divine I boast;
Proteus, a name tremendous o'er the main,
The delegate of Neptune's watery reign.
Watch with insidious care his known abode;
There fast in chains constrain the various god;
Who bound, obedient to superior force,
Unerring will prescribe your destined course.
If, studious on your realms, you then demand

Their state, since last you left your natal land,
Instant the god obsequious will disclose
Bright tracts of glory or a cloud of woes.'

"She ceased; and suppliant thus I made reply:
'O goddess I on thy aid my hopes rely;
Dictate propitious to my duteous ear,
What arts can captivate the changeful seer;
For perilous the assay, unheard the toil,
To elude the prescience of a god by guile.'

"Thus to the goddess mild my suit I end.
Then she: 'Obedient to my rule attend:
When through the zone of heaven the mounted sun
Hath journeyed half, and half remains to run;
The seer, while zephyrs curl the swelling deep,
Basks on the breezy shore, in grateful sleep,
His oozy limbs. Emerging from the wave,
The Phocas swift surround his rocky cave,
Frequent and full; the consecrated train
Of her, whose azure trident awes the main;
There wallowing warm, the enormous herd exhales
An oily steam, and taints the noontide gales.
To that recess, commodious for surprise,
When purple light shall next suffuse the skies,
With me repair; and from thy warrior-band
Three chosen chiefs of dauntless soul command;
Let their auxiliar force befriend the toil;
For strong the god, and perfected in guile.
Strech'd on the shelly shore, he first surveys
The flouncing herd ascending from the seas,
Their number summ'd, reposed in sleep profound
The scaly charge their guardian god surround;
So with his battening flocks the careful swain
Abides pavilion'd on the grassy plain.
With powers united, obstinately bold,
Invade him, couch'd amid the scaly fold;
Instant he wears, elusive of the rape,
The mimic force of every savage shape;
Or glides with liquid lapse a murmuring stream,
Or, wrapp'd in flame, he glows at every limb.
Yet, still retentive, with redoubled might,
Through each vain passive form constrain his flight
But when, his native shape renamed, he stands
Patient of conquest, and your cause demands;
The cause that urged the bold attempt declare,
And soothe the vanquish'd with a victor's prayer.
The bands releas'd, implore the seer to say

What godhead interdicts the watery way.
Who, straight propitious, in prophetic strain
Will teach you to repass the unmeasured main.
She ceased, and bounding from the shelfy shore,
Round the descending nymph the waves resounding roar.

"High wrapp'd in wonder of the future deed,
with joy impetuous to the port I speed:
The wants of nature with repast suffice,
Till night with grateful shade involved the skies,
And shed ambrosial dews. Fast by the deep,
Along the tented shore, in balmy sleep,
Our cares were lost. When o'er the eastern lawn,
In saffron robes, the daughter of the dawn
Advanced her rosy steps, before the bay
Due ritual honours to the gods I pay;
Then seek the place the sea-born nymph assign'd,
With three associates of undaunted mind.
Arrived, to form along the appointed strand
For each a bed, she scoops the hilly sand;
Then, from her azure cave the finny spoils
Of four vast Phocae takes, to veil her wiles;
Beneath the finny spoils extended prone,
Hard toil! the prophet's piercing eye to shun;
New from the corse, the scaly frauds diffuse
Unsavoury stench of oil, and brackish ooze;
But the bright sea-maid's gentle power implored,
With nectar'd drops the sickening sense restored.

"Thus till the sun had travell'd half the skies,
Ambush'd we lie, and wait the bold emprise;
When, thronging quick to bask in open air,
The flocks of ocean to the strand repair;
Couch'd on the sunny sand, the monsters sleep;
Then Proteus, mounting from the hoary deep,
Surveys his charge, unknowing of deceit;
(In order told, we make the sum complete.)
Pleased with the false review, secure he lies,
And leaden slumbers press his drooping eyes.
Rushing impetuous forth, we straight prepare
A furious onset with the sound of war,
And shouting seize the god; our force to evade,
His various arts he soon resumes in aid;
A lion now, he curls a surgy mane;
Sudden our hands a spotted paid restrain;
Then, arm'd with tusks, and lightning in his eyes,
A boar's obscener shape the god belies;
On spiry volumes, there a dragon rides;

Here, from our strict embrace a stream he glides.
At last, sublime, his stately growth he rears
A tree, and well-dissembled foliage wears.
Vain efforts with superior power compress'd,
Me with reluctance thus the seer address'd;
'Say, son of Atreus, say what god inspired
This daring fraud, and what the boon desired?'
I thus: 'O thou, whose certain eye foresees
The fix'd event of fate's remote decrees;
After long woes, and various toil endured,
Still on this desert isle my fleet is moor'd,
Unfriended of the gales. All-knowing, say,
What godhead interdicts the watery way?
What vows repentant will the power appease,
To speed a prosperous voyage o'er the seas.'

"'To Jove (with stern regard the god replies)
And all the offended synod of the skies,
Just hecatombs with due devotion slain,
Thy guilt absolved, a prosperous voyage gain.
To the firm sanction of thy fate attend!
An exile thou, nor cheering face of friend,
Nor sight of natal shore, nor regal dome,
Shalt yet enjoy, but still art doom'd to roam.
Once more the Nile, who from the secret source
Of Jove's high seat descends with sweepy force,
Must view his billows white beneath thy oar,
And altars blaze along his sanguine shore.
Then will the gods with holy pomp adored,
To thy long vows a safe return accord.'

"He ceased: heart wounded with afflictive pain,
(Doom'd to repeat the perils of the main,
A shelfy track and long!) 'O seer' I cry,
'To the stern sanction of the offended sky
My prompt obedience bows. But deign to say
What fate propitious, or what dire dismay,
Sustain those peers, the relics of our host,
Whom I with Nestor on the Phrygian coast
Embracing left? Must I the warriors weep,
Whelm'd in the bottom of the monstrous deep?
Or did the kind domestic friend deplore
The breathless heroes on their native shore?

"'Press not too far,' replied the god: 'but cease
To know what, known, will violate thy peace;
Too curious of their doom! with friendly woe
Thy breast will heave, and tears eternal flow.

Part live! the rest, a lamentable train!
Range the dark bounds of Pluto's dreary reign.
Two, foremost in the roll of Mars renown'd,
Whose arms with conquest in thy cause were crown'd,
Fell by disastrous fate: by tempests toss'd,
A third lives wretched on a distant coast.

"By Neptune rescued from Minerva's hate,
On Gyrae, safe Oilean Ajax sate,
His ship o'erwhelm'd; but, frowning on the floods,
Impious he roar'd defiance to the gods;
To his own prowess all the glory gave:
The power defrauding who vouchsafed to save.
This heard the raging ruler of the main;
His spear, indignant for such high disdain,
He launched; dividing with his forky mace
The aerial summit from the marble base:
The rock rush'd seaward, with impetuous roar
Ingulf'd, and to the abyss the boaster bore.

"By Juno's guardian aid, the watery vast,
Secure of storms, your royal brother pass'd,
Till, coasting nigh the cape where Malen shrouds
Her spiry cliffs amid surrounding clouds,
A whirling gust tumultuous from the shore
Across the deep his labouring vessel bore.
In an ill-fated hour the coast he gain'd,
Where late in regal pomp Thyestes reigned;
But, when his hoary honours bow'd to fate,
Aegysthus govern'd in paternal state,
The surges now subside, the tempest ends;
From his tall ship the king of men descends;
There fondly thinks the gods conclude his toil:
Far from his own domain salutes the soil;
With rapture oft the urge of Greece reviews,
And the dear turf with tears of joy bedews.
Him, thus exulting on the distant stand,
A spy distinguish'd from his airy stand;
To bribe whose vigilance, Aegysthus told
A mighty sum of ill-persuading gold:
There watch'd this guardian of his guilty fear,
Till the twelfth moon had wheel'd her pale career;
And now, admonish'd by his eye, to court
With terror wing'd conveys the dread report.
Of deathful arts expert, his lord employs
The ministers of blood in dark surprise;
And twenty youths, in radiant mail incased,
Close ambush'd nigh the spacious hall he placed.

Then bids prepare the hospitable treat:
Vain shows of love to veil his felon hate!
To grace the victor's welcome from the wars,
A train of coursers and triumphal cars
Magnificent he leads: the royal guest,
Thoughtless of ill, accepts the fraudful feast.
The troop forth-issuing from the dark recess,
With homicidal rage the king oppress!
So, whilst he feeds luxurious in the stall,
The sovereign of the herd is doomed to fall,
The partners of his fame and toils at Troy,
Around their lord, a mighty ruin, lie:
Mix'd with the brave, the base invaders bleed;
Aegysthus sole survives to boast the deed."

He said: chill horrors shook my shivering soul,
Rack'd wish convulsive pangs in dust I roll;
And hate, in madness of extreme despair,
To view the sun, or breathe the vital air.
But when, superior to the rage of woe,
I stood restored and tears had ceased to flow,
Lenient of grief the pitying god began:
'Forget the brother, and resume the man.
To Fate's supreme dispose the dead resign,
That care be Fate's, a speedy passage thine
Still lives the wretch who wrought the death deplored,
But lives a victim for thy vengeful sword;
Unless with filial rage Orestes glow,
And swift prevent the meditated blow:
You timely will return a welcome guest,
With him to share the sad funereal feast."

"He said: new thoughts my beating heart employ,
My gloomy soul receives a gleam of joy.
Fair hope revives; and eager I address'd
The prescient godhead to reveal the rest:
'The doom decreed of those disastrous two
I've heard with pain, but oh! the tale pursue;
What third brave son of Mars the Fates constrain
To roam the howling desert of the main;
Or, in eternal shade of cold he lies,
Provoke new sorrows from these grateful eyes.'

"'That chief (rejoin'd the god) his race derives
From Ithaca, and wondrous woes survives;
Laertes' son: girt with circumfluous tides,
He still calamitous constraint abides.
Him in Calypso's cave of late! view'd,

When streaming grief his faded cheek bedow'd.
But vain his prayer, his arts are vain, to move
The enamour'd goddess, or elude her love:
His vessel sunk, and dear companions lost,
He lives reluctant on a foreign coast.
But oh, beloved by Heaven! reserved to thee
A happier lot the smiling Fates decree:
Free from that law, beneath whose mortal sway
Matter is changed, and varying forms decay,
Elysium shall be thine: the blissful plains
Of utmost earth, where Rhadamanthus reigns.
Joys ever young, unmix'd with pain or fear,
Fill the wide circle of the eternal year:
Stern winter smiles on that auspicious clime:
The fields are florid with unfading prime;
From the bleak pole no winds inclement blow,
Mould the round hail, or flake the fleecy snow;
But from the breezy deep the blest inhale
The fragrant murmurs of the western gale.
This grace peculiar will the gods afford
To thee, the son of Jove, and beauteous Helen's lord.'

"He ceased, and plunging in the vast profound,
Beneath the god and whirling billows bound.
Then speeding back, involved in various thought,
My friends attending at the shore I sought,
Arrived, the rage of hunger we control
Till night with silent shade invests the pole;
Then lose the cares of life in pleasing rest.
Soon as the morn reveals the roseate east,
With sails we wing the masts, our anchors weigh,
Unmoor the fleet, and rush into the sea.
Ranged on the banks, beneath our equal oars
White curl the waves, and the vex'd ocean roars
Then, steering backward from the Pharian isle,
We gain the stream of Jove-descended Nile;
There quit the ships, and on the destined shore
With ritual hecatombs the gods adore;
Their wrath atoned, to Agamemnon's name
A cenotaph I raise of deathless fame.
These rites to piety and grief discharged,
The friendly gods a springing gale enlarged;
The fleet swift tilting o'er the surges flew,
Till Grecian cliffs appear'd a blissful view!

"Thy patient ear hath heard me long relate
A story, fruitful of disastrous fate.
And now, young prince, indulge my fond request;

Be Sparta honoured with his royal guest,
Till, from his eastern goal, the joyous sun
His twelfth diurnal race begins to run.
Meantime my train the friendly gifts prepare,
The sprightly coursers and a polish'd car;
With these a goblet of capacious mould,
Figured with art to dignify the gold
(Form'd for libation to the gods), shall prove
A pledge and monument of sacred love."

"My quick return (young Ithacus rejoin'd),
Damps the warm wishes of my raptured mind;
Did not my fate my needful haste constrain,
Charm'd by your speech so graceful and humane,
Lost in delight the circling year would roll,
While deep attention fix'd my listening soul.
But now to Pyle permit my destined way,
My loved associates chide my long delay:
In dear remembrance of your royal grace,
I take the present of the promised vase;
The coursers, for the champaign sports retain;
That gift our barren rocks will render vain:
Horrid with cliffs, our meagre land allows
Thin herbage for the mountain goat to browse,
But neither mead nor plain supplies, to feed
The sprightly courser, or indulge his speed:
To sea-surrounded realms the gods assign
Small tract of fertile lawn, the least to mine."

His hand the king with tender passion press'd,
And, smiling, thus the royal youth address'd:
"O early worth! a soul so wise, and young,
Proclaims you from the sage Ulysses sprung.
Selected from my stores, of matchless price,
An urn shall recompense your prudent choice;
By Vulcan's art, the verge with gold enchased.
A pledge the sceptred power of Sidon gave,
When to his realm I plough'd the orient wave."

Thus they alternate; while, with artful care,
The menial train the regal feast prepare.
The firstlings of the flock are doom'd to die:
Rich fragrant wines the cheering bowl supply;
A female band the gift of Ceres bring;
And the gilt roofs with genial triumph ring.

Meanwhile, in Ithaca, the suitor powers
In active games divide their jovial hours;

In areas varied with mosaic art,
Some whirl the disk, and some the javelin dart,
Aside, sequester'd from the vast resort,
Antinous sole spectator of the sport;
With great Eurymachus, of worth confess'd,
And high descent, superior to the rest;
Whom young Noemon lowly thus address'd:—

"My ship, equipp'd within the neighboring port,
The prince, departing for the Pylian court,
Requested for his speed; but, courteous, say
When steers he home, or why this long delay?
For Elis I should sail with utmost speed.
To import twelve mares which there luxurious feed,
And twelve young mules, a strong laborious race,
New to the plow, unpractised in the trace."

Unknowing of the course to Pyle design'd,
A sudden horror seized on either mind;
The prince in rural bower they fondly thought,
Numbering his flocks and herds, not far remote.
"Relate (Antinous cries), devoid of guile,
When spread the prince his sale for distant Pyle?
Did chosen chiefs across the gulfy main
Attend his voyage, or domestic train?
Spontaneous did you speed his secret course,
Or was the vessel seized by fraud or force?"

"With willing duty, not reluctant mind
(Noemon cried), the vessel was resign'd,
Who, in the balance, with the great affairs
Of courts presume to weigh their private cares?
With him, the peerage next in power to you;
And Mentor, captain of the lordly crew,
Or some celestial in his reverend form,
Safe from the secret rock and adverse storm,
Pilot's the course; for when the glimmering ray
Of yester dawn disclosed the tender day,
Mentor himself I saw, and much admired,"
Then ceased the youth, and from the court retired.

Confounded and appall'd, the unfinish'd game
The suitors quit, and all to council came.
Antinous first the assembled peers address'd.
Rage sparkling in his eyes, and burning in his breast

"O shame to manhood! shall one daring boy
The scheme of all our happiness destroy?

Fly unperceived, seducing half the flower
Of nobles, and invite a foreign power?
The ponderous engine raised to crush us all,
Recoiling, on his head is sure to fall.
Instant prepare me, on the neighbouring strand,
With twenty chosen mates a vessel mann'd;
For ambush'd close beneath the Samian shore
His ship returning shall my spies explore;
He soon his rashness shall with life atone,
Seek for his father's fate, but find his own."

With vast applause the sentence all approve;
Then rise, and to the feastful hall remove;
Swift to the queen the herald Medon ran,
Who heard the consult of the dire divan:
Before her dome the royal matron stands,
And thus the message of his haste demands;

"What will the suitors? must my servant-train
The allotted labours of the day refrain,
For them to form some exquisite repast?
Heaven grant this festival may prove their last!
Or, if they still must live, from me remove
The double plague of luxury and love!
Forbear, ye sons of insolence! forbear,
In riot to consume a wretched heir.
In the young soul illustrious thought to raise,
Were ye not tutor'd with Ulysses' praise?
Have not your fathers oft my lord defined,
Gentle of speech, beneficent of mind?
Some kings with arbitrary rage devour,
Or in their tyrant-minions vest the power;
Ulysses let no partial favours fall,
The people's parent, he protected all;
But absent now, perfidious and ingrate!
His stores ye ravage, and usurp his state."

He thus: "O were the woes you speak the worst!
They form a deed more odious and accursed;
More dreadful than your boding soul divines;
But pitying Jove avert the dire designs!
The darling object of your royal care
Is marked to perish in a deathful snare;
Before he anchors in his native port,
From Pyle re-sailing and the Spartan court;
Horrid to speak! in ambush is decreed
The hope and heir of Ithaca to bleed!"

Sudden she sunk beneath the weighty woes,
The vital streams a chilling horror froze;
The big round tear stands trembling in her eye,
And on her tongue imperfect accents die.
At length in tender language interwove
With sighs, she thus expressed her anxious love;
"Why rarely would my son his fate explore,
Ride the wild waves, and quit the safer shore?
Did he with all the greatly wretched, crave
A blank oblivion, and untimely grave?"

"Tis not (replied the sage) to Medon given
To know, if some inhabitant of heaven
In his young breast the daring thought inspired
Or if, alone with filial duty fired,
The winds end waves he tempts in early bloom,
Studious to learn his absent father's doom."

The sage retired: unable to control
The mighty griefs that swell her labouring soul
Rolling convulsive on the floor is seen
The piteous object of a prostrate queen.
Words to her dumb complaint a pause supplies,
And breath, to waste in unavailing cries.
Around their sovereign wept the menial fair,
To whom she thus address'd her deep despair:

"Behold a wretch whom all the gods consign
To woe! Did ever sorrows equal mine?
Long to my joys my dearest lord is lost,
His country's buckler, and the Grecian boast;
Now from my fond embrace, by tempests torn,
Our other column of the state is borne;
Nor took a kind adieu, nor sought consent!—
Unkind confederates in his dire intent!
Ill suits it with your shows of duteous zeal,
From me the purposed voyage to conceal;
Though at the solemn midnight hour he rose,
Why did you fear to trouble my repose?
He either had obey'd my fond desire,
Or seen his mother pierced with grief expire.
Bid Dolius quick attend, the faithful slave
Whom to my nuptial train Icarius gave
To tend the fruit groves: with incessant speed
He shall this violence of death decreed
To good Laertes tell. Experienced age
May timely intercept the ruffian rage.
Convene the tribes the murderous plot reveal,

And to their power to save his race appeal."

Then Euryclea thus: "My dearest dread;
Though to the sword I bow this hoary head,
Or if a dungeon be the pain decreed,
I own me conscious of the unpleasing deed;
Auxiliar to his flight, my aid implored,
With wine and viands I the vessel stored;
A solemn oath, imposed, the secret seal'd,
Till the twelfth dawn the light of day reveal'd.
Dreading the effect of a fond mother's fear,
He dared not violate your royal ear.
But bathe, and, in imperial robes array'd,
Pay due devotions to the martial maid,
And rest affianced in her guardian aid.
Send not to good Laertes, nor engage
In toils of state the miseries of age:
Tis impious to surmise the powers divine
To ruin doom the Jove-descended line;
Long shall the race of just Arcesius reign,
And isles remote enlarge his old domain."

The queen her speech with calm attention hears,
Her eyes restrain the silver-streaming tears:
She bathes, and robed, the sacred dome ascends;
Her pious speed a female train attends:
The salted cakes in canisters are laid,
And thus the queen invokes Minerva's aid;

"Daughter divine of Jove, whose arm can wield
The avenging bolt, and shake the dreadful shield
If e'er Ulysses to thy fane preferr'd
The best and choicest of his flock and herd;
Hear, goddess, hear, by those oblations won;
And for the pious sire preserve the son;
His wish'd return with happy power befriend,
And on the suitors let thy wrath descend."

She ceased; shrill ecstasies of joy declare
The favouring goddess present to the prayer;
The suitors heard, and deem'd the mirthful voice
A signal of her hymeneal choice;
Whilst one most jovial thus accosts the board:

"Too late the queen selects a second lord;
In evil hour the nuptial rite intends,
When o'er her son disastrous death impends."
Thus he, unskill'd of what the fates provide!

But with severe rebuke Antinous cried:

"These empty vaunts will make the voyage vain:
Alarm not with discourse the menial train:
The great event with silent hope attend,
Our deeds alone our counsel must commend."
His speech thus ended short, he frowning rose,
And twenty chiefs renowned for valour chose;
Down to the strand he speeds with haughty strides,
Where anchor'd in the bay the vessel rides,
Replete with mail and military store,
In all her tackle trim to quit the shore.
The desperate crew ascend, unfurl the sails
(The seaward prow invites the tardy gales);
Then take repast till Hesperus display'd
His golden circlet, in the western shade.

Meantime the queen, without reflection due,
Heart-wounded, to the bed of state withdrew:
In her sad breast the prince's fortunes roll,
And hope and doubt alternate seize her soul.
So when the woodman's toil her cave surrounds,
And with the hunter's cry the grove resounds,
With grief and rage the mother-lion stung.
Fearless herself, yet trembles for her young
While pensive in the silent slumberous shade,
Sleep's gentle powers her drooping eyes invade;
Minerva, life-like, on embodied air
Impress'd the form of Iphthima the fair;
(Icarius' daughter she, whose blooming charms
Allured Eumelus to her virgin arms;
A sceptred lord, who o'er the fruitful plain
Of Thessaly wide stretched his ample reign:)
As Pallas will'd, along the sable skies,
To calm the queen, the phantom sister flies.
Swift on the regal dome, descending right,
The bolted valves are pervious to her flight.
Close to her head the pleasing vision stands,
And thus performs Minerva's high commands

"O why, Penelope, this causeless fear,
To render sleep's soft blessing unsincere?
Alike devote to sorrow's dire extreme
The day-reflection, and the midnight-dream!
Thy son the gods propitious will restore,
And bid thee cease his absence to deplore."

To whom the queen (whilst yet in pensive mind

Was in the silent gates of sleep confined):
"O sister to my soul forever dear,
Why this first visit to reprove my fear?
How in a realm so distant should you know
From what deep source ceaseless sorrows flow?
To all my hope my royal lord is lost,
His country's buckler, and the Grecian boast;
And with consummate woe to weigh me down,
The heir of all his honours and his crown,
My darling son is fled! an easy prey
To the fierce storms, or men more fierce than they;
Who, in a league of blood associates sworn,
Will intercept the unwary youth's return."

"Courage resume (the shadowy form replied);
In the protecting care of Heaven confide;
On him attends the blue eyed martial maid:
What earthly can implore a surer aid?
Me now the guardian goddess deigns to send,
To bid thee patient his return attend."

The queen replies: "If in the blest abodes,
A goddess, thou hast commerce with the gods;
Say, breathes my lord the blissful realm of light,
Or lies he wrapp'd in ever-during night?"

"Inquire not of his doom, (the phantom cries,)
I speak not all the counsel of the skies;
Nor must indulge with vain discourse, or long,
The windy satisfaction of the tongue."

Swift through the valves the visionary fair
Repass'd, and viewless mix'd with common air.
The queen awakes, deliver'd of her woes;
With florid joy her heart dilating glows:
The vision, manifest of future fate,
Makes her with hope her son's arrival wait.

Meantime the suitors plough the watery plain,
Telemachus in thought already slain!
When sight of lessening Ithaca was lost
Their sail directed for the Samian coast
A small but verdant isle appear'd in view,
And Asteris the advancing pilot knew;
An ample port the rocks projected form,
To break the rolling waves and ruffling storm:
That safe recess they gain with happy speed,
And in close ambush wait the murderous deed.

BOOK V

ARGUMENT

THE DEPARTURE OF ULYSSES FROM CALYPSO

Pallas in a council of the gods complains of the detention of Ulysses in the Island of Calypso: whereupon Mercury is sent to command his removal. The seat of Calypso described. She consents with much difficulty; and Ulysses builds a vessel with his own hands, in which he embarks. Neptune overtakes him with a terrible tempest, in which he is shipwrecked, and in the last danger of death; till Lencothea, a sea-goddess, assists him, and, after innumerable perils, he gets ashore on Phaeacia.

The saffron morn, with early blushes spread,
Now rose refulgent from Tithonus' bed;
With new-born day to gladden mortal sight,
And gild the courts of heaven with sacred light.
Then met the eternal synod of the sky,
Before the god, who thunders from on high,
Supreme in might, sublime in majesty.
Pallas, to these, deplores the unequal fates
Of wise Ulysses and his toils relates:
Her hero's danger touch'd the pitying power,
The nymph's seducements, and the magic bower.
Thus she began her plaint: "Immortal Jove!
And you who fill the blissful seats above!
Let kings no more with gentle mercy sway,
Or bless a people willing to obey,
But crush the nations with an iron rod,
And every monarch be the scourge of God.
If from your thoughts Ulysses you remove,
Who ruled his subjects with a father's love,
Sole in an isle, encircled by the main,
Abandon'd, banish'd from his native reign,
Unbless'd he sighs, detained by lawless charms,
And press'd unwilling in Calypso's arms.
Nor friends are there, nor vessels to convey,
Nor oars to cut the immeasurable way.
And now fierce traitors, studious to destroy
His only son, their ambush'd fraud employ;
Who, pious, following his great father's fame,
To sacred Pylos and to Sparta came."

"What words are these? (replied the power who forms
The clouds of night, and darkens heaven with storms;)
Is not already in thy soul decreed,

The chief's return shall make the guilty bleed?
What cannot Wisdom do? Thou may'st restore
The son in safety to his native shore;
While the fell foes, who late in ambush lay,
With fraud defeated measure back their way."

Then thus to Hermes the command was given:
"Hermes, thou chosen messenger of heaven!
Go, to the nymph be these our orders borne
'Tis Jove's decree, Ulysses shall return:
The patient man shall view his old abodes,
Nor helped by mortal hand, nor guiding gods
In twice ten days shall fertile Scheria find,
Alone, and floating to the wave and wind.
The bold Phaecians there, whose haughty line
Is mixed with gods, half human, half divine,
The chief shall honour as some heavenly guest,
And swift transport him to his place of rest,
His vessels loaded with a plenteous store
Of brass, of vestures, and resplendent ore
(A richer prize than if his joyful isle
Received him charged with Ilion's noble spoil),
His friends, his country, he shall see, though late:
Such is our sovereign will, and such is fate."

He spoke. The god who mounts the winged winds
Fast to his feet the golden pinions binds,
That high through fields of air his flight sustain
O'er the wide earth, and o'er the boundless main:
He grasps the wand that causes sleep to fly,
Or in soft slumber seals the wakeful eye;
Then shoots from heaven to high Pieria's steep,
And stoops incumbent on the rolling deep.
So watery fowl, that seek their fishy food,
With wings expanded o'er the foaming flood,
Now sailing smooth the level surface sweep,
Now dip their pinions in the briny deep;
Thus o'er the word of waters Hermes flew,
Till now the distant island rose in view:
Then, swift ascending from the azure wave,
he took the path that winded to the cave.
Large was the grot, in which the nymph he found
(The fair-hair'd nymph with every beauty crown'd).
The cave was brighten'd with a rising blaze;
Cedar and frankincense, an odorous pile,
Flamed on the hearth, and wide perfumed the isle;
While she with work and song the time divides,
And through the loom the golden shuttle guides.

Without the grot a various sylvan scene
Appear'd around, and groves of living green;
Poplars and alders ever quivering play'd,
And nodding cypress form'd a fragrant shade:
On whose high branches, waving with the storm,
The birds of broadest wing their mansions form,—
The chough, the sea-mew, the loquacious crow,—
and scream aloft, and skim the deeps below.
Depending vines the shelving cavern screen.
With purple clusters blushing through the green.
Four limped fountains from the clefts distil:
And every fountain pours a several rill,
In mazy windings wandering down the hill:
Where bloomy meads with vivid greens were crown'd,
And glowing violets threw odours round.
A scene, where, if a god should cast his sight,
A god might gaze, and wander with delight!
Joy touch'd the messenger of heaven: he stay'd
Entranced, and all the blissful haunts surveyed.
Him, entering in the cave, Calypso knew;
For powers celestial to each other's view
Stand still confess'd, though distant far they lie
To habitants of earth, or sea, or sky.
But sad Ulysses, by himself apart,
Pour'd the big sorrows of his swelling heard;
All on the lonely shore he sate to weep,
And roll'd his eyes around the restless deep:
Toward his loved coast he roll'd his eyes in vain,
Till, dimm'd with rising grief, they stream'd again.

Now graceful seated on her shining throne,
To Hermes thus the nymph divine begun:

"God of the golden wand! on what behest
Arrivest thou here, an unexpected guest?
Loved as thou art, thy free injunctions lay;
'Tis mine with joy and duty to obey.
Till now a stranger, in a happy hour
Approach, and taste the dainties of my bower."

Thus having spoke, the nymph the table spread
(Ambrosial cates, with nectar rosy-red);
Hermes the hospitable rite partook,
Divine refection! then, recruited, spoke:

"What moves this journey from my native sky,
A goddess asks, nor can a god deny.
Hear then the truth. By mighty Jove's command

Unwilling have I trod this pleasing land:
For who, self-moved, with weary wing would sweep
Such length of ocean and unmeasured deep;
A world of waters! far from all the ways
Where men frequent, or sacred altars blaze!
But to Jove's will submission we must pay;
What power so great to dare to disobey?
A man, he says, a man resides with thee,
Of all his kind most worn with misery.
The Greeks, (whose arms for nine long year employ'd
Their force on Ilion, in the tenth destroy'd,)
At length, embarking in a luckless hour,
With conquest proud, incensed Minerva's power:
Hence on the guilty race her vengeance hurl'd,
With storms pursued them through the liquid world.
There all his vessels sunk beneath the wave!
There all his dear companions found their grave!
Saved from the jaws of death by Heaven's decree,
The tempest drove him to these shores and thee.
Him, Jove now orders to his native lands
Straight to dismiss: so destiny commands:
Impatient Fate his near return attends,
And calls him to his country, and his friends."

E'en to her inmost soul the goddess shook;
Then thus her anguish, and her passion broke:
"Ungracious gods! with spite and envy cursed!
Still to your own ethereal race the worst!
Ye envy mortal and immortal joy,
And love, the only sweet of life destroy,
Did ever goddess by her charms engage
A favour'd mortal, and not feel your rage?
So when Aurora sought Orion's love,
Her joys disturbed your blissful hours above,
Till, in Ortygia Dian's winged dart
Had pierced the hapless hunter to the heart,
So when the covert of the thrice-eared field
Saw stately Ceres to her passion yield,
Scarce could Iasion taste her heavenly charms,
But Jove's swift lightning scorched him in her arms.
And is it now my turn, ye mighty powers!
Am I the envy of your blissful bowers?
A man, an outcast to the storm and wave,
It was my crime to pity, and to save;
When he who thunders rent his bark in twain,
And sunk his brave companions in the main,
Alone, abandon'd, in mid-ocean tossed,
The sport of winds, and driven from every coast,

Hither this man of miseries I led,
Received the friendless, and the hungry fed;
Nay promised (vainly promised) to bestow
Immortal life, exempt from age and woe.
'Tis past-and Jove decrees he shall remove;
Gods as we are, we are but slaves to Jove.
Go then he must (he must, if he ordain,
Try all those dangers, all those deeps, again);
But never, never shall Calypso send
To toils like these her husband and her friend.
What ships have I, what sailors to convey,
What oars to cut the long laborious way?
Yet I'll direct the safest means to go;
That last advice is all I can bestow."

To her the power who hears the charming rod;
"Dismiss the man, nor irritate the god;
Prevent the rage of him who reigns above,
For what so dreadful as the wrath of Jove?"
Thus having said, he cut the cleaving sky,
And in a moment vanished from her eye,
The nymph, obedient to divine command,
To seek Ulysses, paced along the sand,
Him pensive on the lonely beach she found,
With streaming eyes in briny torrents drown'd,
And inly pining for his native shore;
For now the soft enchantress pleased no more;
For now, reluctant, and constrained by charms,
Absent he lay in her desiring arms,
In slumber wore the heavy night away,
On rocks and shores consumed the tedious day;
There sate all desolate, and sighed alone,
With echoing sorrows made the mountains groan.
And roll'd his eyes o'er all the restless main,
Till, dimmed with rising grief, they streamed again.

Here, on his musing mood the goddess press'd,
Approaching soft, and thus the chief address'd:
"Unhappy man! to wasting woes a prey,
No more in sorrows languish life away:
Free as the winds I give thee now to rove:
Go, fell the timber of yon lofty grove,
And form a raft, and build the rising ship,
Sublime to bear thee o'er the gloomy deep.
To store the vessel let the care be mine,
With water from the rock and rosy wine,
And life-sustaining bread, and fair array,
And prosperous gales to waft thee on the way.

These, if the gods with my desire comply
(The gods, alas, more mighty far than I,
And better skill'd in dark events to come),
In peace shall land thee at thy native home."

With sighs Ulysses heard the words she spoke,
Then thus his melancholy silence broke:
"Some other motive, goddess! sways thy mind
(Some close design, or turn of womankind),
Nor my return the end, nor this the way,
On a slight raft to pass the swelling sea,
Huge, horrid, vast! where scarce in safety sails
The best-built ship, though Jove inspires the gales.
The bold proposal how shall I fulfil,
Dark as I am, unconscious of thy will?
Swear, then, thou mean'st not what my soul forebodes;
Swear by the solemn oath that binds the gods."

Him, while he spoke, with smiles Calypso eyed,
And gently grasp'd his hand, and thus replied:
"This shows thee, friend, by old experience taught,
And learn'd in all the wiles of human thought,
How prone to doubt, how cautious, are the wise!
But hear, O earth, and hear, ye sacred skies!
And thou, O Styx! whose formidable floods
Glide through the shades, and bind the attesting gods!
No form'd design, no meditated end,
Lurks in the counsel of thy faithful friend;
Kind the persuasion, and sincere my aim;
The same my practice, were my fate the same.
Heaven has not cursed me with a heart of steel,
But given the sense to pity, and to feel."

Thus having said, the goddess marched before:
He trod her footsteps in the sandy shore.
At the cool cave arrived, they took their state;
He filled the throne where Mercury had sate.
For him the nymph a rich repast ordains,
Such as the mortal life of man sustains;
Before herself were placed the the cates divine,
Ambrosial banquet and celestial wine.
Their hunger satiate, and their thirst repress'd,
Thus spoke Calypso to her godlike guest:

"Ulysses! (with a sigh she thus began;)
O sprung from gods! in wisdom more than man!
Is then thy home the passion of thy heart?
Thus wilt thou leave me, are we thus to part?

Farewell! and ever joyful mayst thou be,
Nor break the transport with one thought of me.
But ah, Ulysses! wert thou given to know
What Fate yet dooms these still to undergo,
Thy heart might settle in this scene of ease.
And e'en these slighted charms might learn to please.
A willing goddess, and immortal life.
Might banish from thy mind an absent wife.
Am I inferior to a mortal dame?
Less soft my feature less august my frame?
Or shall the daughters of mankind compare
Their earth born beauties with the heavenly fair?"

"Alas! for this (the prudent man replies)
Against Ulysses shall thy anger rise?
Loved and adored, O goddess as thou art,
Forgive the weakness of a human heart.
Though well I see thy graces far above
The dear, though mortal, object of my love,
Of youth eternal well the difference know,
And the short date of fading charms below;
Yet every day, while absent thus I roam,
I languish to return and die at home.
Whate'er the gods shall destine me to bear;
In the black ocean or the watery war,
'Tis mine to master with a constant mind;
Inured to perils, to the worst resign'd,
By seas, by wars, so many dangers run;
Still I can suffer; their high will he done!"

Thus while he spoke, the beamy sun descends,
And rising night her friendly shade extends,
To the close grot the lonely pair remove,
And slept delighted with the gifts of love.
When rose morning call'd them from their rest,
Ulysses robed him in the cloak and vest.
The nymph's fair head a veil transparent graced,
Her swelling loins a radiant zone embraced
With flowers of gold; an under robe, unbound,
In snowy waves flow'd glittering on the ground.
Forth issuing thus, she gave him first to wield
A weighty axe with truest temper steeled,
And double-edged; the handle smooth and plain,
Wrought of the clouded olive's easy grain;
And next, a wedge to drive with sweepy sway
Then to the neighboring forest led the way.
On the lone island's utmost verge there stood
Of poplars, pine, and firs, a lofty wood,

Whose leafless summits to the skies aspire,
Scorch'd by the sun, or seared by heavenly fire
(Already dried). These pointing out to view,
The nymph just show'd him, and with tears withdrew.

Now toils the hero: trees on trees o'erthrown
Fall crackling round him, and the forests groan:
Sudden, full twenty on the plain are strow'd,
And lopp'd and lighten'd of their branchy load.
At equal angles these disposed to join,
He smooth'd and squared them by the rule and line,
(The wimbles for the work Calypso found)
With those he pierced them and with clinchers bound.
Long and capacious as a shipwright forms
Some bark's broad bottom to out-ride the storms,
So large he built the raft; then ribb'd it strong
From space to space, and nail'd the planks along;
These form'd the sides: the deck he fashion'd last;
Then o'er the vessel raised the taper mast,
With crossing sail-yards dancing in the wind;
And to the helm the guiding rudder join'd
(With yielding osiers fenced, to break the force
Of surging waves, and steer the steady course).
Thy loom, Calypso, for the future sails
Supplied the cloth, capacious of the gales.
With stays and cordage last he rigged the ship,
And, roll'd on levers, launch'd her in the deep.

Four days were pass'd, and now the work complete,
Shone the fifth morn, when from her sacred seat
The nymph dismiss'd him (odorous garments given),
And bathed in fragrant oils that breathed of heaven:
Then fill'd two goatskins with her hands divine,
With water one, and one with sable wine:
Of every kind, provisions heaved aboard;
And the full decks with copious viands stored.
The goddess, last, a gentle breeze supplies,
To curl old Ocean, and to warm the skies.

And now, rejoicing in the prosperous gales,
With beating heart Ulysses spreads his sails;
Placed at the helm he sate, and mark'd the skies,
Nor closed in sleep his ever-watchful eyes.
There view'd the Pleiads, and the Northern Team,
And great Orion's more refulgent beam.
To which, around the axle of the sky,
The Bear, revolving, points his golden eye:
Who shines exalted on the ethereal plain,

Nor bathes his blazing forehead in the main.
Far on the left those radiant fires to keep
The nymph directed, as he sail'd the deep.
Full seventeen nights he cut the foaming way:
The distant land appear'd the following day:
Then swell'd to sight Phaeacia's dusky coast,
And woody mountains, half in vapours lost;
That lay before him indistinct and vast,
Like a broad shield amid the watery waste.

But him, thus voyaging the deeps below,
From far, on Solyme's aerial brow,
The king of ocean saw, and seeing burn'd
(From AEthiopia's happy climes return'd);
The raging monarch shook his azure head,
And thus in secret to his soul he said:
"Heavens! how uncertain are the powers on high!
Is then reversed the sentence of the sky,
In one man's favour; while a distant guest
I shared secure the AEthiopian feast?
Behold how near Phoenecia's land he draws;
The land affix'd by Fate's eternal laws
To end his toils. Is then our anger vain?
No; if this sceptre yet commands the main."

He spoke, and high the forky trident hurl'd,
Rolls clouds on clouds, and stirs the watery world,
At once the face of earth and sea deforms,
Swells all the winds, and rouses all the storms.
Down rushed the night: east, west, together roar;
And south and north roll mountains to the shore.
Then shook the hero, to despair resign'd,
And question'd thus his yet unconquer'd mind;

"Wretch that I am! what farther fates attend
This life of toils, and what my destined end?
Too well, alas! the island goddess knew
On the black sea what perils should ensue.
New horrors now this destined head inclose;
Untill'd is yet the measure of my woes;
With what a cloud the brows of heaven are crown'd;
What raging winds! what roaring waters round!
'Tis Jove himself the swelling tempest rears;
Death, present death, on every side appears.
Happy! thrice happy! who, in battle slain,
Press'd in Atrides' cause the Trojan plain!
Oh! had I died before that well-fought wall!
Had some distinguish'd day renown'd my fall

(Such as was that when showers of javelins fled
From conquering Troy around Achilles dead),
All Greece had paid me solemn funerals then,
And spread my glory with the sons of men.
A shameful fate now hides my hapless head,
Unwept, unnoted, and for ever dead!"

A mighty wave rush'd o'er him as he spoke,
The raft is cover'd, and the mast is broke;
Swept from the deck and from the rudder torn,
Far on the swelling surge the chief was borne;
While by the howling tempest rent in twain
Flew sail and sail-yards rattling o'er the main.
Long-press'd, he heaved beneath the weighty wave,
Clogg'd by the cumbrous vest Calypso gave;
At length, emerging, from his nostrils wide
And gushing mouth effused the briny tide;
E'en then not mindless of his last retreat,
He seized the raft, and leap'd into his seat,
Strong with the fear of death. In rolling flood,
Now here, now there, impell'd the floating wood
As when a heap of gather'd thorns is cast,
Now to, now fro, before the autumnal blast;
Together clung, it rolls around the field;
So roll'd the float, and so its texture held:
And now the south, and now the north, bear sway,
And now the east the foamy floods obey,
And now the west wind whirls it o'er the sea.
The wandering chief with toils on toils oppress'd,
Leucothea saw, and pity touch'd her breast.
(Herself a mortal once, of Cadmus' strain,
But now an azure sister of the main)
Swift as a sea-mew springing from the flood,
All radiant on the raft the goddess stood;
Then thus address'd him: "Thou whom heaven decrees
To Neptune's wrath, stern tyrant of the seas!
(Unequal contest!) not his rage and power,
Great as he is, such virtue shall devour.
What I suggest, thy wisdom will perform:
Forsake thy float, and leave it to the storm;
Strip off thy garments; Neptune's fury brave
With naked strength, and plunge into the wave.
To reach Phaeacia all thy nerves extend,
There Fate decrees thy miseries shall end.
This heavenly scarf beneath thy bosom bind,
And live; give all thy terrors to the wind.
Soon as thy arms the happy shore shall gain,
Return the gift, and cast it in the main:

Observe my orders, and with heed obey,
Cast it far off, and turn thy eyes away."

With that, her hand the sacred veil bestows,
Then down the deeps she dived from whence she rose;
A moment snatch'd the shining form away,
And all was covered with the curling sea.

Struck with amaze, yet still to doubt inclined,
He stands suspended, and explores his mind:
"What shall I do? unhappy me! who knows
But other gods intend me other woes?
Whoe'er thou art, I shall not blindly join
Thy pleaded reason, but consult with mine:
For scarce in ken appears that distant isle
Thy voice foretells me shall conclude my toil.
Thus then I judge: while yet the planks sustain
The wild waves' fury, here I fix'd remain:
But, when their texture to the tempest yields,
I launch adventurous on the liquid fields,
Join to the help of gods the strength of man,
And take this method, since the best I can."

While thus his thoughts an anxious council hold,
The raging god a watery mountain roll'd;
Like a black sheet the whelming billows spread,
Burst o'er the float, and thunder'd on his head.
Planks, beams, disparted fly; the scatter'd wood
Rolls diverse, and in fragments strews the flood.
So the rude Boreas, o'er the field new-shorn,
Tosses and drives the scatter'd heaps of corn.
And now a single beam the chief bestrides:
There poised a while above the bounding tides,
His limbs discumbers of the clinging vest,
And binds the sacred cincture round his breast:
Then prone an ocean in a moment flung,
Stretch'd wide his eager arms, and shot the seas along.
All naked now, on heaving billows laid,
Stern Neptune eyed him, and contemptuous said:

"Go, learn'd in woes, and other foes essay!
Go, wander helpless on the watery way;
Thus, thus find out the destined shore, and then
(If Jove ordains it) mix with happier men.
Whate'er thy fate, the ills our wrath could raise
Shall last remember'd in thy best of days."

This said, his sea-green steeds divide the foam,

And reach high Aegae and the towery dome.
Now, scarce withdrawn the fierce earth-shaking power,
Jove's daughter Pallas watch'd the favouring hour.
Back to their caves she bade the winds to fly;
And hush'd the blustering brethren of the sky.
The drier blasts alone of Boreas away,
And bear him soft on broken waves away;
With gentle force impelling to that shore,
Where fate has destined he shall toil no more.
And now, two nights, and now two days were pass'd,
Since wide he wander'd on the watery waste;
Heaved on the surge with intermitting breath,
And hourly panting in the arms of death.
The third fair morn now blazed upon the main;
Then glassy smooth lay all the liquid plain;
The winds were hush'd, the billows scarcely curl'd,
And a dead silence still'd the watery world;
When lifted on a ridgy wave he spies
The land at distance, and with sharpen'd eyes.
As pious children joy with vast delight
When a loved sire revives before their sight
(Who, lingering along, has call'd on death in vain,
Fix'd by some demon to his bed of pain,
Till heaven by miracle his life restore);
So joys Ulysses at the appearing shore;
And sees (and labours onward as he sees)
The rising forests, and the tufted trees.
And now, as near approaching as the sound
Of human voice the listening ear may wound,
Amidst the rocks he heard a hollow roar
Of murmuring surges breaking on the shore;
Nor peaceful port was there, nor winding bay,
To shield the vessel from the rolling sea,
But cliffs and shaggy shores, a dreadful sight!
All rough with rocks, with foamy billows white.
Fear seized his slacken'd limbs and beating heart,
As thus he communed with his soul apart;

"Ah me! when, o'er a length of waters toss'd,
These eyes at last behold the unhoped-for coast,
No port receives me from the angry main,
But the loud deeps demand me back again.
Above, sharp rocks forbid access; around
Roar the wild waves; beneath, is sea profound!
No footing sure affords the faithless sand,
To stem too rapid, and too deep to stand.
If here I enter, my efforts are vain,
Dash'd on the cliffs, or heaved into the main;

Or round the island if my course I bend,
Where the ports open, or the shores descend,
Back to the seas the rolling surge may sweep,
And bury all my hopes beneath the deep.
Or some enormous whale the god may send
(For many such an Amphitrite attend);
Too well the turns of mortal chance I know,
And hate relentless of my heavenly foe."
While thus he thought, a monstrous wave upbore
The chief, and dash'd him on the craggy shore;
Torn was his skin, nor had the ribs been whole,
But Instant Pallas enter'd in his soul.
Close to the cliff with both his hands he clung,
And stuck adherent, and suspended hung;
Till the huge surge roll'd off; then backward sweep
The refluent tides, and plunge him in the deep.
As when the polypus, from forth his cave
Torn with full force, reluctant beats the wave,
His ragged claws are stuck with stones and sands;
So the rough rock had shagg'd Ulysses hands,
And now had perish'd, whelm'd beneath the main,
The unhappy man; e'en fate had been in vain;
But all-subduing Pallas lent her power,
And prudence saved him in the needful hour.
Beyond the beating surge his course he bore,
(A wider circle, but in sight of shore),
With longing eyes, observing, to survey
Some smooth ascent, or safe sequester'd bay.
Between the parting rocks at length he spied
A failing stream with gentler waters glide;
Where to the seas the shelving shore declined,
And form'd a bay impervious to the wind.
To this calm port the glad Ulysses press'd,
And hail'd the river, and its god address'd:

"Whoe'er thou art, before whose stream unknown
I bend, a suppliant at thy watery throne,
Hear, azure king! nor let me fly in vain
To thee from Neptune and the raging main
Heaven hears and pities hapless men like me,
For sacred even to gods is misery:
Let then thy waters give the weary rest,
And save a suppliant, and a man distress'd."

He pray'd, and straight the gentle stream subsides,
Detains the rushing current of his tides,
Before the wanderer smooths the watery way,
And soft receives him from the rolling sea.

That moment, fainting as he touch'd the shore,
He dropp'd his sinewy arms: his knees no more
Perform'd their office, or his weight upheld:
His swoln heart heaved; his bloated body swell'd:
From mouth and nose the briny torrent ran;
And lost in lassitude lay all the man,
Deprived of voice, of motion, and of breath;
The soul scarce waking in the arms of death.
Soon as warm life its wonted office found,
The mindful chief Leucothea's scarf unbound;
Observant of her word, he turn'd aside
HIs head, and cast it on the rolling tide.
Behind him far, upon the purple waves,
The waters waft it, and the nymph receives.

Now parting from the stream, Ulysses found
A mossy bank with pliant rushes crown'd;
The bank he press'd, and gently kiss'd the ground;
Where on the flowery herb as soft he lay,
Thus to his soul the sage began to say:

"What will ye next ordain, ye powers on high!
And yet, ah yet, what fates are we to try?
Here by the stream, if I the night out-wear,
Thus spent already, how shall nature bear
The dews descending, and nocturnal air;
Or chilly vapours breathing from the flood
When morning rises?—If I take the wood,
And in thick shelter of innumerous boughs
Enjoy the comfort gentle sleep allows;
Though fenced from cold, and though my toil be pass'd,
What savage beasts may wander in the waste?
Perhaps I yet may fall a bloody prey
To prowling bears, or lions in the way."

Thus long debating in himself he stood:
At length he took the passage to the wood,
Whose shady horrors on a rising brow
Waved high, and frown'd upon the stream below.
There grew two olives, closest of the grove,
With roots entwined, the branches interwove;
Alike their leaves, but not alike they smiled
With sister-fruits; one fertile, one was wild.
Nor here the sun's meridian rays had power,
Nor wind sharp-piercing, nor the rushing shower;
The verdant arch so close its texture kept:
Beneath this covert great Ulysses crept.
Of gather'd leaves an ample bed he made

(Thick strewn by tempest through the bowery shade);
Where three at least might winter's cold defy,
Though Boreas raged along the inclement sky.
This store with joy the patient hero found,
And, sunk amidst them, heap'd the leaves around.
As some poor peasant, fated to reside
Remote from neighbours in a forest wide,
Studious to save what human wants require,
In embers heap'd, preserves the seeds of fire:
Hid in dry foliage thus Ulysses lies,
Till Pallas pour'd soft slumbers on his eyes;
And golden dreams (the gift of sweet repose)
Lull'd all his cares, and banish'd all his woes.

BOOK VI

ARGUMENT

Pallas appearing in a dream in to Nausicaa (the daughter of Alcinous, king of Phaeacia, commands her to descend to the river, and wash the robes of state, in preparation for her nuptials. Nausicaa goes with her handmaidens to the river; where, while the garments are spread on the bank, they divert themselves in sports. Their voices awaken Ulysses, who, addressing himself to the princess, is by her relieved and clothed, and receives directions in what manner to apply to the king and queen of the island.

While thus the weary wanderer sunk to rest,
And peaceful slumbers calmed his anxious breast,
The martial maid from heavens aerial height
Swift to Phaeacia wing'd her rapid flight,
In elder times the soft Phaeacian train
In ease possess'd the wide Hyperian plain;
Till the Cyclopean race in arms arose
A lawless nation of gigantic foes;
Then great Nausithous from Hyperia far,
Through seas retreating from the sounds of war,
The recreant nation to fair Scheria led,
Where never science rear'd her laurell'd head;
There round his tribes a strength of wall he raised;
To heaven the glittering domes and temples blazed;
Just to his realms, he parted grounds from grounds,
And shared the lands, and gave the lands their bounds.
Now in the silent grave the monarch lay,
And wise Alcinous held the legal sway.

To his high palace through the fields of air
The goddess shot; Ulysses was her care.
There, as the night in silence roll'd away,

A heaven of charms divine Nausicaa lay:
Through the thick gloom the shining portals blaze;
Two nymphs the portals guard, each nymph a Grace,
Light as the viewless air the warrior maid
Glides through the valves, and hovers round her head;
A favourite virgin's blooming form she took,
From Dymas sprung, and thus the vision spoke:

"Oh Indolent! to waste thy hours away!
And sleep'st thou careless of the bridal day!
Thy spousal ornament neglected lies;
Arise, prepare the bridal train, arise!
A just applause the cares of dress impart,
And give soft transport to a parent's heart.
Haste, to the limpid stream direct thy way,
When the gay morn unveils her smiling ray;
Haste to the stream! companion of thy care,
Lo, I thy steps attend, thy labours share.
Virgin, awake! the marriage hour is nigh,
See from their thrones thy kindred monarchs sigh!
The royal car at early dawn obtain,
And order mules obedient to the rein;
For rough the way, and distant rolls the wave,
Where their fair vests Phaeacian virgins lave,
In pomp ride forth; for pomp becomes the great
And majesty derives a grace from state."
Then to the palaces of heaven she sails,
Incumbent on the wings of wafting gales;
The seat of gods; the regions mild of peace,
Full joy, and calm eternity of ease.
There no rude winds presume to shake the skies,
No rains descend, no snowy vapours rise;
But on immortal thrones the blest repose;
The firmament with living splendours glows.
Hither the goddess winged the aerial way,
Through heaven's eternal gates that blazed with day.

Now from her rosy car Aurora shed
The dawn, and all the orient flamed with red.
Up rose the virgin with the morning light,
Obedient to the vision of the night.
The queen she sought, the queen her hours bestowed
In curious works; the whirling spindle glow'd
With crimson threads, while busy damsels call
The snowy fleece, or twist the purpled wool.
Meanwhile Phaeacia's peers in council sate;
From his high dome the king descends in state;
Then with a filial awe the royal maid

Approach'd him passing, and submissive said:

"Will my dread sire his ear regardful deign,
And may his child the royal car obtain?
Say, with my garments shall I bend my way?
Where through the vales the mazy waters stray?
A dignity of dress adorns the great,
And kings draw lustre from the robe of state.
Five sons thou hast; three wait the bridal day.
And spotless robes become the young and gay;
So when with praise amid the dance they shine,
By these my cares adorn'd that praise is mine."

Thus she: but blushes ill-restrain'd betray
Her thoughts intentive on the bridal day,
The conscious sire the dawning blush survey'd,
And, smiling, thus bespoke the blooming maid
"My child, my darling joy, the car receive;
That, and whate'er our daughter asks, we give."
Swift at the royal nod the attending train
The car prepare, the mules incessant rein,
The blooming virgin with despatchful cares
Tunics, and stoles, and robes imperial, bears.
The queen, assiduous to her train assigns
The sumptuous viands, and the flavorous wines.
The train prepare a cruse of curious mould,
A cruse of fragrance, form'd of burnish'd gold;
Odour divine! whose soft refreshing streams
Sleek the smooth skin, and scent the snowy limbs.

Now mounting the gay seat, the silken reins
Shine in her hand; along the sounding plains
Swift fly the mules; nor rode the nymph alone;
Around, a bevy of bright damsels shone.
They seek the cisterns where Phaeacian dames
Wash their fair garments in the limpid streams;
Where, gathering into depth from falling rills,
The lucid wave a spacious bason fills.
The mules, unharness'd, range beside the main,
Or crop the verdant herbage of the plain.

Then emulous the royal robes they lave,
And plunge the vestures in the cleansing wave
(The vestures cleansed o'erspread the shelly sand,
Their snowy lustre whitens all the strand);
Then with a short repast relieve their toil,
And o'er their limbs diffuse ambrosial oil;
And while the robes imbibe the solar ray,

O'er the green mead the sporting virgins play
(Their shining veils unbound). Along the skies,
Toss'd and retoss'd, the ball incessant flies.
They sport, they feast; Nausicaa lifts her voice,
And, warbling sweet, makes earth and heaven rejoice.

As when o'er Erymanth Diana roves,
Or wide Tuygetus' resounding groves;
A sylvan train the huntress queen surrounds,
Her rattling quiver from her shoulders sounds:
Fierce in the sport, along the mountain's brow
They bay the boar, or chase the bounding roe;
High o'er the lawn, with more majestic pace,
Above the nymphs she treads with stately grace;
Distinguish'd excellence the goddess proves;
Exults Latona as the virgin moves.
With equal grace Nausicaa trod the plain,
And shone transcendent o'er the beauteous train.

Meantime (the care and favourite of the skies
Wrapp'd in imbowering shade, Ulysses lies,
His woes forgot! but Pallas now address'd
To break the bands of all-composing rest.
Forth from her snowy hand Nausicaa threw
The various ball; the ball erroneous flew
And swam the stream; loud shrieks the virgin train,
And the loud shriek redoubles from the main.
Waked by the shrilling sound, Ulysses rose,
And, to the deaf woods wailing, breathed his woes:

"Ah me! on what inhospitable coast,
On what new region is Ulysses toss'd;
Possess'd by wild barbarians fierce in arms;
Or men, whose bosom tender pity warms?
What sounds are these that gather from he shores?
The voice of nymphs that haunt the sylvan bowers,
The fair-hair'd Dryads of the shady wood;
Or azure daughters of the silver flood;
Or human voice? but issuing from the shades,
Why cease I straight to learn what sound invades?"

Then, where the grove with leaves umbrageous bends,
With forceful strength a branch the hero rends;
Around his loins the verdant cincture spreads
A wreathy foliage and concealing shades.
As when a lion in the midnight hours,
Beat by rude blasts, and wet with wintry showers,
Descends terrific from the mountains brow;

With living flames his rolling eye balls glow;
With conscious strength elate, he bends his way,
Majestically fierce, to seize his prey
(The steer or stag;) or, with keen hunger bold,
Spring o'er the fence and dissipates the fold.
No less a terror, from the neighbouring groves
(Rough from the tossing surge) Ulysses moves;
Urged on by want, and recent from the storms;
The brackish ooze his manly grace deforms.
Wide o'er the shore with many a piercing cry
To rocks, to caves, the frightened virgins fly;
All but the nymph; the nymph stood fix'd alone,
By Pallas arm'd with boldness not her own.
Meantime in dubious thought the king awaits,
And, self-considering, as he stands, debates;
Distant his mournful story to declare,
Or prostrate at her knee address the prayer.
But fearful to offend, by wisdom sway'd,
At awful distance he accosts the maid:

"If from the skies a goddess, or if earth
(Imperial virgin) boast thy glorious birth,
To thee I bend! If in that bright disguise
Thou visit earth, a daughter of the skies,
Hail, Dian, hail! the huntress of the groves
So shines majestic, and so stately moves,
So breathes an air divine! But if thy race
Be mortal, and this earth thy native place,
Blest is the father from whose loins you sprung,
Blest is the mother at whose breast you hung.
Blest are the brethren who thy blood divide,
To such a miracle of charms allied:
Joyful they see applauding princes gaze,
When stately in the dance you swim the harmonious maze.
But blest o'er all, the youth with heavenly charms,
Who clasps the bright perfection in his arms!
Never, I never view'd till this blast hour
Such finish'd grace! I gaze, and I adore!
Thus seems the palm with stately honours crown'd
By Phoebus' altars; thus o'erlooks the ground;
The pride of Delos. (By the Delian coast,
I voyaged, leader of a warrior-host,
But ah, how changed I from thence my sorrow flows;
O fatal voyage, source of all my woes;)
Raptured I stood, and as this hour amazed,
With reverence at the lofty wonder gazed:
Raptured I stand! for earth ne'er knew to bear
A plant so stately, or a nymph so fair.

Awed from access, I lift my suppliant hands;
For Misery, O queen! before thee stands.
Twice ten tempestuous nights I roll'd, resign'd
To roaring blows, and the warring wind;
Heaven bade the deep to spare; but heaven, my foe,
Spares only to inflict some mightier woe.
Inured to cares, to death in all its forms;
Outcast I rove, familiar with the storms.
Once more I view the face of human kind:
Oh let soft pity touch thy generous mind!
Unconscious of what air I breathe, I stand
Naked, defenceless on a narrow land.
Propitious to my wants a vest supply
To guard the wretched from the inclement sky:
So may the gods, who heaven and earth control,
Crown the chaste wishes of thy virtuous soul,
On thy soft hours their choicest blessings shed;
Blest with a husband be thy bridal bed;
Blest be thy husband with a blooming race,
And lasting union crown your blissful days.
The gods, when they supremely bless, bestow
Firm union on their favourites below;
Then envy grieves, with inly-pining hate;
The good exult, and heaven is in our state."

To whom the nymph: "O stranger, cease thy care;
Wise is thy soul, but man is bore to bear;
Jove weighs affairs of earth in dubious scales,
And the good suffers, while the bad prevails.
Bear, with a soul resign'd, the will of Jove;
Who breathes, must mourn: thy woes are from above.
But since thou tread'st our hospitable shore,
'Tis mine to bid the wretched grieve no more,
To clothe the naked, and thy way to guide.
Know, the Phaecian tribes this land divide;
From great Alcinous' royal loins I spring,
A happy nation, and a happy king."

Then to her maids: "Why, why, ye coward train,
These fears, this flight? ye fear, and fly in vain.
Dread ye a foe? dismiss that idle dread,
'Tis death with hostile step these shores to tread;
Safe in the love of heaven, an ocean flows
Around our realm, a barrier from the foes;
'Tis ours this son of sorrow to relieve,
Cheer the sad heart, nor let affliction grieve.
By Jove the stranger and the poor are sent;
And what to those we give to Jove is lent.

Then food supply, and bathe his fainting limbs
Where waving shades obscure the mazy streams."

Obedient to the call, the chief they guide
To the calm current of the secret tide;
Close by the stream a royal dress they lay,
A vest and robe, with rich embroidery gay;
Then unguents in a vase of gold supply,
That breathed a fragrance through the balmy sky.

To them the king: "No longer I detain
Your friendly care: retire, ye virgin train!
Retire, while from my wearied limbs I lave
The foul pollution of the briny wave.
Ye gods! since this worn frame refection know,
What scenes have I surveyed of dreadful view!
But, nymphs, recede! sage chastity denies
To raise the blush, or pain the modest eyes."

The nymphs withdrawn, at once into the tide
Active he bounds; the flashing waves divide
O'er all his limbs his hands the waves diffuse,
And from his locks compress the weedy ooze;
The balmy oil, a fragrant shower, be sheds;
Then, dressed, in pomp magnificently treads.
The warrior-goddess gives his frame to shine
With majesty enlarged, and air divine:
Back from his brows a length of hair unfurls,
His hyacinthine locks descend in wavy curls.
As by some artist, to whom Vulcan gives
His skill divine, a breathing statue lives;
By Pallas taught, he frames the wondrous mould,
And o'er the silver pours the fusile gold
So Pallas his heroic frame improves
With heavenly bloom, and like a god he moves.
A fragrance breathes around; majestic grace
Attends his steps: the astonished virgins gaze.
Soft he reclines along the murmuring seas,
Inhaling freshness from the fanning breeze.

The wondering nymph his glorious port survey'd,
And to her damsels, with amazement, said:

"Not without care divine the stranger treads
This land of joy; his steps some godhead leads:
Would Jove destroy him, sure he had been driven
Far from this realm, the favourite isle of heaven.
Late, a sad spectacle of woe, he trod

The desert sands, and now be looks a god.
Oh heaven! in my connubial hour decree
This man my spouse, or such a spouse as he!
But haste, the viands and the bowl provide."
The maids the viands and the bowl supplied:
Eager he fed, for keen his hunger raged,
And with the generous vintage thirst assuaged.

Now on return her care Nausicaa bends,
The robes resumes, the glittering car ascends,
Far blooming o'er the field; and as she press'd
The splendid seat, the listening chief address'd:

"Stranger, arise! the sun rolls down the day.
Lo, to the palace I direct thy way;
Where, in high state, the nobles of the land
Attend my royal sire, a radiant band
But hear, though wisdom in thy soul presides,
Speaks from thy tongue, and every action guides;
Advance at distance, while I pass the plain
Where o'er the furrows waves the golden grain;
Alone I reascend—With airy mounds
A strength of wall the guarded city bounds;
The jutting land two ample bays divides:
Full through the narrow mouths descend the tides;
The spacious basons arching rocks enclose,
A sure defence from every storm that blows.
Close to the bay great Neptune's fane adjoins;
And near, a forum flank'd with marble shines,
Where the bold youth, the numerous fleets to store,
Shape the broad sail, or smooth the taper oar:
For not the bow they bend, nor boast the skill
To give the feather'd arrow wings to kill;
But the tall mast above the vessel rear,
Or teach the fluttering sail to float in air.
They rush into the deep with eager joy,
Climb the steep surge, and through the tempest fly;
A proud, unpolish'd race—To me belongs
The care to shun the blast of slanderous tongues;
Lest malice, prone the virtuous to defame,
Thus with wild censure taint my spotless name:
'What stranger this whom thus Nausicaa leads!
Heavens, with what graceful majesty he treads!
Perhaps a native of some distant shore,
The future consort of her bridal hour:
Or rather some descendant of the skies;
Won by her prayer, the aerial bridegroom flies,
Heaven on that hour its choicest influence shed,

That gave a foreign spouse to crown her bed!
All, all the godlike worthies that adorn
This realm, she flies: Phaeacia is her scorn.'
And just the blame: for female innocence
Not only flies the guilt, but shuns the offence:
The unguarded virgin, as unchaste, I blame;
And the least freedom with the sex is shame,
Till our consenting sires a spouse provide,
And public nuptials justify the bride,
But would'st thou soon review thy native plain?
Attend, and speedy thou shalt pass the main:
Nigh where a grove with verdant poplars crown'd,
To Pallas sacred, shades the holy ground,
We bend our way; a bubbling fount distills
A lucid lake, and thence descends in rills;
Around the grove, a mead with lively green
Falls by degrees, and forms a beauteous scene;
Here a rich juice the royal vineyard pours;
And there the garden yields a waste of flowers.
Hence lies the town, as far as to the ear
Floats a strong shout along the waves of air.
There wait embower'd, while I ascend alone
To great Alcinous on his royal throne.
Arrived, advance, impatient of delay,
And to the lofty palace bend thy way:
The lofty palace overlooks the town,
From every dome by pomp superior known;
A child may point the way. With earnest gait
Seek thou the queen along the rooms of state;
Her royal hand a wondrous work designs,
Around a circle of bright damsels shines;
Part twist the threads, and part the wool dispose,
While with the purple orb the spindle glows.
High on a throne, amid the Scherian powers,
My royal father shares the genial hours:
But to the queen thy mournful tale disclose,
With the prevailing eloquence of woes:
So shalt thou view with joy thy natal shore,
Though mountains rise between and oceans roar."

She added not, but waving, as she wheel'd,
The silver scourge, it glitter'd o'er the field;
With skill the virgin guides the embroider'd rein,
Slow rolls the car before the attending train,
Now whirling down the heavens, the golden day
Shot through the western clouds a dewy ray;
The grove they reach, where, from the sacred shade,
To Pallas thus the pensive hero pray'd:

"Daughter of Jove! whose arms in thunder wield
The avenging bolt, and shake the dreadful shield;
Forsook by thee, in vain I sought thy aid
When booming billows closed above my bead;
Attend, unconquer'd maid! accord my vows,
Bid the Great hear, and pitying, heal my woes."

This heard Minerva, but forbore to fly
(By Neptune awed) apparent from the sky;
Stern god! who raged with vengeance, unrestrain'd.
Till great Ulysses hail'd his native land.

BOOK VII

ARGUMENT

The COURT OF ALCINOUS

The Princess Nausicaa returns to the city and Ulysses soon after follows thither. He is met by Pallas in
the form of a young virgin, who guides him to the palace, and directs him in what manner to address the
queen Arete. She then involves him in a mist which causes him to pass invisible. The palace and gardens
of Alcinous described. Ulysses falling at the feet of the queen, the mist disperses, the Phaecians admire,
and receive him with respect. The queen inquiring by what means he had the garments he then wore,
be relates to her and Alcinous his departure from Calypso, and his arrival in their dominions.

The same day continues, and the book ends with the night.

The patient heavenly man thus suppliant pray'd;
While the slow mules draws on the imperial maid;
Through the proud street she moves, the public gaze;
The turning wheel before the palace stays.
With ready love her brothers, gathering round,
Received the vestures, and the mules unbound.
She seeks the bridal bower: a matron there
The rising fire supplies with busy care,
Whose charms in youth her father's heart inflamed,
Now worn with age, Eurymedusa named;
The captive dame Phaeacian rovers bore,
Snatch'd from Epirus, her sweet native shore
(A grateful prize), and in her bloom bestow'd
On good Alcinous, honor'd as a god;
Nurse of Nausicaa from her infant years,
And tender second to a mother's cares.

Now from the sacred thicket where he lay,

To town Ulysses took the winding way.
Propitious Pallas, to secure her care,
Around him spread a veil of thicken'd air;
To shun the encounter of the vulgar crowd,
Insulting still, inquisitive and loud.
When near the famed Phaeacian walls he drew,
The beauteous city opening to his view,
His step a virgin met, and stood before:
A polish'd urn the seeming virgin bore,
And youthful smiled; but in the low disguise
Lay hid the goddess with the azure eyes.

"Show me, fair daughter (thus the chief demands),
The house of him who rules these happy lands
Through many woes and wanderings, do I come
To good Alcinous' hospitable dome.
Far from my native coast, I rove alone,
A wretched stranger, and of all unknown!"

The goddess answer'd: "Father, I obey,
And point the wandering traveller his way:
Well known to me the palace you inquire,
For fast beside it dwells my honour'd sire:
But silent march, nor greet the common train
With question needless, or inquiry vain;
A race of ragged mariners are these,
Unpolish'd men, and boisterous as their seas
The native islanders alone their care,
And hateful he who breathes a foreign air.
These did the ruler of the deep ordain
To build proud navies, and command the main;
On canvas wings to cut the watery way;
No bird so light, no thought so swift as they."

Thus having spoke, the unknown celestial leads:
The footsteps of the duty he treads,
And secret moves along the crowded space,
Unseen of all the rude Phaeacian race.
(So Pallas order'd, Pallas to their eyes
The mist objected, and condensed the skies.)
The chief with wonder sees the extended streets,
The spreading harbours, and the riding fleets;
He next their princes' lofty domes admires,
In separate islands, crown'd with rising spires;
And deep entrenchments, and high walls of stone.
That gird the city like a marble zone.
At length the kingly palace-gates he view'd;
There stopp'd the goddess, and her speech renew'd;

"My task is done: the mansion you inquire
Appears before you: enter, and admire.
High-throned, and feasting, there thou shalt behold
The sceptred rulers. Fear not, but be bold:
A decent boldness ever meets with friends,
Succeeds, and even a stranger recommends
First to the queen prefer a suppliant's claim,
Alcinous' queen, Arete is her name.
The same her parents, and her power the same.
For know, from ocean's god Nausithous sprung,
And Peribaea, beautiful and young
(Eurymedon's last hope, who ruled of old
The race of giants, impious, proud, and bold:
Perish'd the nation in unrighteous war,
Perish'd the prince, and left this only heir),
Who now, by Neptune's amorous power compress'd,
Produced a monarch that his people bless'd,
Father and prince of the Phaeacian name;
From him Rhexenor and Alcinous came.
The first by Phoebus' hurtling arrows fired,
New from his nuptials, hapless youth! expired.
No son survived; Arete heir'd his state,
And her, Alcinous chose his royal mate.
With honours yet to womankind unknown.
This queen he graces, and divides the throne;
In equal tenderness her sons conspire,
And all the children emulate their sire.
When through the streets she gracious deigns to move
(The public wonder and the public love),
The tongues of all with transport sound her praise,
The eyes of all, as on a goddess, gaze.
She feels the triumph of a generous breast;
To heal divisions, to relieve the oppress'd;
In virtue rich; in blessing others, bless'd.
(to then secure, thy humble suit prefer
And owe thy country and thy friends to her."

With that the goddess deign'd no longer stay,
But o'er the world of waters wing'd her way;
Forsaking Scheria's ever-pleasing shore,
The winds to Marathon the virgin bore:
Thence, where proud Athens rears her towery head,
With opening streets and shining structures spread,
She pass'd, delighted with the well-known seats;
And to Erectheus' sacred dome retreats.

Meanwhile Ulysses at the palace waits,

There stops, and anxious with his soul debates,
Fix'd in amaze before the royal gates.
The front appear'd with radiant splendours gay,
Bright as the lamp of night, or orb of day,
The walls were massy brass: the cornice high
Blue metals crown'd in colours of the sky,
Rich plates of gold the folding doors incase;
The pillars silver, on a brazen base;
Silver the lintels deep-projecting o'er,
And gold the ringlets that command the door.
Two rows of stately dogs, on either hand,
In sculptured gold and labour'd silver stood
These Vulcan form'd with art divine, to wait
Immortal guardians at Alcinous' gate;
Alive each animated frame appears,
And still to live beyond the power of years,
Fair thrones within from space to space were raised,
Where various carpets with embroidery blessed,
The work of matrons: these the princes press'd.
Day following day, a long-continued feast,
Refulgent pedestals the walls surround,
Which boys of gold with illuming torches crown'd;
The polish'd oar, reflecting every ray,
Blazed on the banquets with a double day.
Full fifty handmaids form the household train;
Some turn the mill, or sift the golden grain;
Some ply the loom; their busy fingers move
Like poplar-leaves when Zephyr fans the grove.
Not more renown'd the men of Scheria's isle
For sailing arts and all the naval toil,
Than works of female skill their women's pride,
The flying shuttle through the threads to guide:
Pallas to these her double gifts imparts,
Incentive genius, and industrious arts.

Close to the gates a spacious garden lies,
From storms defended and inclement skies.
Four acres was the allotted space of ground,
Fenced with a green enclosure all around.
Tall thriving trees confess'd the fruitful mould:
The reddening apple ripens here to gold.
Here the blue fig with luscious juice o'erflows,
With deeper red the full pomegranate glows;
The branch here bends beneath the weighty pear,
And verdant olives flourish round the year,
The balmy spirit of the western gale
Eternal breathes on fruits, unthought to fail:
Each dropping pear a following pear supplies,

On apples apples, figs on figs arise:
The same mild season gives the blooms to blow,
The buds to harden, and the fruits to grow.

Here order'd vines in equal ranks appear,
With all the united labours of the year;
Some to unload the fertile branches run,
Some dry the blackening clusters in the sun,
Others to tread the liquid harvest join:
The groaning presses foam with floods of wine
Here are the vines in early flower descried,
Here grapes discolour'd on the sunnyside,
And there in autumn's richest purple dyed,

Beds of all various herbs, for ever green,
In beauteous order terminate the scene.

Two plenteous fountains the whole prospect crown'd
This through the gardens leads its streams around
Visits each plant, and waters all the ground;
While that in pipes beneath the palace flows,
And thence its current on the town bestows:
To various use their various streams they bring,
The people one, and one supplies the king.

Such were the glories which the gods ordain'd,
To grace Alcinous, and his happy land.
E'en from the chief whom men and nations knew,
The unwonted scene surprise and rapture drew;
In pleasing thought he ran the prospect o'er,
Then hasty enter'd at the lofty door.
Night now approaching, in the palace stand,
With goblets crown'd, the rulers of the land;
Prepared for rest, and offering to the god
Who bears the virtue of the sleepy rod,
Unseen he glided through the joyous crowd,
With darkness circled, and an ambient cloud.
Direct to great Alcinous' throne he came,
And prostrate fell before the imperial dame.
Then from around him dropp'd the veil of night;
Sudden he shines, and manifest to sight.
The nobles gaze, with awful fear oppress'd;
Silent they gaze, and eye the godlike guest.

"Daughter of great Rhexenor! (thus began,
Low at her knees, the much-enduring man)
To thee, thy consort, and this royal train,
To all that share the blessings of your reign,

A suppliant bends: oh pity human woe!
'Tis what the happy to the unhappy owe.
A wretched exile to his country send,
Long worn with griefs, and long without a friend
So may the gods your better days increase,
And all your joys descend on all your race;
So reign for ever on your country's breast,
Your people blessing, by your people bless'd!"

Then to the genial hearth he bow'd his face,
And humbled in the ashes took his place.
Silence ensued. The eldest first began,
Echeneus sage, a venerable man!
Whose well-taught mind the present age surpass'd,
And join'd to that the experience of the last.
Fit words attended on his weighty sense,
And mild persuasion flow'd in eloquence.

"Oh sight (he cried) dishonest and unjust!
A guest, a stranger, seated in the dust!
To raise the lowly suppliant from the ground
Befits a monarch. Lo! the peers around
But wait thy word, the gentle guest to grace,
And seat him fair in some distinguish'd place.
Let first the herald due libation pay
To Jove, who guides the wanderer on his way:
Then set the genial banquet in his view,
And give the stranger-guest a stranger's due."

His sage advice the listening king obeys,
He stretch'd his hand the prudent chief to raise,
And from his seat Laodamas removed
(The monarch's offspring, and his best-beloved);
There next his side the godlike hero sate;
With stars of silver shone the bed of state.
The golden ewer a beauteous handmaid brings,
Replenish'd from the cool translucent springs,
Whose polish'd vase with copious streams supplies
A silver layer of capacious size.
The table next in regal order spread,
The glittering canisters are heap'd with bread:
Viands of various kinds invite the taste,
Of choicest sort and savour, rich repast!
Thus feasting high, Alcinous gave the sign,
And bade the herald pour the rosy wine;
"Let all around the due libation pay
To Jove, who guides the wanderer on his way."

He said. Pontonous heard the king's command;
The circling goblet moves from hand to hand;
Each drinks the juice that glads the heart of man.
Alcinous then, with aspect mild, began:

"Princes and peers, attend; while we impart
To you the thoughts of no inhuman heart.
Now pleased and satiate from the social rite
Repair we to the blessings of the night;
But with the rising day, assembled here,
Let all the elders of the land appear,
Pious observe our hospitable laws,
And Heaven propitiate in the stranger's cause;
Then join'd in council, proper means explore
Safe to transport him to the wished-for shore
(How distant that, imports us not to know,
Nor weigh the labour, but relieve the woe).
Meantime, nor harm nor anguish let him bear
This interval, Heaven trusts him to our care
But to his native land our charge resign'd,
Heaven's is his life to come, and all the woes behind.
Then must he suffer what the Fates ordain;
For Fate has wove the thread of life with pain?
And twins, e'en from the birth, are Misery and Man!
But if, descended from the Olympian bower,
Gracious approach us some immortal power;
If in that form thou comest a guest divine:
Some high event the conscious gods design.
As yet, unbid they never graced our feast,
The solemn sacrifice call'd down the guest;
Then manifest of Heaven the vision stood,
And to our eyes familiar was the god.
Oft with some favour'd traveller they stray,
And shine before him all the desert way;
With social intercourse, and face to face,
The friends and guardians of our pious race.
So near approach we their celestial kind,
By justice, truth, and probity of mind;
As our dire neighbours of Cyclopean birth
Match in fierce wrong the giant-sons of earth."

"Let no such thought (with modest grace rejoin'd
The prudent Greek) possess the royal mind.
Alas! a mortal, like thyself, am I;
No glorious native of yon azure sky:
In form, ah how unlike their heavenly kind!
How more inferior in the gifts of mind!
Alas, a mortal! most oppress'd of those

Whom Fate has loaded with a weight of woes;
By a sad train of Miseries alone
Distinguish'd long, and second now to none!
By Heaven's high will compell'd from shore to shore;
With Heaven's high will prepared to suffer more.
What histories of toil could I declare!
But still long-wearied nature wants repair;
Spent with fatigue, and shrunk with pining fast,
My craving bowels still require repast.
Howe'er the noble, suffering mind may grieve
Its load of anguish, and disdain to live,
Necessity demands our daily bread;
Hunger is insolent, and will be fed.
But finish, oh ye peers! what you propose,
And let the morrow's dawn conclude my woes.
Pleased will I suffer all the gods ordain,
To see my soil, my son, my friends again.
That view vouchsafed, let instant death surprise
With ever-during shade these happy eyes!"

The assembled peers with general praise approved
His pleaded reason, and the suit he moved.
Each drinks a full oblivion of his cares,
And to the gifts of balmy sleep repairs,
Ulysses in the regal walls alone
Remain'd: beside him, on a splendid throne,
Divine Arete and Alcinous shone.
The queen, an nearer view, the guest survey'd,
Rob'd in the garments her own hands had made,
Not without wonder seen. Then thus began,
Her words addressing to the godlike man:

"Camest thou hither, wondrous stranger I say,
From lands remote and o'er a length of sea?
Tell, then, whence art thou? whence, that princely air?
And robes like these, so recent and so fair?"

"Hard is the task, O princess! you impose
(Thus sighing spoke the man of many woes),
The long, the mournful series to relate
Of all my sorrows sent by Heaven and Fate!
Yet what you ask, attend. An island lies
Beyond these tracts, and under other skies,
Ogygia named, in Ocean's watery arms;
Where dwells Calypso, dreadful in her charms!
Remote from gods or men she holds her reign,
Amid the terrors of a rolling main.
Me, only me, the hand of fortune bore,

Unblest! to tread that interdicted shore:
When Jove tremendous in the sable deeps
Launch'd his red lightning at our scattered ships;
Then, all my fleet and all my followers lost.
Sole on a plank on boiling surges toss'd,
Heaven drove my wreck the Ogygian Isle to find,
Full nine days floating to the wave and wind.
Met by the goddess there with open arms,
She bribed my stay with more than human charms;
Nay, promised, vainly promised, to bestow
Immortal life, exempt from age and woe;
But all her blandishments successless prove,
To banish from my breast my country's love.
I stay reluctant seven continued years,
And water her ambrosial couch with tears,
The eighth she voluntary moves to part,
Or urged by Jove, or her own changeful heart.
A raft was formed to cross the surging sea;
Herself supplied the stores and rich array,
And gave the gales to waft me on my way,
In seventeen days appear'd your pleasing coast,
And woody mountains half in vapours lost.
Joy touched my soul; my soul was joy'd in vain,
For angry Neptune roused the raging main;
The wild winds whistle, and the billows roar;
The splitting raft the furious tempest tore;
And storms vindictive intercept the shore.
Soon as their rage subsides, the seas I brave
With naked force, and shoot along the wave,
To reach this isle; but there my hopes were lost,
The surge impell'd me on a craggy coast.
I chose the safer sea, and chanced to find
A river's mouth impervious to the wind,
And clear of rocks. I fainted by the flood;
Then took the shelter of the neighbouring wood.
'Twas night, and, covered in the foliage deep,
Jove plunged my senses in the death of sleep.
All night I slept, oblivious of my pain:
Aurora dawned and Phoebus shined in vain,
Nor, till oblique he sloped his evening ray,
Had Somnus dried the balmy dews away.
Then female voices from the shore I heard:
A maid amidst them, goddess-like appear'd;
To her I sued, she pitied my distress;
Like thee in beauty, nor in virtue less.
Who from such youth could hope considerate care?
In youth and beauty wisdom is but rare!
She gave me life, relieved with just supplies

My wants, and lent these robes that strike your eyes.
This is the truth: and oh, ye powers on high!
Forbid that want should sink me to a lie."

To this the king: "Our daughter but express'd
Her cares imperfect to our godlike guest.
Suppliant to her, since first he chose to pray,
Why not herself did she conduct the way,
And with her handmaids to our court convey?"

"Hero and king (Ulysses thus replied)
Nor blame her faultless nor suspect of pride:
She bade me follow in the attendant train;
But fear and reverence did my steps detain,
Lest rash suspicion might alarm thy mind:
Man's of a jealous and mistaken kind."

"Far from my soul (he cried) the gods efface
All wrath ill-grounded, and suspicion base!
Whate'er is honest, stranger, I approve,
And would to Phoebus, Pallas, and to Jove,
Such as thou art, thy thought and mine were one,
Nor thou unwilling to be called my son.
In such alliance couldst thou wish to join,
A palace stored with treasures should be thine.
But if reluctant, who shall force thy stay?
Jove bids to set the stranger on his way,
And ships shall wait thee with the morning ray.
Till then, let slumber cross thy careful eyes:
The wakeful mariners shall watch the skies,
And seize the moment when the breezes rise:
Then gently waft thee to the pleasing shore,
Where thy soul rests, and labour is no more.
Far as Euboea though thy country lay,
Our ships with ease transport thee in a day.
Thither of old, earth's giant son to view,
On wings of wind with Rhadamanth they flew;
This land, from whence their morning course begun,
Saw them returning with the setting sun.
Your eyes shall witness and confirm my tale,
Our youth how dexterous, and how fleet our sail,
When justly timed with equal sweep they row,
And ocean whitens in long tracks below."

Thus he. No word the experienced man replies,
But thus to heaven (and heavenward lifts his eyes):
"O Jove! O father! what the king accords
Do thou make perfect! sacred be his words!

Wide o'er the world Alcinous' glory shine!
Let fame be his, and ah! my country mine!"

Meantime Arete, for the hour of rest,
Ordains the fleecy couch, and covering vest;
Bids her fair train the purple quilts prepare,
And the thick carpets spread with busy care.
With torches blazing in their hands they pass'd,
And finish'd all their queen's command with haste:
Then gave the signal to the willing guest:
He rose with pleasure, and retired to rest.
There, soft extended, to the murmuring sound
Of the high porch, Ulysses sleeps profound!
Within, released from cares, Alcinous lies;
And fast beside were closed Arete's eyes.

BOOK VIII

ARGUMENT

Alcinous calls a council, in which it is resolved to transport Ulysses into his country. After which splendid entertainments are made, where the celebrated musician and poet, Demodocus, plays and sings to the guests. They next proceed to the games, the race, the wrestling, discus, &c., where Ulysses casts a prodigious length, to the admiration of all the spectators. They return again to the banquet and Demodocus sings the loves of Mars and Venus. Ulysses, after a compliment to the poet, desires him to sing the introduction of the wooden horse into Troy, which subject provoking his tears, Alcinous inquires of his guest his name, parentage, and fortunes.

Now fair Aurora lifts her golden ray,
And all the ruddy orient flames with day:
Alcinous, and the chief, with dawning light,
Rose instant from the slumbers of the night;
Then to the council-seat they bend their way,
And fill the shining thrones along the bay.

Meanwhile Minerva, in her guardian care,
Shoots from the starry vault through fields of air;
In form, a herald of the king, she flies
From peer to peer, and thus incessant cries;

"Nobles and chiefs who rule Phaeacia's states,
The king in council your attendance waits;
A prince of grace divine your aid implores,
O'er unknown seas arrived from unknown shores."

She spoke, and sudden with tumultuous sounds

Of thronging multitudes the shore rebounds:
At once the seats they fill; and every eye
Glazed, as before some brother of the sky.
Pallas with grace divine his form improves,
More high he treads, and more enlarged he moves:
She sheds celestial bloom, regard to draw;
And gives a dignity of mien, to awe;
With strength, the future prize of fame to play,
And gather all the honours of the day.

Then from his glittering throne Alcinous rose;
"Attend (he cried) while we our will disclose.
Your present aid this godlike stranger craves,
Toss'd by rude tempest through a war of waves;
Perhaps from realms that view the rising day,
Or nations subject to the western ray.
Then grant, what here all sons of wine obtain
(For here affliction never pleads in vain);
Be chosen youth prepared, expert to try
The vast profound and hid the vessel fly;
Launch the tall back, and order every oar;
Then in our court indulge the genial hour.
Instant, you sailors to this task attend;
Swift to the palace, all ye peers ascend;
Let none to strangers honours due disclaim:
Be there Demodocus the bard of fame,
Taught by the gods to please, when high he sings
The vocal lay, responsive to the strings."

Thus spoke the prince; the attending peers obey;
In state they move; Alcinous heads the way
Swift to Demodocus the herald flies,
At once the sailors to their charge arise;
They launch the vessel, and unfurl the sails,
And stretch the swelling canvas to the gales;
Then to the palace move: a gathering throng,
Youth, and white age, tumultuous pour along.
Now all accesses to the dome are fill'd;
Eight boars, the choicest of the herd, are kill'd;
Two beeves, twelve fatlings, from the flock they bring
To crown the feast; so wills the bounteous king,
The herald now arrives, and guides along
The sacred master of celestial song;
Dear to the Muse! who gave his days to flow
With mighty blessings, mix'd with mighty woe;
With clouds of darkness quench'd his visual ray,
But gave him skill to raise the lofty lay.
High on a radiant throne sublime in state,

Encircled by huge multitudes, he sate;
With silver shone the throne; his lyre, well strung
To rapturous sounds, at hand Poutonous hung.
Before his seat a polish'd table shines,
And a full goblet foams with generous wines;
His food a herald bore; and now they fed;
And now the rage of craving hunger fled.

Then, fired by all the Muse, aloud he sings
The mighty deeds of demigods and kings;
From that fierce wrath the noble song arose,
That made Ulysses and Achilles foes;
How o'er the feast they doom the fall of Troy;
The stern debate Atrides hears with joy;
For Heaven foretold the contest, when he trod
The marble threshold of the Delphic god,
Curious to learn the counsels of the sky,
Ere yet he loosed the rage of war on Troy.

Touch'd at the song, Ulysses straight resign'd
To soft affliction all his manly mind.
Before his eyes the purple vest he drew,
Industrious to conceal the falling dew;
But when the music paused, he ceased to shed
The flowing tear, and raised his drooping head;
And, lifting to the gods a goblet crown'd,
He pour'd a pure libation to the ground.

Transported with the song, the listening train
Again with loud applause demand the strain;
Again Ulysses veil'd his pensive head.
Again unmann'd, a shower of sorrows shed;
Conceal'd he wept; the king observed alone
The silent tear, and heard the secret groan;
Then to the bard aloud—"O cease to sing,
Dumb be thy voice and mute the harmonious string;
Enough the feast has pleased, enough the power
Of heavenly song has crown'd the genial hour!
Incessant in the games your strength display,
Contest, ye brave the honours of the day!
That pleased the admiring stranger may proclaim
In distant regions the Phaeacian fame:
None wield the gauntlet with so dire a sway,
Or swifter in the race devour the way;
None in the leap spring with so strong a bound,
Or firmer, in the wrestling, press the ground."

Thus spoke the king; the attending peers obey;

In state they move, Alcinous lends the way;
His golden lyre Demodocus unstrung,
High on a column in the palace hung;
And guided by a herald's guardian cares,
Majestic to the lists of Fame repairs.

Now swarms the populace: a countless throng,
Youth and boar age; and man drives man along.
The games begin; ambitious of the prize,
Acroneus, Thoon, and Eretmeus rise;
The prize Ocyalus and Prymneus claim,
Anchialus and Ponteus, chiefs of fame.
There Proreus, Nautes, Eratreus, appear
And famed Amphialus, Polyneus' heir;
Euryalus, like Mars terrific, rose,
When clad in wrath he withers hosts of foes;
Naubolides with grace unequall'd shone,
Or equall'd by Laodamas alone.
With these came forth Ambasineus the strong:
And three brave sons, from great Alcinous sprung.

Ranged in a line the ready racers stand,
Start from the goal, and vanish o'er the strand:
Swift as on wings of winds, upborne they fly,
And drifts of rising dust involve the sky.
Before the rest, what space the hinds allow
Between the mule and ox, from plough to plough,
Clytonius sprung: he wing'd the rapid way,
And bore the unrivall'd honours of the day.
With fierce embrace the brawny wrestlers join;
The conquest, great Euryalus, is thine.
Amphialus sprung forward with a bound,
Superior in the leap, a length of ground.
From Elatreus' strong arm the discus flies,
And sings with unmatch'd force along the skies.
And Laodam whirls high, with dreadful sway,
The gloves of death, victorious in the fray.

While thus the peerage in the games contends,
In act to speak, Laodamas ascends.

"O friends (he cries), the stranger seems well skill'd
To try the illustrious labours of the field:
I deem him brave: then grant the brave man's claim,
Invite the hero to his share of fame.
What nervous arms he boasts! how firm his tread!
His limbs how turn'd! how broad his shoulders spread!
By age unbroke!—but all-consuming care

Destroys perhaps the strength that time would spare:
Dire is the ocean, dread in all its forms!
Man must decay when man contends with storms."

"Well hast thou spoke (Euryalus replies):
Thine is the guest, invite him thou to rise."
Swift as the word, advancing from the crowd,
He made obeisance, and thus spoke aloud:

"Vouchsafes the reverend stranger to display
His manly worth, and share the glorious day?
Father, arise! for thee thy port proclaims
Expert to conquer in the solemn games.
To fame arise! for what more fame can yield
Than the swift race, or conflict of the field?
Steal from corroding care one transient day,
To glory give the space thou hast to stay;
Short is the time, and lo! e'en now the gales
Call thee aboard, and stretch the swelling sails."

To whom with sighs Ulysses gave reply:
"Ah why the ill-suiting pastime must I try?
To gloomy care my thoughts alone are free;
Ill the gay sorts with troubled hearts agree;
Sad from my natal hour my days have ran,
A much-afflicted, much-enduring man!
Who, suppliant to the king and peers, implores
A speedy voyage to his native shore."
"Wise wanders, Laodam, thy erring tongue
The sports of glory to the brave belong
(Retorts Euryalus): he bears no claim
Among the great, unlike the sons of Fame.
A wandering merchant he frequents the main
Some mean seafarer in pursuit of gain;
Studious of freight, in naval trade well skill'd,
But dreads the athletic labours of the field."
Incensed, Ulysses with a frown replies:
"O forward to proclaim thy soul unwise!
With partial hands the gods their gifts dispense;
Some greatly think, some speak with manly sense;
Here Heaven an elegance of form denies,
But wisdom the defect of form supplies;
This man with energy of thought controls,
And steals with modest violence our souls;
He speaks reservedly, but he speaks with force,
Nor can one word be changed but for a worse;
In public more than mortal he appears,
And as he moves, the praising crowd reveres;

While others, beauteous as the etherial kind,
The nobler portion went, a knowing mind,
In outward show Heaven gives thee to excel.
But Heaven denies the praise of thinking well
I'll bear the brave a rude ungovern'd tongue,
And, youth, my generous soul resents the wrong.
Skill'd in heroic exercise, I claim
A post of honour with the sons of Fame.
Such was my boast while vigour crown'd my days,
Now care surrounds me, and my force decays;
Inured a melancholy part to bear
In scenes of death, by tempest and by war
Yet thus by woes impair'd, no more I waive
To prove the hero—slander stings the brave."

Then gliding forward with a furious bound
He wrench'd a rocky fragment from the ground
By far more ponderous, and more huge by far
Than what Phaeacia's sons discharged in air.
Fierce from his arm the enormous load he flings;
Sonorous through the shaded air it sings;
Couch'd to the earth, tempestuous as it flies,
The crowd gaze upward while it cleaves the skies.
Beyond all marks, with many a giddy round
Down-rushing, it up-turns a hill of ground.

That Instant Pallas, bursting from a cloud,
Fix'd a distinguish'd mark, and cried aloud:

"E'en he who, sightless, wants his visual ray
May by his touch alone award the day:
Thy signal throw transcends the utmost bound
Of every champion by a length of ground:
Securely bid the strongest of the train
Arise to throw; the strongest throws in vain."

She spoke: and momentary mounts the sky:
The friendly voice Ulysses hears with joy.
Then thus aloud (elate with decent pride)
"Rise, ye Phaecians, try your force (he cried):
If with this throw the strongest caster vie,
Still, further still, I bid the discus fly.
Stand forth, ye champions, who the gauntlet wield,
Or ye, the swiftest racers of the field!
Stand forth, ye wrestlers, who these pastimes grace!
I wield the gauntlet, and I run the race.
In such heroic games I yield to none,
Or yield to brave Laodamas alone:

Shall I with brave Laodamas contend?
A friend is sacred, and I style him friend.
Ungenerous were the man, and base of heart,
Who takes the kind, and pays the ungrateful part:
Chiefly the man, in foreign realms confined,
Base to his friend, to his own interest blind:
All, all your heroes I this day defy;
Give me a man that we our might may try.
Expert in every art, I boast the skill
To give the feather'd arrow wings to kill;
Should a whole host at once discharge the bow,
My well-aim'd shaft with death prevents the foe:
Alone superior in the field of Troy,
Great Philoctetes taught the shaft to fly.
From all the sons of earth unrivall'd praise
I justly claim; but yield to better days,
To those famed days when great Alcides rose,
And Eurytus, who bade the gods be foes
(Vain Eurytus, whose art became his crime,
Swept from the earth, he perish'd in his prime:
Sudden the irremeable way he trod,
Who boldly durst defy the bowyer god).
In fighting fields as far the spear I throw
As flies an arrow from the well-drawn bow.
Sole in the race the contest I decline,
Stiff are my weary joints, and I resign;
By storms and hunger worn; age well may fail,
When storms and hunger doth at once assail."

Abash'd, the numbers hear the godlike man,
Till great Alcinous mildly thus began:

"Well hast thou spoke, and well thy generous tongue
With decent pride refutes a public wrong:
Warm are thy words, but warm without offence;
Fear only fools, secure in men of sense;
Thy worth is known. Then hear our country's claim,
And bear to heroes our heroic fame:
In distant realms our glorious deeds display,
Repeat them frequent in the genial day;
When, blest with ease, thy woes and wanderings end,
Teach them thy consort, bid thy sons attend;
How, loved of Jove, he crown'd our sires with praise,
How we their offspring dignify our race.

"Let other realms the deathful gauntlet wield,
Or boast the glories of the athletic field:
We in the course unrivall'd speed display,

Or through cerulean billows plough the way;
To dress, to dance, to sing, our sole delight,
The feast or bath by day, and love by night:
Rise, then, ye skill'd in measures; let him bear
Your fame to men that breathe a distant air;
And faithful say, to you the powers belong
To race, to sail, to dance, to chant the song.

"But, herald, to the palace swift repair,
And the soft lyre to grace our pastimes bear."

Swift at the word, obedient to the king,
The herald flies the tuneful lyre to bring.
Up rose nine seniors, chosen to survey
The future games, the judges of the day
With instant care they mark a spacious round
And level for the dance the allotted ground:
The herald bears the lyre: intent to play,
The bard advancing meditates the lay.
Skill'd in the dance, tall youths, a blooming band,
Graceful before the heavenly minstrel stand:
Light bounding from the earth, at once they rise,
Their feet half-viewless quiver in the skies:
Ulysses gazed, astonish'd to survey
The glancing splendours as their sandals play.
Meantime the bard, alternate to the strings,
The loves of Mars and Cytherea sings:
How the stern god, enamour'd with her charms
Clasp'd the gay panting goddess in his arms,
By bribes seduced; and how the sun, whose eye
Views the broad heavens, disclosed the lawless joy.
Stung to the soul, indignant through the skies
To his black forge vindictive Vulcan flies:
Arrived, his sinewy arms incessant place
The eternal anvil on the massy base.
A wondrous net he labours, to betray
The wanton lovers, as entwined they lay,
Indissolubly strong; Then instant bears
To his immortal dome the finish'd snares:
Above, below, around, with art dispread,
The sure inclosure folds the genial bed:
Whose texture even the search of gods deceives,
Thin as the filmy threads the spider weaves,
Then, as withdrawing from the starry bowers,
He feigns a journey to the Lemnian shores,
His favourite isle: observant Mars descries
His wish'd recees, and to the goddess flies;
He glows, he burns, the fair-hair'd queen of love

Descends, smooth gliding from the courts of Jove,
Gay blooming in full charms: her hand he press'd
With eager joy, and with a sigh address'd:

"Come, my beloved! and taste the soft delights:
Come, to repose the genial bed invites:
Thy absent spouse, neglectful of thy charms,
Prefers his barbarous Sintians to thy arms!"

Then, nothing loth, the enamour'd fair he led,
And sunk transported on the conscious bed.
Down rush'd the toils, inwrapping as they lay
The careless lovers in their wanton play:
In vain they strive; the entangling snares deny
(Inextricably firm) the power to fly.
Warn'd by the god who sheds the golden day,
Stern Vulcan homeward treads the starry way:
Arrived, he sees, he grieves, with rage he burns:
Full horribly he roars, his voice all heaven returns.

"O Jove (he cried) O all ye powers above,
See the lewd dalliance of the queen of love!
Me, awkward me, she scorns; and yields her charms
To that fair lecher, the strong god of arms.
If I am lame, that stain my natal hour
By fate imposed; such me my parent bore.
Why was I born? See how the wanton lies!
Oh sight tormenting to a husband's eyes!
But yet, I trust, this once e'en Mars would fly
His fair-one's arms—he thinks her, once, too nigh.
But there remain, ye guilty, in my power,
Till Jove refunds his shameless daughter's dower.
Too dear I prized a fair enchanting face:
Beauty unchaste is beauty in disgrace."

Meanwhile the gods the dome of Vulcan throng;
Apollo comes, and Neptune comes along;
With these gay Hermes trod the starry plain;
But modesty withheld the goddess train.
All heaven beholds, imprison'd as they lie,
And unextinguish'd laughter shakes the sky.
Then mutual, thus they spoke: "Behold on wrong
Swift vengeance waits; and art subdues the strong!
Dwells there a god on all the Olympian brow
More swift than Mars, and more than Vulcan slow?
Yet Vulcan conquers, and the god of arms
Must pay the penalty for lawless charms."

Thus serious they; but he who gilds the skies,
The gay Apollo, thus to Hermes cries:
"Wouldst thou enchain'd like Mars, O Hermes, lie
And bear the shame like Mars to share the joy?"

"O envied shame! (the smiling youth rejoin'd;)
And thrice the chains, and thrice more firmly bind;
Gaze all ye gods, and every goddess gaze,
Yet eager would I bless the sweet disgrace."

Loud laugh the rest, e'en Neptune laughs aloud,
Yet sues importunate to loose the god.
"And free, (he cries) O Vulcan! free from shame
Thy captives; I ensure the penal claim."

"Will Neptune (Vulcan then) the faithless trust?
He suffers who gives surety for the unjust:
But say, if that lewd scandal of the sky,
To liberty restored, perfidious fly:
Say, wilt thou bear the mulct?" He instant cries,
"The mulct I bear, if Mars perfidious flies."

To whom appeased: "No more I urge delay;
When Neptune sues, my part is to obey."
Then to the snares his force the god applies;
They burst; and Mars to Thrace indignant flies:
To the soft Cyprian shores the goddess moves,
To visit Paphos and her blooming groves,
Where to the Power an hundred altars rise,
And breathing odours scent the balmy skies;
Concealed she bathes in consecrated bowers,
The Graces unguents shed, ambrosial showers,
Unguents that charm the gods! she last assumes
Her wondrous robes; and full the goddess blooms.

Thus sung the bard: Ulysses hears with joy,
And loud applauses read the vaulted sky.

Then to the sports his sons the king commands,
Each blooming youth before the monarch stands,
In dance unmatch'd! A wondrous ball is brought
(The work of Polypus, divinely wrought);
This youth with strength enormous bids it fly,
And bending backward whirls it to the sky;
His brother, springing with an active bound,
At distance intercepts it from the ground.
The ball dismissed, in dance they skim the strand,
Turn and return, and scarce imprint the sand.

The assembly gazes with astonished eyes,
And sends in shouts applauses to the skies.

Then thus Ulysses: "Happy king, whose name
The brightest shines in all the rolls of fame!
In subjects happy with surprise I gaze;
Thy praise was just; their skill transcends thy praise."

Pleas'd with his people's fame, the monarch hears,
And thus benevolent accosts the peers:
"Since wisdom's sacred guidance he pursues,
Give to the stranger-guest a stranger's dues:
Twelve princes in our realm dominion share,
O'er whom supreme, imperial power I bear;
Bring gold, a pledge of love: a talent bring,
A vest, a robe, and imitate your king.
Be swift to give: that he this night may share
The social feast of joy, with joy sincere.
And thou, Euryalus, redeem thy wrong;
A generous heart repairs a slanderous tongue."

The assenting peers, obedient to the king,
In haste their heralds send the gifts to bring.
Then thus Euryalus: "O prince, whose sway
Rules this bless'd realm, repentant I obey;
Be his this sword, whose blade of brass displays
A ruddy gleam; whose hilt a silver blaze;
Whose ivory sheath, inwrought with curious pride,
Adds graceful terror to the wearer's side."

He said, and to his hand the sword consign'd:
"And if (he cried) my words affect thy mind,
Far from thy mind those words, ye whirlwinds, bear,
And scatter them, ye storms, in empty air!
Crown, O ye heavens, with joy his peaceful hours,
And grant him to his spouse, and native shores."

"And blest be thou, my friend, (Ulysses cries,)
Crown him with every joy, ye favouring skies
To thy calm hours continued peace afford,
And never, never mayst thou want this sword,"

He said, and o'er his shoulder flung the blade.
Now o'er the earth ascends the evening shade:
The precious gifts the illustrious heralds bear,
And to the court the embodied peers repair.
Before the queen Alcinous' sons unfold
The vests, the robes, and heaps of shining gold;

Then to the radiant thrones they move in state:
Aloft, the king in pomp imperial sate.

Thence to the queen: "O partner of our reign,
O sole beloved! command thy menial train
A polish'd chest and stately robes to bear,
And healing waters for the bath prepare;
That, bathed, our guest may bid his sorrows cease,
Hear the sweet song, and taste the feast in peace.
A bowl that flames with gold, of wondrous frame,
Ourself we give, memorial of our name;
To raise in offerings to almighty Jove,
And every god that treads the courts above."

Instant the queen, observant of the king,
Commands her train a spacious vase to bring,
The spacious vase with ample streams suffice,
Heap the high wood, and bid the flames arise.
The flames climb round it with a fierce embrace,
The fuming waters bubble o'er the blaze.
Herself the chest prepares; in order roll'd
The robes, the vests are ranged, and heaps of gold
And adding a rich dress inwrought with art,
A gift expressive of her bounteous heart.
Thus spoke to Ithacus: "To guard with bands
Insolvable these gifts, thy care demands;
Lest, in thy slumbers on the watery main,
The hand of rapine make our bounty vain."

Then bending with full force around he roll'd
A labyrinth of bands in fold on fold,
Closed with Circaean art. A train attends
Around the bath: the bath the king ascends
(Untasted joy, since that disastrous hour,
He sail'd ill-fated from Calypso's bower);
Where, happy as the gods that range the sky,
He feasted every sense with every joy.
He bathes; the damsels with officious toil,
Shed sweets, shed unguents, in a shower of oil;
Then o'er his limbs a gorgeous robe he spreads,
And to the feast magnificently treads.
Full where the dome its shining valves expands,
Nausicaa blooming as a goddess stands;
With wondering eyes the hero she survey'd,
And graceful thus began the royal maid:

"Hail, godlike stranger! and when heaven restores
To thy fond wish thy long-expected shores,

This ever grateful in remembrance bear:
To me thou owest, to me, the vital air."

"O royal maid! (Ulysses straight returns)
Whose worth the splendours of thy race adorns,
So may dread Jove (whose arm in vengeance forms
The writhen bolt, and blackens heaven with storms),
Restore me safe, through weary wanderings toss'd,
To my dear country's ever-pleasing coast,
As while the spirit in this bosom glows,
To thee, my goddess, I address my vows;
My life, thy gift I boast!" He said, and sate
Fast by Alcinous on a throne of state.

Now each partakes the feast, the wine prepares,
Portions the food, and each his portion shares.
The bard a herald guides; the gazing throng
Pay low obeisance as he moves along:
Beneath a sculptur'd arch he sits enthroned,
The peers encircling form an awful round.
Then, from the chine, Ulysses carves with art
Delicious food, an honorary part:
"This, let the master of the lyre receive,
A pledge of love! 'tis all a wretch can give.
Lives there a man beneath the spacious skies
Who sacred honours to the bard denies?
The Muse the bard inspires, exalts his mind;
The muse indulgent loves the harmonious kind."

The herald to his hand the charge conveys,
Not fond of flattery, nor unpleased with praise.

When now the rage of hunger was allay'd,
Thus to the lyrist wise Ulysses said:
"O more than man! thy soul the muse inspires,
Or Phoebus animates with all his fires;
For who, by Phoebus uninform'd, could know
The woe of Greece, and sing so well the woe?
Just to the tale, as present at the fray,
Or taught the labours of the dreadful day:
The song recalls past horrors to my eyes,
And bids proud Ilion from her ashes rise.
Once more harmonious strike the sounding string,
The Epaean fabric, framed by Pallas, sing:
How stern Ulysses, furious to destroy,
With latent heroes sack'd imperial Troy.
If faithful thou record the tale of Fame,
The god himself inspires thy breast with flame

And mine shall be the task henceforth to raise
In every land thy monument of praise."

Full of the god he raised his lofty strain:
How the Greeks rush'd tumultuous to the main;
How blazing tents illumined half the skies,
While from the shores the winged navy flies;
How e'en in Ilion's walls, in deathful bands,
Came the stern Greeks by Troy's assisting hands:
All Troy up-heaved the steed; of differing mind,
Various the Trojans counsell'd: part consign'd
The monster to the sword, part sentence gave
To plunge it headlong in the whelming wave;
The unwise award to lodge it in the towers,
An offering sacred to the immortal powers:
The unwise prevail, they lodge it in the walls,
And by the gods' decree proud Ilion falls:
Destruction enters in the treacherous wood,
And vengeful slaughter, fierce for human blood.

He sung the Greeks stern-issuing from the steed,
How Ilion burns, how all her fathers bleed;
How to thy dome, Deiphobus! ascends
The Spartan king; how Ithacus attends
(Horrid as Mars); and how with dire alarms
He fights—subdues, for Pallas strings his arms

Thus while he sung, Ulysses' griefs renew,
Tears bathe his cheeks, and tears the ground bedew
As some fond matron views in mortal fight
Her husband falling in his country's right;
Frantic through clashing swords she runs, she flies,
As ghastly pale he groans, and faints and dies;
Close to his breast she grovels on the ground,
And bathes with floods of tears the gaping wound;
She cries, she shrieks: the fierce insulting foe
Relentless mocks her violence of woe:
To chains condemn'd, as wildly she deplores;
A widow, and a slave on foreign shores.

So from the sluices of Ulysses' eyes
Fast fell the tears, and sighs succeeded sighs:
Conceal'd he grieved: the king observed alone
The silent tear, and heard the secret groan;
Then to the bard aloud: "O cease to sing,
Dumb be thy voice, and mute the tuneful string;
To every note his tears responsive flow,
And his great heart heaves with tumultuous woe;

Thy lay too deeply moves: then cease the lay,
And o'er the banquet every heart be gay:
This social right demands: for him the sails,
Floating in air, invite the impelling gales:
His are the gifts of love: the wise and good
Receive the stranger as a brother's blood.

"But, friend, discover faithful what I crave;
Artful concealment ill becomes the brave:
Say what thy birth, and what the name you bore,
Imposed by parents in the natal hour?
(For from the natal hour distinctive names,
One common right, the great and lowly claims:)
Say from what city, from what regions toss'd,
And what inhabitants those regions boast?
So shalt thou instant reach the realm assign'd,
In wondrous ships, self-moved, instinct with mind;
No helm secures their course, no pilot guides;
Like man intelligent, they plough the tides,
Conscious of every coast, and every bay,
That lies beneath the sun's all-seeing ray;
Though clouds and darkness veil the encumber'd sky,
Fearless through darkness and through clouds they fly;
Though tempests rage, though rolls the swelling main,
The seas may roll, the tempests rage in vain;
E'en the stern god that o'er the waves presides,
Safe as they pass, and safe repass the tides,
With fury burns; while careless they convey
Promiscuous every guest to every bay,
These ears have heard my royal sire disclose
A dreadful story, big with future woes;
How Neptune raged, and how, by his command,
Firm rooted in a surge a ship should stand
A monument of wrath; how mound on mound
Should bury these proud towers beneath the ground.
But this the gods may frustrate or fulfil,
As suits the purpose of the Eternal Will.
But say through what waste regions hast thou stray'd
What customs noted, and what coasts survey'd;
Possess'd by wild barbarians fierce in arms,
Or men whose bosom tender pity warms?
Say why the fate of Troy awaked thy cares,
Why heaved thy bosom, and why flowed thy tears?
Just are the ways of Heaven: from Heaven proceed
The woes of man; Heaven doom'd the Greeks to bleed,
A theme of future song! Say, then, if slain
Some dear-loved brother press'd the Phrygian plain?
Or bled some friend, who bore a brother's part,

And claim'd by merit, not by blood, the heart?"

BOOK IX

ARGUMENT

THE ADVENTURES OF THE CICONS, LOTOPHAGI AND CYCLOPS

Ulysses begins the relation of his adventures: how, after the destruction of Troy, he with his companions made an incursion on the Cicons, by whom they were repulsed; and, meeting with a storm, were driven to the coast of the Lotophagi. From there they sailed to the land of the Cyclops, whose manners and situation are particularly characterised. The giant Polyphemus and his cave described; the usage Ulysses and his companions met with there; and, lastly, the method and artifice by which he escaped.

Then thus Ulysses: "Thou whom first in sway,
As first in virtue, these thy realms obey;
How sweet the products of a peaceful reign!
The heaven-taught poet and enchanting strain;
The well-filled palace, the perpetual feast,
A land rejoicing, and a people bless'd!
How goodly seems it ever to employ
Man's social days in union and in joy;
The plenteous hoard high-heap'd with cates divine,
And o'er the foaming bowl the laughing wine!

"Amid these joys, why seels thy mind to know
The unhappy series of a wanderer's woe?
Rememberance sad, whose image to review,
Alas, I must open all my wounds anew!
And oh, what first, what last shall I relate,
Of woes unnumbered sent by Heaven and Fate?

"Know first the man (though now a wretch distress'd)
Who hopes thee, monarch, for his future guest.
Behold Ulysses! no ignoble name,
Earth sounds my wisdom and high heaven my fame.

"My native soil is Ithaca the fair,
Where high Neritus waves his woods in air;
Dulichium, Same and Zaccynthus crown'd
With shady mountains spread their isles around.
(These to the north and night's dark regions run,
Those to Aurora and the rising sun).
Low lies our isle, yet bless'd in fruitful stores;
Strong are her sons, though rocky are her shores;
And none, ah none no lovely to my sight,

Of all the lands that heaven o'erspreads with light.
In vain Calypso long constrained my stay,
With sweet, reluctant, amorous delay;
With all her charms as vainly Circe strove,
And added magic to secure my love.
In pomps or joys, the palace or the grot,
My country's image never was forgot;
My absent parents rose before my sight,
And distant lay contentment and delight.

"Hear, then, the woes which mighty Jove ordain'd
To wait my passage from the Trojan land.
The winds from Ilion to the Cicons' shore,
Beneath cold Ismarus our vessels bore.
We boldly landed on the hostile place,
And sack'd the city, and destroy'd the race,
Their wives made captive, their possessions shared,
And every soldier found a like reward
I then advised to fly; not so the rest,
Who stay'd to revel, and prolong the feast:
The fatted sheep and sable bulls they slay,
And bowls flow round, and riot wastes the day.
Meantime the Cicons, to their holds retired,
Call on the Cicons, with new fury fired;
With early morn the gather'd country swarms,
And all the continent is bright with arms;
Thick as the budding leaves or rising flowers
O'erspread the land, when spring descends in showers:
All expert soldiers, skill'd on foot to dare,
Or from the bounding courser urge the war.
Now fortune changes (so the Fates ordain);
Our hour was come to taste our share of pain.
Close at the ships the bloody fight began,
Wounded they wound, and man expires on man.
Long as the morning sun increasing bright
O'er heaven's pure azure spreads the glowing light,
Promiscuous death the form of war confounds,
Each adverse battle gored with equal wounds;
But when his evening wheels o'erhung the main,
Then conquest crown'd the fierce Ciconian train.
Six brave companions from each ship we lost,
The rest escape in haste, and quit the coast,
With sails outspread we fly the unequal strife,
Sad for their loss, but joyful of our life.
Yet as we fled, our fellows' rites we paid,
And thrice we call'd on each unhappy shade,

"Meanwhile the god, whose hand the thunder forms,

Drives clouds on clouds, and blackens heaven with storms:
Wide o'er the waste the rage of Boreas sweeps,
And night rush'd headlong on the shaded deeps.
Now here, now there, the giddy ships are borne,
And all the rattling shrouds in fragments torn.
We furl'd the sail, we plied the labouring oar,
Took down our masts, and row'd our ships to shore.
Two tedious days and two long nights we lay,
O'erwatch'd and batter'd in the naked bay.
But the third morning when Aurora brings,
We rear the masts, we spread the canvas wings;
Refresh'd and careless on the deck reclined,
We sit, and trust the pilot and the wind.
Then to my native country had I sail'd:
But, the cape doubled, adverse winds prevail'd.
Strong was the tide, which by the northern blast
Impell'd, our vessels on Cythera cast,
Nine days our fleet the uncertain tempest bore
Far in wide ocean, and from sight of shore:
The tenth we touch'd, by various errors toss'd,
The land of Lotus and the flowery coast.
We climb'd the beach, and springs of water found,
Then spread our hasty banquet on the ground.
Three men were sent, deputed from the crew
(A herald one) the dubious coast to view,
And learn what habitants possess'd the place.
They went, and found a hospitable race:
Not prone to ill, nor strange to foreign guest,
They eat, they drink, and nature gives the feast
The trees around them all their food produce:
Lotus the name: divine, nectareous juice!
(Thence call'd Lo'ophagi); which whose tastes,
Insatiate riots in the sweet repasts,
Nor other home, nor other care intends,
But quits his house, his country, and his friends.
The three we sent, from off the enchanting ground
We dragg'd reluctant, and by force we bound.
The rest in haste forsook the pleasing shore,
Or, the charm tasted, had return'd no more.
Now placed in order on their banks, they sweep
The sea's smooth face, and cleave the hoary deep:
With heavy hearts we labour through the tide,
To coasts unknown, and oceans yet untried.

"The land of Cyclops first, a savage kind,
Nor tamed by manners, nor by laws confined:
Untaught to plant, to turn the glebe, and sow,
They all their products to free nature owe:

The soil, untill'd, a ready harvest yields,
With wheat and barley wave the golden fields;
Spontaneous wines from weighty clusters pour,
And Jove descends in each prolific shower,
By these no statues and no rights are known,
No council held, no monarch fills the throne;
But high on hills, or airy cliffs, they dwell,
Or deep in caves whose entrance leads to hell.
Each rules his race, his neighbour not his care,
Heedless of others, to his own severe.

"Opposed to the Cyclopean coast, there lay
An isle, whose hill their subject fields survey;
Its name Lachaea, crown'd with many a grove,
Where savage goats through pathless thickets rove:
No needy mortals here, with hunger bold,
Or wretched hunters through the wintry cold
Pursue their flight; but leave them safe to bound
From hill to hill, o'er all the desert ground.
Nor knows the soil to feed the fleecy care,
Or feels the labours of the crooked share;
But uninhabited, untill'd, unsown,
It lies, and breeds the bleating goat alone.
For there no vessel with vermilion prore,
Or bark of traffic, glides from shore to shore;
The rugged race of savages, unskill'd
The seas to traverse, or the ships to build,
Gaze on the coast, nor cultivate the soil,
Unlearn'd in all the industrious art of toil,
Yet here all produces and all plants abound,
Sprung from the fruitful genius of the ground;
Fields waving high with heavy crops are seen,
And vines that flourish in eternal green,
Refreshing meads along the murmuring main,
And fountains streaming down the fruitful plain.

"A port there is, inclosed on either side,
Where ships may rest, unanchor'd and untied;
Till the glad mariners incline to sail,
And the sea whitens with the rising gale,
High at the head, from out the cavern'd rock,
In living rills a gushing fountain broke:
Around it, and above, for ever green,
The busy alders form'd a shady scene;
Hither some favouring god, beyond our thought,
Through all surrounding shade our navy brought;
For gloomy night descended on the main,
Nor glimmer'd Phoebe in the ethereal plain:

But all unseen the clouded island lay,
And all unseen the surge and rolling sea,
Till safe we anchor'd in the shelter'd bay:
Our sails we gather'd, cast our cables o'er,
And slept secure along the sandy shore.
Soon as again the rosy morning shone,
Reveal'd the landscape and the scene unknown,
With wonder seized, we view the pleasing ground,
And walk delighted, and expatiate round.
Roused by the woodland nymphs at early dawn,
The mountain goats came bounding o'er the lawn:
In haste our fellows to the ships repair,
For arms and weapons of the sylvan war;
Straight in three squadrons all our crew we part,
And bend the bow, or wing the missile dart;
The bounteous gods afford a copious prey,
And nine fat goats each vessel bears away:
The royal bark had ten. Our ships complete
We thus supplied (for twelve were all the fleet).

"Here, till the setting sun roll'd down the light,
We sat indulging in the genial rite:
Nor wines were wanting; those from ample jars
We drain'd, the prize of our Ciconian wars.
The land of Cyclops lay in prospect near:
The voice of goats and bleating flocks we hear,
And from their mountains rising smokes appear.
Now sunk the sun, and darkness cover'd o'er
The face of things: along the sea-beat shore
Satiate we slept: but, when the sacred dawn
Arising glitter'd o'er the dewy lawn,
I call'd my fellows, and these words address'd
'My dear associates, here indulge your rest;
While, with my single ship, adventurous, I
Go forth, the manners of you men to try;
Whether a race unjust, of barbarous might,
Rude and unconscious of a stranger's right;
Or such who harbour pity in their breast,
Revere the gods, and succour the distress'd,'

"This said, I climb'd my vessel's lofty side;
My train obey'd me, and the ship untied.
In order seated on their banks, they sweep
Neptune's smooth face, and cleave the yielding deep.
When to the nearest verge of land we drew,
Fast by the sea a lonely cave we view,
High, and with darkening laurels covered o'er;
Were sheep and goats lay slumbering round the shore

Near this, a fence of marble from the rock,
Brown with o'eraching pine and spreading oak.
A giant shepherd here his flock maintains
Far from the rest, and solitary reigns,
In shelter thick of horrid shade reclined;
And gloomy mischiefs labour in his mind.
A form enormous! far unlike the race
Of human birth, in stature, or in face;
As some lone mountain's monstrous growth he stood,
Crown'd with rough thickets, and a nodding wood.
I left my vessel at the point of land,
And close to guard it, gave our crew command:
With only twelve, the boldest and the best,
I seek the adventure, and forsake the rest.
Then took a goatskin fill'd with precious wine,
The gift of Maron of Evantheus' line
(The priest of Phoebus at the Ismarian shrine).
In sacred shade his honour'd mansion stood
Amidst Apollo's consecrated wood;
Him, and his house, Heaven moved my mind to save,
And costly presents in return he gave;
Seven golden talents to perfection wrought,
A silver bowl that held a copious draught,
And twelve large vessels of unmingled wine,
Mellifluous, undecaying, and divine!
Which now, some ages from his race conceal'd,
The hoary sire in gratitude reveal'd.
Such was the wine: to quench whose fervent steam
Scarce twenty measures from the living stream
To cool one cup sufficed: the goblet crown'd
Breathed aromatic fragrances around.
Of this an ample vase we heaved aboard,
And brought another with provisions stored.
My soul foreboded I should find the bower
Of some fell monster, fierce with barbarous power;
Some rustic wretch, who lived in Heaven's despite,
Contemning laws, and trampling on the right.
The cave we found, but vacant all within
(His flock the giant tended on the green):
But round the grot we gaze; and all we view,
In order ranged our admiration drew:
The bending shelves with loads of cheeses press'd,
The folded flocks each separate from the rest
(The larger here, and there the lesser lambs,
The new-fallen young here bleating for their dams:
The kid distinguish'd from the lambkin lies);
The cavern echoes with responsive cries.
Capacious chargers all around were laid.

Full pails, and vessels of the milking trade.
With fresh provisions hence our fleet to store
My friends advise me, and to quit the shore.
Or drive a flock of sheep and goats away,
Consult our safety, and put off to sea.
Their wholesome counsel rashly I declined,
Curious to view the man of monstrous kind,
And try what social rites a savage lends:
Dire rites, alas! and fatal to my friends

"Then first a fire we kindle, and prepare
For his return with sacrifice and prayer;
The loaden shelves afford us full repast;
We sit expecting. Lo! he comes at last,
Near half a forest on his back he bore,
And cast the ponderous burden at the door.
It thunder'd as it fell. We trembled then,
And sought the deep recesses of the den.
New driven before him through the arching rock,
Came tumbling, heaps on heaps, the unnumber'd flock.
Big-udder'd ewes, and goats of female kind
(The males were penn'd in outward courts behind);
Then, heaved on high, a rock's enormous weight
To the cave's mouth he roll'd, and closed the gate
(Scarce twenty four-wheel'd cars, compact and strong,
The massy load could bear, or roll along).
He next betakes him to his evening cares,
And, sitting down, to milk his flocks prepares;
Of half their udders eases first the dams,
Then to the mother's teat submits the lambs;
Half the white stream to hardening cheese be press'd,
And high in wicker-baskets heap'd: the rest,
Reserved in bowls, supplied his nightly feast.
His labour done, he fired the pile, that gave
A sudden blaze, and lighted all the cave.
We stand discover'd by the rising fires;
Askance the giant glares, and thus inquires:

"'What are ye, guests? on what adventure, say,
Thus far ye wander through the watery way?
Pirates perhaps, who seek through seas unknown
The lives of others, and expose your own?'

"His voice like thunder through the cavern sounds;
My bold companions thrilling fear confounds,
Appall'd at sight of more than mortal man!
At length, with heart recover'd, I began:

"'From Troy's famed fields, sad wanderers o'er the main,
Behold the relics of the Grecian train:
Through various seas, by various perils toss'd,
And forced by storms, unwilling on your coast;
Far from our destined course and native land,
Such was our fate, and such high Jove's command!
Nor what we are befits us to disclaim,
Atrides' friends (in arms a mighty name),
Who taught proud Troy and all her sons to bow;
Victors of late, but humble suppliants now!
Low at thy knee thy succour we implore;
Respect us, human, and relieve us, poor.
At least, some hospitable gift bestow;
'Tis what the happy to the unhappy owe;
'Tis what the gods require: those gods revere;
The poor and stranger are their constant care;
To Jove their cause, and their revenge belongs,
He wanders with them, and he feels their wrongs."

"'Fools that ye are (the savage thus replies,
His inward fury blazing at his eyes),
Or strangers, distant far from our abodes,
To bid me reverence or regard the gods.
Know then, we Cyclops are a race above
Those air-bred people, and their goat-nursed Jove;
And learn, our power proceeds with thee and thine,
Not as he wills, but as ourselves incline.
But answer, the good ship that brought ye o'er,
Where lies she anchor'd? near or off the shore?'

"Thus he. His meditated fraud I find
(Versed in the turns of various human-kind):
And, cautious thus: 'Against a dreadful rock,
Fast by your shore the gallant vessel broke.
Scarce with these few I 'scaped; of all my train,
Whom angry Neptune, whelm'd beneath the main,
The scattered wreck the winds blew back again.'

"He answer'd with his deed: his bloody hand
Snatch'd two, unhappy! of my martial band;
And dash'd like dogs against the stony floor:
The pavement swims with brains and mingled gore.
Torn limb from limb, he spreads his horrid feast,
And fierce devours it like a mountain beast:
He sucks the marrow, and the blood he drains,
Nor entrails, flesh, nor solid bone remains.
We see the death from which we cannot move,
And humbled groan beneath the hand of Jove.

His ample maw with human carnage fill'd,
A milky deluge next the giant swill'd;
Then stretch'd in length o'er half the cavern'd rock,
Lay senseless, and supine, amidst the flock.
To seize the time, and with a sudden wound
To fix the slumbering monster to the ground,
My soul impels me! and in act I stand
To draw the sword; but wisdom held my hand.
A deed so rash had finished all our fate,
No mortal forces from the lofty gate
Could roll the rock. In hopeless grief we lay,
And sigh, expecting the return of day.
Now did the rosy-fingered morn arise,
And shed her sacred light along the skies;
He wakes, he lights the fire, he milks the dams,
And to the mother's teats submits the lambs.
The task thus finish'd of his morning hours,
Two more he snatches, murders, and devours.
Then pleased, and whistling, drives his flock before,
Removes the rocky mountain from the door,
And shuts again: with equal ease disposed,
As a light quiver's lid is oped and closed.
His giant voice the echoing region fills:
His flocks, obedient, spread o'er all the hills.

"Thus left behind, even in the last despair
I thought, devised, and Pallas heard my prayer.
Revenge, and doubt, and caution, work'd my breast;
But this of many counsels seem'd the best:
The monster's club within the cave I spied,
A tree of stateliest growth, and yet undried,
Green from the wood: of height and bulk so vast,
The largest ship might claim it for a mast.
This shorten'd of its top, I gave my train
A fathom's length, to shape it and to plane;
The narrower end I sharpen'd to a spire,
Whose point we harden'd with the force of fire,
And hid it in the dust that strew'd the cave,
Then to my few companions, bold and brave,
Proposed, who first the venturous deed should try,
In the broad orbit of his monstrous eye
To plunge the brand and twirl the pointed wood,
When slumber next should tame the man of blood.
Just as I wished, the lots were cast on four:
Myself the fifth. We stand and wait the hour.
He comes with evening: all his fleecy flock
Before him march, and pour into the rock:
Not one, or male or female, stayed behind

(So fortune chanced, or so some god designed);
Then heaving high the stone's unwieldy weight,
He roll'd it on the cave and closed the gate.
First down he sits, to milk the woolly dams,
And then permits their udder to the lambs.
Next seized two wretches more, and headlong cast,
Brain'd on the rock; his second dire repast.
I then approach'd him reeking with their gore,
And held the brimming goblet foaming o'er;
'Cyclop! since human flesh has been thy feast,
Now drain this goblet, potent to digest;
Know hence what treasures in our ship we lost,
And what rich liquors other climates boast.
We to thy shore the precious freight shall bear,
If home thou send us and vouchsafe to spare.
But oh! thus furious, thirsting thus for gore,
The sons of men shall ne'er approach thy shore,
And never shalt thou taste this nectar more,'

"He heard, he took, and pouring down his throat,
Delighted, swill'd the large luxurious draught,
'More! give me more (he cried): the boon be thine,
Whoe'er thou art that bear'st celestial wine!
Declare thy name: not mortal is this juice,
Such as the unbless'd Cyclopaean climes produce
(Though sure our vine the largest cluster yields,
And Jove's scorn'd thunder serves to drench our fields);
But this descended from the bless'd abodes,
A rill of nectar, streaming from the gods.'

"He said, and greedy grasped the heady bowl,
Thrice drained, and poured the deluge on his soul.
His sense lay covered with the dozy fume;
While thus my fraudful speech I reassume.
'Thy promised boon, O Cyclop! now I claim,
And plead my title; Noman is my name.
By that distinguish'd from my tender years,
'Tis what my parents call me, and my peers.

"The giant then: 'Our promis'd grace receive,
The hospitable boon we mean to give:
When all thy wretched crew have felt my power,
Noman shall be the last I will devour.'

"He said: then nodding with the fumes of wine
Droop'd his huge head, and snoring lay supine.
His neck obliquely o'er his shoulders hung,
Press'd with the weight of sleep that tames the strong:

There belch'd the mingled streams of wine and blood,
And human flesh, his indigested food.
Sudden I stir the embers, and inspire
With animating breath the seeds of fire:
Each drooping spirit with bold words repair,
And urged my train the dreadful deed to dare.
The stake now glow'd beneath the burning bed
(Green as it was) and sparkled fiery red,
Then forth the vengeful instrument I bring;
With beating hearts my fellows form a ring.
Urged my some present god, they swift let fall
The pointed torment on his visual ball.
Myself above them from a rising ground
Guide the sharp stake, and twirl it round and round.
As when a shipwright stands his workmen o'er,
Who ply the wimble, some huge beam to bore;
Urged on all hands, it nimbly spins about,
The grain deep-piercing till it scoops it out:
In his broad eye he whirls the fiery wood;
From the pierced pupil spouts the boiling blood;
Singed are his brows; the scorching lids grow black;
The jelly bubbles, and the fibres crack.
And as when armourers temper in the ford
The keen-edged pole-axe, or the shining sword,
The red-hot metal hisses in the lake,
Thus in his eye-ball hiss'd the plunging stake.
He sends a dreadful groan, the rocks around
Through all their inmost winding caves resound.
Scared we recoiled. Forth with frantic hand,
He tore and dash'd on earth and gory brand;
Then calls the Cyclops, all that round him dwell,
With voice like thunder, and a direful yell.
From all their dens the one-eyed race repair,
From rifted rocks, and mountains bleak in air.
All haste assembled, at his well-known roar,
Inquire the cause, and crowd the cavern door.

"'What hurts thee, Polypheme? what strange affright
Thus breaks our slumbers, and disturbs the night?
Does any mortal, in the unguarded hour
Of sleep, oppress thee, or by fraud or power?
Or thieves insidious thy fair flock surprise?'
Thus they; the Cyclop from his den replies:

"'Friends, Noman kills me; Noman in the hour
Of sleep, oppresses me with fraudful power.'
'If no man hurt thee, but the hand divine
Inflict disease, it fits thee to resign:

To Jove or to thy father Neptune pray.'
The brethren cried, and instant strode away.
"Joy touch'd my secret soul and conscious heart,
Pleased with the effect of conduct and of art.
Meantime the Cyclop, raging with his wound,
Spreads his wide arms, and searches round and round:
At last, the stone removing from the gate,
With hands extended in the midst he sate;
And search'd each passing sheep, and fell it o'er,
Secure to seize us ere we reach'd the door
(Such as his shallow wit he deem'd was mine);
But secret I revolved the deep design:
'Twas for our lives my labouring bosom wrought;
Each scheme I turn'd, and sharpen'd every thought;
This way and that I cast to save my friends,
Till one resolve my varying counsel ends.

"Strong were the rams, with native purple fair,
Well fed, and largest of the fleecy care,
These, three and three, with osier bands we tied
(The twining bands the Cyclop's bed supplied);
The midmost bore a man, the outward two
Secured each side: so bound we all the crew,
One ram remain'd, the leader of the flock:
In his deep fleece my grasping hands I lock,
And fast beneath, in wooly curls inwove,
There cling implicit, and confide in Jove.
When rosy morning glimmer'd o'er the dales,
He drove to pasture all the lusty males:
The ewes still folded, with distended thighs
Unmilk'd lay bleating in distressful cries.
But heedless of those cares, with anguish stung,
He felt their fleeces as they pass'd along
(Fool that he was.) and let them safely go,
All unsuspecting of their freight below.

"The master ram at last approach'd the gate,
Charged with his wool, and with Ulysses' fate.
Him while he pass'd, the monster blind bespoke:
'What makes my ram the lag of all the flock?
First thou wert wont to crop the flowery mead,
First to the field and river's bank to lead,
And first with stately step at evening hour
Thy fleecy fellows usher to their bower.
Now far the last, with pensive pace and slow
Thou movest, as conscious of thy master's woe!
Seest thou these lids that now unfold in vain?
(The deed of Noman and his wicked train!)

Oh! did'st thou feel for thy afflicted lord,
And would but Fate the power of speech afford.
Soon might'st thou tell me, where in secret here
The dastard lurks, all trembling with his fear:
Swung round and round, and dash'd from rock to rock,
His battered brains should on the pavement smoke
No ease, no pleasure my sad heart receives,
While such a monster as vile Noman lives.'

"The giant spoke, and through the hollow rock
Dismiss'd the ram, the father of the flock.
No sooner freed, and through the inclosure pass'd,
First I release myself, my fellows last:
Fat sheep and goats in throngs we drive before,
And reach our vessel on the winding shore.
With joy the sailors view their friends return'd,
And hail us living whom as dead they mourn'd
Big tears of transport stand in every eye:
I check their fondness, and command to fly.
Aboard in haste they heave the wealthy sheep,
And snatch their oars, and rush into the deep.
"Now off at sea, and from the shallows clear,
As far as human voice could reach the ear,
With taunts the distant giant I accost:
'Hear me, O Cyclop! hear, ungracious host!
'Twas on no coward, no ignoble slave,
Thou meditatest thy meal in yonder cave;
But one, the vengeance fated from above
Doom'd to inflict; the instrument of Jove.
Thy barbarous breach of hospitable bands,
The god, the god revenges by my hands.'

"These words the Cyclop's burning rage provoke;
From the tall hill he rends a pointed rock;
High o'er the billows flew the massy load,
And near the ship came thundering on the flood.
It almost brush'd the helm, and fell before:
The whole sea shook, and refluent beat the shore,
The strong concussion on the heaving tide
Roll'd back the vessel to the island's side:
Again I shoved her off: our fate to fly,
Each nerve we stretch, and every oar we ply.
Just 'scaped impending death, when now again
We twice as far had furrow'd back the main,
Once more I raise my voice; my friends, afraid,
With mild entreaties my design dissuade:
'What boots the godless giant to provoke,
Whose arm may sink us at a single stroke?

Already when the dreadful rock he threw,
Old Ocean shook, and back his surges flew.
The sounding voice directs his aim again;
The rock o'erwhelms us, and we 'scaped in vain.'

"But I, of mind elate, and scorning fear,
Thus with new taunts insult the monster's ear:
'Cyclop! if any, pitying thy disgrace.
Ask, who disfigured thus that eyeless face?
Say 'twas Ulysses: 'twas his deed declare,
Laertes' son, of Ithaca the fair;
Ulysses, far in fighting fields renown'd,
Before whose arm Troy tumbled to the ground.'

"The astonished savage with a roar replies:
'Oh heavens! oh faith of ancient prophecies!
This, Telemus Eurymedes foretold
(The mighty seer who on these hills grew old;
Skill'd the dark fates of mortals to declare,
And learn'd in all wing'd omens of the air);
Long since he menaced, such was Fate's command;
And named Ulysses as the destined hand.
I deem'd some godlike giant to behold,
Or lofty hero, haughty, brave, and bold;
Not this weak pigmy wretch, of mean design,
Who, not by strength subdued me, but by wine.
But come, accept our gifts, and join to pray
Great Neptune's blessing on the watery way;
For his I am, and I the lineage own;
The immortal father no less boasts the son.
His power can heal me, and relight my eye;
And only his, of all the gods on high.'
"'Oh! could this arm (I thus aloud rejoin'd)
From that vast bulk dislodge thy bloody mind,
And send thee howling to the realms of night!
As sure as Neptune cannot give thee sight.'
"Thus I; while raging he repeats his cries,
With hands uplifted to the starry skies?
'Hear me, O Neptune; thou whose arms are hurl'd
From shore to shore, and gird the solid world;
If thine I am, nor thou my birth disown,
And if the unhappy Cyclop be thy son,
Let not Ulysses breathe his native air,
Laertes' son, of Ithaca the fair.
If to review his country be his fate,
Be it through toils and sufferings long and late;
His lost companions let him first deplore;
Some vessel, not his own, transport him o'er;

And when at home from foreign sufferings freed,
More near and deep, domestic woes succeed!'
With imprecations thus he fill'd the air,
And angry Neptune heard the unrighteous prayer,
A larger rock then heaving from the plain,
He whirl'd it round: it sung across the main;
It fell, and brush'd the stern: the billows roar,
Shake at the weight, and refluent beat the shore.
With all our force we kept aloof to sea,
And gain'd the island where our vessels lay.
Our sight the whole collected navy cheer'd.
Who, waiting long, by turns had hoped and fear'd.
There disembarking on the green sea side,
We land our cattle, and the spoil divide;
Of these due shares to every sailor fall;
The master ram was voted mine by all;
And him (the guardian of Ulysses' fate)
With pious mind to heaven I consecrate.
But the great god, whose thunder rends the skies,
Averse, beholds the smoking sacrifice;
And sees me wandering still from coast to coast,
And all my vessels, all my people, lost!
While thoughtless we indulge the genial rite,
As plenteous cates and flowing bowls invite;
Till evening Phoebus roll'd away the light;
Stretch'd on the shore in careless ease we rest,
Till ruddy morning purpled o'er the east;
Then from their anchors all our ships unbind,
And mount the decks, and call the willing wind.
Now, ranged in order on our banks we sweep.
With hasty strokes the hoarse-resounding deep;
Blind to the future, pensive with our fears,
Glad for the living, for the dead in tears."

BOOK X

ARGUMENT

ADVENTURES WITH AEOLUS, THE LAESTRYGONS, AND CIRCE

Ulysses arrives at the island of AEolus, who gives him prosperous winds, and incloses the adverse ones
in a bag, which his companions untying, they are driven back again and rejected. Then they sail to the
Laestrygons, where they lose eleven ships, and, with only one remaining, proceed to the island of Circe.
Eurylochus is sent first with some companions, all which, except Eurylochus, are transformed into swine.
Ulysses then undertakes the adventure, and, by the help of Mercury, who gives him the herb Moly,

overcomes the enchantress, and procures the restoration of his men. After a year's stay with her, he prepares, at her instigation, for his voyage to the infernal shades.

"At length we reach'd AEolias's sea-girt shore,
Where great Hippotades the sceptre bore,
A floating isle! high-raised by toil divine,
Strong walls of brass the rocky coast confine.
Six blooming youths, in private grandeur bred,
And six fair daughters, graced the royal bed;
These sons their sisters wed, and all remain
Their parents' pride, and pleasure of their reign.
All day they feast, all day the bowls flow round,
And joy and music through the isle resound;
At night each pair on splendid carpets lay,
And crown'd with love the pleasures of the day.
This happy port affords our wandering fleet
A month's reception, and a safe retreat.
Full oft the monarch urged me to relate
The fall of Ilion, and the Grecian fate;
Full oft I told: at length for parting moved;
The king with mighty gifts my suit approved.
The adverse winds in leathern bags he braced,
Compress'd their force, and lock'd each struggling blast.
For him the mighty sire of gods assign'd
The tempest's lood, the tyrant of the wind;
His word alone the listening storms obey,
To smooth the deep, or swell the foamy sea.
These in my hollow ship the monarch hung,
Securely fetter'd by a silver thong:
But Zephyrus exempt, with friendly gales
He charged to fill, and guide the swelling sails:
Rare gift! but O, what gift to fools avails!

"Nine prosperous days we plied the labouring oar;
The tenth presents our welcome native shore:
The hills display the beacon's friendly light,
And rising mountains gain upon our sight.
Then first my eyes, by watchful toils oppress'd,
Complied to take the balmy gifts of rest:
Then first my hands did from the rudder part
(So much the love of home possess'd my heart):
When lo! on board a fond debate arose;
What rare device those vessels might inclose?
What sum, what prize from AEolus I brought?
Whilst to his neighbour each express'd his thought:

"'Say, whence ye gods, contending nations strive
Who most shall please, who most our hero give?

Long have his coffers groan'd with Trojan spoils:
Whilst we, the wretched partners of his toils,
Reproach'd by want, our fruitless labours mourn,
And only rich in barren fame return.
Now AEolus, ye see, augments his store:
But come, my friends, these mystic gifts explore,'
They said: and (oh cursed fate!) the thongs unbound!
The gushing tempest sweeps the ocean round;
Snatch'd in the whirl, the hurried navy flew,
The ocean widen'd and the shores withdrew.
Roused from my fatal sleep I long debate
If still to live, or desperate plunge to fate;
Thus doubting, prostrate on the deck I lay,
Till all the coward thoughts of death gave way.

"Meanwhile our vessels plough the liquid plain,
And soon the known AEolian coast regain;
Our groan the rocks remurmur'd to the main.
We leap'd on shore, and with a scanty feast
Our thirst and hunger hastily repress'd;
That done, two chosen heralds straight attend
Our second progress to my royal friend;
And him amidst his jovial sons we found;
The banquet steaming, and the goblets crown'd;
There humbly stoop'd with conscious shame and awe,
Nor nearer than the gate presumed to draw.
But soon his sons their well-known guest descried,
And starting from their couches loudly cried:
'Ulysses here! what demon could'st thou meet
To thwart thy passage, and repel thy fleet?
Wast thou not furnish'd by our choicest care
For Greece, for home and all thy soul held dear?'
Thus they, In silence long my fate I mourn'd;
At length these words with accents low return'd:
`Me, lock'd in sleep, my faithless crew bereft
Of all the blessing of your godlike gift!
But grant, oh grant, our loss we may retrieve;
A favour you, and you alone can give.'

"Thus I with art to move their pity tried,
And touch'd the youths; but their stern sire replied:
'Vile wretch, begone! this instant I command
Thy fleet accursed to leave our hallow'd land.
His baneful suit pollutes these bless'd abodes,
Whose fate proclaims him hateful to the gods.'

"Thus fierce he said: we sighing went our way,
And with desponding hearts put off to sea.

The sailors spent with toils their folly mourn,
But mourn in vain; no prospect of return
Six days and nights a doubtful course we steer,
The next proud Lamos' stately towers appear,
And Laestrygonia's gates arise distinct in air.
The shepherd, quitting here at night the plain,
Calls, to succeed his cares, the watchful swain;
But he that scorns the chains of sleep to wear,
And adds the herdsman's to the shepherd's care,
So near the pastures, and so short the way,
His double toils may claim a double pay,
And join the labours of the night and day.

"Within a long recess a bay there lies,
Edged round with cliffs high pointing to the skies;
The jutting shores that swell on either side
Contract its mouth, and break the rushing tide.
Our eager sailors seize the fair retreat,
And bound within the port their crowded fleet:
For here retired the sinking billows sleep,
And smiling calmness silver'd o'er the deep.
I only in the bay refused to moor,
And fix'd without, my halsers to the shore.

"From thence we climb'd a point, whose airy brow
Commands the prospect of the plains below;
No tracks of beasts, or signs of men, we found,
But smoky volumes rolling from the ground.
Two with our herald thither we command,
With speed to learn what men possess'd the land.
They went, and kept the wheel's smooth-beaten road
Which to the city drew the mountain wood;
When lo! they met, beside a crystal spring,
The daughter of Antiphates the king;
She to Artacia's silver streams came down;
(Artacia's streams alone supply the town);
The damsel they approach, and ask'd what race
The people were? who monarch of the place?
With joy the maid the unwary strangers heard
And show'd them where the royal dome appear'd.
They went; but as they entering saw the queen
Of size enormous, and terrific mien
(Not yielding to some bulky mountain's height),
A sudden horror struck their aching sight.
Swift at her call her husband scour'd away
To wreak his hunger on the destined prey;
One for his food the raging glutton slew,
But two rush'd out, and to the navy flew.

"Balk'd of his prey, the yelling monster flies,
And fills the city with his hideous cries;
A ghastly band of giants hear the roar,
And, pouring down the mountains, crowd the shore.
Fragments they rend from off the craggy brow
And dash the ruins on the ships below;
The crackling vessels burst; hoarse groans arise,
And mingled horrors echo to the skies;
The men like fish, they struck upon the flood,
And cramm'd their filthy throats with human food.
Whilst thus their fury rages at the bay,
My sword our cables cut, I call'd to weigh;
And charged my men, as they from fate would fly,
Each nerve to strain, each bending oar to ply.
The sailors catch the word, their oars they seize,
And sweep with equal strokes the smoky seas;
Clear of the rocks the impatient vessel flies;
Whilst in the port each wretch encumber'd dies.
With earnest haste my frighted sailors press,
While kindling transports glow'd at our success;
But the sad fate that did our friends destroy,
Cool'd every breast, and damp'd the rising joy.

"Now dropp'd our anchors in the Aeaean bay,
Where Circe dwelt, the daughter of the Day!
Her mother Perse, of old Ocean's strain,
Thus from the Lun descended, and the Main
(From the same lineage stern Aeaetes came,
The far-famed brother of the enchantress dame);
Goddess, the queen, to whom the powers belong
Of dreadful magic and commanding song.
Some god directing to this peaceful bay
Silent we came, and melancholy lay,
Spent and o'erwatch'd. Two days and nights roll'd on,
And now the third succeeding morning shone.
I climb'd a cliff, with spear and sword in hand,
Whose ridge o'erlook'd a shady length of land;
To learn if aught of mortal works appear,
Or cheerful voice of mortal strike the ear?
From the high point I mark'd, in distant view,
A stream of curling smoke ascending blue,
And spiry tops, the tufted trees above,
Of Circe's palace bosom'd in the grove.

"Thither to haste, the region to explore,
Was first my thought: but speeding back to shore
I deem'd it best to visit first my crew,

And send our spies the dubious coast to view.
As down the hill I solitary go,
Some power divine, who pities human woe,
Sent a tall stag, descending from the wood,
To cool his fervour in the crystal flood;
Luxuriant on the wave-worn bank he lay,
Stretch'd forth and panting in the sunny ray.
I launch'd my spear, and with a sudden wound
Transpierced his back, and fix'd him to the ground.
He falls, and mourns his fate with human cries:
Through the wide wound the vital spirit flies.
I drew, and casting on the river's side
The bloody spear, his gather'd feet I tied
With twining osiers which the bank supplied.
An ell in length the pliant wisp I weaved,
And the huge body on my shoulders heaved:
Then leaning on my spear with both my hands,
Upbore my load, and press'd the sinking sands
With weighty steps, till at the ship I threw
The welcome burden, and bespoke my crew:

"'Cheer up, my friends! it is not yet our fate
To glide with ghosts through Pluto's gloomy gate.
Food in the desert land, behold! is given!
Live, and enjoy the providence of heaven.'

"The joyful crew survey his mighty size,
And on the future banquet feast their eyes,
As huge in length extended lay the beast;
Then wash their hands, and hasten to the feast.
There, till the setting sun roll'd down the light,
They sate indulging in the genial rite.
When evening rose, and darkness cover'd o'er
The face of things, we slept along the shore.
But when the rosy morning warm'd the east,
My men I summon'd, and these words address'd:
"'Followers and friends, attend what I propose:
Ye sad companions of Ulysses' woes!
We know not here what land before us lies,
Or to what quarter now we turn our eyes,
Or where the sun shall set, or where shall rise.
Here let us think (if thinking be not vain)
If any counsel, any hope remain.
Alas! from yonder promontory's brow
I view'd the coast, a region flat and low;
An isle encircled with the boundless flood;
A length of thickets, and entangled wood.
Some smoke I saw amid the forest rise,

And all around it only seas and skies!'

"With broken hearts my sad companions stood,
Mindful of Cyclops and his human food,
And horrid Laestrygons, the men of blood.
Presaging tears apace began to rain;
But tears in mortal miseries are vain.
In equal parts I straight divide my band,
And name a chief each party to command;
I led the one, and of the other side
Appointed brave Eurylochus the guide.
Then in the brazen helm the lots we throw,
And fortune casts Eurylochus to go;
He march'd with twice eleven in his train;
Pensive they march, and pensive we remain.

"The palace in a woody vale they found,
High raised of stone; a shaded space around;
Where mountain wolves and brindled lions roam,
(By magic tamed,) familiar to the dome.
With gentle blandishment our men they meet,
And wag their tails, and fawning lick their feet.
As from some feast a man returning late,
His faithful dogs all meet him at the gate,
Rejoicing round, some morsel to receive,
(Such as the good man ever used to give,)
Domestic thus the grisly beasts drew near;
They gaze with wonder not unmix'd with fear.
Now on the threshold of the dome they stood,
And heard a voice resounding through the wood:
Placed at her loom within, the goddess sung;
The vaulted roofs and solid pavement rung.
O'er the fair web the rising figures shine,
Immortal labour! worthy hands divine.
Polites to the rest the question moved
(A gallant leader, and a man I loved):

"'What voice celestial, chanting to the loom
(Or nymph, or goddess), echoes from the room?
Say, shall we seek access?' With that they call;
And wide unfold the portals of the hall.

"The goddess, rising, asks her guests to stay,
Who blindly follow where she leads the way.
Eurylochus alone of all the band,
Suspecting fraud, more prudently remain'd.
On thrones around with downy coverings graced,
With semblance fair, the unhappy men she placed.

Milk newly press'd, the sacred flour of wheat,
And honey fresh, and Pramnian wines the treat:
But venom'd was the bread, and mix'd the bowl,
With drugs of force to darken all the soul:
Soon in the luscious feast themselves they lost,
And drank oblivion of their native coast.
Instant her circling wand the goddess waves,
To hogs transforms them, and the sty receives.
No more was seen the human form divine;
Head, face, and members, bristle into swine:
Still cursed with sense, their minds remain alone,
And their own voice affrights them when they groan.
Meanwhile the goddess in disdain bestows
The mast and acorn, brutal food! and strows
The fruits and cornel, as their feast, around;
Now prone and grovelling on unsavoury ground.

"Eurylochus, with pensive steps and slow.
Aghast returns; the messenger of woe,
And bitter fate. To speak he made essay,
In vain essay'd, nor would his tongue obey.
His swelling heart denied the words their way:
But speaking tears the want of words supply,
And the full soul bursts copious from his eye.
Affrighted, anxious for our fellows' fates,
We press to hear what sadly he relates:

"We went, Ulysses! (such was thy command)
Through the lone thicket and the desert land.
A palace in a woody vale we found
Brown with dark forests, and with shades around.
A voice celestial echoed through the dome,
Or nymph or goddess, chanting to the loom.
Access we sought, nor was access denied:
Radiant she came: the portals open'd wide:
The goddess mild invites the guests to stay:
They blindly follow where she leads the way.
I only wait behind of all the train:
I waited long, and eyed the doors in vain:
The rest are vanish'd, none repass'd the gate,
And not a man appears to tell their fate.'

"I heard, and instant o'er my shoulder flung
The belt in which my weighty falchion hung
(A beamy blade): then seized the bended bow,
And bade him guide the way, resolved to go.
He, prostrate falling, with both hands embraced
My knees, and weeping thus his suit address'd:

"'O king, beloved of Jove, thy servant spare,
And ah, thyself the rash attempt forbear!
Never, alas! thou never shalt return,
Or see the wretched for whose loss we mourn.
With what remains from certain ruin fly,
And save the few not fated yet to die.'

"I answer'd stern: 'Inglorious then remain,
Here feast and loiter, and desert thy train.
Alone, unfriended, will I tempt my way;
The laws of fate compel, and I obey.'
This said, and scornful turning from the shore
My haughty step, I stalk'd the valley o'er.
Till now approaching nigh the magic bower,
Where dwelt the enchantress skill'd in herbs of power,
A form divine forth issued from the wood
(Immortal Hermes with the golden rod)
In human semblance. On his bloomy face
Youth smiled celestial, with each opening grace.
He seized my hand, and gracious thus began:
'Ah whither roam'st thou, much-enduring man?
O blind to fate! what led thy steps to rove
The horrid mazes of this magic grove?
Each friend you seek in yon enclosure lies,
All lost their form, and habitants of sties.
Think'st thou by wit to model their escape?
Sooner shalt thou, a stranger to thy shape,
Fall prone their equal: first thy danger know,
Then take the antidote the gods bestow.
The plant I give through all the direful bower
Shall guard thee, and avert the evil hour.
Now hear her wicked arts: Before thy eyes
The bowl shall sparkle, and the banquet rise;
Take this, nor from the faithless feast abstain,
For temper'd drugs and poison shall be vain.
Soon as she strikes her wand, and gives the word,
Draw forth and brandish thy refulgent sword,
And menace death: those menaces shall move
Her alter'd mind to blandishment and love.
Nor shun the blessing proffer'd to thy arms,
Ascend her bed, and taste celestial charms;
So shall thy tedious toils a respite find,
And thy lost friends return to human kind.
But swear her first by those dread oaths that tie
The powers below, the blessed in the sky;
Lest to thee naked secret fraud be meant,
Or magic bind thee cold and impotent.

"Thus while he spoke, the sovereign plant he drew
Where on the all-bearing earth unmark'd it grew,
And show'd its nature and its wondrous power:
Black was the root, but milky white the flower;
Moly the name, to mortals hard to find,
But all is easy to the ethereal kind.
This Hermes gave, then, gliding off the glade,
Shot to Olympus from the woodland shade.
While, full of thought, revolving fates to come,
I speed my passage to the enchanted dome.
Arrived, before the lofty gates I stay'd;
The lofty gates the goddess wide display'd;
She leads before, and to the feast invites;
I follow sadly to the magic rites.
Radiant with starry studs, a silver seat
Received my limbs: a footstool eased my feet,
She mix'd the potion, fraudulent of soul;
The poison mantled in the golden bowl.
I took, and quaff'd it, confident in heaven.
Then waved the wand, and then the word was given.
'Hence to thy fellows! (dreadful she began:)
Go, be a beast!'—I heard, and yet was man.

"Then, sudden whirling, like a waving flame,
My beamy falchion, I assault the dame.
Struck with unusual fear, she trembling cries,
She faints, she falls; she lifts her weeping eyes.

"'What art thou? say! from whence, from whom you came?
O more than human! tell thy race, thy name.
Amazing strength, these poisons to sustain!
Not mortal thou, nor mortal is thy brain.
Or art thou he, the man to come (foretold
By Hermes, powerful with the wand of gold),
The man from Troy, who wander'd ocean round;
The man for wisdom's various arts renown'd,
Ulysses? Oh! thy threatening fury cease;
Sheathe thy bright sword, and join our hands in peace!
Let mutual joys our mutual trust combine,
And love, and love-born confidence, be thine.'

"'And how, dread Circe! (furious I rejoin)
Can love, and love-born confidence, be mine,
Beneath thy charms when my companions groan,
Transform'd to beasts, with accents not their own?
O thou of fraudful heart, shall I be led
To share thy feast-rites, or ascend thy bed;

That, all unarm'd, thy vengeance may have vent,
And magic bind me, cold and impotent?
Celestial as thou art, yet stand denied;
Or swear that oath by which the gods are tied,
Swear, in thy soul no latent frauds remain,
Swear by the vow which never can be vain.'

"The goddess swore: then seized my hand, and led
To the sweet transports of the genial bed.
Ministrant to the queen, with busy care
Four faithful handmaids the soft rites prepare;
Nymphs sprung from fountains, or from shady woods,
Or the fair offspring of the sacred floods.
One o'er the couches painted carpets threw,
Whose purple lustre glow'd against the view:
White linen lay beneath. Another placed
The silver stands, with golden flaskets graced:
With dulcet beverage this the beaker crown'd,
Fair in the midst, with gilded cups around:
That in the tripod o'er the kindled pile
The water pours; the bubbling waters boil;
An ample vase receives the smoking wave;
And, in the bath prepared, my limbs I lave:
Reviving sweets repair the mind's decay,
And take the painful sense of toil away.
A vest and tunic o'er me next she threw,
Fresh from the bath, and dropping balmy dew;
Then led and placed me on the sovereign seat,
With carpets spread; a footstool at my feet.
The golden ewer a nymph obsequious brings,
Replenish'd from the cool translucent springs;
With copious water the bright vase supplies
A silver laver of capacious size.
I wash'd. The table in fair order spread,
They heap the glittering canisters with bread:
Viands of various kinds allure the taste,
Of choicest sort and savour, rich repast!
Circe in vain invites the feast to share;
Absent I ponder, and absorb'd in care;
While scenes of woe rose anxious in my breast,
The queen beheld me, and these words address'd:

"'Why sits Ulysses silent and apart,
Some hoard of grief close harbour'd at his heart
Untouch'd before thee stand the cates divine,
And unregarded laughs the rosy wine.
Can yet a doubt or any dread remain,
When sworn that oath which never can be vain?'

"I answered: 'Goddess! human is my breast,
By justice sway'd, by tender pity press'd:
Ill fits it me, whose friends are sunk to beasts,
To quaff thy bowls, or riot in thy feasts.
Me would'st thou please? for them thy cares employ,
And them to me restore, and me to joy.'

"With that she parted: in her potent hand
She bore the virtue of the magic wand.
Then, hastening to the sties, set wide the door,
Urged forth, and drove the bristly herd before;
Unwieldy, out they rush'd with general cry,
Enormous beasts, dishonest to the eye.
Now touch'd by counter-charms they change again,
And stand majestic, and recall'd to men.
Those hairs of late that bristled every part,
Fall off, miraculous effect of art!
Till all the form in full proportion rise,
More young, more large, more graceful to my eyes.
They saw, they knew me, and with eager pace
Clung to their master in a long embrace:
Sad, pleasing sight! with tears each eye ran o'er,
And sobs of joy re-echoed through the bower;
E'en Circe wept, her adamantine heart
Felt pity enter, and sustain'd her part.

"'Son of Laertes! (then the queen began)
Oh much-enduring, much experienced man!
Haste to thy vessel on the sea-beat shore,
Unload thy treasures, and the galley moor;
Then bring thy friends, secure from future harms,
And in our grottoes stow thy spoils and arms,'

"She said. Obedient to her high command
I quit the place, and hasten to the strand,
My sad companions on the beach I found,
Their wistful eyes in floods of sorrow drown'd.

"As from fresh pastures and the dewy field
(When loaded cribs their evening banquet yield)
The lowing herds return; around them throng
With leaps and bounds their late imprison'd young,
Rush to their mothers with unruly joy,
And echoing hills return the tender cry:
So round me press'd, exulting at my sight,
With cries and agonies of wild delight,
The weeping sailors; nor less fierce their joy

Than if return'd to Ithaca from Troy.
'Ah master! ever honour'd, ever dear!
(These tender words on every side I hear)
What other joy can equal thy return?
Not that loved country for whose sight we mourn,
The soil that nursed us, and that gave us breath:
But ah! relate our lost companions' death.'

"I answer'd cheerful: 'Haste, your galley moor,
And bring our treasures and our arms ashore:
Those in yon hollow caverns let us lay,
Then rise, and follow where I lead the way.
Your fellows live; believe your eyes, and come
To taste the joys of Circe's sacred dome.'

"With ready speed the joyful crew obey:
Alone Eurylochus persuades their stay.

"'Whither (he cried), ah whither will ye run?
Seek ye to meet those evils ye should shun?
Will you the terrors of the dome explore,
In swine to grovel, or in lions roar,
Or wolf-like howl away the midnight hour
In dreadful watch around the magic bower?
Remember Cyclops, and his bloody deed;
The leader's rashness made the soldiers bleed.'

"I heard incensed, and first resolved to speed
My flying falchion at the rebel's head.
Dear as he was, by ties of kindred bound,
This hand had stretch'd him breathless on the ground.
But all at once my interposing train
For mercy pleaded, nor could plead in vain.
'Leave here the man who dares his prince desert,
Leave to repentance and his own sad heart,
To guard the ship. Seek we the sacred shades
Of Circe's palace, where Ulysses leads.'

"This with one voice declared, the rising train
Left the black vessel by the murmuring main.
Shame touch'd Eurylochus' alter'd breast:
He fear'd my threats, and follow'd with the rest.

"Meanwhile the goddess, with indulgent cares
And social joys, the late transform'd repairs;
The bath, the feast, their fainting soul renews:
Rich in refulgent robes, and dropping balmy dews:
Brightening with joy, their eager eyes behold,

Each other's face, and each his story told;
Then gushing tears the narrative confound,
And with their sobs the vaulted roof resound.
When hush'd their passion, thus the goddess cries:
'Ulysses, taught by labours to be wise,
Let this short memory of grief suffice.
To me are known the various woes ye bore.
In storms by sea, in perils on the shore;
Forget whatever was in Fortune's power,
And share the pleasures of this genial hour.
Such be your mind as ere ye left your coast,
Or learn'd to sorrow for a country lost.
Exiles and wanderers now, where'er ye go,
Too faithful memory renews your woe:
The cause removed, habitual griefs remain,
And the soul saddens by the use of pain.'

"Her kind entreaty moved the general breast;
Tired with long toil, we willing sunk to rest.
We plied the banquet, and the bowl we crown'd,
Till the full circle of the year came round.
But when the seasons following in their train,
Brought back the months, the days, and hours again;
As from a lethargy at once they rise,
And urge their chief with animating cries:

"'Is this, Ulysses, our inglorious lot?
And is the name of Ithaca forgot?
Shall never the dear land in prospect rise,
Or the loved palace glitter in our eyes?
"Melting I heard; yet till the sun's decline
Prolong'd the feast, and quaff'd the rosy wine
But when the shades came on at evening hour,
And all lay slumbering in the dusky bower,
I came a suppliant to fair Circe's bed,
The tender moment seized, and thus I said:
'Be mindful, goddess! of thy promise made;
Must sad Ulysses ever be delay'd?
Around their lord my sad companions mourn,
Each breast beats homeward, anxious to return:
If but a moment parted from thy eyes,
Their tears flow round me, and my heart complies.'

"'Go then (she cried), ah go! yet think, not I,
Not Circe, but the Fates, your wish deny.
Ah, hope not yet to breathe thy native air!
Far other journey first demands thy care;
To tread the uncomfortable paths beneath,

And view the realms of darkness and of death.
There seek the Theban bard, deprived of sight;
Within, irradiate with prophetic light;
To whom Persephone, entire and whole,
Gave to retain the unseparated soul:
The rest are forms, of empty ether made;
Impassive semblance, and a flitting shade.'

"Struck at the word, my very heart was dead:
Pensive I sate: my tears bedew'd the bed:
To hate the light and life my soul begun,
And saw that all was grief beneath the sun:
Composed at length the gushing tears suppress'd,
And my toss'd limbs now wearied into rest.
'How shall I tread (I cried), ah, Circe! say,
The dark descent, and who shall guide the way?
Can living eyes behold the realms below?
What bark to waft me, and what wind to blow?'

"'Thy fated road (the magic power replied),
Divine Ulysses! ask no mortal guide.
Rear but the mast, the spacious sail display,
The northern winds shall wing thee on thy way.
Soon shalt thou reach old Ocean's utmost ends,
Where to the main the shelving shore descends;
The barren trees of Proserpine's black woods,
Poplars and willows trembling o'er the floods:
There fix thy vessel in the lonely bay,
And enter there the kingdoms void of day,
Where Phlegethon's loud torrents, rushing down,
Hiss in the flaming gulf of Acheron;
And where, slow rolling from the Stygian bed,
Cocytus' lamentable waters spread:
Where the dark rock o'erhangs the infernal lake,
And mingling streams eternal murmurs make.
First draw thy falchion, and on every side
Trench the black earth a cubit long and wide:
To all the shades around libations pour,
And o'er the ingredients strew the hallow'd flour:
New wine and milk, with honey temper'd bring,
And living water from the crystal spring.
Then the wan shades and feeble ghosts implore,
With promised offerings on thy native shore;
A barren cow, the stateliest of the isle,
And heap'd with various wealth, a blazing pile:
These to the rest; but to the seer must bleed
A sable ram, the pride of all thy breed.
These solemn vows and holy offerings paid

To all the phantom nations of the dead,
Be next thy care the sable sheep to place
Full o'er the pit, and hellward turn their face:
But from the infernal rite thine eye withdraw,
And back to Ocean glance with reverend awe.
Sudden shall skim along the dusky glades
Thin airy shoals, and visionary shades.
Then give command the sacrifice to haste,
Let the flay'd victims in the flame be cast,
And sacred vows and mystic song applied
To grisly Pluto and his gloomy bride.
Wide o'er the pool thy falchion waved around
Shall drive the spectres from unbidden ground:
The sacred draught shall all the dead forbear,
Till awful from the shades arise the seer.
Let him, oraculous, the end, the way,
The turns of all thy future fate display,
Thy pilgrimage to come, and remnant of thy day.'

"So speaking, from the ruddy orient shone
The morn, conspicuous on her golden throne.
The goddess with a radiant tunic dress'd
My limbs, and o'er me cast a silken vest.
Long flowing robes, of purest white, array
The nymph, that added lustre to the day:
A tiar wreath'd her head with many a fold;
Her waist was circled with a zone of gold.
Forth issuing then, from place to place I flew;
Rouse man by man, and animate my crew.
'Rise, rise, my mates! 'tis Circe gives command:
Our journey calls us; haste, and quit the land.'
All rise and follow, yet depart not all,
For Fate decreed one wretched man to fall.

"A youth there was, Elpenor was he named,
Not much for sense, nor much for courage famed:
The youngest of our band, a vulgar soul,
Born but to banquet, and to drain the bowl.
He, hot and careless, on a turret's height
With sleep repair'd the long debauch of night:
The sudden tumult stirred him where he lay,
And down he hasten'd, but forgot the way;
Full headlong from the roof the sleeper fell,
And snapp'd the spinal joint, and waked in hell.

"The rest crowd round me with an eager look;
I met them with a sigh, and thus bespoke:
'Already, friends! ye think your toils are o'er,

Your hopes already touch your native shore:
Alas! far otherwise the nymph declares,
Far other journey first demands our cares;
To tread the uncomfortable paths beneath,
The dreary realms of darkness and of death;
To seek Tiresias' awful shade below,
And thence our fortunes and our fates to know.'

"My sad companions heard in deep despair;
Frantic they tore their manly growth of hair;
To earth they fell: the tears began to rain;
But tears in mortal miseries are vain,
Sadly they fared along the sea-beat shore;
Still heaved their hearts, and still their eyes ran o'er.
The ready victims at our bark we found,
The sable ewe and ram together bound.
For swift as thought the goddess had been there,
And thence had glided, viewless as the air:
The paths of gods what mortal can survey?
Who eyes their motion? who shall trace their way?"

BOOK XI

ARGUMENT

THE DESCENT INTO HELL

Ulysses continues his narration. How he arrived at the land of the Cimmerians, and what ceremonies he performed to invoke the dead. The manner of his descent, and the apparition of the shades: his conversation with Elpenor, and with Tiresias, who informs him in a prophetic manner of his fortunes to come. He meets his mother Anticles, from whom he learns the state of his family. He sees the shades of the ancient heroines, afterwards of the heroes, and converses in particular with Agamemnon and Achilles. Ajax keeps at a sullen distance, and disdains to answer him. He then beholds Tityus, Tantalus, Sisyphus, Hercules; till he is deterred from further curiosity by the apparition of horrid spectres, and the cries of the wicked in torments.

"Now to the shores we bend, a mournful train,
Climb the tall bark, and launch into the main;
At once the mast we rear, at once unbind
The spacious sheet, and stretch it to the wind;
Then pale and pensive stand, with cares oppress'd,
And solemn horror saddens every breast.
A freshening breeze the magic power supplied,
While the wing'd vessel flew along the tide;
Our oars we shipp'd; all day the swelling sails
Full from the guiding pilot catch'd the gales.

"Now sunk the sun from his aerial height,
And o'er the shaded billows rush'd the night;
When lo! we reach'd old Ocean's utmost bounds,
Where rocks control his waves with ever-during mounds.

"There in a lonely land, and gloomy cells,
The dusky nation of Cimmeria dwells;
The sun ne'er views the uncomfortable seats,
When radiant he advances, or retreats:
Unhappy race! whom endless night invades,
Clouds the dull air, and wraps them round in shades.

"The ship we moor on these obscure abodes;
Disbark the sheep, an offering to the gods;
And, hellward bending, o'er the beach descry
The doleful passage to the infernal sky.
The victims, vow'd to each Tartarian power,
Eurylochus and Perimedes bore.

"Here open'd hell, all hell I here implored,
And from the scabbard drew the shining sword:
And trenching the black earth on every side,
A cavern form'd, a cubit long and wide.
New wine, with honey-temper'd milk, we bring,
Then living waters from the crystal spring:
O'er these was strew'd the consecrated flour,
And on the surface shone the holy store.

"Now the wan shades we hail, the infernal gods,
To speed our course, and waft us o'er the floods:
So shall a barren heifer from the stall
Beneath the knife upon your altars fall;
So in our palace, at our safe return,
Rich with unnumber'd gifts the pile shall burn;
So shall a ram, the largest of the breed,
Black as these regions, to Tiresias bleed.

"Thus solemn rites and holy vows we paid
To all the phantom-nations of the dead;
Then died the sheep: a purple torrent flow'd,
And all the caverns smoked with streaming blood.
When lo! appear'd along the dusky coasts,
Thin, airy shoals of visionary ghosts:
Fair, pensive youths, and soft enamour'd maids;
And wither'd elders, pale and wrinkled shades;
Ghastly with wounds the forms of warriors slain
Stalk'd with majestic port, a martial train:

These and a thousand more swarm'd o'er the ground,
And all the dire assembly shriek'd around.
Astonish'd at the sight, aghast I stood,
And a cold fear ran shivering through my blood;
Straight I command the sacrifice to haste,
Straight the flay'd victims to the flames are cast,
And mutter'd vows, and mystic song applied
To grisly Pluto, and his gloomy bride.

"Now swift I waved my falchion o'er the blood;
Back started the pale throngs, and trembling stood,
Round the black trench the gore untasted flows,
Till awful from the shades Tiresias rose.

"There wandering through the gloom I first survey'd,
New to the realms of death, Elpenor's shade:
His cold remains all naked to the sky
On distant shores unwept, unburied lie.
Sad at the sight I stand, deep fix'd in woe,
And ere I spoke the tears began to flow.

"'O say what angry power Elpenor led
To glide in shades, and wander with the dead?
How could thy soul, by realms and seas disjoin'd,
Outfly the nimble sail, and leave the lagging wind?

"The ghost replied: 'To hell my doom I owe,
Demons accursed, dire ministers of woe!
My feet, through wine unfaithful to their weight,
Betray'd me tumbling from a towery height:
Staggering I reel'd, and as I reel'd I fell,
Lux'd the neck-joint—my soul descends to hell.
But lend me aid, I now conjure thee lend,
By the soft tie and sacred name of friend!
By thy fond consort! by thy father's cares!
By loved Telemachus' blooming years?
For well I know that soon the heavenly powers
Will give thee back to-day, and Circe's shores:
There pious on my cold remains attend,
There call to mind thy poor departed friend.
The tribute of a tear is all I crave,
And the possession of a peaceful grave.
But if, unheard, in vain compassion plead,
Revere the gods. The gods avenge the dead!
A tomb along the watery margin raise,
The tomb with manly arms and trophies grace,
To show posterity Elpenor was.
There high in air, memorial of my name,

Fix the smooth oar, and bid me live to fame.'

"To whom with tears: 'These rites, O mournful shade,
Due to thy ghost, shall to thy ghost be paid.'

"Still as I spoke the phantom seem'd to moan,
Tear follow'd tear, and groan succeeded groan.
But, as my waving sword the blood surrounds,
The shade withdrew, and mutter'd empty sounds.

"There as the wondrous visions I survey'd,
All pale ascends my royal mother's shade:
A queen, to Troy she saw our legions pass;
Now a thin form is all Anticlea was!
Struck at the sight I melt with filial woe,
And down my cheek the pious sorrows flow,
Yet as I shook my falchion o'er the blood,
Regardless of her son the parent stood.

"When lo! the mighty Theban I behold,
To guide his steps he bore a staff of gold;
Awful he trod; majestic was his look!
And from his holy lips these accents broke:

"'Why, mortal, wanderest thou from cheerful day,
To tread the downward, melancholy way?
What angry gods to these dark regions led
Thee, yet alive, companion of the deed?
But sheathe thy poniard, while my tongue relates
Heaven's steadfast purpose, and thy future fates.'

"While yet he spoke, the prophet I obey'd,
And in the scabbard plunged the glittering blade:
Eager he quaff'd the gore, and then express'd
Dark things to come, the counsels of his breast.

"Weary of light, Ulysses here explores
A prosperous voyage to his native shores;
But know—by me unerring Fates disclose
New trains of dangers, and new scenes of woes.
I see, I see, thy bark by Neptune toss'd,
For injured Cyclops, and his eyeball lost!
Yet to thy woes the gods decree an end,
If Heaven thou please: and how to please attend
Where on Trinacrian rocks the ocean roars,
Graze numerous herds along the verdant shores;
Though hunger press, yet fly the dangerous prey,
The herds are sacred to the god of day,

Who all surveys with his extensive eye,
Above, below, on earth, and in the sky!
Rob not the god; and so propitious gales
Attend thy voyage, and impel thy sails:
But, if his herds ye seize, beneath the waves
I see thy friends o'erwhelm'd in liquid graves!
The direful wreck Ulysses scarce survives!
Ulysses at his country scarce arrives!
Strangers thy guides! nor there thy labours end;
New foes arise; domestic ills attend!
There foul adulterers to thy bride resort,
And lordly gluttons riot in thy court.
But vengeance hastes amain! These eyes behold
The deathful scene, princes on princes roll'd!
That done, a people far from sea explore,
Who ne'er knew salt, or heard the billows roar,
Or saw gay vessel stem the watery plain,
A painted wonder flying on the main!
Bear on thy back an oar: with strange amaze
A shepherd meeting thee, the oar surveys,
And names a van: there fix it on the plain,
To calm the god that holds the watery reign;
A threefold offering to his altar bring,
A bull, a ram, a boar; and hail the ocean king.
But home return'd, to each ethereal power
Slay the due victim in the genial hour:
So peaceful shalt thou end thy blissful days,
And steal thyself from life by slow decays:
Unknown to pain, in age resign thy breath,
When late stern Neptune points the shaft with death:
To the dark grave retiring as to rest,
Thy people blessing, by thy people bless'd!

"Unerring truths, O man, my lips relate;
This is thy life to come, and this is fate.'

"To whom unmoved: 'If this the gods prepare,
What Heaven ordains the wise with courage bear.
But say, why yonder on the lonely strands,
Unmindful of her son, Anticlea stands?
Why to the ground she bends her downcast eye?
Why is she silent, while her son is nigh?
The latent cause, O sacred seer, reveal!'

"'Nor this (replies the seer) will I conceal.
Know, to the spectres that thy beverage taste,
The scenes of life recur, and actions past:
They, seal'd with truth, return the sure reply;

The rest, repell'd, a train oblivious fly.'

"The phantom-prophet ceased, and sunk from sight,
To the black palace of eternal night.

"Still in the dark abodes of death I stood,
When near Anticlea moved, and drank the blood.
Straight all the mother in her soul awakes,
And, owning her Ulysses, thus she speaks;
'Comest thou, my son, alive, to realms beneath,
The dolesome realms of darkness and of death!
Comest thou alive from pure, ethereal day?
Dire is the region, dismal is the way!
Here lakes profound, there floods oppose their waves,
There the wide sea with all his billows raves!
Or (since to dust proud Troy submits her towers)
Comest thou a wanderer from the Phrygian shores?
Or say, since honour call'd thee to the field,
Hast thou thy Ithaca, thy bride, beheld?'

"'Source of my life,' I cried, 'from earth I fly
To seek Tiresias in the nether sky,
To learn my doom; for, toss'd from woe to woe,
In every land Ulysses finds a foe:
Nor have these eyes beheld my native shores,
Since in the dust proud Troy submits her towers.

"'But, when thy soul from her sweet mansion fled,
Say, what distemper gave thee to the dead?
Has life's fair lamp declined by slow decays,
Or swift expired it in a sudden blaze?
Say, if my sire, good old Laertes, lives?
If yet Telemachus, my son, survives?
Say, by his rule is my dominion awed,
Or crush'd by traitors with an iron rod?
Say, if my spouse maintains her royal trust;
Though tempted, chaste, and obstinately just?
Or if no more her absent lord she wails,
But the false woman o'er the wife prevails?'

"Thus I, and thus the parent-shade returns:
'Thee, ever thee, thy faithful consort mourns:
Whether the night descends or day prevails,
Thee she by night, and thee by day bewails.
Thee in Telemachus thy realm obeys;
In sacred groves celestial rites he pays,
And shares the banquet in superior state,
Graced with such honours as become the great

Thy sire in solitude foments his care:
The court is joyless, for thou art not there!
No costly carpets raise his hoary head,
No rich embroidery shines to grace his bed;
Even when keen winter freezes in the skies,
Rank'd with his slaves, on earth the monarch lies:
Deep are his sighs, his visage pale, his dress
The garb of woe and habit of distress.
And when the autumn takes his annual round,
The leafy honours scattering on the ground,
Regardless of his years, abroad he lies,
His bed the leaves, his canopy the skies.
Thus cares on cares his painful days consume,
And bow his age with sorrow to the tomb!

"'For thee, my son, I wept my life away;
For thee through hell's eternal dungeons stray:
Nor came my fate by lingering pains and slow,
Nor bent the silver-shafted queen her bow;
No dire disease bereaved me of my breath;
Thou, thou, my son, wert my disease and death;
Unkindly with my love my son conspired,
For thee I lived, for absent thee expired.'

"Thrice in my arms I strove her shade to bind,
Thrice through my arms she slipp'd like empty wind,
Or dreams, the vain illusions of the mind.
Wild with despair, I shed a copious tide
Of flowing tears, and thus with sighs replied:

"'Fliest thou, loved shade, while I thus fondly mourn!
Turn to my arms, to my embraces turn!
Is it, ye powers that smile at human harms!
Too great a bliss to weep within her arms?
Or has hell's queen an empty image sent,
That wretched I might e'en my joys lament?'

"'O son of woe,' the pensive shade rejoin'd;
'O most inured to grief of all mankind!
"'Tis not the queen of hell who thee deceives;
All, all are such, when life the body leaves:
No more the substance of the man remains,
Nor bounds the blood along the purple veins:
These the funereal flames in atoms bear,
To wander with the wind in empty air:
While the impassive soul reluctant flies,
Like a vain dream, to these infernal skies.
But from the dark dominions speed the way,

And climb the steep ascent to upper day:
To thy chaste bride the wondrous story tell,
The woes, the horrors, and the laws of hell.'

"Thus while she spoke, in swarms hell's empress brings
Daughters and wives of heroes and of kings;
Thick and more thick they gather round the blood,
Ghost thronged on ghost (a dire assembly) stood!
Dauntless my sword I seize: the airy crew,
Swift as it flash'd along the gloom, withdrew;
Then shade to shade in mutual forms succeeds,
Her race recounts, and their illustrious deeds.

"Tyro began, whom great Salmoneus bred;
The royal partner of famed Cretheus' bed.
For fair Enipeus, as from fruitful urns
He pours his watery store, the virgin burns;
Smooth flows the gentle stream with wanton pride,
And in soft mazes rolls a silver tide.
As on his banks the maid enamour'd roves,
The monarch of the deep beholds and loves;
In her Enipeus' form and borrow'd charms
The amorous god descends into her arms:
Around, a spacious arch of waves he throws,
And high in air the liquid mountain rose;
Thus in surrounding floods conceal'd, he proves
The pleasing transport, and completes his loves.
Then, softly sighing, he the fair address'd,
And as he spoke her tender hand he press'd.
'Hail, happy nymph! no vulgar births are owed
To the prolific raptures of a god:
Lo! when nine times the moon renews her horn,
Two brother heroes shall from thee be born;
Thy early care the future worthies claim,
To point them to the arduous paths of fame;
But in thy breast the important truth conceal,
Nor dare the secret of a god reveal:
For know, thou Neptune view'st! and at my nod
Earth trembles, and the waves confess their god.'

"He added not, but mounting spurn'd the plain,
Then plunged into the chambers of the main,

"Now in the time's full process forth she brings
Jove's dread vicegerents in two future kings;
O'er proud Iolcos Pelias stretch'd his reign,
And godlike Neleus ruled the Pylian plain:
Then, fruitful, to her Cretheus' royal bed

She gallant Pheres and famed Aeson bred;
From the same fountain Amythaon rose,
Pleased with the din of scar; and noble shout of foes.

"There moved Antiope, with haughty charms,
Who bless'd the almighty Thunderer in her arms:
Hence sprung Amphion, hence brave Zethus came,
Founders of Thebes, and men of mighty name;
Though bold in open field, they yet surround
The town with walls, and mound inject on mound;
Here ramparts stood, there towers rose high in air,
And here through seven wide portals rush'd the war.

"There with soft step the fair Alcmena trod,
Who bore Alcides to the thundering god:
And Megara, who charm'd the son of Jove,
And soften'd his stern soul to tender love.

"Sullen and sour, with discontented mien,
Jocasta frown'd, the incestuous Theban queen;
With her own son she join'd in nuptial bands,
Though father's blood imbrued his murderous hands
The gods and men the dire offence detest,
The gods with all their furies rend his breast;
In lofty Thebes he wore the imperial crown,
A pompous wretch! accursed upon a throne.
The wife self-murder'd from a beam depends,
And her foul soul to blackest hell descends;
Thence to her son the choicest plagues she brings,
And the fiends haunt him with a thousand stings.

"And now the beauteous Chloris I descry,
A lovely shade, Amphion's youngest joy!
With gifts unnumber'd Neleus sought her arms,
Nor paid too dearly for unequall'd charms;
Great in Orchomenos, in Pylos great,
He sway'd the sceptre with imperial state.
Three gallant sons the joyful monarch told,
Sage Nestor, Periclimenus the bold,
And Chromius last; but of the softer race,
One nymph alone, a myracle of grace.
Kings on their thrones for lovely Pero burn;
The sire denies, and kings rejected mourn.
To him alone the beauteous prize he yields,
Whose arm should ravish from Phylacian fields
The herds of Iphyclus, detain'd in wrong;
Wild, furious herds, unconquerably strong!
This dares a seer, but nought the seer prevails,

In beauty's cause illustriously he fails;
Twelve moons the foe the captive youth detains
In painful dungeons, and coercive chains;
The foe at last from durance where he lay,
His heart revering, give him back to day;
Won by prophetic knowledge, to fulfil
The steadfast purpose of the Almighty will.

"With graceful port advancing now I spied,
Leda the fair, the godlike Tyndar's bride:
Hence Pollux sprung, who wields the furious sway
The deathful gauntlet, matchless in the fray;
And Castor, glorious on the embattled plain,
Curbs the proud steeds, reluctant to the rein:
By turns they visit this ethereal sky,
And live alternate, and alternate die:
In hell beneath, on earth, in heaven above,
Reign the twin-gods, the favourite sons of Jove.

"There Ephimedia trod the gloomy plain,
Who charm'd the monarch of the boundless main:
Hence Ephialtes, hence stern Otus sprung,
More fierce than giants, more than giants strong;
The earth o'erburden'd groan'd beneath their weight,
None but Orion e'er surpassed their height:
The wondrous youths had scarce nine winters told,
When high in air, tremendous to behold,
Nine ells aloft they rear'd their towering head,
And full nine cubits broad their shoulders spread.
Proud of their strength, and more than mortal size,
The gods they challenge, and affect the skies:
Heaved on Olympus tottering Ossa stood;
On Ossa, Pelion nods with all his wood.
Such were they youths I had they to manhood grown
Almighty Jove had trembled on his throne,
But ere the harvest of the beard began
To bristle on the chin, and promise man,
His shafts Apollo aim'd; at once they sound,
And stretch the giant monsters o'er the ground.

"There mournful Phaedra with sad Procris moves,
Both beauteous shades, both hapless in their loves;
And near them walk'd with solemn pace and slow,
Sad Adriadne, partner of their woe:
The royal Minos Ariadne bred,
She Theseus loved, from Crete with Theseus fled:
Swift to the Dian isle the hero flies,
And towards his Athens bears the lovely prize;

There Bacchus with fierce rage Diana fires,
The goddess aims her shaft, the nymph expires.

"There Clymene and Mera I behold,
There Eriphyle weeps, who loosely sold
Her lord, her honour, for the lust of gold.
But should I all recount, the night would fail,
Unequal to the melancholy tale:
And all-composing rest my nature craves,
Here in the court, or yonder on the waves;
In you I trust, and in the heavenly powers,
To land Ulysses on his native shores."

He ceased; but left so charming on their ear
His voice, that listening still they seem'd to hear,
Till, rising up, Arete silence broke,
Stretch'd out her snowy hand, and thus she spoke:

"What wondrous man heaven sends us in our guest;
Through all his woes the hero shines confess'd;
His comely port, his ample frame express
A manly air, majestic in distress.
He, as my guest, is my peculiar care:
You share the pleasure, then in bounty share
To worth in misery a reverence pay,
And with a generous hand reward his stay;
For since kind heaven with wealth our realm has bless'd,
Give it to heaven by aiding the distress'd."

Then sage Echeneus, whose grave reverend brow
The hand of time had silvered o'er with snow,
Mature in wisdom rose: "Your words (he cries)
Demand obedience, for your words are wise.
But let our king direct the glorious way
To generous acts; our part is to obey."

"While life informs these limbs (the king replied),
Well to deserve, be all my cares employed:
But here this night the royal guest detain,
Till the sun flames along the ethereal plain.
Be it my task to send with ample stores
The stranger from our hospitable shores:
Tread you my steps! 'Tis mine to lead the race,
The first in glory, as the first in place."

To whom the prince: "This night with joy I stay
O monarch great in virtue as in sway!
If thou the circling year my stay control,

To raise a bounty noble as thy soul;
The circling year I wait, with ampler stores
And fitter pomp to hail my native shores:
Then by my realms due homage would be paid;
For wealthy kings are loyally obeyed!"

"O king! for such thou art, and sure thy blood
Through veins (he cried) of royal fathers flow'd:
Unlike those vagrants who on falsehood live,
Skill'd in smooth tales, and artful to deceive;
Thy better soul abhors the liar's part,
Wise is thy voice, and noble is thy heart.
Thy words like music every breast control,
Steal through the ear, and win upon the soul;
soft, as some song divine, thy story flows,
Nor better could the Muse record thy woes.

"But say, upon the dark and dismal coast,
Saw'st thou the worthies of the Grecian host?
The godlike leaders who, in battle slain,
Fell before Troy, and nobly press'd the plain?
And lo! a length of night behind remains,
The evening stars still mount the ethereal plains.
Thy tale with raptures I could hear thee tell,
Thy woes on earth, the wondrous scenes in hell,
Till in the vault of heaven the stars decay.
And the sky reddens with the rising day."

"O worthy of the power the gods assign'd
(Ulysses thus replies), a king in mind:
Since yet the early hour of night allows
Time for discourse, and time for soft repose,
If scenes of misery can entertain,
Woes I unfold, of woes a dismal train.
Prepare to heir of murder and of blood;
Of godlike heroes who uninjured stood
Amidst a war of spears in foreign lands,
Yet bled at home, and bled by female hands.

"Now summon'd Proserpine to hell's black hall
The heroine shades: they vanish'd at her call.
When lo! advanced the forms of heroes slain
By stern AEgysthus, a majestic train:
And, high above the rest Atrides press'd the plain.
He quaff'd the gore; and straight his soldier knew,
And from his eyes pour'd down the tender dew:
His arms he stretch'd; his arms the touch deceive,
Nor in the fond embrace, embraces give:

His substance vanish'd, and his strength decay'd,
Now all Atrides is an empty shade.

"Moved at the sight, I for a apace resign'd
To soft affliction all my manly mind;
At last with tears: 'O what relentless doom,
Imperial phantom, bow'd thee to the tomb?
Say while the sea, and while the tempest raves,
Has Fate oppress'd thee in the roaring waves,
Or nobly seized thee in the dire alarms
Of war and slaughter, and the clash of arms?'

"The ghost returns: 'O chief of human kind
For active courage and a patient mind;
Nor while the sea, nor while the tempest raves
Has Fate oppress'd me on the roaring waves!
Nor nobly seized me in the dire alarms
Of war and slaughter, and the clash of arms
Stabb'd by a murderous hand Atrides died,
A foul adulterer, and a faithless bride;
E'en in my mirth, and at the friendly feast,
O'er the full bowl, the traitor stabb'd his guest;
Thus by the gory arm of slaughter falls
The stately ox, and bleeds within the stalls.
But not with me the direful murder ends,
These, these expired! their crime, they were my friends:
Thick as the boars, which some luxurious lord
Kills for the feast, to crown the nuptial board.
When war has thunder'd with its loudest storms,
Death thou hast seen in all her ghastly forms:
In duel met her on the listed ground,
When hand to hand they wound return for wound;
But never have the eyes astonish'd view'd
So vile a deed, so dire a scene of blood.
E'en in the flow of joy, when now the bowl
Glows in our veins, and opens every soul,
We groan, we faint; with blood the doom is dyed.
And o'er the pavement floats the dreadful tide—
Her breast all gore, with lamentable cries,
The bleeding innocent Cassandra dies!
Then though pale death froze cold in every vein,
My sword I strive to wield, but strive in vain;
Nor did my traitress wife these eyelids close,
Or decently in death my limbs compose.
O woman, woman, when to ill thy mind
Is bent, all hell contains no fouler fiend:
And such was mine! who basely plunged her sword
Through the fond bosom where she reign'd adored!

Alas! I hoped the toils of war o'ercome,
To meet soft quiet and repose at home;
Delusive hope! O wife, thy deeds disgrace
The perjured sex, and blacken all the race;
And should posterity one virtuous find,
Name Clytemnestra, they will curse the kind.'

"Oh injured shade (I cried) what mighty woes
To thy imperial race from woman rose!
By woman here thou tread'st this mournful strand,
And Greece by woman lies a desert land.'

"'Warn'd by my ills beware, (the shade replies,)
Nor trust the sex that is so rarely wise;
When earnest to explore thy secret breast,
Unfold some trifle, but conceal the rest.
But in thy consort cease to fear a foe,
For thee she feels sincerity of woe;
When Troy first bled beneath the Grecian arms,
She shone unrivall'd with a blaze of charms;
Thy infant son her fragrant bosom press'd,
Hung at her knee, or wanton'd at her breast;
But now the years a numerous train have ran;
The blooming boy is ripen'd into man;
Thy eyes shall see him burn with noble fire,
The sire shall bless his son, the son his sire;
But my Orestes never met these eyes,
Without one look the murder'd father dies;
Then from a wretched friend this wisdom learn,
E'en to thy queen disguised, unknown, return;
For since of womankind so few are just,
Think all are false, nor e'en the faithful trust.

"'But, say, resides my son in royal port,
In rich Orchomenos, or Sparta's court?
Or say in Pyle? for yet he views the light,
Nor glides a phantom through the realms of night.'

"Then I: 'Thy suit is vain, nor can I say
If yet he breathes in realms of cheerful day;
Or pale or wan beholds these nether skies;
Truth I revere; for wisdom never lies.'

"Thus in a tide of tears our sorrows flow,
And add new horror to the realms of woe;
Till side by side along the dreary coast
Advanced Achilles' and Patroclus' ghost,
A friendly pair! near these the Pylian stray'd,

And towering Ajax, an illustrious shade!
War was his joy, and pleased with loud alarms,
None but Pelides brighter shone in arms.

"Through the thick gloom his friend Achilles knew,
And as he speaks the tears descend in dew.

"'Comest thou alive to view the Stygian bounds,
Where the wan spectres walk eternal rounds;
Nor fear'st the dark and dismal waste to tread,
Throng'd with pale ghosts, familiar with the dead?'

"To whom with sighs: 'I pass these dreadful gates
To seek the Theban, and consult the Fates;
For still, distress'd, I rove from coast to coast,
Lost to my friends, and to my country lost.
But sure the eye of Time beholds no name
So bless'd as thine in all the rolls of fame;
Alive we hail'd thee with our guardian gods,
And dead thou rulest a king in these abodes.'

"'Talk not of ruling in this dolorous gloom,
Nor think vain words (he cried) can ease my doom.
Rather I'd choose laboriously to bear
A weight of woes, and breathe the vital air,
A slave to some poor hind that toils for bread,
Than reign the sceptred monarch of the dead.
But say, if in my steps my son proceeds,
And emulates his godlike father's deeds?
If at the clash of arms, and shout of foes,
Swells his bold heart, his bosom nobly glows?
Say if my sire, the reverend Peleus, reigns,
Great in his Phthia, and his throne maintains;
Or, weak and old, my youthful arm demands,
To fix the sceptre steadfast in his hands?
O might the lamp of life rekindled burn,
And death release me from the silent urn!
This arm, that thunder'd o'er the Phrygian plain,
And swell'd the ground with mountains of the slain,
Should vindicate my injured father's fame,
Crush the proud rebel, and assert his claim.'

"'Illustrious shade (I cried), of Peleus' fates
No circumstance the voice of Fame relates:
But hear with pleased attention the renown,
The wars and wisdom of thy gallant son.
With me from Scyros to the field of fame
Radiant in arms the blooming hero came.

When Greece assembled all her hundred states,
To ripen counsels, and decide debates,
Heavens! how he charm'd us with a flow of sense,
And won the heart with manly eloquence!
He first was seen of all the peers to rise,
The third in wisdom, where they all were wise!
But when, to try the fortune of the day,
Host moved toward host in terrible array,
Before the van, impatient for the fight,
With martial port he strode, and stern delight:
Heaps strew'd on heaps beneath his falchion groan'd,
And monuments of dead deform'd the ground.
The time would fail should I in order tell
What foes were vanquish'd, and what numbers fell:
How, lost through love, Eurypylus was slain,
And round him bled his bold Cetaean train.
To Troy no hero came of nobler line,
Or if of nobler, Memnon, it was thine.

"When Ilion in the horse received her doom,
And unseen armies ambush'd in its womb,
Greece gave her latent warriors to my care,
'Twas mine on Troy to pour the imprison'd war:
Then when the boldest bosom beat with fear,
When the stern eyes of heroes dropp'd a tear,
Fierce in his look his ardent valour glow'd,
Flush'd in his cheek, or sallied in his blood;
Indignant in the dark recess he stands,
Pants for the battle, and the war demands:
His voice breathed death, and with a martial air
He grasp'd his sword, and shook his glittering spear.
And when the gods our arms with conquest crown'd,
When Troy's proud bulwarks smoked upon the ground,
Greece, to reward her soldier's gallant toils,
Heap'd high his navy with unnumber'd spoils.

"Thus great in glory, from the din of war
Safe he return'd, without one hostile scar;
Though spears in iron tempests rain'd around,
Yet innocent they play'd, and guiltless of a wound.'

"While yet I spoke, the shade with transport glow'd,
Rose in his majesty, and nobler trod;
With haughty stalk he sought the distant glades
Of warrior kings, and join'd the illustrious shades.

"Now without number ghost by ghost arose,
All wailing with unutterable woes.

Alone, apart, in discontented mood,
A gloomy shade the sullen Ajax stood;
For ever sad, with proud disdain he pined,
And the lost arms for ever stung his mind;
Though to the contest Thetis gave the laws,
And Pallas, by the Trojans, judged the cause.
O why was I victorious in the strife?
O dear bought honour with so brave a life!
With him the strength of war, the soldier's pride,
Our second hope to great Achilles, died!
Touch'd at the sight from tears I scarce refrain,
And tender sorrow thrills in every vein;
Pensive and sad I stand, at length accost
With accents mild the inexorable ghost:
'Still burns thy rage? and can brave souls resent
E'en after death? Relent, great shade, relent!
Perish those arms which by the gods' decree
Accursed our army with the loss of thee!
With thee we fall; Greece wept thy hapless fates,
And shook astonish'd through her hundred states;
Not more, when great Achilles press'd the ground,
And breathed his manly spirit through the wound.
O deem thy fall not owed to man's decree,
Jove hated Greece, and punish'd Greece in thee!
Turn then; oh peaceful turn, thy wrath control,
And calm the raging tempest of thy soul.'

"While yet I speak, the shade disdains to stay,
In silence turns, and sullen stalks away.

"Touch'd at his sour retreat, through deepest night,
Through hell's black bounds I had pursued his flight,
And forced the stubborn spectre to reply;
But wondrous visions drew my curious eye.
High on a throne, tremendous to behold,
Stern Minos waves a mace of burnish'd gold;
Around ten thousand thousand spectres stand
Through the wide dome of Dis, a trembling band
Still as they plead, the fatal lots he rolls,
Absolves the just, and dooms the guilty souls.

"The huge Orion, of portentous size,
Swift through the gloom a giant-hunter flies:
A ponderous mace of brass with direful sway
Aloft he whirls, to crush the savage prey!
Stern beasts in trains that by his truncheon fell,
Now grisly forms, shoot o'er the lawns of hell.

"There Tityus large and long, in fetters bound,
O'erspreads nine acres of infernal ground;
Two ravenous vultures, furious for their food,
Scream o'er the fiend, and riot in his blood,
Incessant gore the liver in his breast,
The immortal liver grows, and gives the immortal feast.
For as o'er Panope's enamell'd plains
Latona journey'd to the Pythian fanes,
With haughty love the audacious monster strove
To force the goddess, and to rival Jove.

"There Tantalus along the Stygian bounds
Pours out deep groans (with groans all hell resounds);
E'en in the circling floods refreshment craves,
And pines with thirst amidst a sea of waves;
When to the water he his lip applies,
Back from his lip the treacherous water flies.
Above, beneath, around his hapless head,
Trees of all kinds delicious fruitage spread;
There figs, sky-dyed, a purple hue disclose,
Green looks the olive, the pomegranate glows.
There dangling pears exalting scents unfold.
And yellow apples ripen into gold;
The fruit he strives to seize; but blasts arise,
Toss it on high, and whirl it to the skies.

"I turn'd my eye, and as I turn'd survey'd
A mournful vision! the Sisyphian shade;
With many a weary step, and many a groan,
Up the high hill he heaves a huge round stone;
The huge round stone, resulting with a bound,
Thunders impetuous down, and smokes along the ground.
Again the restless orb his toil renews,
Dust mounts in clouds, and sweat descends in dews.

"Now I the strength of Hercules behold,
A towering spectre of gigantic mould,
A shadowy form! for high in heaven's abodes
Himself resides, a god among the gods;
There in the bright assemblies of the skies.
He nectar quaffs, and Hebe crowns his joys.
Here hovering ghosts, like fowl, his shade surround,
And clang their pinions with terrific sound;
Gloomy as night he stands, in act to throw
The aerial arrow from the twanging bow.
Around his breast a wondrous zone is roll'd,
Where woodland monsters grin in fretted gold;
There sullen lions sternly seem to roar,

The bear to growl to foam the tusky boar;
There war and havoc and destruction stood,
And vengeful murder red with human blood.
Thus terribly adorned the figures shine,
Inimitably wrought with skill divine.
The mighty good advanced with awful look,
And, turning his grim visage, sternly spoke:

"'O exercise in grief! by arts refined;
O taught to bear the wrongs of base mankind!
Such, such was I! Still toss'd from care to care,
While in your world I drew the vital air!
E'en I, who from the Lord of Thunders rose,
Bore toils and dangers, and a weight of woes;
To a base monarch still a slave confined,
(The hardest bondage to a generous mind!)
Down to these worlds I trod the dismal way,
And dragg'd the three-mouth'd dog to upper day
E'en hell I conquer'd, through the friendly aid
Of Maia's offspring, and the martial maid.

"Thus he, nor deign'd for our reply to stay,
But, turning, stalk'd with giant-strides away.

"Curious to view the kings of ancient days,
The mighty dead that live in endless praise,
Resolved I stand; and haply had survey'd
The godlike Theseus, and Pirithous' shade;
But swarms of spectres rose from deepest hell,
With bloodless visage, and with hideous yell.
They scream, they shriek; and groans and dismal sounds
Stun my scared ears, and pierce hell's utmost bounds.
No more my heart the dismal din sustains,
And my cold blood hangs shivering in my veins;
Lest Gorgon, rising from the infernal lakes,
With horrors arm'd, and curls of hissing snakes,
Should fix me stiffen'd at the monstrous sight,
A stony image, in eternal night!
Straight from the direful coast to purer air
I speed my flight, and to my mates repair.
My mates ascend the ship; they strike their oars;
The mountains lessen, and retreat the shores;
Swift o'er the waves we fly; the freshening gales
Sing through the shrouds, and stretch the swelling sails."

BOOK XII

THE SIRENE, SCYLLA, AND CHARYBDIS

He relates how, after his return from the shades, he was sent by Circe on his voyage, by the coast of the Sirens, and by the strait of Scylla and Charybdis: the manner in which he escaped those dangers: how, being cast on the island Trinacria, his companions destroyed the oxen of the Sun: the vengeance that followed; how all perished by shipwreck except himself, who, swimming on the mast of the ship, arrived on the island of Calypso. With which his narration concludes.

"Thus o'er the rolling surge the vessel flies,
Till from the waves the AEaean hills arise.
Here the gay Morn resides in radiant bowers,
Here keeps here revels with the dancing Hours;
Here Phoebus, rising in the ethereal way,
Through heaven's bright portals pours the beamy day.
At once we fix our halsers on the land.
At once descend, and press the desert sand:
There, worn and wasted, lose our cares in sleep,
To the hoarse murmurs of the rolling deep.

"Soon as the morn restored the day, we paid
Sepulchral honours to Elpenor's shade.
Now by the axe the rushing forest bends,
And the huge pile along the shore ascends.
Around we stand, a melancholy train,
And a loud groan re-echoes from the main.
Fierce o'er the pyre, by fanning breezes spread,
The hungry flames devour the silent dead.
A rising tomb, the silent dead to grace,
Fast by the roarings of the main we place;
The rising tomb a lofty column bore,
And high above it rose the tapering oar.

"Meantime the goddess our return survey'd
From the pale ghosts and hell's tremendous shade.
Swift she descends: a train of nymphs divine
Bear the rich viands and the generous wine:
In act to speak the power of magic stands,
And graceful thus accosts the listening bands;

"'O sons of woe? decreed by adverse fates
Alive to pass through hell's eternal gates!
All, soon or late, are doom'd that path to tread;
More wretched you! twice number'd with the dead!
This day adjourn your cares, exalt your souls,
Indulge the taste, and drain the sparkling bowls;

And when the morn unveils her saffron ray,
Spread your broad sails, and plough the liquid way:
Lo, I this night, your faithful guide, explain
Your woes by land, your dangers on the main.'

"The goddess spoke. In feasts we waste the day,
Till Phoebus downward plunged his burning ray;
Then sable night ascends, and balmy rest
Seals every eye, and calms the troubled breast.
Then curious she commands me to relate
The dreadful scenes of Pluto's dreary state.
She sat in silence while the tale I tell,
The wondrous visions and the laws of hell.

"Then thus: 'The lot of man the gods dispose;
These ills are past: now hear thy future woes
O prince attend; some favouring power be kind,
And print the important story on thy mind!

"'Next, where the Sirens dwells, you plough the seas;
Their song is death, and makes destruction please.
Unblest the man, whom music wins to stay
Nigh the cursed shore and listen to the lay.
No more that wretch shall view the joys of life
His blooming offspring, or his beauteous wife!
In verdant meads they sport; and wide around
Lie human bones that whiten all the ground:
The ground polluted floats with human gore,
And human carnage taints the dreadful shore
Fly swift the dangerous coast: let every ear
Be stopp'd against the song! 'tis death to hear!
Firm to the mast with chains thyself be bound,
Nor trust thy virtue to the enchanting sound.
If, mad with transport, freedom thou demand,
Be every fetter strain'd, and added band to band.

"'These seas o'erpass'd, be wise! but I refrain
To mark distinct thy voyage o'er the main:
New horrors rise! let prudence be thy guide,
And guard thy various passage through the tide.

"'High o'er the main two rocks exalt their brow,'
The boiling billows thundering roll below;
Through the vast waves the dreadful wonders move,
Hence named Erratic by the gods above.
No bird of air, no dove of swiftest wing,
That bears ambrosia to the ethereal king,
Shuns the dire rocks: in vain she cuts the skies;

The dire rocks meet, and crush her as she flies:
Not the fleet bark, when prosperous breezes play,
Ploughs o'er that roaring surge its desperate way;
O'erwhelm'd it sinks: while round a smoke expires,
And the waves flashing seem to burn with fires.
Scarce the famed Argo pass'd these raging floods,
The sacred Argo, fill'd with demigods!
E'en she had sunk, but Jove's imperial bride
Wing'd her fleet sail, and push'd her o'er the tide.

"'High in the air the rock its summit shrouds
In brooding tempests, and in rolling clouds;
Loud storms around, and mists eternal rise,
Beat its bleak brow, and intercept the skies.
When all the broad expansion, bright with day,
Glows with the autumnal or the summer ray,
The summer and the autumn glow in vain,
The sky for ever lowers, for ever clouds remain.
Impervious to the step of man it stands,
Though borne by twenty feet, though arm'd with twenty hands;
Smooth as the polish of the mirror rise
The slippery sides, and shoot into the skies.
Full in the centre of this rock display'd,
A yawning cavern casts a dreadful shade:
Nor the fleet arrow from the twanging bow,
Sent with full force, could reach the depth below.
Wide to the west the horrid gulf extends,
And the dire passage down to hell descends.
O fly the dreadful sight! expand thy sails,
Ply the strong oar, and catch the nimble gales;
Here Scylla bellows from the dire abodes,
Tremendous pest, abhorr'd by man and gods!
Hideous her voice, and with less terrors roar
The whelps of lions in the midnight hour.
Twelve feet, deform'd and foul, the fiend dispreads;
Six horrid necks she rears, and six terrific heads;
Her jaws grin dreadful with three rows of teeth;
Jaggy they stand, the gaping den of death;
Her parts obscene the raging billows hide;
Her bosom terribly o'erlooks the tide.
When stung with hunger she embroils the flood,
The sea-dog and the dolphin are her food;
She makes the huge leviathan her prey,
And all the monsters of the watery way;
The swiftest racer of the azure plain
Here fills her sails, and spreads her oars in vain;
Fell Scylla rises, in her fury roars,
At once six mouths expands, at once six men devours.

"'Close by, a rock of less enormous height
Breaks the wild waves, and forms a dangerous strait;
Full on its crown a fig's green branches rise,
And shoot a leafy forest to the skies;
Beneath, Charybdis holds her boisterous reign
'Midst roaring whirlpools, and absorbs the main;
Thrice in her gulfs the boiling seas subside,
Thrice in dire thunders she refunds the tide.
Oh, if thy vessel plough the direful waves,
When seas retreating roar within her caves,
Ye perish all! though he who rules the main
Lends his strong aid, his aid he lends in vain.
Ah, shun the horrid gulf! by Scylla fly.
'Tis better six to lose, than all to die.'

"I then: 'O nymph propitious to my prayer,
Goddess divine, my guardian power, declare,
Is the foul fiend from human vengeance freed?
Or, if I rise in arms, can Scylla bleed?'

"Then she: 'O worn by toils, O broke in fight,
Still are new toils and war thy dire delight?
Will martial flames for ever fire thy mind,
And never, never be to Heaven resign'd?
How vain thy efforts to avenge the wrong!
Deathless the pest! impenetrably strong!
Furious and fell, tremendous to behold!
E'en with a look she withers all the bold!
She mocks the weak attempts of human might;
Oh, fly her rage! thy conquest is thy flight.
If but to seize thy arms thou make delay,
Again thy fury vindicates her prey;
Her six mouths yawn, and six are snatch'd away.
From her foul wound Crataeis gave to air
This dreadful pest! To her direct thy prayer,
To curb the monster in her dire abodes,
And guard thee through the tumult of the floods.
Thence to Trinacria's shore you bend your way,
Where graze thy herds, illustrious source of day!
Seven herds, seven flocks enrich the sacred plains,
Each herd, each flock full fifty heads contains;
The wondrous kind a length of age survey,
By breed increase not, nor by death decay.
Two sister goddesses possess the plain,
The constant guardian of the woolly train;
Lampetie fair, and Phaethusa young,
From Phoebus and the bright Neaea sprung;

Here, watchful o'er the flocks, in shady bowers
And flowery meads, they waste the joyous hours.
Rob not the gods! and so propitious gales
Attend thy voyage, and impel thy sails;
But if thy impious hands the flocks destroy,
The gods, the gods avenge it, and ye die!
'Tis thine alone (thy friends and navy lost)
Through tedious toils to view thy native coast.'

She ceased: and now arose the morning ray;
Swift to her dome the goddess held her way.
Then to my mates I measured back the plain,
Climb'd the tall bark, and rush'd into the main;
Then, bending to the stroke, their oars they drew
To their broad breasts, and swift the galley flew.
Up sprung a brisker breeze; with freshening gales
The friendly goddess stretch'd the swelling sails;
We drop our oars; at ease the pilot guides;
The vessel light along the level glides.
When, rising sad and slow, with pensive look,
Thus to the melancholy train I spoke:

"'O friends, oh ever partners of my woes,
Attend while I what Heaven foredooms disclose.
Hear all! Fate hangs o'er all; on you it lies
To live or perish! to be safe, be wise!

"'In flowery meads the sportive Sirens play,
Touch the soft lyre, and tune the vocal lay;
Me, me alone, with fetters firmly bound,
The gods allow to hear the dangerous sound.
Hear and obey; if freedom I demand,
Be every fetter strain'd, be added band to band.'

"While yet I speak the winged galley flies,
And lo! the Siren shores like mists arise.
Sunk were at once the winds; the air above,
And waves below, at once forgot to move;
Some demon calm'd the air and smooth'd the deep,
Hush'd the loud winds, and charm'd the waves to sleep.
Now every sail we furl, each oar we ply;
Lash'd by the stroke, the frothy waters fly.
The ductile wax with busy hands I mould,
And cleft in fragments, and the fragments roll'd;
The aerial region now grew warm with day,
The wax dissolved beneath the burning ray;
Then every ear I barr'd against the strain,
And from access of frenzy lock'd the brain.

Now round the masts my mates the fetters roll'd,
And bound me limb by limb with fold on fold.
Then bending to the stroke, the active train
Plunge all at once their oars, and cleave the main.

"While to the shore the rapid vessel flies,
Our swift approach the Siren choir descries;
Celestial music warbles from their tongue,
And thus the sweet deluders tune the song:

"'Oh stay, O pride of Greece! Ulysses, stay!
Oh cease thy course, and listen to our lay!
Blest is the man ordain'd our voice to hear,
The song instructs the soul, and charms the ear.
Approach! thy soul shall into raptures rise!
Approach! and learn new wisdom from the wise!
We know whate'er the kings of mighty name
Achieved at Ilion in the field of fame;
Whate'er beneath the sun's bright journey lies.
Oh stay, and learn new wisdom from the wise!'

"Thus the sweet charmers warbled o'er the main;
My soul takes wing to meet the heavenly strain;
I give the sign, and struggle to be free;
Swift row my mates, and shoot along the sea;
New chains they add, and rapid urge the way,
Till, dying off, the distant sounds decay;
Then scudding swiftly from the dangerous ground,
The deafen'd ear unlock'd, the chains unbound.

"Now all at once tremendous scenes unfold;
Thunder'd the deeps, the smoky billows roll'd!
Tumultuous waves embroil the bellowing flood,
All trembling, deafen'd, and aghast we stood!
No more the vessel plough'd the dreadful wave,
Fear seized the mighty, and unnerved the brave;
Each dropp'd his oar; but swift from man to man
With looks serene I turn'd, and thus began:
'O friends! O often tried in adverse storms!
With ills familiar in more dreadful forms!
Deep in the dire Cyclopean den you lay,
Yet safe return'd—Ulysses led the way.
Learn courage hence, and in my care confide;
Lo! still the same Ulysses is your guide.
Attend my words! your oars incessant ply;
Strain every nerve, and bid the vessel fly.
If from yon jostling rocks and wavy war
Jove safety grants, he grants it to your care.

And thou, whose guiding hand directs our way,
Pilot, attentive listen and obey!
Bear wide thy course, nor plough those angry waves
Where rolls yon smoke, yon tumbling ocean raves;
Steer by the higher rock; lest whirl'd around
We sink, beneath the circling eddy drown'd.'
While yet I speak, at once their oars they seize,
Stretch to the stroke, and brush the working seas.
Cautious the name of Scylla I suppress'd;
That dreadful sound had chill'd the boldest breast.

"Meantime, forgetful of the voice divine,
All dreadful bright my limbs in armour shine;
High on the deck I take my dangerous stand,
Two glittering javelins lighten in my hand;
Prepared to whirl the whizzing spear I stay,
Till the fell fiend arise to seize her prey.
Around the dungeon, studious to behold
The hideous pest, my labouring eyes I roll'd;
In vain! the dismal dungeon, dark as night,
Veils the dire monster, and confounds the sight.

"Now through the rocks, appall'd with deep dismay,
We bend our course, and stem the desperate way;
Dire Scylla there a scene of horror forms,
And here Charybdis fills the deep with storms.
When the tide rushes from her rumbling caves,
The rough rock roars, tumultuous boil the waves;
They toss, they foam, a wild confusion raise,
Like waters bubbling o'er the fiery blaze;
Eternal mists obscure the aerial plain,
And high above the rock she spouts the main;
When in her gulfs the rushing sea subsides,
She drains the ocean with the refluent tides;
The rock re-bellows with a thundering sound;
Deep, wondrous deep, below appears the ground.

"Struck with despair, with trembling hearts we view'd
The yawning dungeon, and the tumbling flood;
When lo! fierce Scylla stoop'd to seize her prey,
Stretch'd her dire jaws, and swept six men away.
Chiefs of renown! loud-echoing shrieks arise;
I turn, and view them quivering in the skies;
They call, and aid with outstretch'd arms implore;
In vain they call! those arms are stretch'd no more.
As from some rock that overhangs the flood
The silent fisher casts the insidious food,
With fraudful care he waits the finny prize,

And sudden lifts it quivering to the skies:
So the foul monster lifts her prey on high,
So pant the wretches struggling in the sky;
In the wide dungeon she devours her food,
And the flesh trembles while she churns the blood.
Worn as I am with griefs, with care decay'd,
Never, I never scene so dire survey'd!
My shivering blood, congeal'd, forgot to flow;
Aghast I stood, a monument of woe!

"Now from the rocks the rapid vessel flies,
And the hoarse din like distant thunder dies;
To Sol's bright isle our voyage we pursue,
And now the glittering mountains rise to view.
There, sacred to the radiant god of day,
Graze the fair herds, the flocks promiscuous stray:
Then suddenly was heard along the main
To low the ox, to blest the woolly train.
Straight to my anxious thoughts the sound convey'd
The words of Circe and the Theban shade;
Warn'd by their awful voice these shores to shun,
With cautious fears oppress'd I thus begun:

"'O friends! O ever exorcised in care!
Hear Heaven's commands, and reverence what ye hear!
To fly these shores the prescient Theban shade
And Circe warn! Oh be their voice obey'd
Some mighty woe relentless Heaven forebodes:
Fly these dire regions, and revere the gods!'

"While yet I spoke, a sudden sorrow ran
Through every breast, and spread from man to man,
Till wrathful thus Eurylochus began:

"'O cruel thou! some Fury sure has steel'd
That stubborn soul, by toil untaught to yield!
From sleep debarr'd, we sink from woes to woes:
And cruel' enviest thou a short repose?
Still must we restless rove, new seas explore,
The sun descending, and so near the shore?
And lo! the night begins her groomy reign,
And doubles all the terrors of the main:
Oft in the dead of night loud winds rise,
Lash the wild surge, and bluster in the skies.
Oh, should the fierce south-west his rage display,
And toss with rising storms the watery way,
Though gods descend from heaven's aerial plain
To lend us aid, the gods descend in vain.

Then while the night displays her awful shade,
Sweet time of slumber! be the night obey'
Haste ye to land! and when the morning ray
Sheds her bright beam, pursue the destined way.'
A sudden joy in every bosom rose:
So will'd some demon, minister of woes!

"To whom with grief: 'O swift to be undone!
Constrain'd I act what wisdom bids me shun.
But yonder herbs and yonder flocks forbear;
Attest the heavens, and call the gods to hear:
Content, an innocent repast display,
By Circe given, and fly the dangerous prey.'

'Thus I: and while to shore the vessel flies,
With hands uplifted they attest the skies:
Then, where a fountain's gurgling waters play,
They rush to land, and end in feasts the day:
They feed; they quaff; and now (their hunger fled)
Sigh for their friends devour'd, and mourn the dead;
Nor cease the tears' till each in slumber shares
A sweet forgetfulness of human cares.
Now far the night advanced her gloomy reign,
And setting stars roll'd down the azure plain:
When at the voice of Jove wild whirlwinds rise,
And clouds and double darkness veil the skies;
The moon, the stars, the bright ethereal host
Seem as extinct, and all their splendours lost:
The furious tempest roars with dreadful sound:
Air thunders, rolls the ocean, groans the ground.
All night it raged: when morning rose to land
We haul'd our bark, and moor'd it on the strand,
Where in a beauteous grotto's cool recess
Dance the green Nerolds of the neighbouring seas.

"There while the wild winds whistled o'er the main,
Thus careful I address'd the listening train:

"'O friends, be wise! nor dare the flocks destroy
Of these fair pastures: if ye touch, ye die.
Warn'd by the high command of Heaven, be awed:
Holy the flocks, and dreadful is the god!
That god who spreads the radiant beams of light,
And views wide earth and heaven's unmeasured height.'

"And now the moon had run her monthly round,
The south-east blustering with a dreadful sound:
Unhurt the beeves, untouch'd the woolly train,

Low through the grove, or touch the flowery plain:
Then fail'd our food: then fish we make our prey,
Or fowl that screaming haunt the watery way.
Till now from sea or flood no succour found,
Famine and meagre want besieged us round.
Pensive and pale from grove to grove I stray'd,
From the loud storms to find a sylvan shade;
There o'er my hands the living wave I pour;
And Heaven and Heaven's immortal thrones implore,
To calm the roarings of the stormy main,
And guide me peaceful to my realms again.
Then o'er my eyes the gods soft slumbers shed,
While thus Eurylochus arising said:

"'O friends, a thousand ways frail mortals lead
To the cold tomb, and dreadful all to tread;
But dreadful most, when by a slow decay
Pale hunger wastes the manly strength away.
Why cease ye then to implore the powers above,
And offer hecatombs to thundering Jove?
Why seize ye not yon beeves, and fleecy prey?
Arise unanimous; arise and slay!
And if the gods ordain a safe return,
To Phoebus shrines shall rise, and altars burn.
But should the powers that o'er mankind preside
Decree to plunge us in the whelming tide,
Better to rush at once to shades below
Than linger life away, and nourish woe.'

"Thus he: the beeves around securely stray,
When swift to ruin they invade the prey;
They seize, they kill!—but for the rite divine.
The barley fail'd, and for libations wine.
Swift from the oak they strip the shady pride;
And verdant leaves the flowery cake supplied.

"With prayer they now address the ethereal train,
Slay the selected beeves, and flay the slain;
The thighs, with fat involved, divide with art,
Strew'd o'er with morsels cut from every part.
Water, instead of wine, is brought in urns,
And pour'd profanely as the victim burns.
The thighs thus offer'd, and the entrails dress'd,
They roast the fragments, and prepare the feast.

"'Twas then soft slumber fled my troubled brain;
Back to the bark I speed along the main.
When lo! an odour from the feast exhales,

Spreads o'er the coast and scents the tainted gales;
A chilly fear congeal'd my vital blood,
And thus, obtesting Heaven, I mourn'd aloud;

"'O sire of men and gods, immortal Jove!
O all ye blissful powers that reign above!
Why were my cares beguiled in short repose?
O fatal slumber, paid with lasting woes!
A deed so dreadful all the gods alarms,
Vengeance is on the wing, and Heaven in arms!'

"Meantime Lampetie mounts the aerial way,
And kindles into rage the god of day;

"'Vengeance, ye powers (he cries), and then whose hand
Aims the red bolt, and hurls the writhen brand!
Slain are those herds which I with pride survey,
When through the ports of heaven I pour the day,
Or deep in ocean plunge the burning ray.
Vengeance, ye gods! or I the skies forego,
And bear the lamp of heaven to shades below.'

"To whom the thundering Power: 'O source of day
Whose radiant lamp adorns the azure way,
Still may thy beams through heaven's bright portal rise,
The joy of earth, the glory of the skies:
Lo! my red arm I bare, my thunders guide,
To dash the offenders in the whelming tide.'

"To fair Calypso, from the bright abodes,
Hermes convey'd these counsels of the gods.

"Meantime from man to man my tongue exclaims,
My wrath is kindled, and my soul in flames.
In vain! I view perform'd the direful deed,
Beeves, slain in heaps, along the ocean bleed.

"Now heaven gave signs of wrath: along the ground
Crept the raw hides, and with a bellowing sound
Roar'd the dead limbs; the burning entrails groan'd.
Six guilty days my wretched mates employ
In impious feasting, and unhallowed joy;
The seventh arose, and now the sire of gods
Rein'd the rough storms; and calm'd the tossing floods:
With speed the bark we climb; the spacious sails.
Loosed from the yards invite the impelling gales.
Past sight of shore, along the surge we bound,
And all above is sky, and ocean all around;

When lo! a murky cloud the thunderer forms
Full o'er our heads, and blackens heaven with storms.
Night dwells o'er all the deep: and now outflies
The gloomy west, and whistles in the skies.
The mountain-billows roar! the furious blast
Howls o'er the shroud, and rends it from the mast:
The mast gives way, and, crackling as it bends,
Tears up the deck; then all at once descends:
The pilot by the tumbling ruin slain,
Dash'd from the helm, falls headlong in the main.
Then Jove in anger bids his thunders roll,
And forky lightnings flash from pole to pole:
Fierce at our heads his deadly bolt he aims,
Red with uncommon wrath, and wrapp'd in flames:
Full on the bark it fell; now high, now low,
Toss'd and retoss'd, it reel'd beneath the blow;
At once into the main the crew it shook:
Sulphurous odours rose, and smouldering smoke.
Like fowl that haunt the floods, they sink, they rise,
Now lost, now seen, with shrieks and dreadful cries;
And strive to gain the bark, but Jove denies.
Firm at the helm I stand, when fierce the main
Rush'd with dire noise, and dash'd the sides in twain;
Again impetuous drove the furious blast,
Snapp'd the strong helm, and bore to sea the mast.
Firm to the mast with cords the helm I bind,
And ride aloft, to Providence resign'd,
Through tumbling billows and a war of wind.
"Now sunk the west, and now a southern breeze,
More dreadful than the tempest lash'd the seas;
For on the rocks it bore where Scylla raves,
And dire Charybdis rolls her thundering waves.
All night I drove; and at the dawn of day,
Fast by the rocks beheld the desperate way;
Just when the sea within her gulfs subsides,
And in the roaring whirlpools rush the tides,
Swift from the float I vaulted with a bound,
The lofty fig-tree seized, and clung around;
So to the beam the bat tenacious clings,
And pendent round it clasps his leather wings.
High in the air the tree its boughs display'd,
And o'er the dungeon cast a dreadful shade;
All unsustain'd between the wave and sky,
Beneath my feet the whirling billows fly.
What time the judge forsakes the noisy bar
To take repast, and stills the wordy war,
Charybdis, rumbling from her inmost caves,
The mast refunded on her refluent waves.

Swift from the tree, the floating mass to gain,
Sudden I dropp'd amidst the flashing main;
Once more undaunted on the ruin rode,
And oar'd with labouring arms along the flood.
Unseen I pass'd by Scylla's dire abodes.
So Jove decreed (dread sire of men and gods).
Then nine long days I plow'd the calmer seas,
Heaved by the surge, and wafted by the breeze.
Weary and wet the Ogygian shores I gain,
When the tenth sun descended to the main.
There, in Calypso's ever-fragrant bowers,
Refresh'd I lay, and joy beguiled the hours.
"My following fates to thee, O king, are known,
And the bright partner of thy royal throne.
Enough: in misery can words avail?
And what so tedious as a twice-told tale?"

BOOK XIII

ARGUMENT

THE ARRIVAL OF ULYSSES IN ITHACA

Ulysses takes his leave of Alcinous and Arete, and embarks in the evening. Next morning the ship arrives
at Ithaca; where the sailors, as Ulysses is yet sleeping, lay him on the shore with all his treasures. On
their return, Neptune changes their ship into a rock. In the meantime Ulysses, awaking, knows not his
native Ithaca, by reason of a mist which Pallas had cast around him. He breaks into loud lamentations;
till the goddess appearing to him in the form of a shepherd, discovers the country to him, and points out
the particular places. He then tells a feigned story of his adventures, upon which she manifests herself,
and they consult together of the measures to be taken to destroy the suitors. To conceal his return, and
disguise his person the more effectually, she changes him into the figure of an old beggar.

He ceased; but left so pleasing on their ear
His voice, that listening still they seem'd to hear.
A pause of silence hush'd the shady rooms:
The grateful conference then the king resumes:

"Whatever toils the great Ulysses pass'd,
Beneath this happy roof they end at last;
No longer now from shore to shore to roam,
Smooth seas and gentle winds invite him home.
But hear me, princes! whom these walls inclose,
For whom my chanter sings: and goblet flows
With wine unmix'd (an honour due to age,
To cheer the grave, and warm the poet's rage);
Though labour'd gold and many a dazzling vest

Lie heap'd already for our godlike guest;
Without new treasures let him not remove,
Large, and expressive of the public love:
Each peer a tripod, each a vase bestow,
A general tribute, which the state shall owe."

This sentence pleased: then all their steps address'd
To separate mansions, and retired to rest.

Now did the rosy-finger'd morn arise,
And shed her sacred light along the skies.
Down to the haven and the ships in haste
They bore the treasures, and in safety placed.
The king himself the vases ranged with care;
Then bade his followers to the feast prepare.
A victim ox beneath the sacred hand
Of great Alcinous falls, and stains the sand.
To Jove the Eternal (power above all powers!
Who wings the winds, and darkens heaven with showers)
The flames ascend: till evening they prolong
The rites, more sacred made by heavenly song;
For in the midst, with public honours graced,
Thy lyre divine, Demodocus! was placed.
All, but Ulysses, heard with fix'd delight;
He sate, and eyed the sun, and wish'd the night;
Slow seem'd the sun to move, the hours to roll,
His native home deep-imaged in his soul.
As the tired ploughman, spent with stubborn toil,
Whose oxen long have torn the furrow'd soil,
Sees with delight the sun's declining ray,
When home with feeble knees he bends his way
To late repast (the day's hard labour done);
So to Ulysses welcome set the sun;
Then instant to Alcinous and the rest
(The Scherian states) he turn'd, and thus address'd:

"O thou, the first in merit and command!
And you the peers and princes of the land!
May every joy be yours! nor this the least,
When due libation shall have crown'd the feast,
Safe to my home to send your happy guest.
Complete are now the bounties you have given,
Be all those bounties but confirm'd by Heaven!
So may I find, when all my wanderings cease,
My consort blameless, and my friends in peace.
On you be every bliss; and every day,
In home-felt joys, delighted roll away;
Yourselves, your wives, your long-descending race,

May every god enrich with every grace!
Sure fix'd on virtue may your nation stand,
And public evil never touch the land!"

His words well weigh'd, the general voice approved
Benign, and instant his dismission moved,
The monarch to Pontonus gave the sign.
To fill the goblet high with rosy wine;
"Great Jove the Father first (he cried) implore;'
Then send the stranger to his native shore."

The luscious wine the obedient herald brought;
Around the mansion flow'd the purple draught;
Each from his seat to each immortal pours,
Whom glory circles in the Olympian bowers
Ulysses sole with air majestic stands,
The bowl presenting to Arete's hands;
Then thus: "O queen, farewell! be still possess'd
Of dear remembrance, blessing still and bless'd!
Till age and death shall gently call thee hence,
(Sure fate of every mortal excellence!)
Farewell! and joys successive ever spring
To thee, to thine, the people, and the king!"

Thus he: then parting prints the sandy shore
To the fair port: a herald march'd before,
Sent by Alcinous; of Arete's train
Three chosen maids attend him to the main;
This does a tunic and white vest convey,
A various casket that, of rich inlay,
And bread and wine the third. The cheerful mates
Safe in the hollow poop dispose the cates;
Upon the deck soft painted robes they spread
With linen cover'd, for the hero's bed.
He climbed the lofty stern; then gently press'd
The swelling couch, and lay composed to rest.

Now placed in order, the Phaeacian train
Their cables loose, and launch into the main;
At once they bend, and strike their equal oars,
And leave the sinking hills and lessening shores.
While on the deck the chief in silence lies,
And pleasing slumbers steal upon his eyes.
As fiery coursers in the rapid race
Urged by fierce drivers through the dusty space,
Toss their high heads, and scour along the plain,
So mounts the bounding vessel o'er the main.
Back to the stern the parted billows flow,

And the black ocean foams and roars below.

Thus with spread sails the winged galley flies;
Less swift an eagle cuts the liquid skies;
Divine Ulysses was her sacred load,
A man, in wisdom equal to a god!
Much danger, long and mighty toils he bore,
In storms by sea, and combats on the shore;
All which soft sleep now banish'd from his breast,
Wrapp'd in a pleasing, deep, and death-like rest.

But when the morning-star with early ray
Flamed in the front of heaven, and promised day;
Like distant clouds the mariner descries
Fair Ithaca's emerging hills arise.
Far from the town a spacious port appears,
Sacred to Phorcys' power, whose name it bears;
Two craggy rocks projecting to the main,
The roaring wind's tempestuous rage restrain;
Within the waves in softer murmurs glide,
And ships secure without their halsers ride.
High at the head a branching olive grows,
And crowns the pointed cliffs with shady boughs.
Beneath, a gloomy grotto's cool recess
Delights the Nereids of the neighbouring seas,
Where bowls and urns were form'd of living stone,
And massy beams in native marble shone,
On which the labours of the nymphs were roll'd,
Their webs divine of purple mix'd with gold.
Within the cave the clustering bees attend
Their waxen works, or from the roof depend.
Perpetual waters o'er the pavement glide;
Two marble doors unfold on either side;
Sacred the south, by which the gods descend;
But mortals enter at the northern end.
Thither they bent, and haul'd their ship to land
(The crooked keel divides the yellow sand).
Ulysses sleeping on his couch they bore,
And gently placed him on the rocky shore.
His treasures next, Alcinous' gifts, they laid
In the wild olive's unfrequented shade,
Secure from theft; then launch'd the bark again,
Resumed their oars, and measured back the main,
Nor yet forgot old Ocean's dread supreme,
The vengeance vow'd for eyeless Polypheme.
Before the throne of mighty Jove lie stood,
And sought the secret counsels of the god.

"Shall then no more, O sire of gods! be mine
The rights and honours of a power divine?
Scorn'd e'en by man, and (oh severe disgrace!)
By soft Phaeacians, my degenerate race!
Against yon destined head in vain I swore,
And menaced vengeance, ere he reach'd his shore;
To reach his natal shore was thy decree;
Mild I obey'd, for who shall war with thee?
Behold him landed, careless and asleep,
From all the eluded dangers of the deep;
Lo where he lies, amidst a shining store
Of brass, rich garments, and refulgent ore;
And bears triumphant to his native isle
A prize more worth than Ilion's noble spoil."

To whom the Father of the immortal powers,
Who swells the clouds, and gladdens earth with showers,
"Can mighty Neptune thus of man complain?
Neptune, tremendous o'er the boundless main!
Revered and awful e'en in heaven's abodes,
Ancient and great! a god above the gods!
If that low race offend thy power divine
(Weak, daring creatures!) is not vengeance thine?
Go, then, the guilty at thy will chastise."
He said. The shaker of the earth replies:

"This then, I doom: to fix the gallant ship,
A mark of vengeance on the sable deep;
To warn the thoughtless, self-confiding train,
No more unlicensed thus to brave the main.
Full in their port a Shady hill shall rise,
If such thy will."—" We will it (Jove replies).
E'en when with transport blackening all the strand,
The swarming people hail their ship to land,
Fix her for ever, a memorial stone:
Still let her seem to sail, and seem alone.
The trembling crowds shall see the sudden shade
Of whelming mountains overhang their head!"

With that the god whose earthquakes rock the ground
Fierce to Phaeacia cross'd the vast profound.
Swift as a swallow sweeps the liquid way,
The winged pinnace shot along the sea.
The god arrests her with a sudden stroke,
And roots her down an everlasting rock.
Aghast the Scherians stand in deep surprise;
All press to speak, all question with their eyes.
What hands unseen the rapid bark restrain!

And yet it swims, or seems to swim, the main!
Thus they, unconscious of the deed divine;
Till great Alcinous, rising, own'd the sign.

"Behold the long predestined day I (he cries;)
O certain faith of ancient prophecies
These ears have heard my royal sire disclose
A dreadful story, big with future woes;
How, moved with wrath, that careless we convey
Promiscuous every guest to every bay,
Stern Neptune raged; and how by his command
Firm rooted in the surge a ship should stand
(A monument of wrath); and mound on mound
Should hide our walls, or whelm beneath the ground.

"The Fates have follow'd as declared the seer.
Be humbled, nations! and your monarch hear.
No more unlicensed brave the deeps, no more
With every stranger pass from shore to shore;
On angry Neptune now for mercy call;
To his high name let twelve black oxen fall.
So may the god reverse his purposed will,
Nor o'er our city hang the dreadful hill."

The monarch spoke: they trembled and obey'd,
Forth on the sands the victim oxen led;
The gathered tribes before the altars stand,
And chiefs and rulers, a majestic band.
The king of ocean all the tribes implore;
The blazing altars redden all the shore.

Meanwhile Ulysses in his country lay,
Released from sleep, and round him might survey
The solitary shore and rolling sea.
Yet had his mind through tedious absence lost
The dear resemblance of his native coast;
Besides, Minerva, to secure her care,
Diffused around a veil of thickened air;
For so the gods ordain'd to keep unseen
His royal person from his friends and queen;
Till the proud suitors for their crimes afford
An ample vengeance to their injured lord.

Now all the land another prospect bore,
Another port appear'd, another shore.
And long-continued ways, and winding floods,
And unknown mountains, crown'd with unknown woods
Pensive and slow, with sudden grief oppress'd,

The king arose, and beat his careful breast,
Cast a long look o'er all the coast and main,
And sought, around, his native realm in vain;
Then with erected eyes stood fix'd in woe,
And as he spoke, the tears began to flow.

"Ye gods (he cried), upon what barren coast,
In what new region, is Ulysses toss'd?
Possess'd by wild barbarians, fierce in arms?
Or men whose bosom tender pity warms?
Where shall this treasure now in safely be?
And whither, whither its sad owner fly?
Ah, why did I Alcinous' grace implore?
Ah, why forsake Phaeacia's happy shore?
Some juster prince perhaps had entertain'd,
And safe restored me to my native land.
Is this the promised, long-expected coast,
And this the faith Phaeacia's rulers boast?
O righteous gods! of all the great, how few
Are just to Heaven, and to their promise true!
But he, the power to whose all-seeing eyes
The deeds of men appear without disguise,
'Tis his alone to avenge the wrongs I bear;
For still the oppress'd are his peculiar care.
To count these presents, and from thence to prove,
Their faith is mine; the rest belongs to Jove."

Then on the sands he ranged his wealthy store,
The gold, the vests, the tripods number'd o'er:
All these he found, but still in error lost,
Disconsolate he wanders on the coast,
Sighs for his country, and laments again
To the deaf rocks, and hoarse-resounding main.
When lo! the guardian goddess of the wise,
Celestial Pallas, stood before his eyes;
In show a youthful swain, of form divine,
Who seem'd descended from some princely line.
A graceful robe her slender body dress'd;
Around her shoulders flew the waving vest;
Her decent hand a shining javelin bore,
And painted sandals on her feet she wore.
To whom the king: "Whoe'er of human race
Thou art, that wanderest in this desert place,
With joy to thee, as to some god I bend,
To thee my treasures and myself commend.
O tell a wretch in exile doom'd to stray,
What air I breathe, what country I survey?
The fruitful continent's extremest bound,

Or some fair isle which Neptune's arms surround?

"From what far clime (said she) remote from fame
Arrivest thou here, a stranger to our name?
Thou seest an island, not to those unknown
Whose hills are brighten'd by the rising sun,
Nor those that placed beneath his utmost reign
Behold him sinking in the western main.
The rugged soil allows no level space
For flying chariots, or the rapid race;
Yet, not ungrateful to the peasant's pain,
Suffices fulness to the swelling grain;
The loaded trees their various fruits produce,
And clustering grapes afford a generous juice;
Woods crown our mountains, and in every grove
The bounding goats and frisking heifers rove;
Soft rains and kindly dews refresh the field,
And rising springs eternal verdure yield.
E'en to those shores is Ithaca renown'd,
Where Troy's majestic ruins strew the ground."

At this, the chief with transport was possess'd;
His panting heart exulted in his breast;
Yet, well dissembling his untimely joys,
And veiling truth in plausible disguise,
Thus, with an air sincere, in fiction bold,
His ready tale the inventive hero told:

"Oft have I heard in Crete this island's name;
For 'twas from Crete, my native soil, I came,
Self-banished thence. I sail'd before the wind,
And left my children and my friends behind.
From fierce Idomeneus' revenge I flew,
Whose son, the swift Orsilochus, I slew
(With brutal force he seized my Trojan prey,
Due to the toils of many a bloody day).
Unseen I 'scaped, and favour'd by the night,
In a Phoenician vessel took my flight,
For Pyle or Elis bound; but tempests toss'd
And raging billows drove us on your coast.
In dead of night an unknown port we gain'd;
Spent with fatigue, and slept secure on land.
But ere the rosy morn renew'd the day,
While in the embrace of pleasing sleep I lay,
Sudden, invited by auspicious gales,
They land my goods, and hoist their flying sails.
Abandon'd here, my fortune I deplore
A hapless exile on a foreign shore,"

Thus while he spoke, the blue-eyed maid began
With pleasing smiles to view the godlike man;
Then changed her form: and now, divinely bright,
Jove's heavenly daughter stood confess'd to sight;
Like a fair virgin in her beauty's bloom,
Skill'd in the illustrious labours of the loom.

"O still the same Ulysses! (she rejoin'd,)
In useful craft successfully refined!
Artful in speech, in action, and in mind!
Sufficed it not, that, thy long labours pass'd,
Secure thou seest thy native shore at last?
But this to me? who, like thyself, excel
In arts of counsel and dissembling well;
To me? whose wit exceeds the powers divine,
No less than mortals are surpass'd by thine.
Know'st thou not me; who made thy life my care,
Through ten years' wandering, and through ten years' war;
Who taught thee arts, Alcinous to persuade,
To raise his wonder, and engage his aid;
And now appear, thy treasures to protect,
Conceal thy person, thy designs direct,
And tell what more thou must from Fate expect;
Domestic woes far heavier to be borne!
The pride of fools, and slaves' insulting scorn?
But thou be silent, nor reveal thy state;
Yield to the force of unresisted Fate,
And bear unmoved the wrongs of base mankind,
The last, and hardest, conquest of the mind."

"Goddess of wisdom! (Ithacus replies,)
He who discerns thee must be truly wise,
So seldom view'd and ever in disguise!
When the bold Argives led their warring powers,
Against proud Ilion's well-defended towers,
Ulysses was thy care, celestial maid!
Graced with thy sight, and favoured with thy aid.
But when the Trojan piles in ashes lay,
And bound for Greece we plough'd the watery way;
Our fleet dispersed, and driven from coast to coast,
Thy sacred presence from that hour I lost;
Till I beheld thy radiant form once more,
And heard thy counsels on Phaeacia's shore.
But, by the almighty author of thy race,
Tell me, oh tell, is this my native place?
For much I fear, long tracts of land and sea
Divide this coast from distant Ithaca;

The sweet delusion kindly you impose,
To soothe my hopes, and mitigate my woes."

Thus he. The blue-eyed goddess thus replies;
"How prone to doubt, how cautious are the wise!
Who, versed in fortune, fear the flattering show,
And taste not half the bliss the gods bestow.
The more shall Pallas aid thy just desires,
And guard the wisdom which herself inspires.
Others long absent from their native place,
Straight seek their home, and fly with eager pace
To their wives' arms, and children's dear embrace.
Not thus Ulysses; he decrees to prove
His subjects' faith, and queen's suspected love;
Who mourn'd her lord twice ten revolving years,
And wastes the days in grief, the nights in tears.
But Pallas knew (thy friends and navy lost)
Once more 'twas given thee to behold thy coast;
Yet how could I with adverse Fate engage,
And mighty Neptune's unrelenting rage?
Now lift thy longing eyes, while I restore
The pleasing prospect of thy native shore.
Bebold the port of Phorcys! fenced around
With rocky mountains, and with olives crown'd,
Behold the gloomy grot! whose cool recess
Delights the Nereids of the neighbouring seas;
Whose now-neglected altars in thy reign
Blush'd with the blood of sheep and oxen slain,
Behold! where Neritus the clouds divides,
And shakes the waving forests on his sides."

So spake the goddess; and the prospect clear'd,
The mists dispersed, and all the coast appeared.
The king with joy confess'd his place of birth,
And on his knees salutes his mother earth;
Then, with his suppliant hands upheld in air,
Thus to the sea-green sisters sends his prayer;

"All hail! ye virgin daughters of the main!
Ye streams, beyond my hopes, beheld again!
To you once more your own Ulysses bows;
Attend his transports, and receive his vows!
If Jove prolong my days, and Pallas crown
The growing virtues of my youthful son,
To you shall rites divine be ever paid,
And grateful offerings on your altars laid."

Thus then Minerva: "From that anxious breast

Dismiss those cares, and leave to heaven the rest.
Our task be now thy treasured stores to save,
Deep in the close recesses of the cave;
Then future means consult." She spoke, and trod
The shady grot, that brighten'd with the god.
The closest caverns of the grot she sought;
The gold, the brass, the robes, Ulysses brought;
These in the secret gloom the chief disposed;
The entrance with a rock the goddess closed.

Now, seated in the olive's sacred shade,
Confer the hero and the martial maid.
The goddess of the azure eyes began:
"Son of Laertes! much-experienced man!
The suitor-train thy earliest care demand,
Of that luxurious race to rid the land;
Three years thy house their lawless rule has seen,
And proud addresses to the matchless queen.
But she thy absence mourns from day to day,
And inly bleeds, and silent wastes away;
Elusive of the bridal hour, she gives
Fond hopes to all, and all with hopes deceives."

To this Ulysses: "O celestial maid!
Praised be thy counsel, and thy timely aid;
Else had I seen my native walls in vain,
Like great Atrides, just restored and slain.
Vouchsafe the means of vengeance to debate,
And plan with all thy arts the scene of fate.
Then, then be present, and my soul inspire,
As when we wrapp'd Troy's heaven-built walls in fire.
Though leagued against me hundred heroes stand.
Hundreds shall fall, if Pallas aid my hand."

She answer'd: "In the dreadful day of fight
Know, I am with thee, strong in all my might.
If thou but equal to thyself be found,
What gasping numbers then shall press the ground!
What human victims stain the feastful floor!
How wide the pavements float with guilty gore!
It fits thee now to wear a dark disguise,
And secret walk unknown to mortal eyes.
For this, my hand shall wither every grace,
And every elegance of form and face;
O'er thy smooth skin a bark of wrinkles spread,
Turn hoar the auburn honours of thy head;
Disfigure every limb with coarse attire,
And in thy eyes extinguish all the fire;

Add all the wants and the decays of life;
Estrange thee from thy own; thy son, thy wife;
From the loathed object every sight shall turn,
And the blind suitors their destruction scorn.

"Go first the master of thy herds to find,
True to his charge, a loyal swain and kind;
For thee he sighs; and to the loyal heir
And chaste Penelope extends his care.
At the Coracian rock he now resides,
Where Arethusa's sable water glides;
The sable water and the copious mast
Swell the fat herd; luxuriant, large repast!
With him rest peaceful in the rural cell,
And all you ask his faithful tongue shall tell.
Me into other realms my cares convey,
To Sparta, still with female beauty gay;
For know, to Sparta thy loved offspring came,
To learn thy fortunes from the voice of Fame."

At this the father, with a father's care:
"Must he too suffer? he, O goddess! bear
Of wanderings and of woes a wretched share?
Through the wild ocean plough the dangerous way,
And leave his fortunes and his house a prey?
Why would'st not thou, O all-enlighten'd mind!
Inform him certain, and protect him, kind?"

To whom Minerva: "Be thy soul at rest;
And know, whatever heaven ordains is best.
To fame I sent him, to acquire renown;
To other regions is his virtue known;
Secure he sits, near great Atrides placed;
With friendships strengthen'd, and with honours graced,
But lo! an ambush waits his passage o'er;
Fierce foes insidious intercept the shore;
In vain; far sooner all the murderous brood
This injured land shall fatten with their blood."

She spake, then touch'd him with her powerful wand:
The skin shrunk up, and wither'd at her hand;
A swift old age o'er all his members spread;
A sudden frost was sprinkled on his head;
Nor longer in the heavy eye-ball shined
The glance divine, forth-beaming from the mind.
His robe, which spots indelible besmear,
In rags dishonest flutters with the air:
A stag's torn hide is lapp'd around his reins;

A rugged staff his trembling hand sustains;
And at his side a wretched scrip was hung,
Wide-patch'd, and knotted to a twisted thong.
So looked the chief, so moved: to mortal eyes
Object uncouth! a man of miseries!
While Pallas, cleaving the wild fields of air,
To Sparta flies, Telemachus her care.

BOOK XIV

ARGUMENT

THE CONVERSATION WITH EUMAEUS

Ulysses arrives in disguise at the house of Eumaeus, where he is received, entertained, and lodged with
the utmost hospitality. The several discourses of that faithful old servant, with the feigned story told by
Ulysses to conceal himself, and other conversations on various subjects, take up this entire book.

But he, deep-musing, o'er the mountains stray'd
Through mazy thickets of the woodland shade,
And cavern'd ways, the shaggy coast along
With cliffs and nodding forests overhung.
Eumaeus at his sylvan lodge he sought,
A faithful servant, and without a fault.
Ulysses found him busied as he sate
Before the threshold of his rustic gate;
Around the mansion in a circle shone
A rural portico of rugged stone
(In absence of his lord with honest toil
His own industrious hands had raised the pile).
The wall was stone from neighbouring quarries borne,
Encircled with a fence of native thorn,
And strong with pales, by many a weary stroke
Of stubborn labour hewn from heart of oak:
Frequent and thick. Within the space were rear'd
Twelve ample cells, the lodgments of his herd.
Full fifty pregnant females each contain'd;
The males without (a smaller race) remain'd;
Doom'd to supply the suitors' wasteful feast,
A stock by daily luxury decreased;
Now scarce four hundred left. These to defend,
Four savage dogs, a watchful guard, attend.
Here sat Eumaeus, and his cares applied
To form strong buskins of well-season'd hide.
Of four assistants who his labour share,
Three now were absent on the rural care;
The fourth drove victims to a suitor train:

But he, of ancient faith, a simple swain,
Sigh'd, while he furnish'd the luxurious board,
And wearied Heaven with wishes for his lord.

Soon as Ulysses near the inclosure drew,
With open mouths the furious mastiffs flew:
Down sat the sage, and cautious to withstand,
Let fall the offensive truncheon from his hand.
Sudden, the master runs; aloud he calls;
And from his hasty hand the leather falls:
With showers of stones he drives then far away:
The scattering dogs around at distance bay.

"Unhappy stranger! (thus the faithful swain
Began with accent gracious and humane),
What sorrow had been mine, if at my gate
Thy reverend age had met a shameful fate!
Enough of woes already have I known;
Enough my master's sorrows and my own.
While here (ungrateful task!) his herds I feed,
Ordain'd for lawless rioters to bleed!
Perhaps, supported at another's board!
Far from his country roams my hapless lord;
Or sigh'd in exile forth his latest breath,
Now cover'd with the eternal shade of death!

"But enter this my homely roof, and see
Our woods not void of hospitality.
Then tell me whence thou art, and what the share
Of woes and wanderings thou wert born to bear."

He said, and, seconding the kind request,
With friendly step precedes his unknown guest.
A shaggy goat's soft hide beneath him spread,
And with fresh rushes heap'd an ample bed;
Jove touch'd the hero's tender soul, to find
So just reception from a heart so kind:
And "Oh, ye gods! with all your blessings grace
(He thus broke forth) this friend of human race!"

The swain replied: "It never was our guise
To slight the poor, or aught humane despise:
For Jove unfold our hospitable door,
'Tis Jove that sends the stranger and the poor,
Little, alas! is all the good I can
A man oppress'd, dependent, yet a man:
Accept such treatment as a swain affords,
Slave to the insolence of youthful lords!

Far hence is by unequal gods removed
That man of bounties, loving and beloved!
To whom whate'er his slave enjoys is owed,
And more, had Fate allow'd, had been bestow'd:
But Fate condemn'd him to a foreign shore;
Much have I sorrow'd, but my Master more.
Now cold he lies, to death's embrace resign'd:
Ah, perish Helen! perish all her kind!
For whose cursed cause, in Agamemnon's name,
He trod so fatally the paths of fame."

His vest succinct then girding round his waist,
Forth rush'd the swain with hospitable haste.
Straight to the lodgments of his herd he run,
Where the fat porkers slept beneath the sun;
Of two, his cutlass launch'd the spouting blood;
These quarter'd, singed, and fix'd on forks of wood,
All hasty on the hissing coals he threw;
And smoking, back the tasteful viands drew.
Broachers and all then an the board display'd
The ready meal, before Ulysses laid
With flour imbrown'd; next mingled wine yet new,
And luscious as the bees' nectareous dew:
Then sate, companion of the friendly feast,
With open look; and thus bespoke his guest:
"Take with free welcome what our hands prepare,
Such food as falls to simple servants' share;
The best our lords consume; those thoughtless peers,
Rich without bounty, guilty without fears;
Yet sure the gods their impious acts detest,
And honour justice and the righteous breast.
Pirates and conquerors of harden'd mind,
The foes of peace, and scourges of mankind,
To whom offending men are made a prey
When Jove in vengeance gives a land away;
E'en these, when of their ill-got spoils possess'd,
Find sure tormentors in the guilty breast:
Some voice of God close whispering from within,
'Wretch! this is villainy, and this is sin.'
But these, no doubt, some oracle explore,
That tells, the great Ulysses is no more.
Hence springs their confidence, and from our sighs
Their rapine strengthens, and their riots rise:
Constant as Jove the night and day bestows,
Bleeds a whole hecatomb, a vintage flows.
None match'd this hero's wealth, of all who reign
O'er the fair islands of the neighbouring main.
Nor all the monarchs whose far-dreaded sway

The wide-extended continents obey:
First, on the main land, of Ulysses' breed
Twelve herds, twelve flocks, on ocean's margin feed;
As many stalls for shaggy goats are rear'd;
As many lodgments for the tusky herd;
Two foreign keepers guard: and here are seen
Twelve herds of goats that graze our utmost green;
To native pastors is their charge assign'd,
And mine the care to feed the bristly kind;
Each day the fattest bleeds of either herd,
All to the suitors' wasteful board preferr'd."
Thus he, benevolent: his unknown guest
With hunger keen devours the savoury feast;
While schemes of vengeance ripen in his breast.
Silent and thoughtful while the board he eyed,
Eumaeus pours on high the purple tide;
The king with smiling looks his joy express'd,
And thus the kind inviting host address'd:

"Say now, what man is he, the man deplored,
So rich, so potent, whom you style your lord?
Late with such affluence and possessions bless'd,
And now in honour's glorious bed at rest.
Whoever was the warrior, he must be
To fame no stranger, nor perhaps to me:
Who (so the gods and so the Fates ordain'd)
Have wander'd many a sea, and many a land."

"Small is the faith the prince and queen ascribe
(Replied Eumaeus) to the wandering tribe.
For needy strangers still to flattery fly,
And want too oft betrays the tongue to lie.
Each vagrant traveller, that touches here,
Deludes with fallacies the royal ear,
To dear remembrance makes his image rise,
And calls the springing sorrows from her eyes.
Such thou mayst be. But he whose name you crave
Moulders in earth, or welters on the wave,
Or food for fish or dogs his relics lie,
Or torn by birds are scatter'd through the sky.
So perish'd he: and left (for ever lost)
Much woe to all, but sure to me the most.
So mild a master never shall I find;
Less dear the parents whom I left behind,
Less soft my mother, less my father kind.
Not with such transport would my eyes run o'er,
Again to hail them in their native shore,
As loved Ulysses once more to embrace,

Restored and breathing in his natal place.
That name for ever dread, yet ever dear,
E'en in his absence I pronounce with fear:
In my respect, he bears a prince's part;
But lives a very brother in my heart."

Thus spoke the faithful swain, and thus rejoin'd
The master of his grief, the man of patient mind:
"Ulysses, friend! shall view his old abodes
(Distrustful as thou art), nor doubt the gods.
Nor speak I rashly, but with faith averr'd,
And what I speak attesting Heaven has heard.
If so, a cloak and vesture be my meed:
Till his return no title shall I plead,
Though certain be my news, and great my need.
Whom want itself can force untruths to tell,
My soul detests him as the gates of hell.

"Thou first be witness, hospitable Jove!
And every god inspiring social love!
And witness every household power that waits,
Guard of these fires, and angel of these gates!
Ere the next moon increase or this decay,
His ancient realms Ulysses shall survey,
In blood and dust each proud oppressor mourn,
And the lost glories of his house return."

"Nor shall that meed be thine, nor ever more
Shall loved Ulysses hail this happy shore.
(Replied Eumaeus): to the present hour
Now turn thy thought, and joys within our power.
From sad reflection let my soul repose;
The name of him awakes a thousand woes.
But guard him, gods! and to these arms restore!
Not his true consort can desire him more;
Not old Laertes, broken with despair:
Not young Telemachus, his blooming heir.
Alas, Telemachus! my sorrows flow
Afresh for thee, my second cause of woe!
Like some fair plant set by a heavenly hand,
He grew, he flourish'd, and he bless'd the land;
In all the youth his father's image shined,
Bright in his person, brighter in his mind.
What man, or god, deceived his better sense,
Far on the swelling seas to wander hence?
To distant Pylos hapless is he gone,
To seek his father's fate and find his own!
For traitors wait his way, with dire design

To end at once the great Arcesian line.
But let us leave him to their wills above;
The fates of men are in the hand of Jove.
And now, my venerable guest! declare
Your name, your parents, and your native air:
Sincere from whence begun, your course relate,
And to what ship I owe the friendly freight?"

Thus he: and thus (with prompt invention bold)
The cautious chief his ready story told.

"On dark reserve what better can prevail,
Or from the fluent tongue produce the tale,
Than when two friends, alone, in peaceful place
Confer, and wines and cates the table grace;
But most, the kind inviter's cheerful face?
Thus might we sit, with social goblets crown'd,
Till the whole circle of the year goes round:
Not the whole circle of the year would close
My long narration of a life of woes.
But such was Heaven's high will! Know then, I came
From sacred Crete, and from a sire of fame:
Castor Hylacides (that name he bore),
Beloved and honour'd in his native shore;
Bless'd in his riches, in his children more.
Sprung of a handmaid, from a bought embrace,
I shared his kindness with his lawful race:
But when that fate, which all must undergo,
From earth removed him to the shades below,
The large domain his greedy sons divide,
And each was portion'd as the lots decide.
Little, alas! was left my wretched share,
Except a house, a covert from the air:
But what by niggard fortune was denied,
A willing widow's copious wealth supplied.
My valour was my plea, a gallant mind,
That, true to honour, never lagg'd behind
(The sex is ever to a soldier kind).
Now wasting years my former strength confound,
And added woes have bow'd me to the ground;
Yet by the stubble you may guess the grain,
And mark the ruins of no vulgar man.
Me, Pallas gave to lead the martial storm,
And the fair ranks of battle to deform;
Me, Mars inspired to turn the foe to flight,
And tempt the secret ambush of the night.
Let ghastly Death in all his forms appear,
I saw him not, it was not mine to fear.

Before the rest I raised my ready steel,
The first I met, he yielded, or he fell.
But works of peace my soul disdain'd to bear,
The rural labour, or domestic care.
To raise the mast, the missile dart to wing,
And send swift arrows from the bounding string,
Were arts the gods made grateful to my mind;
Those gods, who turn (to various ends design'd)
The various thoughts and talents of mankind.
Before the Grecians touch'd the Trojan plain,
Nine times commander or by land or main,
In foreign fields I spread my glory far,
Great in the praise, rich in the spoils of war;
Thence charged with riches, as increased in fame,
To Crete return'd, an honourable name.
But when great Jove that direful war decreed,
Which roused all Greece, and made the mighty bleed;
Our states myself and Idomen employ
To lead their fleets, and carry death to Troy.
Nine years we warr'd; the tenth saw Ilion fall;
Homeward we sail'd, but heaven dispersed us all.
One only month my wife enjoy'd my stay;
So will'd the god who gives and takes away.
Nine ships I mann'd, equipp'd with ready stores,
Intent to voyage to the Aegyptian shores;
In feast and sacrifice my chosen train
Six days consum'd; the seventh we plough'd the main.
Crete's ample fields diminish to our eye;
Before the Boreal blast the vessels fly;
Safe through the level seas we sweep our way;
The steersman governs, and the ships obey.
The fifth fair morn we stem the Aegyptian tide,
And tilting o'er the bay the vessels ride:
To anchor there my fellows I command,
And spies commission to explore the land.
But, sway'd by lust of gain, and headlong will,
The coasts they ravage, and the natives kill.
The spreading clamour to their city flies,
And horse and foot in mingled tumult rise.
The reddening dawn reveals the circling fields,
Horrid with bristly spears, and glancing shields.
Jove thunder'd on their side. Our guilty head
We turn'd to flight; the gathering vengeance spread
On all parts round, and heaps on heaps lie dead.
I then explored my thought, what course to prove
(And sure the thought was dictated by Jove):
Oh, had he left me to that happier doom,
And saved a life of miseries to come!

The radiant helmet from my brows unlaced,
And low on earth my shield and javelin cast,
I meet the monarch with a suppliant's face,
Approach his chariot, and his knees embrace,
He heard, he saved, he placed me at his side;
My state he pitied, and my tears he dried,
Restrain'd the rage the vengeful foe express'd,
And turn'd the deadly weapons from my breast.
Pious! to guard the hospitable rite,
And fearing Jove, whom mercy's works delight.

"In Aegypt thus with peace and plenty bless'd,
I lived (and happy still have lived) a guest.
On seven bright years successive blessings wait;
The next changed all the colour of my fate.
A false Phoenician, of insiduous mind,
Versed in vile arts, and foe to humankind,
With semblance fair invites me to his home;
I seized the proffer (ever fond to roam):
Domestic in his faithless roof I stay'd,
Till the swift sun his annual circle made.
To Libya then he mediates the way;
With guileful art a stranger to betray,
And sell to bondage in a foreign land:
Much doubting, yet compell'd I quit the strand,
Through the mid seas the nimble pinnace sails,
Aloof from Crete, before the northern gales:
But when remote her chalky cliffs we lost,
And far from ken of any other coast,
When all was wild expanse of sea and air,
Then doom'd high Jove due vengeance to prepare.
He hung a night of horrors o'er their head
(The shaded ocean blacken'd as it spread):
He launch'd the fiery bolt: from pole to pole
Broad burst the lightnings, deep the thunders roll;
In giddy rounds the whirling ship is toss'd,
An all in clouds of smothering sulphur lost.
As from a hanging rock's tremendous height,
The sable crows with intercepted flight
Drop endlong; scarr'd, and black with sulphurous hue,
So from the deck are hurl'd the ghastly crew.
Such end the wicked found! but Jove's intent
Was yet to save the oppress'd and innocent.
Placed on the mast (the last resource of life)
With winds and waves I held unequal strife:
For nine long days the billows tilting o'er,
The tenth soft wafts me to Thesprotia's shore.
The monarch's son a shipwreck'd wretch relieved,

The sire with hospitable rites received,
And in his palace like a brother placed,
With gifts of price and gorgeous garments graced
While here I sojourn'd, oft I heard the fame
How late Ulysses to the country came.
How loved, how honour'd in this court he stay'd,
And here his whole collected treasure laid;
I saw myself the vast unnumber'd store
Of steel elaborate, and refulgent ore,
And brass high heap'd amidst the regal dome;
Immense supplies for ages yet to come!
Meantime he voyaged to explore the will
Of Jove, on high Dodona's holy hill,
What means might best his safe return avail,
To come in pomp, or bear a secret sail?
Full oft has Phidon, whilst he pour'd the wine,
Attesting solemn all the powers divine,
That soon Ulysses would return, declared
The sailors waiting, and the ships prepared.
But first the king dismiss'd me from his shores,
For fair Dulichium crown'd with fruitful stores;
To good Acastus' friendly care consign'd:
But other counsels pleased the sailors' mind:
New frauds were plotted by the faithless train,
And misery demands me once again.
Soon as remote from shore they plough the wave,
With ready hands they rush to seize their slave;
Then with these tatter'd rags they wrapp'd me round
(Stripp'd of my own), and to the vessel bound.
At eve, at Ithaca's delightful land
The ship arriv'd: forth issuing on the sand,
They sought repast; while to the unhappy kind,
The pitying gods themselves my chains unbind.
Soft I descended, to the sea applied
My naked breast, and shot along the tide.
Soon pass'd beyond their sight, I left the flood,
And took the spreading shelter of the wood.
Their prize escaped the faithless pirates mourn'd;
But deem'd inquiry vain, and to their ships return'd.
Screen'd by protecting gods from hostile eyes,
They led me to a good man and a wise,
To live beneath thy hospitable care,
And wait the woes Heaven dooms me yet to bear."

"Unhappy guest! whose sorrows touch my mind!
(Thus good Eumaeus with a sigh rejoin'd,)
For real sufferings since I grieve sincere,
Check not with fallacies the springing tear:

Nor turn the passion into groundless joy
For him whom Heaven has destined to destroy.
Oh! had he perish'd on some well-fought day,
Or in his friend's embraces died away!
That grateful Greece with streaming eyes might raise
Historic marbles to record his praise;
His praise, eternal on the faithful stone,
Had with transmissive honours graced his son.
Now, snatch'd by harpies to the dreary coast,
Sunk is the hero, and his glory lost!
While pensive in this solitary den,
Far from gay cities and the ways of men,
I linger life; nor to the court repair,
But when my constant queen commands my care;
Or when, to taste her hospitable board,
Some guest arrives, with rumours of her lord;
And these indulge their want, and those their woe,
And here the tears and there the goblets flow.
By many such have I been warn'd; but chief
By one Aetolian robb'd of all belief,
Whose hap it was to this our roof to roam,
For murder banish'd from his native home.
He swore, Ulysses on the coast of Crete
Stay'd but a season to refit his fleet;
A few revolving months should waft him o'er,
Fraught with bold warriors, and a boundless store
O thou! whom age has taught to understand,
And Heaven has guided with a favouring hand!
On god or mortal to obtrude a lie
Forbear, and dread to flatter as to die.
Nor for such ends my house and heart are free,
But dear respect to Jove, and charity."

"And why, O swain of unbelieving mind!
(Thus quick replied the wisest of mankind)
Doubt you my oath? yet more my faith to try,
A solemn compact let us ratify,
And witness every power that rules the sky!
If here Ulysses from his labours rest,
Be then my prize a tunic and a vest;
And where my hopes invite me, straight transport
In safety to Dulichium's friendly court.
But if he greets not thy desiring eye,
Hurl me from yon dread precipice on high:
The due reward of fraud and perjury."

"Doubtless, O guest! great laud and praise were mine
(Replied the swain, for spotless faith divine),

If after social rites and gifts bestow'd,
I stain'd my hospitable hearth with blood.
How would the gods my righteous toils succeed,
And bless the hand that made a stranger bleed?
No more—the approaching hours of silent night
First claim refection, then to rest invite;
Beneath our humble cottage let us haste,
And here, unenvied, rural dainties taste."

Thus communed these; while to their lowly dome
The full-fed swine return'd with evening home;
Compell'd, reluctant, to their several sties,
With din obstreperous, and ungrateful cries.
Then to the slaves: "Now from the herd the best
Select in honour of our foreign guest:
With him let us the genial banquet share,
For great and many are the griefs we bear;
While those who from our labours heap their board
Blaspheme their feeder, and forget their lord."

Thus speaking, with despatchful hand he took
A weighty axe, and cleft the solid oak;
This on the earth he piled; a boar full fed,
Of five years' age, before the pile was led:
The swain, whom acts of piety delight,
Observant of the gods, begins the rite;
First shears the forehead of the bristly boar,
And suppliant stands, invoking every power
To speed Ulysses to his native shore.
A knotty stake then aiming at his head,
Down dropped he groaning, and the spirit fled.
The scorching flames climb round on every side;
Then the singed members they with skill divide;
On these, in rolls of fat involved with art,
The choicest morsels lay from every part.
Some in the flames bestrew'd with flour they threw;
Some cut in fragments from the forks they drew:
These while on several tables they dispose.
A priest himself the blameless rustic rose;
Expert the destined victim to dispart
In seven just portions, pure of hand and heart.
One sacred to the nymphs apart they lay:
Another to the winged sons of May;
The rural tribe in common share the rest,
The king the chine, the honour of the feast,
Who sate delighted at his servant's board;
The faithful servant joy'd his unknown lord.
"Oh be thou dear (Ulysses cried) to Jove,

As well thou claim'st a grateful stranger's love!"

"Be then thy thanks (the bounteous swain replied)
Enjoyment of the good the gods provide.
From God's own hand descend our joys and woes;
These he decrees, and he but suffers those:
All power is his, and whatsoe'er he wills,
The will itself, omnipotent, fulfils."
This said, the first-fruits to the gods he gave;
Then pour'd of offer'd wine the sable wave:
In great Ulysses' hand he placed the bowl,
He sate, and sweet refection cheer'd his soul.
The bread from canisters Mesaulius gave
(Eumaeus' proper treasure bought this slave,
And led from Taphos, to attend his board,
A servant added to his absent lord);
His task it was the wheaten loaves to lay,
And from the banquet take the bowls away.
And now the rage of hunger was repress'd,
And each betakes him to his couch to rest.

Now came the night, and darkness cover'd o'er
The face of things; the winds began to roar;
The driving storm the watery west-wind pours,
And Jove descends in deluges of showers.
Studious of rest and warmth, Ulysses lies,
Foreseeing from the first the storm would rise
In mere necessity of coat and cloak,
With artful preface to his host he spoke:
"Hear me, my friends! who this good banquet grace;
'Tis sweet to play the fool in time and place,
And wine can of their wits the wise beguile,
Make the sage frolic, and the serious smile,
The grave in merry measures frisk about,
And many a long-repented word bring out.
Since to be talkative I now commence,
Let wit cast off the sullen yoke of sense.
Once I was strong (would Heaven restore those days!)
And with my betters claim'd a share of praise.
Ulysses, Menelaus, led forth a band,
And join'd me with them ('twas their own command);
A deathful ambush for the foe to lay,
Beneath Troy walls by night we took our way:
There, clad in arms, along the marshes spread,
We made the osier-fringed bank our bed.
Full soon the inclemency of heaven I feel,
Nor had these shoulders covering, but of steel.
Sharp blew the north; snow whitening all the fields

Froze with the blast, and gathering glazed our shields.
There all but I, well fenced with cloak and vest,
Lay cover'd by their ample shields at rest.
Fool that I was! I left behind my own,
The skill of weather and of winds unknown,
And trusted to my coat and shield alone!
When now was wasted more than half the night,
And the stars faded at approaching light,
Sudden I jogg'd Ulysses, who was laid
Fast by my side, and shivering thus I said:

"'Here longer in this field I cannot lie;
The winter pinches, and with cold I die,
And die ashamed (O wisest of mankind),
The only fool who left his cloak behind.'

"He thought and answer'd: hardly waking yet,
Sprung in his mind a momentary wit
(That wit, which or in council or in fight,
Still met the emergence, and determined right).
'Hush thee (he cried, soft whispering in my ear),
Speak not a word, lest any Greek may hear'—
And then (supporting on his arm his head),
'Hear me, companions! (thus aloud he said:)
Methinks too distant from the fleet we lie:
E'en now a vision stood before my eye,
And sure the warning vision was from high:
Let from among us some swift courier rise,
Haste to the general, and demand supplies.'

"Up started Thoas straight, Andraemon's son,
Nimbly he rose, and cast his garment down!
Instant, the racer vanish'd off the ground;
That instant in his cloak I wrapp'd me round:
And safe I slept, till brightly-dawning shone
The morn conspicuous on her golden throne.

"Oh were my strength as then, as then my age!
Some friend would fence me from the winter's rage.
Yet, tatter'd as I look, I challenged then
The honours and the offices of men:
Some master, or some servant would allow
A cloak and vest—but I am nothing now!"

"Well hast thou spoke (rejoin'd the attentive swain):
Thy lips let fall no idle word or vain!
Nor garment shalt thou want, nor aught beside,
Meet for the wandering suppliant to provide.

But in the morning take thy clothes again,
For here one vest suffices every swain:
No change of garments to our hinds is known;
But when return'd, the good Ulysses' son
With better hand shall grace with fit attires
His guest, and send thee where thy soul desires."

The honest herdsman rose, as this he said,
And drew before the hearth the stranger's bed;
The fleecy spoils of sheep, a goat's rough hide
He spreads; and adds a mantle thick and wide;
With store to heap above him, and below,
And guard each quarter as the tempests blow.
There lay the king, and all the rest supine;
All, but the careful master of the swine:
Forth hasted he to tend his bristly care;
Well arm'd, and fenced against nocturnal air:
His weighty falchion o'er his shoulder tied:
His shaggy cloak a mountain goat supplied:
With his broad spear the dread of dogs and men,
He seeks his lodging in the rocky den.
There to the tusky herd he bends his way,
Where, screen'd from Boreas, high o'erarch'd they lay.

BOOK XV

ARGUMENT

THE RETURN OF TELEMACHUS

The goddess Minerva commands Telemachus in a vision to return to Ithaca. Pisistratus and he take leave
of Menelaus, and arrive at Pylos, where they part: and Telemachus sets sail, after having received on
board Theoclymenus the soothsayer. The scene then changes to the cottage of Eumaeus, who
entertains Ulysses with a recital of his adventures. In the meantime Telemachus arrives on the coast,
and sending the vessel to the town, proceeds by himself to the lodge of Eumaeus.

Now had Minerva reach'd those ample plains,
Famed for the dance, where Menelaus reigns:
Anxious she flies to great Ulysses' heir,
His instant voyage challenged all her care.
Beneath the royal portico display'd,
With Nestor's son Telemachus was laid:
In sleep profound the son of Nestor lies;
Not thine, Ulysses! Care unseal'd his eyes:
Restless he grieved, with various fears oppress'd,
And all thy fortunes roll'd within his breast.

When, "O Telemachus! (the goddess said)
Too long in vain, too widely hast thou stray'd,
Thus leaving careless thy paternal right
The robbers' prize, the prey to lawless might.
On fond pursuits neglectful while you roam,
E'en now the hand of rapine sacks the dome.
Hence to Atrides; and his leave implore
To launch thy vessel for thy natal shore;
Fly, whilst thy mother virtuous yet withstands
Her kindred's wishes, and her sire's commands;
Through both, Eurymachus pursues the dame,
And with the noblest gifts asserts his claim.
Hence, therefore, while thy stores thy own remain;
Thou know'st the practice of the female train,
Lost in the children of the present spouse,
They slight the pledges of their former vows;
Their love is always with the lover past;
Still the succeeding flame expels the last.
Let o'er thy house some chosen maid preside,
Till Heaven decrees to bless thee in a bride.
But now thy more attentive ears incline,
Observe the warnings of a power divine;
For thee their snares the suitor lords shall lay
In Samos' sands, or straits of Ithaca;
To seize thy life shall lurk the murderous band,
Ere yet thy footsteps press thy native land.
No!—sooner far their riot and their lust
All-covering earth shall bury deep in dust!
Then distant from the scatter'd islands steer,
Nor let the night retard thy full career;
Thy heavenly guardian shall instruct the gales
To smooth thy passage and supply thy sails:
And when at Ithaca thy labour ends,
Send to the town the vessel with thy friends;
But seek thou first the master of the swine
(For still to thee his loyal thoughts incline);
There pass the night: while he his course pursues
To bring Penelope the wish'd-for news,
That thou, safe sailing from the Pylian strand,
Art come to bless her in thy native land."
Thus spoke the goddess, and resumed her flight
To the pure regions of eternal light,
Meanwhile Pisistratus he gently shakes,
And with these words the slumbering youth awakes:

"Rise, son of Nestor; for the road prepare,
And join the harness'd coursers to the car."

"What cause (he cried) can justify our flight
To tempt the dangers of forbidding night?
Here wait we rather, till approaching day
Shall prompt our speed, and point the ready way.
Nor think of flight before the Spartan king
Shall bid farewell, and bounteous presents bring;
Gifts, which to distant ages safely stored,
The sacred act of friendship shall record."

Thus he. But when the dawn bestreak'd the east,
The king from Helen rose, and sought his guest.
As soon as his approach the hero knew,
The splendid mantle round him first he threw,
Then o'er his ample shoulders whirl'd the cloak,
Respectful met the monarch, and bespoke:

"Hail, great Atrides, favour'd of high Jove!
Let not thy friends in vain for licence move.
Swift let us measure back the watery way,
Nor check our speed, impatient of delay."

"If with desire so strong thy bosom glows,
Ill (said the king) should I thy wish oppose;
For oft in others freely I reprove
The ill-timed efforts of officious love;
Who love too much, hate in the like extreme,
And both the golden mean alike condemn.
Alike he thwarts the hospitable end,
Who drives the free, or stays the hasty friend:
True friendship's laws are by this rule express'd,
Welcome the coming, speed the parting guest.
Yet, stay, my friends, and in your chariot take
The noblest presents that our love can make;
Meantime commit we to our women's care
Some choice domestic viands to prepare;
The traveller, rising from the banquet gay,
Eludes the labours of the tedious way,
Then if a wider course shall rather please,
Through spacious Argos and the realms of Greece,
Atrides in his chariot shall attend;
Himself thy convoy to each royal friend.
No prince will let Ulysses' heir remove
Without some pledge, some monument of love:
These will the caldron, these the tripod give;
From those the well-pair'd mules we shall receive,
Or bowl emboss'd whose golden figures live."

To whom the youth, for prudence famed, replied:

"O monarch, care of heaven! thy people's pride!
No friend in Ithaca my place supplies,
No powerful hands are there, no watchful eyes:
My stores exposed and fenceless house demand
The speediest succour from my guardian hand;
Lest, in a search too anxious and too vain,
Of one lost joy, I lose what yet remain."

His purpose when the generous warrior heard,
He charged the household cates to be prepared.
Now with the dawn, from his adjoining home,
Was Boethoedes Eteoneus come;
Swift at the word he forms the rising blaze,
And o'er the coals the smoking fragments lays.
Meantime the king, his son, and Helen went
Where the rich wardrobe breathed a costly scent;
The king selected from the glittering rows
A bowl; the prince a silver beaker chose.
The beauteous queen revolved with careful eyes
Her various textures of unnumber'd dyes,
And chose the largest; with no vulgar art
Her own fair hands embroider'd every part;
Beneath the rest it lay divinely bright,
Like radiant Hesper o'er the gems of night,
Then with each gift they hasten'd to their guest,
And thus the king Ulysses' heir address'd:
"Since fix'd are thy resolves, may thundering Jove
With happiest omens thy desires approve!
This silver bowl, whose costly margins shine
Enchased with old, this valued gift be thine;
To me this present, of Vulcanian frame,
From Sidon's hospitable monarch came;
To thee we now consign the precious load,
The pride of kings, and labour of a god."

Then gave the cup, while Megapenthe brought
The silver vase with living sculpture wrought.
The beauteous queen, advancing next, display'd
The shining veil, and thus endearing said:

"Accept, dear youth, this monument of love,
Long since, in better days, by Helen wove:
Safe in thy mother's care the vesture lay,
To deck thy bride and grace thy nuptial day.
Meantime may'st thou with happiest speed regain
Thy stately palace, and thy wide domain."

She said, and gave the veil; with grateful look

The prince the variegated present took.
And now, when through the royal dome they pass'd,
High on a throne the king each stranger placed.
A golden ewer the attendant damsel brings,
Replete with water from the crystal springs;
With copious streams the shining vase supplies
A silver layer of capacious size.
They wash. The tables in fair order spread,
The glittering canisters are crown'd with bread;
Viands of various kinds allure the taste,
Of choicest sort and savour; rich repast!
Whilst Eteoneus portions out the shares
Atrides' son the purple draught prepares,
And now (each sated with the genial feast,
And the short rage of thirst and hunger ceased)
Ulysses' son, with his illustrious friend,
The horses join, the polish'd car ascend,
Along the court the fiery steeds rebound,
And the wide portal echoes to the sound.
The king precedes; a bowl with fragrant wine
(Libation destined to the powers divine)
His right hand held: before the steed he stands,
Then, mix'd with prayers, he utters these commands:

"Farewell, and prosper, youths! let Nestor know
What grateful thoughts still in this bosom glow,
For all the proofs of his paternal care,
Through the long dangers of the ten years' war."
"Ah! doubt not our report (the prince rejoin'd)
Of all the virtues of thy generous mind.
And oh! return'd might we Ulysses meet!
To him thy presents show, thy words repeat:
How will each speech his grateful wonder raise!
How will each gift indulge us in thy praise!"

Scarce ended thus the prince, when on the right
Advanced the bird of Jove: auspicious sight!
A milk-white fowl his clinching talons bore,
With care domestic pampered at the floor.
Peasants in vain with threatening cries pursue,
In solemn speed the bird majestic flew
Full dexter to the car; the prosperous sight
Fill'd every breast with wonder and delight.

But Nestor's son the cheerful silence broke,
And in these words the Spartan chief bespoke:
"Say if to us the gods these omens send,
Or fates peculiar to thyself portend?"

Whilst yet the monarch paused, with doubts oppress'd
The beauteous queen relieved his labouring breast:
"Hear me (she cried), to whom the gods have given
To read this sign, and mystic sense of heaven,
As thus the plumy sovereign of the air
Left on the mountain's brow his callow care,
And wander'd through the wide ethereal way
To pour his wrath on yon luxurious prey;
So shall thy godlike father, toss'd in vain
Through all the dangers of the boundless main,
Arrive (or if perchance already come)
From slaughter'd gluttons to release the dome."

"Oh! if this promised bliss by thundering Jove
(The prince replied) stand fix'd in fate above;
To thee, as to some god, I'll temples raise.
And crown thy altars with the costly blaze."

He said; and bending o'er his chariot, flung
Athwart the fiery steeds the smarting thong;
The bounding shafts upon the harness play,
Till night descending intercepts the way.
To Diocles at Pherae they repair,
Whose boasted sire was sacred Alpheus' heir;
With him all night the youthful stranger stay'd,
Nor found the hospitable rites unpaid,
But soon as morning from her orient bed
Had tinged the mountains with her earliest red,
They join'd the steeds, and on the chariot sprung,
The brazen portals in their passage rung.

To Pylos soon they came; when thus begun
To Nestor's heir Ulysses' godlike son:

"Let not Pisistratus in vain be press'd,
Nor unconsenting hear his friend's request;
His friend by long hereditary claim,
In toils his equal, and in years the same.
No farther from our vessel, I implore,
The courses drive; but lash them to the shore.
Too long thy father would his friend detain;
I dread his proffer'd kindness urged in vain."

The hero paused, and ponder'd this request,
While love and duty warr'd within his breast.
At length resolved, he turn'd his ready hand,
And lash'd his panting coursers to the strand.

There, while within the poop with care he stored
The regal presents of the Spartan lord,
"With speed begone (said he); call every mate,
Ere yet to Nestor I the tale relate:
'Tis true, the fervour of his generous heart
Brooks no repulse, nor couldst thou soon depart:
Himself will seek thee here, nor wilt thou find,
In words alone, the Pylian monarch kind.
But when, arrived, he thy return shall know
How will his breast with honest fury glow!"
This said, the sounding strokes his horses fire,
And soon he reached the palace of his sire.

"Now (cried Telemachus) with speedy care
Hoist every sail, and every oar prepare."
Swift as the word his willing mates obey,
And seize their seats, impatient for the sea.

Meantime the prince with sacrifice adores
Minerva, and her guardian aid implores;
When lo! a wretch ran breathless to the shore,
New from his crime; and reeking yet with gore.
A seer he was, from great Melampus sprung,
Melampus, who in Pylos flourish'd long,
Till, urged by wrongs, a foreign realm he chose,
Far from the hateful cause of all his woes.
Neleus his treasures one long year detains,
As long he groan'd in Philacus' chains:
Meantime, what anguish and what rage combined
For lovely Pero rack'd his labouring mind!
Yet 'scaped he death; and vengeful of his wrong
To Pylos drove the lowing herds along:
Then (Neleus vanquish'd, and consign'd the fair
To Bias' arms) he so sought a foreign air;
Argos the rich for his retreat he chose,
There form'd his empire; there his palace rose.
From him Antiphates and Mantius came:
The first begot Oicleus great in fame,
And he Amphiaraus, immortal name!
The people's saviour, and divinely wise,
Beloved by Jove, and him who gilds the skies;
Yet short his date of life! by female pride he dies.
From Mantius Clitus, whom Aurora's love
Snatch'd for his beauty to the thrones above;
And Polyphides, on whom Phoebus shone
With fullest rays, Amphiaraus now gone;
In Hyperesia's groves he made abode,
And taught mankind the counsels of the god.

From him sprung Theoclymenus, who found
(The sacred wine yet foaming on the ground)
Telemachus: whom, as to Heaven he press'd
His ardent vows, the stranger thus address'd:

"O thou! that dost thy happy course prepare
With pure libations and with solemn prayer:
By that dread power to whom thy vows are paid;
By all the lives of these; thy own dear head,
Declare sincerely to no foe's demand
Thy name, thy lineage, and paternal land."

"Prepare, then (said Telemachus), to know
A tale from falsehood free, not free from woe.
From Ithaca, of royal birth I came,
And great Ulysses (ever honour'd name!)
Once was my sire, though now, for ever lost,
In Stygian gloom he glides a pensive ghost!
Whose fate inquiring through the world we rove;
The last, the wretched proof of filial love."

The stranger then: "Nor shall I aught conceal,
But the dire secret of my fate reveal.
Of my own tribe an Argive wretch I slew;
Whose powerful friends the luckless deed pursue
With unrelenting rage, and force from home
The blood-stain'd exile, ever doom'd to roam.
But bear, oh bear me o'er yon azure flood;
Receive the suppliant! spare my destined blood!"

"Stranger (replied the prince) securely rest
Affianced in our faith; henceforth our guest."
Thus affable, Ulysses' godlike heir
Takes from the stranger's hand the glittering spear:
He climbs the ship, ascends the stern with haste
And by his side the guest accepted placed.
The chief his order gives: the obedient band,
With due observance wait the chief's command:
With speed the mast they rear, with speed unbind
The spacious sheet, and stretch it to the wind.
Minerva calls; the ready gales obey
With rapid speed to whirl them o'er the sea.
Crunus they pass'd, next Chalcis roll'd away,
With thickening darkness closed the doubtful day;
The silver Phaea's glittering rills they lost,
And skimm'd along by Elis' sacred coast.
Then cautious through the rocky reaches wind,
And turning sudden, shun the death design'd.

Meantime, the king, Eumaeus, and the rest,
Sate in the cottage, at their rural feast:
The banquet pass'd, and satiate every man,
To try his host, Ulysses thus began:

"Yet one night more, my friends, indulge your guest;
The last I purpose in your walls to rest:
To-morrow for myself I must provide,
And only ask your counsel, and a guide;
Patient to roam the street, by hunger led,
And bless the friendly hand that gives me bread.
There in Ulysses' roof I may relate
Ulysses' wanderings to his royal mate;
Or, mingling with the suitors' haughty train,
Not undeserving some support obtain.
Hermes to me his various gifts imparts.
Patron of industry and manual arts:
Few can with me in dexterous works contend,
The pyre to build, the stubborn oak to rend;
To turn the tasteful viand o'er the flame;
Or foam the goblet with a purple stream.
Such are the tasks of men of mean estate,
Whom fortune dooms to serve the rich and great."

"Alas! (Eumaeus with a sigh rejoin'd).
How sprung a thought so monstrous in thy mind?
If on that godless race thou would'st attend,
Fate owes thee sure a miserable end!
Their wrongs and blasphemies ascend the sky,
And pull descending vengeance from on high.
Not such, my friend, the servants of their feast:
A blooming train in rich embroidery dress'd,
With earth's whole tribute the bright table bends,
And smiling round celestial youth attends.
Stay, then: no eye askance beholds thee here;
Sweet is thy converse to each social ear;
Well pleased, and pleasing, in our cottage rest,
Till good Telemachus accepts his guest
With genial gifts, and change of fair attires,
And safe conveys thee where thy soul desires."

To him the man of woes; "O gracious Jove!
Reward this stranger's hospitable love!
Who knows the son of sorrow to relieve,
Cheers the sad heart, nor lets affliction grieve.
Of all the ills unhappy mortals know,
A life of wanderings is the greatest woe;

On all their weary ways wait care and pain,
And pine and penury, a meagre train.
To such a man since harbour you afford,
Relate the farther fortunes of your lord;
What cares his mother's tender breast engage,
And sire forsaken on the verge of age;
Beneath the sun prolong they yet their breath,
Or range the house of darkness and of death?"

To whom the swain: "Attend what you enquire;
Laertes lives, the miserable sire,
Lives, but implores of every power to lay
The burden down, and wishes for the day.
Torn from his offspring in the eve of life,
Torn from the embraces of his tender wife,
Sole, and all comfortless, he wastes away
Old age, untimely posting ere his day.
She too, sad mother! for Ulysses lost
Pined out her bloom, and vanish'd to a ghost;
(So dire a fate, ye righteous gods! avert
From every friendly, every feeling heart!)
While yet she was, though clouded o'er with grief.
Her pleasing converse minister'd relief:
With Climene, her youngest daughter, bred,
One roof contain'd us, and one table fed.
But when the softly-stealing pace of time
Crept on from childhood into youthful prime,
To Samos' isle she sent the wedded fair;
Me to the fields; to tend the rural care;
Array'd in garments her own hands had wove,
Nor less the darling object of her love.
Her hapless death my brighter days o'ercast,
Yet Providence deserts me not at last;
My present labours food and drink procure,
And more, the pleasure to relieve the poor.
Small is the comfort from the queen to hear
Unwelcome news, or vex the royal ear;
Blank and discountenanced the servants stand,
Nor dare to question where the proud command;
No profit springs beneath usurping powers;
Want feeds not there where luxury devours,
Nor harbours charity where riot reigns:
Proud are the lords, and wretched are the swains."

The suffering chief at this began to melt;
And, "O Eumaeus! thou (he cries) hast felt
The spite of fortune too! her cruel hand
Snatch'd thee an infant from thy native land!

Snatch'd from thy parents' arms, thy parents' eyes,
To early wants! a man of miseries!
The whole sad story, from its first, declare:
Sunk the fair city by the rage of war,
Where once thy parents dwelt? or did they keep,
In humbler life, the lowing herds and sheep?
So left perhaps to tend the fleecy train,
Rude pirates seized, and shipp'd thee o'er the main?
Doom'd a fair prize to grace some prince's board,
The worthy purchase of a foreign lord."

"If then my fortunes can delight my friend,
A story fruitful of events attend:
Another's sorrow may thy ears enjoy,
And wine the lengthen'd intervals employ.
Long nights the now declining year bestows;
A part we consecrate to soft repose,
A part in pleasing talk we entertain;
For too much rest itself becomes a pain.
Let those, whom sleep invites, the call obey,
Their cares resuming with the dawning day:
Here let us feast, and to the feast be join'd
Discourse, the sweeter banquet of the mind;
Review the series of our lives, and taste
The melancholy joy of evils pass'd:
For he who much has suffer'd, much will know,
And pleased remembrance builds delight on woe.

"Above Ortygia lies an isle of fame,
Far hence remote, and Syria is the name
(There curious eyes inscribed with wonder trace
The sun's diurnal, and his annual race);
Not large, but fruitful; stored with grass to keep
The bellowing oxen and the bleating sheep;
Her sloping hills the mantling vines adorn,
And her rich valleys wave with golden corn.
No want, no famine, the glad natives know,
Nor sink by sickness to the shades below;
But when a length of years unnerves the strong,
Apollo comes, and Cynthia comes along.
They bend the silver bow with tender skill,
And, void of pain, the silent arrows kill.
Two equal tribes this fertile land divide,
Where two fair cities rise with equal pride.
But both in constant peace one prince obey,
And Ctesius there, my father, holds the sway.
Freighted, it seems, with toys of every sort,
A ship of Sidon anchor'd in our port;

What time it chanced the palace entertain'd,
Skill'd in rich works, a woman of their land:
This nymph, where anchor'd the Phoenician train,
To wash her robes descending to the main,
A smooth tongued sailor won her to his mind
(For love deceives the best of womankind).
A sudden trust from sudden liking grew;
She told her name, her race, and all she knew,
'I too (she cried) from glorious Sidon came,
My father Arybas, of wealthy fame:
But, snatch'd by pirates from my native place,
The Taphians sold me to this man's embrace.'

"'Haste then (the false designing youth replied),
Haste to thy country; love shall be thy guide;
Haste to thy father's house, thy father's breast,
For still he lives, and lives with riches blest.'

"'Swear first (she cried), ye sailors! to restore
A wretch in safety to her native shore.'
Swift as she ask'd, the ready sailors swore.
She then proceeds: 'Now let our compact made
Be nor by signal nor by word betray'd,
Nor near me any of your crew descried,
By road frequented, or by fountain side.
Be silence still our guard. The monarch's spies
(For watchful age is ready to surmise)
Are still at hand; and this, revealed, must be
Death to yourselves, eternal chains to me.
Your vessel loaded, and your traffic pass'd,
Despatch a wary messenger with haste;
Then gold and costly treasures will I bring,
And more, the infant offspring of the king.
Him, child-like wandering forth, I'll lead away
(A noble prize!) and to your ship convey.'

"Thus spoke the dame, and homeward took the road.
A year they traffic, and their vessel load.
Their stores complete, and ready now to weigh,
A spy was sent their summons to convey:
An artist to my father's palace came,
With gold and amber chains, elaborate frame:
Each female eye the glittering links employ;
They turn, review, and cheapen every toy.
He took the occasion, as they stood intent,
Gave her the sign, and to his vessel went.
She straight pursued, and seized my willing arm;
I follow'd, smiling, innocent of harm.

Three golden goblets in the porch she found
(The guests not enter'd, but the table crown'd);
Hid in her fraudful bosom these she bore:
Now set the sun, and darken'd all the shore.
Arriving then, where tilting on the tides
Prepared to launch the freighted vessel rides,
Aboard they heave us, mount their decks, and sweep
With level oar along the glassy deep.
Six calmy days and six smooth nights we sail,
And constant Jove supplied the gentle gale.
The seventh, the fraudful wretch (no cause descried),
Touch'd by Diana's vengeful arrow, died.
Down dropp'd the caitiff-corse, a worthless load,
Down to the deep; there roll'd, the future food
Of fierce sea-wolves, and monsters of the flood.
An helpless infant I remain'd behind;
Thence borne to Ithaca by wave and wind;
Sold to Laertes by divine command,
And now adopted to a foreign land."

To him the king: "Reciting thus thy cares,
My secret soul in all thy sorrow shares;
But one choice blessing (such is Jove's high will)
Has sweeten'd all thy bitter draught of ill:
Torn from thy country to no hapless end,
The gods have, in a master, given a friend.
Whatever frugal nature needs is thine
(For she needs little), daily bread and wine.
While I, so many wanderings past, and woes,
Live but on what thy poverty bestows."

So passed in pleasing dialogue away
The night; then down to short repose they lay;
Till radiant rose the messenger of day.
While in the port of Ithaca, the band
Of young Telemachus approach'd the land;
Their sails they loosed, they lash'd the mast aside,
And cast their anchors, and the cables tied:
Then on the breezy shore, descending, join
In grateful banquet o'er the rosy wine.
When thus the prince: "Now each his course pursue;
I to the fields, and to the city you.
Long absent hence, I dedicate this day
My swains to visit, and the works survey.
Expect me with the morn, to pay the skies
Our debt of safe return in feast and sacrifice."

Then Theoclymenus: "But who shall lend,

Meantime, protection to thy stranger friend?
Straight to the queen and palace shall I fly,
Or yet more distant, to some lord apply?"

The prince return'd: "Renown'd in days of yore
Has stood our father's hospitable door;
No other roof a stranger should receive,
No other hands than ours the welcome give.
But in my absence riot fills the place,
Nor bears the modest queen a stranger's face;
From noiseful revel far remote she flies,
But rarely seen, or seen with weeping eyes.
No—let Eurymachus receive my guest,
Of nature courteous, and by far the best;
He woos the queen with more respectful flame,
And emulates her former husband's fame,
With what success, 'tis Jove's alone to know,
And the hoped nuptials turn to joy or woe."

Thus speaking, on the right up-soar'd in air
The hawk, Apollo's swift-wing'd messenger:
His dreadful pounces tore a trembling dove;
The clotted feathers, scatter'd from above,
Between the hero and the vessel pour
Thick plumage mingled with a sanguine shower.

The observing augur took the prince aside,
Seized by the hand, and thus prophetic cried:
"Yon bird, that dexter cuts the aerial road,
Rose ominous, nor flies without a god:
No race but thine shall Ithaca obey,
To thine, for ages, Heaven decrees the sway."

"Succeed the omens, gods! (the youth rejoin'd:)
Soon shall my bounties speak a grateful mind,
And soon each envied happiness attend
The man who calls Telemachus his friend."
Then to Peiraeus: "Thou whom time has proved
A faithful servant, by thy prince beloved!
Till we returning shall our guest demand,
Accept this charge with honour, at our hand."

To this Peiraeus: "Joyful I obey,
Well pleased the hospitable rites to pay.
The presence of thy guest shall best reward
(If long thy stay) the absence of my lord."

With that, their anchors he commands to weigh,

Mount the tall bark, and launch into the sea.
All with obedient haste forsake the shores,
And, placed in order, spread their equal oars.
Then from the deck the prince his sandals takes;
Poised in his hand the pointed javelin shakes.
They part; while, lessening from the hero's view
Swift to the town the well-row'd galley flew:
The hero trod the margin of the main,
And reach'd the mansion of his faithful swain.

BOOK XVI

ARGUMENT

THE DISCOVERY OF ULYSSES TO TELEMACHUS

Telemachus arriving at the lodge of Eumaeus, sends him to carry Penelope the news of his return.
Minerva appearing to Ulysses, commands him to discover himself to his son. The princes, who had lain
in ambush to intercept Telemachus in his way, their project being defeated, return to Ithaca.

Soon as the morning blush'd along the plains,
Ulysses, and the monarch of the swains,
Awake the sleeping fires, their meals prepare,
And forth to pasture send the bristly care.
The prince's near approach the dogs descry,
And fawning round his feet confess their joy.
Their gentle blandishment the king survey'd,
Heard his resounding step, and instant said:

"Some well-known friend, Eumaeus, bends this way;
His steps I hear; the dogs familiar play."

While yet he spoke, the prince advancing drew
Nigh to the lodge, and now appear'd in view.
Transported from his seat Eumaeus sprung,
Dropp'd the full bowl, and round his bosom hung;
Kissing his cheek, his hand, while from his eye
The tears rain'd copious in a shower of joy,
As some fond sire who ten long winters grieves,
From foreign climes an only son receives
(Child of his age), with strong paternal joy,
Forward he springs, and clasps the favourite boy:
So round the youth his arms Eumaeus spread,
As if the grave had given him from the dead.

"And is it thou? my ever-dear delight!

Oh, art thou come to bless my longing sight?
Never, I never hoped to view this day,
When o'er the waves you plough'd the desperate way.
Enter, my child! Beyond my hopes restored,
Oh give these eyes to feast upon their lord.
Enter, oh seldom seen! for lawless powers
Too much detain thee from these sylvan bowers,"
The prince replied: "Eumaeus, I obey;
To seek thee, friend, I hither took my way.
But say, if in the court the queen reside
Severely chaste, or if commenced a bride?"

Thus he; and thus the monarch of the swains:
"Severely chaste Penelope remains;
But, lost to every joy, she wastes the day
In tedious cares, and weeps the night away."

He ended, and (receiving as they pass
The javelin pointed with a star of brass),
They reach'd the dome; the dome with marble shined.
His seat Ulysses to the prince resign'd.
"Not so (exclaims the prince with decent grace)
For me, this house shall find an humbler place:
To usurp the honours due to silver hairs
And reverend strangers modest youth forbears."
Instant the swain the spoils of beasts supplies,
And bids the rural throne with osiers rise.
There sate the prince: the feast Eumaeus spread,
And heap'd the shining canisters with bread.
Thick o'er the board the plenteous viands lay,
The frugal remnants of the former day.
Then in a bowl he tempers generous wines,
Around whose verge a mimic ivy twines.
And now, the rage of thirst and hunger fled,
Thus young Ulysses to Eumaeus said:

"Whence, father, from what shore this stranger, say?
What vessel bore him o'er the watery way?
To human step our land impervious lies,
And round the coast circumfluent oceans rise."

The swain returns: "A tale of sorrows hear:
In spacious Crete he drew his natal air;
Long doom'd to wander o'er the land and main,
For Heaven has wove his thread of life with pain.
Half breathless 'scaping to the land he flew
From Thesprot mariners, a murderous crew.
To thee, my son, the suppliant I resign;

I gave him my protection, grant him thine."

"Hard task (he cries) thy virtue gives thy friend,
Willing to aid, unable to defend.
Can strangers safely in the court reside,
'Midst the swell'd insolence of lust and pride?
E'en I unsafe: the queen in doubt to wed,
Or pay due honours to the nuptial bed.
Perhaps she weds regardless of her fame,
Deaf to the mighty Ulyssean name.
However, stranger! from our grace receive
Such honours as befit a prince to give;
Sandals, a sword and robes, respect to prove,
And safe to sail with ornaments of love.
Till then, thy guest amid the rural train,
Far from the court, from danger far, detain.
'Tis mine with food the hungry to supply,
And clothe the naked from the inclement sky.
Here dwell in safety from the suitors' wrongs,
And the rude insults of ungovern'd tongues.
For should'st thou suffer, powerless to relieve,
I must behold it, and can only grieve.
The brave, encompass'd by an hostile train,
O'erpower'd by numbers, is but brave in vain."

To whom, while anger in his bosom glows,
With warmth replies the man of mighty woes:
"Since audience mild is deign'd, permit my tongue
At once to pity and resent thy wrong.
My heart weeps blood to see a soul so brave
Live to base insolence or power a slave,
But tell me, dost thou, prince, dost thou behold,
And hear their midnight revels uncontroll'd?
Say, do thy subjects in bold faction rise,
Or priests in fabled oracles advise?
Or are thy brothers, who should aid thy power,
Turn'd mean deserters in the needful hour?
Oh that I were from great Ulysses sprung,
Or that these wither'd nerves like thine were strung,
Or, heavens! might he return! (and soon appear
He shall, I trust; a hero scorns despair:)
Might he return, I yield my life a prey
To my worst foe, if that avenging day
Be not their last: but should I lose my life,
Oppress'd by numbers in the glorious strife,
I chose the nobler part, and yield my breath,
Rather than bear dishonor, worse than death;
Than see the hand of violence invade

The reverend stranger and the spotless maid;
Than see the wealth of kings consumed in waste,
The drunkard's revel, and the gluttons' feast."

Thus he, with anger flashing from his eye;
Sincere the youthful hero made reply:
"Nor leagued in factious arms my subjects rise,
Nor priests in fabled oracles advise;
Nor are my brothers, who should aid my power,
Turn'd mean deserters in the needful hour.
Ah me! I boast no brother; heaven's dread King
Gives from our stock an only branch to spring:
Alone Laertes reign'd Arcesius' heir,
Alone Ulysses drew the vital air,
And I alone the bed connubial graced,
An unbless'd offspring of a sire unbless'd!
Each neighbouring realm, conducive to our woe,
Sends forth her peers, and every peer a foe:
The court proud Samos and Dulichium fills,
And lofty Zacinth crown'd with shady hills.
E'en Ithaca and all her lords invade
The imperial sceptre, and the regal bed:
The queen, averse to love, yet awed by power,
Seems half to yield, yet flies the bridal hour:
Meantime their licence uncontroll'd I bear;
E'en now they envy me the vital air:
But Heaven will sure revenge, and gods there are.

"But go Eumaeus! to the queen impart
Our safe return, and ease a mother's heart.
Yet secret go; for numerous are my foes,
And here at least I may in peace repose."

To whom the swain: "I hear and I obey:
But old Laertes weeps his life away,
And deems thee lost: shall I speed employ
To bless his age: a messenger of joy?
The mournful hour that tore his son away
Sent the sad sire in solitude to stray;
Yet busied with his slaves, to ease his woe,
He dress'd the vine, and bade the garden blow,
Nor food nor wine refused; but since the day
That you to Pylos plough'd the watery way,
Nor wine nor food he tastes; but, sunk in woes,
Wild springs the vine, no more the garden blows,
Shut from the walks of men, to pleasure lost,
Pensive and pale he wanders half a ghost."

"Wretched old man! (with tears the prince returns)
Yet cease to go—what man so blest but mourns?
Were every wish indulged by favouring skies,
This hour should give Ulysses to my eyes.
But to the queen with speed dispatchful bear,
Our safe return, and back with speed repair;
And let some handmaid of her train resort
To good Laertes in his rural court."

While yet he spoke, impatient of delay,
He braced his sandals on, and strode away:
Then from the heavens the martial goddess flies
Through the wild fields of air, and cleaves the skies:
In form, a virgin in soft beauty's bloom,
Skill'd in the illustrious labours of the loom.
Alone to Ithaca she stood display'd,
But unapparent as a viewless shade
Escaped Telemachus (the powers above,
Seen or unseen, o'er earth at pleasure move):
The dogs intelligent confess'd the tread
Of power divine, and howling, trembling, fled.
The goddess, beckoning, waves her deathless hands:
Dauntless the king before the goddess stands:

"Then why (she said), O favour'd of the skies!
Why to thy godlike son this long disguise?
Stand forth reveal'd; with him thy cares employ
Against thy foes; be valiant and destroy!
Lo! I descend in that avenging hour,
To combat by thy side, thy guardian power."

She said, and o'er him waves her wand of gold
Imperial robes his manly limbs infold;
At once with grace divine his frame improves;
At once with majesty enlarged he moves:
Youth flush'd his reddening cheek, and from his brows
A length of hair in sable ringlets flows;
His blackening chin receives a deeper shade;
Then from his eyes upsprung the warrior-maid.

The hero reascends: the prince o'erawed
Scarce lifts his eyes, and bows as to a god,
Then with surprise (surprise chastised by fears):
"How art thou changed! (he cried)—a god appears!
Far other vests thy limbs majestic grace,
Far other glories lighten from thy face!
If heaven be thy abode, with pious care,
Lo! I the ready sacrifice prepare:

Lo! gifts of labour'd gold adorn thy shrine,
To win thy grace: O save us, power divine!"

"Few are my days (Ulysses made reply),
Nor I, alas! descendant of the sky.
I am thy father. O my son! my son!
That father, for whose sake thy days have run
One scene of woe! to endless cares consign'd,
And outraged by the wrongs of base mankind."

Then, rushing to his arms, he kiss'd his boy
With the strong raptures of a parent's joy.
Tears bathe his cheek, and tears the ground bedew:
He strain'd him close, as to his breast he grew.
"Ah me! (exclaims the prince with fond desire)
Thou art not—no, thou canst not be my sire.
Heaven such illusion only can impose,
By the false joy to aggravate my woes.
Who but a god can change the general doom,
And give to wither'd age a youthful bloom!
Late, worn with years, in weeds obscene you trod;
Now, clothed in majesty, you move a god!"

"Forbear (he cried,) for Heaven reserve that name;
Give to thy father but a father's claim;
Other Ulysses shalt thou never see,
I am Ulysses, I, my son, am he.
Twice ten sad years o'er earth and ocean toss'd,
'Tis given at length to view my native coast.
Pallas, unconquer'd maid, my frame surrounds
With grace divine: her power admits no bounds;
She o'er my limbs old age and wrinkles shed;
Now strong as youth, magnificent I tread.
The gods with ease frail man depress or raise,
Exalt the lowly, or the proud debase."

He spoke and sate. The prince with transport flew,
Hung round his neck, while tears his cheek bedew;
Nor less the father pour'd a social flood;
They wept abundant, and they wept aloud.
As the bold eagle with fierce sorrow stung,
Or parent vulture, mourns her ravish'd young;
They cry, they scream, their unfledged brood a prey
To some rude churl, and borne by stealth away:
So they aloud: and tears in tides had run,
Their grief unfinish'd with the setting sun;
But checking the full torrent in its flow,
The prince thus interrupts the solemn woe.

"What ship transported thee, O father, say;
And what bless'd hands have oar'd thee on the way?"

"All, all (Ulysses instant made reply),
I tell thee all, my child, my only joy!
Phaeacians bore me to the port assign'd,
A nation ever to the stranger kind;
Wrapp'd in the embrace of sleep, the faithful train
O'er seas convey'd me to my native reign:
Embroider'd vestures, gold, and brass, are laid
Conceal'd in caverns in the sylvan shade.
Hither, intent the rival rout to slay,
And plan the scene of death, I bend my way;
So Pallas wills—but thou, my son, explain
The names and numbers of the audacious train;
'Tis mine to judge if better to employ
Assistant force, or singly to destroy."

"O'er earth (returns the prince) resounds thy name,
Thy well-tried wisdom, and thy martial fame,
Yet at thy words I start, in wonder lost;
Can we engage, not decades but an host?
Can we alone in furious battle stand,
Against that numerous and determined band?
Hear then their numbers; from Dulichium came
Twice twenty-six, all peers of mighty name.
Six are their menial train: twice twelve the boast
Of Samos; twenty from Zacynthus' coast:
And twelve our country's pride; to these belong
Medon and Phemius, skill'd in heavenly song.
Two sewers from day to day the revels wait,
Exact of taste, and serve the feast in state.
With such a foe the unequal fight to try,
Were by false courage unrevenged to die.
Then what assistant powers you boast relate,
Ere yet we mingle in the stern debate."

"Mark well my voice, (Ulysses straight replies:)
What need of aids, if favour'd by the skies?
If shielded to the dreadful fight we move,
By mighty Pallas, and by thundering Jove?"

"Sufficient they (Telemachus rejoin'd)
Against the banded powers of all mankind:
They, high enthroned above the rolling clouds,
Wither the strength of man, and awe the gods."

"Such aids expect (he cries,) when strong in might

We rise terrific to the task of fight.
But thou, when morn salutes the aerial plain,
The court revisit and the lawless train:
Me thither in disguise Eumaeus leads,
An aged mendicant in tatter'd weeds.
There, if base scorn insult my reverend age,
Bear it, my son! repress thy rising rage.
If outraged, cease that outrage to repel;
Bear it, my son! howe'er thy heart rebel.
Yet strive by prayer and counsel to restrain
Their lawless insults, though thou strive in vain:
For wicked ears are deaf to wisdom's call,
And vengeance strikes whom Heaven has doom'd to fall.
Once more attend: when she whose power inspires
The thinking mind, my soul to vengeance fires,
I give the sign: that instant, from beneath,
Aloft convey the instruments of death,
Armour and arms; and, if mistrust arise,
Thus veil the truth in plausible disguise:

"'These glittering weapons, ere he sail'd to Troy,
Ulysses view'd with stern heroic joy:
Then, beaming o'er the illumined wall they shone;
Now dust dishonours, all their lustre gone.
I bear them hence (so Jove my soul inspires),
From the pollution of the fuming fires;
Lest when the bowl inflames, in vengeful mood
Ye rush to arms, and stain the feast with blood:
Oft ready swords in luckless hour incite
The hand of wrath, and arm it for the fight.'

"Such be the plea, and by the plea deceive:
For Jove infatuates all, and all believe.
Yet leave for each of us a sword to wield,
A pointed javelin, and a fenceful shield.
But by my blood that in thy bosom glows,
By that regard a son his father owes;
The secret, that thy father lives, retain
Lock'd in thy bosom from the household train;
Hide it from all; e'en from Eumaeus hide,
From my dear father, and my dearer bride.
One care remains, to note the loyal few
Whose faith yet lasts among the menial crew;
And noting, ere we rise in vengeance, prove
Who love his prince; for sure you merit love."

To whom the youth: "To emulate, I aim,
The brave and wise, and my great father's fame.

But reconsider, since the wisest err,
Vengeance resolved, 'tis dangerous to defer.
What length of time must we consume in vain,
Too curious to explore the menial train!
While the proud foes, industrious to destroy
Thy wealth, in riot the delay enjoy.
Suffice it in this exigence alone
To mark the damsels that attend the throne:
Dispersed the youth reside; their faith to prove
Jove grants henceforth, if thou hast spoke from Jove."

While in debate they waste the hours away,
The associates of the prince repass'd the bay:
With speed they guide the vessel to the shores;
With speed debarking land the naval stores:
Then, faithful to their charge, to Clytius bear,
And trust the presents to his friendly care.
Swift to the queen a herald flies to impart
Her son's return, and ease a parent's heart:
Lest a sad prey to ever-musing cares,
Pale grief destroy what time awhile forbears.
The incautious herald with impatience burns,
And cries aloud, "Thy son, O queen, returns;"
Eumaeus sage approach'd the imperial throne,
And breathed his mandate to her ear alone,
Then measured back the way. The suitor band,
Stung to the soul, abash'd, confounded, stand;
And issuing from the dome, before the gate,
With clouded looks, a pale assembly sate.

At length Eurymachus: "Our hopes are vain;
Telemachus in triumph sails the main.
Haste, rear the mast, the swelling shroud display;
Haste, to our ambush'd friends the news convey!"

Scarce had he spake, when, turning to the strand,
Amphinomos survey'd the associate band;
Full to the bay within the winding shores
With gather'd sails they stood, and lifted oars.
"O friends!" he cried, elate with rising joy,
"See to the port secure the vessel fly!
Some god has told them, or themselves survey
The bark escaped; and measure back their way."

Swift at the word descending to the shores,
They moor the vessel and unlade the stores:
Then, moving from the strand, apart they sate,
And full and frequent form'd a dire debate.

"Lives then the boy? he lives (Antinous cries),
The care of gods and favourite of the skies.
All night we watch'd, till with her orient wheels
Aurora flamed above the eastern hills,
And from the lofty brow of rocks by day
Took in the ocean with a broad survey
Yet safe he sails; the powers celestial give
To shun the hidden snares of death, and live.
But die he shall, and thus condemn'd to bleed,
Be now the scene of instant death decreed.
Hope ye success? undaunted crush the foe.
Is he not wise? know this, and strike the blow.
Wait ye, till he to arms in council draws
The Greeks, averse too justly to our cause?
Strike, ere, the states convened, the foe betray
Our murderous ambush on the watery way.
Or choose ye vagrant from their rage to fly,
Outcasts of earth, to breathe an unknown sky?
The brave prevent misfortune; then be brave,
And bury future danger in his grave.
Returns he? ambush'd we'll his walk invade,
Or where he hides in solitude and shade;
And give the palace to the queen a dower,
Or him she blesses in the bridal hour.
But if submissive you resign the sway,
Slaves to a boy, go, flatter and obey.
Retire we instant to our native reign,
Nor be the wealth of kings consumed in vain;
Then wed whom choice approves: the queen be given
To some blest prince, the prince decreed by Heaven."

Abash'd, the suitor train his voice attends;
Till from his throne Amphinomus ascends,
Who o'er Dulichium stretch'd his spacious reign,
A land of plenty, bless'd with every grain:
Chief of the numbers who the queen address'd,
And though displeasing, yet displeasing least.
Soft were his words; his actions wisdom sway'd;
Graceful awhile he paused, then mildly said:

"O friends, forbear! and be the thought withstood:
'Tis horrible to shed imperial blood!
Consult we first the all-seeing powers above,
And the sure oracles of righteous Jove.
If they assent, e'en by this hand he dies;
If they forbid, I war not with the skies."

He said: the rival train his voice approved,
And rising instant to the palace moved.
Arrived, with wild tumultuous noise they sate,
Recumbent on the shining thrones of state.

The Medon, conscious of their dire debates,
The murderous counsel to the queen relates.
Touch'd at the dreadful story, she descends:
Her hasty steps a damsel train attends.
Full where the dome its shining valves expands,
Sudden before the rival powers she stands;
And, veiling, decent, with a modest shade
Her cheek, indignant to Antinous said:

"O void of faith! of all bad men the worst!
Renown'd for wisdom, by the abuse accursed!
Mistaking fame proclaims thy generous mind:
Thy deeds denote thee of the basest kind.
Wretch! to destroy a prince that friendship gives,
While in his guest his murderer he receives;
Nor dread superior Jove, to whom belong
The cause of suppliants, and revenge of wrong.
Hast thou forgot, ungrateful as thou art,
Who saved thy father with a friendly part?
Lawless he ravaged with his martial powers
The Taphian pirates on Thesprotia's shores;
Enraged, his life, his treasures they demand;
Ulysses saved him from the avenger's hand.
And would'st thou evil for his good repay?
His bed dishonour, and his house betray?
Afflict his queen, and with a murderous hand
Destroy his heir!—but cease, 'tis I command."

"Far hence those fears (Eurymachus replied,)
O prudent princess! bid thy soul confide.
Breathes there a man who dares that hero slay,
While I behold the golden light of day?
No: by the righteous powers of heaven I swear,
His blood in vengeance smokes upon my spear.
Ulysses, when my infant days I led,
With wine sufficed me, and with dainties fed:
My generous soul abhors the ungrateful part,
And my friend's son lives nearest to my heart.
Then fear no mortal arm; if Heaven destroy,
We must resign: for man is born to die."

Thus smooth he ended, yet his death conspired:
Then sorrowing, with sad step the queen retired,

With streaming eyes, all comfortless deplored,
Touch'd with the dear remembrance of her lord:
Nor ceased till Pallas bids her sorrows fly,
And in soft slumber seal'd her flowing eye.

And now Eumaeus, at the evening hour,
Came late, returning to his sylvan bower.
Ulysses and his son had dress'd with art
A yearling boar, and gave the gods their part.
Holy repast! That instant from the skies
The martial goddess to Ulysses flies:
She waves her golden wand, and reassumes
From every feature every grace that blooms;
At once his vestures change; at once she sheds
Age o'er his limbs, that tremble as he treads:
Lest to the queen the swain with transport fly,
Unable to contain the unruly joy;
When near he drew, the prince breaks forth: "Proclaim
What tidings, friend? what speaks the voice of fame?
Say, if the suitors measure back the main,
Or still in ambush thirst for blood in vain?"

"Whether (he cries) they measure back the flood,
Or still in ambush thirst in vain for blood,
Escaped my care: where lawless suitors sway,
Thy mandate borne my soul disdain'd to stay.
But from the Hermaean height I cast a view,
Where to the port a bark high-bounding flew;
Her freight a shining band: with martial air
Each poised his shield, and each advanced his spear;
And, if aright these searching eyes survey,
The eluded suitors stem the watery way."

The prince, well pleased to disappoint their wiles,
Steals on his sire a glance, and secret smiles.
And now, a short repast prepared, they fed
Till the keen rage of craving hunger fled:
Then to repose withdrawn, apart they lay,
And in soft sleep forgot the cares of day.

BOOK XVII

ARGUMENT

Telemachus returning to the city, relates to Penelope the sum of his travels. Ulysses is conducted by
Eumaeus to the palace, where his old dog Argus acknowledges his master, after an absence of twenty

years, and dies with joy. Eumaeus returns into the country, and Ulysses remains among the suitors, whose behaviour is described.

Soon as Aurora, daughter of the dawn,
Sprinkled with roseate light the dewy lawn,
In haste the prince arose, prepared to part;
His hand impatient grasps the pointed dart;
Fair on his feet the polish'd sandals shine,
And thus he greets the master of the swine:

"My friend, adieu! let this short stay suffice;
I haste to meet my mother's longing eyes,
And end her tears, her sorrows and her sighs.
But thou, attentive, what we order heed:
This hapless stranger to the city lead:
By public bounty let him there be fed,
And bless the hand that stretches forth the bread.
To wipe the tears from all afflicted eyes,
My will may covet, but my power denies.
If this raise anger in the stranger's thought,
The pain of anger punishes the fault:
The very truth I undisguised declare;
For what so easy as to be sincere?"

To this Ulysses: "What the prince requires
Of swift removal, seconds my desires.
To want like mine the peopled town can yield
More hopes of comfort than the lonely field:
Nor fits my age to till the labour'd lands,
Or stoop to tasks a rural lord demands.
Adieu! but since this ragged garb can bear
So ill the inclemencies of morning air,
A few hours' space permit me here to stay:
My steps Eumaeus shall to town convey,
With riper beams when Phoebus warms the day."

Thus he: nor aught Telemachus replied,
But left the mansion with a lofty stride:
Schemes of revenge his pondering breast elate,
Revolving deep the suitors' sudden fate,
Arriving now before the imperial hall,
He props his spear against the pillar'd wall;
Then like a lion o'er the threshold bounds;
The marble pavement with his steps resounds:
His eye first glanced where Euryclea spreads
With furry spoils of beasts the splendid beds:
She saw, she wept, she ran with eager pace,
And reach'd her master with a long embrace.

All crowded round, the family appears
With wild entrancement, and ecstatic tears.
Swift from above descends the royal fair
(Her beauteous cheeks the blush of Venus wear,
Chasten'd with coy Diana's pensive air);
Hangs o'er her son, in his embraces dies;
Rains kisses on his neck, his face, his eyes:
Few words she spoke, though much she had to say;
And scarce those few, for tears, could force their way.

"Light of my eyes: he comes! unhoped-for joy!
Has Heaven from Pylos brought my lovely boy?
So snatch'd from all our cares!—Tell, hast thou known
Thy father's fate, and tell me all thy own."

"Oh dearest! most revered of womankind!
Cease with those tears to melt a manly mind
(Replied the prince); nor be our fates deplored,
From death and treason to thy arms restored.
Go bathe, and robed in white ascend the towers;
With all thy handmaids thank the immortal powers;
To every god vow hecatombs to bleed.
And call Jove's vengeance on their guilty deed.
While to the assembled council I repair:
A stranger sent by Heaven attends me there;
My new accepted guest I haste to find,
Now to Peiraeus' honour'd charge consign'd."

The matron heard, nor was his word in vain.
She bathed; and, robed in white, with all her train,
To every god vow'd hecatombs to bleed,
And call'd Jove's vengeance on the guilty deed,
Arm'd with his lance, the prince then pass'd the gate,
Two dogs behind, a faithful guard, await;
Pallas his form with grace divine improves:
The gazing crowd admires him as he moves.
Him, gathering round, the haughty suitors greet
With semblance fair, but inward deep deceit,
Their false addresses, generous, he denied.
Pass'd on, and sate by faithful Mentor's side;
With Antiphus, and Halitherses sage
(His father's counsellors, revered for age).
Of his own fortunes, and Ulysses' fame,
Much ask'd the seniors; till Peiraeus came.
The stranger-guest pursued him close behind;
Whom when Telemachus beheld, he join'd.
He (when Peiraeus ask'd for slaves to bring
The gifts and treasures of the Spartan king)

Thus thoughtful answer'd: "Those we shall not move,
Dark and unconscious of the will of Jove;
We know not yet the full event of all:
Stabb'd in his palace if your prince must fall,
Us, and our house, if treason must o'erthrow,
Better a friend possess them than a foe;
If death to these, and vengeance Heaven decree,
Riches are welcome then, not else, to me.
Till then retain the gifts."—The hero said,
And in his hand the willing stranger led.
Then disarray'd, the shining bath they sought
(With unguents smooth) of polish'd marble wrought:
Obedient handmaids with assistant toil
Supply the limpid wave, and fragrant oil:
Then o'er their limbs refulgent robes they threw,
And fresh from bathing to their seats withdrew.
The golden ewer a nymph attendant brings,
Replenish'd from the pure translucent springs;
With copious streams that golden ewer supplies
A silver layer of capacious size.
They wash: the table, in fair order spread,
Is piled with viands and the strength of bread.
Full opposite, before the folding gate,
The pensive mother sits in humble state;
Lowly she sate, and with dejected view
The fleecy threads her ivory fingers drew.
The prince and stranger shared the genial feast,
Till now the rage of thirst and hunger ceased.

When thus the queen: "My son! my only friend!
Say, to my mournful couch shall I ascend?
(The couch deserted now a length of years;
The couch for ever water'd with my tears;)
Say, wilt thou not (ere yet the suitor crew
Return, and riot shakes our walls anew),
Say, wilt thou not the least account afford?
The least glad tidings of my absent lord?"

To her the youth. "We reach'd the Pylian plains,
Where Nestor, shepherd of his people, reigns.
All arts of tenderness to him are known,
Kind to Ulysses' race as to his own;
No father with a fonder grasp of joy
Strains to his bosom his long-absent boy.
But all unknown, if yet Ulysses breathe,
Or glide a spectre in the realms beneath;
For farther search, his rapid steeds transport
My lengthen'd journey to the Spartan court.

There Argive Helen I beheld, whose charms
(So Heaven decreed) engaged the great in arms.
My cause of coming told, he thus rejoin'd;
And still his words live perfect in my mind:

"'Heavens! would a soft, inglorious, dastard train
An absent hero's nuptial joys profane
So with her young, amid the woodland shades,
A timorous hind the lion's court invades,
Leaves in that fatal lair her tender fawns,
And climbs the cliffs, or feeds along the lawns;
Meantime returning, with remorseless sway
The monarch savage rends the panting prey:
With equal fury, and with equal fame,
Shall great Ulysses reassert his claim.
O Jove! supreme! whom men and gods revere;
And thou whose lustre gilds the rolling sphere!
With power congenial join'd, propitious aid
The chief adopted by the martial maid!
Such to our wish the warrior soon restore,
As when, contending on the Lesbian shore,
His prowess Philomelides confess'd,
And loud acclaiming Greeks the victor bless'd:
Then soon the invaders of his bed, and throne,
Their love presumptuous shall by death atone.
Now what you question of my ancient friend,
With truth I answer; thou the truth attend.
Learn what I heard the sea-born seer relate,
Whose eye can pierce the dark recess of fate
Sole in an isle, imprison'd by the main,
The sad survivor of his numerous train,
Ulysses lies; detain'd by magic charms,
And press'd unwilling in Calypso's arms.
No sailors there, no vessels to convey,
No oars to cut the immeasurable way.'
This told Atrides, and he told no more.
Then safe I voyaged to my native shore."

He ceased; nor made the pensive queen reply,
But droop'd her head, and drew a secret sigh.
When Theoclymenus the seer began:
"O suffering consort of the suffering man!
What human knowledge could, those kings might tell,
But I the secrets of high heaven reveal.
Before the first of gods be this declared,
Before the board whose blessings we have shared;
Witness the genial rites, and witness all
This house holds sacred in her ample wall!

E'en now, this instant, great Ulysses, laid
At rest, or wandering in his country's shade,
Their guilty deeds, in hearing, and in view,
Secret revolves; and plans the vengeance due.
Of this sure auguries the gods bestow'd,
When first our vessel anchor'd in your road."
"Succeed those omens, Heaven! (the queen rejoin'd)
So shall our bounties speak a grateful mind;
And every envied happiness attend
The man who calls Penelope his friend."
Thus communed they: while in the marble court
(Scene of their insolence) the lords resort:
Athwart the spacious square each tries his art,
To whirl the disk, or aim the missile dart.
Now did the hour of sweet repast arrive,
And from the field the victim flocks they drive:
Medon the herald (one who pleased them best,
And honour'd with a portion of their feast),
To bid the banquet, interrupts their play:
Swift to the hall they haste; aside they lay
Their garments, and succinct the victims slay.
Then sheep, and goats, and bristly porkers bled,
And the proud steer was o'er the marble spread.
While thus the copious banquet they provide,
Along the road, conversing side by side,
Proceed Ulysses and the faithful swain;
When thus Eumaeus, generous and humane:
"To town, observant of our lord's behest,
Now let us speed; my friend no more my guest!
Yet like myself I wish thee here preferr'd,
Guard of the flock, or keeper of the herd,
But much to raise my master's wrath I fear;
The wrath of princes ever is severe.
Then heed his will, and be our journey made
While the broad beams of Phoebus are display'd,
Or ere brown evening spreads her chilly shade."
"Just thy advice (the prudent chief rejoin'd),
And such as suits the dictate of my mind.
Lead on: but help me to some staff to stay
My feeble step, since rugged is the way."
Across his shoulders then the scrip he flung,
Wide-patch'd, and fasten'd by a twisted thong.
A staff Eumaeus gave. Along the way
Cheerly they fare: behind, the keepers stay:
These with their watchful dogs (a constant guard)
Supply his absence, and attend the herd.
And now his city strikes the monarch's eyes,
Alas! how changed! a man of miseries;

Propp'd on a staff, a beggar old and bare
In rags dishonest fluttering with the air!
Now pass'd the rugged road, they journey down
The cavern'd way descending to the town,
Where, from the rock, with liquid drops distils
A limpid fount; that spread in parting rills
Its current thence to serve the city brings;
An useful work, adorn'd by ancient kings.
Neritus, Ithacus, Polyctor, there,
In sculptured stone immortalized their care,
In marble urns received it from above,
And shaded with a green surrounding grove;
Where silver alders, in high arches twined,
Drink the cool stream, and tremble to the wind.
Beneath, sequester'd to the nymphs, is seen
A mossy altar, deep embower'd in green;
Where constant vows by travellers are paid,
And holy horrors solemnize the shade.

Here with his goats (not vow'd to sacred fame,
But pamper'd luxury) Melanthias came:
Two grooms attend him. With an envious look
He eyed the stranger, and imperious spoke:

"The good old proverb how this pair fulfil!
One rogue is usher to another still.
Heaven with a secret principle endued
Mankind, to seek their own similitude.
Where goes the swineherd with that ill-look'd guest?
That giant-glutton, dreadful at a feast!
Full many a post have those broad shoulders worn,
From every great man's gate repulsed with scorn:
To no brave prize aspired the worthless swain,
'Twas but for scraps he ask'd, and ask'd in vain.
To beg, than work, he better understands,
Or we perhaps might take him off thy hands.
For any office could the slave be good,
To cleanse the fold, or help the kids to food.
If any labour those big joints could learn,
Some whey, to wash his bowels, he might earn.
To cringe, to whine, his idle hands to spread,
Is all, by which that graceless maw is fed.
Yet hear me! if thy impudence but dare
Approach yon wall, I prophesy thy fare:
Dearly, full dearly, shalt thou buy thy bread
With many a footstool thundering at thy head."

He thus: nor insolent of word alone,

Spurn'd with his rustic heel his king unknown;
Spurn'd, but not moved: he like a pillar stood,
Nor stirr'd an inch, contemptuous, from the road:
Doubtful, or with his staff to strike him dead,
Or greet the pavement with his worthless head.
Short was that doubt; to quell his rage inured,
The hero stood self-conquer'd, and endured.
But hateful of the wretch, Eumaeus heaved
His hands obtesting, and this prayer conceived:
"Daughters of Jove! who from the ethereal bowers
Descend to swell the springs, and feed the flowers!
Nymphs of this fountain! to whose sacred names
Our rural victims mount in blazing flames!
To whom Ulysses' piety preferr'd
The yearly firstlings of his flock and herd;
Succeed my wish, your votary restore:
Oh, be some god his convoy to our shore!
Due pains shall punish then this slave's offence,
And humble all his airs of insolence,
Who, proudly stalking, leaves the herds at large,
Commences courtier, and neglects his charge."

"What mutters he? (Melanthius sharp rejoins;)
This crafty miscreant, big with dark designs?
The day shall come—nay, 'tis already near—
When, slave! to sell thee at a price too dear
Must be my care; and hence transport thee o'er,
A load and scandal to this happy shore.
Oh! that as surely great Apollo's dart,
Or some brave suitor's sword, might pierce the heart
Of the proud son; as that we stand this hour
In lasting safety from the father's power!"

So spoke the wretch, but, shunning farther fray,
Turn'd his proud step, and left them on their way.
Straight to the feastful palace he repair'd,
Familiar enter'd, and the banquet shared;
Beneath Eurymachus, his patron lord,
He took his place, and plenty heap'd the board.

Meantime they heard, soft circling in the sky
Sweet airs ascend, and heavenly minstrelsy
(For Phemius to the lyre attuned the strain):
Ulysses hearken'd, then address'd the swain:

"Well may this palace admiration claim,
Great and respondent to the master's fame!
Stage above stage the imperial structure stands,

Holds the chief honours, and the town commands:
High walls and battlements the courts inclose,
And the strong gates defy a host of foes.
Far other cares its dwellers now employ;
The throng'd assembly and the feast of joy:
I see the smokes of sacrifice aspire,
And hear (what graces every feast) the lyre."

Then thus Eumaeus: "Judge we which were best;
Amidst yon revellers a sudden guest
Choose you to mingle, while behind I stay?
Or I first entering introduce the way?
Wait for a space without, but wait not long;
This is the house of violence and wrong:
Some rude insult thy reverend age may bear;
For like their lawless lords the servants are."

"Just is, O friend! thy caution, and address'd
(Replied the chief, to no unheedful breast:)
The wrongs and injuries of base mankind
Fresh to my sense, and always in my mind.
The bravely-patient to no fortune yields:
On rolling oceans, and in fighting fields,
Storms have I pass'd, and many a stern debate;
And now in humbler scene submit to fate.
What cannot want? The best she will expose,
And I am learn'd in all her train of woes;
She fills with navies, hosts, and loud alarms,
The sea, the land, and shakes the world with arms!"

Thus, near the gates conferring as they drew,
Argus, the dog, his ancient master knew:
He not unconscious of the voice and tread,
Lifts to the sound his ear, and rears his head;
Bred by Ulysses, nourish'd at his board,
But, ah! not fated long to please his lord;
To him, his swiftness and his strength were vain;
The voice of glory call'd him o'er the main.
Till then in every sylvan chase renown'd,
With Argus, Argus, rung the woods around;
With him the youth pursued the goat or fawn,
Or traced the mazy leveret o'er the lawn.
Now left to man's ingratitude he lay,
Unhoused, neglected in the public way;
And where on heaps the rich manure was spread,
Obscene with reptiles, took his sordid bed.

He knew his lord; he knew, and strove to meet;

In vain he strove to crawl and kiss his feet;
Yet (all he could) his tail, his tears, his eyes,
Salute his master, and confess his joys.
Soft pity touch'd the mighty master's soul;
Adown his cheek a tear unbidden stole,
Stole unperceived: he turn'd his head and dried
The drop humane: then thus impassion'd cried:

"What noble beast in this abandon'd state
Lies here all helpless at Ulysses' gate?
His bulk and beauty speak no vulgar praise:
If, as he seems, he was in better days,
Some care his age deserves; or was he prized
For worthless beauty? therefore now despised;
Such dogs and men there are, mere things of state;
And always cherish'd by their friends, the great."

"Not Argus so, (Eumaeus thus rejoin'd,)
But served a master of a nobler kind,
Who, never, never shall behold him more!
Long, long since perish'd on a distant shore!
Oh had you seen him, vigorous, bold, and young,
Swift as a stag, and as a lion strong:
Him no fell savage on the plain withstood,
None 'scaped him bosom'd in the gloomy wood;
His eye how piercing, and his scent how true,
To wind the vapour on the tainted dew!
Such, when Ulysses left his natal coast:
Now years unnerve him, and his lord is lost!
The women keep the generous creature bare,
A sleek and idle race is all their care:
The master gone, the servants what restrains?
Or dwells humanity where riot reigns?
Jove fix'd it certain, that whatever day
Makes man a slave, takes half his worth away."

This said, the honest herdsman strode before;
The musing monarch pauses at the door:
The dog, whom Fate had granted to behold
His lord, when twenty tedious years had roll'd,
Takes a last look, and having seen him, dies;
So closed for ever faithful Argus' eyes!

And now Telemachus, the first of all,
Observed Eumaeus entering in the hall;
Distant he saw, across the shady dome;
Then gave a sign, and beckon'd him to come:
There stood an empty seat, where late was placed,

In order due, the steward of the feast,
(Who now was busied carving round the board,)
Eumaeus took, and placed it near his lord.
Before him instant was the banquet spread,
And the bright basket piled with loaves of bread.

Next came Ulysses lowly at the door,
A figure despicable, old, and poor.
In squalid vests, with many a gaping rent,
Propp'd or a staff, and trembling as he went.
Then, resting on the threshold of the gate,
Against a cypress pillar lean'd his weight
Smooth'd by the workman to a polish'd plane);
The thoughtful son beheld, and call'd his swain

"These viands, and this bread, Eumaeus! bear,
And let yon mendicant our plenty share:
And let him circle round the suitors' board,
And try the bounty of each gracious lord.
Bold let him ask, encouraged thus by me:
How ill, alas! do want and shame agree!"

His lord's command the faithful servant bears:
The seeming beggar answers with his prayers:
"Bless'd be Telemachus! in every deed
Inspire him. Jove! in every wish succeed!"
This said, the portion from his son convey'd
With smiles receiving on his scrip he laid.
Long has the minstrel swept the sounding wire,
He fed, and ceased when silence held the lyre.
Soon as the suitors from the banquet rose,
Minerva prompts the man of mighty woes
To tempt their bounties with a suppliant's art,
And learn the generous from the ignoble heart
(Not but his soul, resentful as humane,
Dooms to full vengeance all the offending train);
With speaking eyes, and voice of plaintive sound,
Humble he moves, imploring all around.
The proud feel pity, and relief bestow,
With such an image touch'd of human woe;
Inquiring all, their wonder they confess,
And eye the man, majestic in distress.

While thus they gaze and question with their eyes,
The bold Melanthius to their thought replies:
"My lords! this stranger of gigantic port
The good Eumaeus usher'd to your court.
Full well I mark'd the features of his face,

Though all unknown his clime, or noble race."

"And is this present, swineherd! of thy band?
Bring'st thou these vagrants to infest the land?
(Returns Antinous with retorted eye)
Objects uncouth, to check the genial joy.
Enough of these our court already grace;
Of giant stomach, and of famish'd face.
Such guests Eumaeus to his country brings,
To share our feast, and lead the life of kings."

To whom the hospitable swain rejoins:
"Thy passion, prince, belies thy knowing mind.
Who calls, from distant nations to his own,
The poor, distinguish'd by their wants alone?
Round the wide world are sought those men divine
Who public structures raise, or who design;
Those to whose eyes the gods their ways reveal,
Or bless with salutary arts to heal;
But chief to poets such respect belongs,
By rival nations courted for their songs;
These states invite, and mighty kings admire,
Wide as the sun displays his vital fire.
It is not so with want! how few that feed
A wretch unhappy, merely for his need!
Unjust to me, and all that serve the state,
To love Ulysses is to raise thy hate.
For me, suffice the approbation won
Of my great mistress, and her godlike son."

To him Telemachus: "No more incense
The man by nature prone to insolence:
Injurious minds just answers but provoke"—
Then turning to Antinous, thus he spoke:
"Thanks to thy care! whose absolute command
Thus drives the stranger from our court and land.
Heaven bless its owner with a better mind!
From envy free, to charity inclined.
This both Penelope and I afford:
Then, prince! be bounteous of Ulysses' board.
To give another's is thy hand so slow?
So much more sweet to spoil than to bestow?"

"Whence, great Telemachus! this lofty strain?
(Antinous cries with insolent disdain):
Portions like mine if every suitor gave,
Our walls this twelvemonth should not see the slave."

He spoke, and lifting high above the board
His ponderous footstool, shook it at his lord.
The rest with equal hand conferr'd the bread:
He fill'd his scrip, and to the threshold sped;
But first before Antinous stopp'd, and said:
"Bestow, my friend! thou dost not seem the worst
Of all the Greeks, but prince-like and the first;
Then, as in dignity, be first in worth,
And I shall praise thee through the boundless earth.
Once I enjoy'd in luxury of state
Whate'er gives man the envied name of great;
Wealth, servants, friends, were mine in better days
And hospitality was then my praise;
In every sorrowing soul I pour'd delight,
And poverty stood smiling in my sight.
But Jove, all-governing, whose only will
Determines fate, and mingles good with ill,
Sent me (to punish my pursuit of gain)
With roving pirates o'er the Egyptian main
By Egypt's silver flood our ships we moor;
Our spies commission'd straight the coast explore;
But impotent of mind, the lawless will
The country ravage, and the natives kill.
The spreading clamour to their city flies,
And horse and foot in mingled tumults rise:
The reddening dawn reveals the hostile fields,
Horrid with bristly spears, and gleaming shields:
Jove thunder'd on their side: our guilty head
We turn'd to flight; the gathering vengeance spread
On all parts round, and heaps on heaps lay dead.
Some few the foe in servitude detain;
Death ill exchanged for bondage and for pain!
Unhappy me a Cyprian took aboard,
And gave to Dmetor, Cyprus' haughty lord:
Hither, to 'scape his chains, my course I steer,
Still cursed by Fortune, and insulted here!"

To whom Antinous thus his rage express'd:
"What god has plagued us with this gourmand guest?
Unless at distance, wretch! thou keep behind,
Another isle, than Cyprus more unkind,
Another Egypt shalt thou quickly find.
From all thou begg'st, a bold audacious slave;
Nor all can give so much as thou canst crave.
Nor wonder I, at such profusion shown;
Shameless they give, who give what's not their own."

The chief, retiring: "Souls, like that in thee,

Ill suits such forms of grace and dignity.
Nor will that hand to utmost need afford
The smallest portion of a wasteful board,
Whose luxury whole patrimonies sweeps,
Yet starving want, amidst the riot, weeps."

The haughty suitor with resentment burns,
And, sourly smiling, this reply returns:
"Take that, ere yet thou quit this princely throng;
And dumb for ever be thy slanderous tongue!"
He said, and high the whirling tripod flung.
His shoulder-blade received the ungentle shock;
He stood, and moved not, like a marble rock;
But shook his thoughtful head, nor more complain'd,
Sedate of soul, his character sustain'd,
And inly form'd revenge; then back withdrew:
Before his feet the well fill'd scrip he threw,
And thus with semblance mild address'd the crew:

"May what I speak your princely minds approve,
Ye peers and rivals in this noble love!
Not for the hurt I grieve, but for the cause.
If, when the sword our country's quarrel draws,
Or if, defending what is justly dear,
From Mars impartial some broad wound we bear,
The generous motive dignifies the scar.
But for mere want, how hard to suffer wrong!
Want brings enough of other ills along!
Yet, if injustice never be secure,
If fiends revenge, and gods assert the poor,
Death shall lay low the proud aggressor's head,
And make the dust Antinous' bridal bed."

"Peace, wretch! and eat thy bread without offence
(The suitor cried), or force shall drag thee hence,
Scourge through the public street, and cast thee there,
A mangled carcase for the hounds to tear."

His furious deed the general anger moved,
All, even the worst, condemn'd; and some reproved.
"Was ever chief for wars like these renown'd?
Ill fits the stranger and the poor to wound.
Unbless'd thy hand! if in this low disguise
Wander, perhaps, some inmate of the skies;
They (curious oft of mortal actions) deign
In forms like these to round the earth and main,
Just and unjust recording in their mind,
And with sure eyes inspecting all mankind."

Telemachus, absorb'd in thought severe,
Nourish'd deep anguish, though he shed no tear;
But the dark brow of silent sorrow shook:
While thus his mother to her virgins spoke:

"On him and his may the bright god of day
That base, inhospitable blow repay!"
The nurse replies: "If Jove receives my prayer,
Not one survives to breathe to-morrow's air."

"All, all are foes, and mischief is their end;
Antinous most to gloomy death a friend
(Replies the queen): the stranger begg'd their grace,
And melting pity soften'd every face;
From every other hand redress he found,
But fell Antinous answer'd with a wound."
Amidst her maids thus spoke the prudent queen,
Then bade Eumaeus call the pilgrim in.
"Much of the experienced man I long to hear,
If or his certain eye, or listening ear,
Have learn'd the fortunes of my wandering lord?"
Thus she, and good Eumaeus took the word:

"A private audience if thy grace impart,
The stranger's words may ease the royal heart.
His sacred eloquence in balm distils,
And the soothed heart with secret pleasure fills.
Three days have spent their beams, three nights have run
Their silent journey, since his tale begun,
Unfinish'd yet; and yet I thirst to hear!
As when some heaven-taught poet charms the ear
(Suspending sorrow with celestial strain
Breathed from the gods to soften human pain)
Time steals away with unregarded wing,
And the soul hears him, though he cease to sing

"Ulysses late he saw, on Cretan ground
(His fathers guest), for Minos' birth renown'd.
He now but waits the wind to waft him o'er,
With boundless treasure, from Thesprotia's shore."

To this the queen: "The wanderer let me hear,
While yon luxurious race indulge their cheer,
Devour the grazing ox, and browsing goat,
And turn my generous vintage down their throat.
For where's an arm, like thine, Ulysses! strong,
To curb wild riot, and to punish wrong?"

She spoke. Telemachus then sneezed aloud;
Constrain'd, his nostril echoed through the crowd.
The smiling queen the happy omen bless'd:

"So may these impious fall, by Fate oppress'd!"
Then to Eumaeus: "Bring the stranger, fly!
And if my questions meet a true reply,
Graced with a decent robe he shall retire,
A gift in season which his wants require."

Thus spoke Penelope. Eumaeus flies
In duteous haste, and to Ulysses cries:
"The queen invites thee, venerable guest!
A secret instinct moves her troubled breast,
Of her long absent lord from thee to gain
Some light, and soothe her soul's eternal pain.
If true, if faithful thou, her grateful mind
Of decent robes a present has design'd:
So finding favour in the royal eye,
Thy other wants her subjects shall supply."

"Fair truth alone (the patient man replied)
My words shall dictate, and my lips shall guide.
To him, to me, one common lot was given,
In equal woes, alas! involved by Heaven.
Much of his fates I know; but check'd by fear
I stand; the hand of violence is here:
Here boundless wrongs the starry skies invade,
And injured suppliants seek in vain for aid.
Let for a space the pensive queen attend,
Nor claim my story till the sun descend;
Then in such robes as suppliants may require,
Composed and cheerful by the genial fire,
When loud uproar and lawless riot cease,
Shall her pleased ear receive my words in peace."

Swift to the queen returns the gentle swain:
"And say (she cries), does fear or shame detain
The cautious stranger? With the begging kind
Shame suits but ill." Eumaeus thus rejoin'd:

"He only asks a more propitious hour,
And shuns (who would not?) wicked men in power;
At evening mild (meet season to confer)
By turns to question, and by turns to hear."

"Whoe'er this guest (the prudent queen replies)

His every step and every thought is wise.
For men like these on earth he shall not find
In all the miscreant race of human kind."
Thus she. Eumaeus all her words attends,
And, parting, to the suitor powers descends;
There seeks Telemachus, and thus apart
In whispers breathes the fondness of his heart:

"The time, my lord, invites me to repair
Hence to the lodge; my charge demands my care.
These sons of murder thirst thy life to take;
O guard it, guard it, for thy servant's sake!"

"Thanks to my friend (he cries): but now the hour
Of night draws on, go seek the rural bower:
But first refresh: and at the dawn of day
Hither a victim to the gods convey.
Our life to Heaven's immortal powers we trust,
Safe in their care, for Heaven protects the just."

Observant of his voice, Eumaeus sate
And fed recumbent on a chair of state.
Then instant rose, and as he moved along,
'Twas riot all amid the suitor throng,
They feast, they dance, and raise the mirthful song
Till now, declining towards the close of day,
The sun obliquely shot his dewy ray.

BOOK XVIII

ARGUMENT

THE FIGHT OF ULYSSES AND IRUS

The beggar Irus insults Ulysses; the suitors promote the quarrel, in which Irus is worsted, and miserably
handled. Penelope descends, and receives the presents of the suitors. The dialogue of Ulysses with
Eurymachus.

While fix'd in thought the pensive hero sate,
A mendicant approach'd the royal gate;
A surly vagrant of the giant kind,
The stain of manhood, of a coward mind:
From feast to feast, insatiate to devour,
He flew, attendant on the genial hour.
Him on his mother's knees, when babe he lay,
She named Arnaeus on his natal day:

But Irus his associates call'd the boy,
Practised the common messenger to fly;
Irus, a name expressive of the employ.

From his own roof, with meditated blows,
He strove to drive the man of mighty woes:

"Hence, dotard! hence, and timely speed thy way,
Lest dragg'd in vengeance thou repent thy stay;
See how with nods assent yon princely train!
But honouring age, in mercy I refrain:
In peace away! lest, if persuasions fail,
This arm with blows more eloquent prevail."
To whom, with stern regard: "O insolence,
Indecently to rail without offence!
What bounty gives without a rival share;
I ask, what harms not thee, to breathe this air:
Alike on alms we both precarious live:
And canst thou envy when the great relieve?
Know, from the bounteous heavens all riches flow,
And what man gives, the gods by man bestow;
Proud as thou art, henceforth no more be proud,
Lest I imprint my vengeance in thy blood;
Old as I am, should once my fury burn,
How would'st thou fly, nor e'en in thought return!"

"Mere woman-glutton! (thus the churl replied;)
A tongue so flippant, with a throat so wide!
Why cease I gods! to dash those teeth away,
Like some wild boar's, that, greedy of his prey,
Uproots the bearded corn? Rise, try the fight,
Gird well thy loins, approach, and feel my might:
Sure of defeat, before the peers engage:
Unequal fight, when youth contends with age!"

Thus in a wordy war their tongues display
More fierce intents, preluding to the fray;
Antinous hears, and in a jovial vein,
Thus with loud laughter to the suitor train:

"This happy day in mirth, my friends, employ,
And lo! the gods conspire to crown our joy;
See ready for the fight, and hand to hand,
Yon surly mendicants contentious stand:
Why urge we not to blows!" Well pleased they spring
Swift from their seats, and thickening form a ring.

To whom Antinous: "Lo! enrich'd with blood,

A kid's well-fatted entrails (tasteful food)
On glowing embers lie; on him bestow
The choicest portion who subdues his foe;
Grant him unrivall'd in these walls to stay,
The sole attendant on the genial day."

The lords applaud: Ulysses then with art,
And fears well-feign'd, disguised his dauntless heart.

"Worn as I am with age, decay'd with woe;
Say, is it baseness to decline the foe?
Hard conflict! when calamity and age
With vigorous youth, unknown to cares, engage!
Yet, fearful of disgrace, to try the day
Imperious hunger bids, and I obey;
But swear, impartial arbiters of right,
Swear to stand neutral, while we cope in fight."

The peers assent: when straight his sacred head
Telemachus upraised, and sternly said:
"Stranger, if prompted to chastise the wrong
Of this bold insolent, confide, be strong!
The injurious Greek that dares attempt a blow,
That instant makes Telemachus his foe;
And these my friends shall guard the sacred ties
Of hospitality, for they are wise."

Then, girding his strong loins, the king prepares
To close in combat, and his body bares;
Broad spread his shoulders, and his nervous thighs
By just degrees, like well-turn'd columns, rise
Ample his chest, his arms are round and long,
And each strong joint Minerva knits more strong
(Attendant on her chief): the suitor-crowd
With wonder gaze, and gazing speak aloud:
"Irus! alas! shall Irus be no more?
Black fate impends, and this the avenging hour!
Gods! how his nerves a matchless strength proclaim,
Swell o'er his well-strong limbs, and brace his frame!"

Then pale with fears, and sickening at the sight;
They dragg'd the unwilling Irus to the fight;
From his blank visage fled the coward blood,
And his flesh trembled as aghast he stood.

"O that such baseness should disgrace the light?
O hide it, death, in everlasting night!
(Exclaims Antinous;) can a vigorous foe

Meanly decline to combat age and woe?
But hear me wretch! if recreant in the fray
That huge bulk yield this ill-contested day,
Instant thou sail'st, to Eschetus resign'd;
A tyrant, fiercest of the tyrant kind,
Who casts thy mangled ears and nose a prey
To hungry dogs, and lops the man away."

While with indignant scorn he sternly spoke,
In every joint the trembling Irus shook.
Now front to front each frowning champion stands,
And poises high in air his adverse hands.
The chief yet doubts, or to the shades below
To fell the giant at one vengeful blow,
Or save his life, and soon his life to save
The king resolves, for mercy sways the brave
That instant Irus his huge arm extends,
Full on his shoulder the rude weight descends;
The sage Ulysses, fearful to disclose
The hero latent in the man of woes,
Check'd half his might; yet rising to the stroke,
His jawbone dash'd, the crashing jawbone broke:
Down dropp'd he stupid from the stunning wound;
His feet extended quivering, beat the ground;
His mouth and nostrils spout a purple flood;
His teeth, all shatter'd, rush inmix'd with blood.

The peers transported, as outstretch'd he lies,
With bursts of laughter rend the vaulted skies;
Then dragg'd along, all bleeding from the wound,
His length of carcase trailing prints the ground:
Raised on his feet, again he reels, he falls,
Till propp'd, reclining on the palace walls:
Then to his hand a staff the victor gave,
And thus with just reproach address'd the slave:
"There terrible, affright with dogs, and reign
A dreaded tyrant o'er the bestial train!
But mercy to the poor and stranger show,
Lest Heaven in vengeance send some mightier woe."

Scornful he spoke, and o'er his shoulder flung
The broad-patch'd scrip in tatters hung
Ill join'd, and knotted to a twisted thong.
Then, turning short, disdain'd a further stay;
But to the palace measured back the way.
There, as he rested gathering in a ring,
The peers with smiles address'd their unknown king:
"Stranger, may Jove and all the aerial powers

With every blessing crown thy happy hours!
Our freedom to thy prowess'd arm we owe
From bold intrusion of thy coward foe:
Instant the flying sail the slave shall wing
To Eschetus, the monster of a king."

While pleased he hears, Antinous bears the food,
A kid's well-fatted entrails, rich with blood;
The bread from canisters of shining mould
Amphinomus; and wines that laugh in gold:
"And oh! (he mildly cries) may Heaven display
A beam of glory o'er thy future day!
Alas, the brave too oft is doom'd to bear
The gripes of poverty and stings of care."

To whom with thought mature the king replies:
"The tongue speaks wisely, when the soul is wise:
Such was thy father! in imperial state,
Great without vice, that oft attends the great;
Nor from the sire art thou, the son, declin'd;
Then hear my words, and grace them in thy mind!
Of all that breathes, or grovelling creeps on earth,
Most man in vain! calamitous by birth:
To-day, with power elate, in strength he blooms;
The haughty creature on that power presumes:
Anon from Heaven a sad reverse he feels:
Untaught to bear, 'gainst Heaven the wretch rebels.
For man is changeful, as his bliss or woe!
Too high when prosperous, when distress'd too low.
There was a day, when with the scornful great
I swell'd in pomp and arrogance of state;
Proud of the power that to high birth belongs;
And used that power to justify my wrongs.
Then let not man be proud; but firm of mind,
Bear the best humbly; and the worst resign'd;
Be dumb when Heaven afflicts! unlike yon train
Of haughty spoilers, insolently vain;
Who make their queen and all her wealth a prey:
But vengeance and Ulysses wing their way.
O may'st thou, favour'd by some guardian power,
Far, far be distant in that deathful hour!
For sure I am, if stern Ulysses breathe,
These lawless riots end in blood and death."

Then to the gods the rosy juice he pours,
And the drain'd goblet to the chief restores.
Stung to the soul, o'ercast with holy dread,
He shook the graceful honours of his head;

His boding mind the future woe forestalls,
In vain! by great Telemachus he falls,
For Pallas seals his doom: all sad he turns
To join the peers; resumes his throne, and mourns.

Meanwhile Minerva with instinctive fires
Thy soul, Penelope, from Heaven inspires;
With flattering hopes the suitors to betray,
And seem to meet, yet fly, the bridal day:
Thy husband's wonder, and thy son's to raise;
And crown the mother and the wife with praise.
Then, while the streaming sorrow dims her eyes,
Thus, with a transient smile, the matron cries:

"Eurynome! to go where riot reigns
I feel an impulse, though my soul disdains;
To my loved son the snares of death to show,
And in the traitor friend, unmask the foe;
Who, smooth of tongue, in purpose insincere,
Hides fraud in smiles, while death is ambush'd there."

"Go, warn thy son, nor be the warning vain
(Replied the sagest of the royal train);
But bathed, anointed, and adorn'd, descend;
Powerful of charms, bid every grace attend;
The tide of flowing tears awhile suppress;
Tears but indulge the sorrow, not repress.
Some joy remains: to thee a son is given,
Such as, in fondness, parents ask of Heaven."

"Ah me! forbear!" returns the queen, "forbear,
Oh! talk not, talk not of vain beauty's care;
No more I bathe, since he no longer sees
Those charms, for whom alone I wish to please.
The day that bore Ulysses from this coast
Blasted the little bloom these cheeks could boast.
But instant bid Autonoe descend,
Instant Hippodame our steps attend;
Ill suits it female virtue, to be seen
Alone, indecent, in the walks of men."

Then while Eurynome the mandate bears,
From heaven Minerva shoots with guardian cares;
O'er all her senses, as the couch she press'd,
She pours, a pleasing, deep and death-like rest,
With every beauty every feature arms,
Bids her cheeks glow, and lights up all her charms;
In her love-darting eyes awakes the fires

(Immortal gifts! to kindle soft desires);
From limb to limb an air majestic sheds,
And the pure ivory o'er her bosom spreads.
Such Venus shines, when with a measured bound
She smoothly gliding swims the harmonious round,
When with the Graces in the dance she moves,
And fires the gazing gods with ardent loves.

Then to the skies her flight Minerva bends,
And to the queen the damsel train descends;
Waked at their steps, her flowing eyes unclose;
The tears she wipes, and thus renews her woes:
"Howe'er 'tis well that sleep awhile can free,
With soft forgetfulness a wretch like me;
Oh! were it given to yield this transient breath,
Send, O Diana! send the sleep of death!
Why must I waste a tedious life in tears,
Nor bury in the silent grave my cares?
O my Ulysses! ever honour'd name!
For thee I mourn till death dissolves my frame."

Thus wailing, slow and sadly she descends,
On either band a damsel train attends:
Full where the dome its shining valves expands,
Radiant before the gazing peers she stands;
A veil translucent o'er her brow display'd,
Her beauty seems, and only seems, to shade:
Sudden she lightens in their dazzled eyes,
And sudden flames in every bosom rise;
They send their eager souls with every look.
Till silence thus the imperial matron broke:

"O why! my son, why now no more appears
That warmth of soul that urged thy younger years?
Thy riper days no growing worth impart,
A man in stature, still a boy in heart!
Thy well-knit frame unprofitably strong,
Speaks thee a hero, from a hero sprung:
But the just gods in vain those gifts bestow,
O wise alone in form, and grave in show!
Heavens! could a stranger feel oppression's hand
Beneath thy roof, and couldst thou tamely stand!
If thou the stranger's righteous cause decline
His is the sufferance, but the shame is thine."

To whom, with filial awe, the prince returns:
"That generous soul with just resentment burns;
Yet, taught by time, my heart has learn'd to glow

For others' good, and melt at others' woe;
But, impotent those riots to repel,
I bear their outrage, though my soul rebel;
Helpless amid the snares of death I tread,
And numbers leagued in impious union dread;
But now no crime is theirs: this wrong proceeds
From Irus, and the guilty Irus bleeds.
Oh would to Jove! or her whose arms display
The shield of Jove, or him who rules the day!
That yon proud suitors, who licentious tread
These courts, within these courts like Irus bled:
Whose loose head tottering, as with wine oppress'd,
Obliquely drops, and nodding knocks his breast;
Powerless to move, his staggering feet deny
The coward wretch the privilege to fly."

Then to the queen Eurymachus replies:
"O justly loved, and not more fair than wise!
Should Greece through all her hundred states survey
Thy finish'd charms, all Greece would own thy sway
In rival crowds contest the glorious prize.
Dispeopling realms to gaze upon thy eyes:
O woman! loveliest of the lovely kind,
In body perfect, and complete in mind."

"Ah me! (returns the queen) when from this shore
Ulysses sail'd, then beauty was no more!
The gods decreed these eyes no more should keep
Their wonted grace, but only serve to weep.
Should he return, whate'er my beauties prove,
My virtues last; my brightest charm is love.
Now, grief, thou all art mine! the gods o'ercast
My soul with woes, that long, ah long must last!
Too faithfully my heart retains the day
That sadly tore my royal lord away:
He grasp'd my hand, and, 'O, my spouse! I leave
Thy arms (he cried), perhaps to find a grave:
Fame speaks the Trojans bold; they boast the skill
To give the feather'd arrow wings to kill,
To dart the spear, and guide the rushing car
With dreadful inroad through the walks of war.
My sentence is gone forth, and 'tis decreed
Perhaps by righteous Heaven that I must bleed!
My father, mother, all I trust to three;
To them, to them, transfer the love of me:
But, when my son grows man, the royal sway
Resign, and happy be thy bridal day!'
Such were his words; and Hymen now prepares

To light his torch, and give me up to cares;
The afflictive hand of wrathful Jove to bear:
A wretch the most complete that breathes the air!
Fall'n e'en below the rights to woman due!
Careless to please, with insolence ye woo!
The generous lovers, studious to succeed,
Bid their whole herds and flocks in banquets bleed;
By precious gifts the vow sincere display:
You, only you, make her ye love your prey."

Well-pleased Ulysses hears his queen deceive
The suitor-train, and raise a thirst to give:
False hopes she kindles, but those hopes betray,
And promise, yet elude, the bridal day.

While yet she speaks, the gay Antinous cries:
"Offspring of kings, and more than woman wise!
'Tis right; 'tis man's prerogative to give,
And custom bids thee without shame receive;
Yet never, never, from thy dome we move,
Till Hymen lights the torch of spousal love."

The peers despatch'd their heralds to convey
The gifts of love; with speed they take the way.
A robe Antinous gives of shining dyes,
The varying hues in gay confusion rise
Rich from the artist's hand! Twelve clasps of gold
Close to the lessening waist the vest infold!
Down from the swelling loins the vest unbound
Floats in bright waves redundant o'er the ground,
A bracelet rich with gold, with amber gay,
That shot effulgence like the solar ray,
Eurymachus presents: and ear-rings bright,
With triple stars, that casts a trembling light.
Pisander bears a necklace wrought with art:
And every peer, expressive of his heart,
A gift bestows: this done, the queen ascends,
And slow behind her damsel train attends.

Then to the dance they form the vocal strain,
Till Hesperus leads forth the starry train;
And now he raises, as the daylight fades,
His golden circlet in the deepening shades:
Three vases heap'd with copious fires display
O'er all the palace a fictitious day;
From space to space the torch wide-beaming burns,
And sprightly damsels trim the rays by turns.

To whom the king: "Ill suits your sex to stay
Alone with men! ye modest maids, away!
Go, with the queen; the spindle guide; or cull
(The partners of her cares) the silver wool;
Be it my task the torches to supply
E'en till the morning lamp adorns the sky;
E'en till the morning, with unwearied care,
Sleepless I watch; for I have learn'd to bear."

Scornful they heard: Melantho, fair and young,
(Melantho, from the loins of Dolius sprung,
Who with the queen her years an infant led,
With the soft fondness of a daughter bred,)
Chiefly derides: regardless of the cares
Her queen endures, polluted joys she shares
Nocturnal with Eurymachus: with eyes
That speak disdain, the wanton thus replies:
"Oh! whither wanders thy distemper'd brain,
Thou bold intruder on a princely train?
Hence, to the vagrants' rendezvous repair;
Or shun in some black forge the midnight air.
Proceeds this boldness from a turn of soul,
Or flows licentious from the copious bowl?
Is it that vanquish'd Irus swells thy mind?
A foe may meet thee of a braver kind,
Who, shortening with a storm of blows thy stay,
Shall send thee howling all in blood away!"

To whom with frowns: "O impudent in wrong!
Thy lord shall curb that insolence of tongue;
Know, to Telemachus I tell the offence;
The scourge, the scourge shall lash thee into sense."

With conscious shame they hear the stern rebuke,
Nor longer durst sustain the sovereign look.

Then to the servile task the monarch turns
His royal hands: each torch refulgent burns
With added day: meanwhile in museful mood,
Absorb'd in thought, on vengeance fix'd he stood.
And now the martial maid, by deeper wrongs
To rouse Ulysses, points the suitors' tongues:
Scornful of age, to taunt the virtuous man,
Thoughtless and gay, Eurymachus began:

"Hear me (he cries), confederates and friends!
Some god, no doubt, this stranger kindly sends;
The shining baldness of his head survey,

It aids our torchlight, and reflects the ray."

Then to the king that levell'd haughty Troy:
"Say, if large hire can tempt thee to employ
Those hands in work; to tend the rural trade,
To dress the walk, and form the embowering shade.
So food and raiment constant will I give:
But idly thus thy soul prefers to live,
And starve by strolling, not by work to thrive."

To whom incensed: "Should we, O prince, engage
In rival tasks beneath the burning rage
Of summer suns; were both constrain'd to wield
Foodless the scythe along the burden'd field;
Or should we labour while the ploughshare wounds,
With steers of equal strength, the allotted grounds,
Beneath my labours, how thy wondering eyes
Might see the sable field at once arise!
Should Jove dire war unloose, with spear and shield,
And nodding helm, I tread the ensanguined field,
Fierce in the van: then wouldst thou, wouldst thou,—say,—
Misname me glutton, in that glorious day?
No, thy ill-judging thoughts the brave disgrace
'Tis thou injurious art, not I am base.
Proud to seem brave among a coward train!
But now, thou art not valorous, but vain.
God! should the stern Ulysses rise in might,
These gates would seem too narrow for thy flight."

While yet he speaks, Eurymachus replies,
With indignation flashing from his eyes:

"Slave, I with justice might deserve the wrong,
Should I not punish that opprobrious tongue.
Irreverent to the great, and uncontroll'd,
Art thou from wine, or innate folly, bold?
Perhaps these outrages from Irus flow,
A worthless triumph o'er a worthless foe!"

He said, and with full force a footstool threw;
Whirl'd from his arm, with erring rage it flew:
Ulysses, cautious of the vengeful foe,
Stoops to the ground, and disappoints the blow.
Not so a youth, who deals the goblet round,
Full on his shoulder it inflicts a wound;
Dash'd from his hand the sounding goblet flies,
He shrieks, he reels, he falls, and breathless lies.
Then wild uproar and clamour mount the sky,

Till mutual thus the peers indignant cry:
"Oh had this stranger sunk to realms beneath,
To the black realms of darkness and of death,
Ere yet he trod these shores! to strife he draws
Peer against peer; and what the weighty cause?
A vagabond! for him the great destroy,
In vile ignoble jars, the feast of joy."

To whom the stern Telemachus uprose;
"Gods! what wild folly from the goblet flows!
Whence this unguarded openness of soul,
But from the license of the copious bowl?
Or Heaven delusion sends: but hence away!
Force I forbear, and without force obey."

Silent, abash'd, they hear the stern rebuke,
Till thus Amphinomus the silence broke:

"True are his words, and he whom truth offends,
Not with Telemachus, but truth contends;
Let not the hand of violence invade
The reverend stranger, or the spotless maid;
Retire we hence, but crown with rosy wine
The flowing goblet to the powers divine!
Guard he his guest beneath whose roof he stands:
This justice, this the social rite demands."

The peers assent: the goblet Mulius crown'd
With purple juice, and bore in order round:
Each peer successive his libation pours
To the blest gods who fill'd the ethereal bowers:
Then swill'd with wine, with noise the crowds obey,
And rushing forth, tumultuous reel away.

BOOK XIX

ARGUMENT

THE DISCOVERY OF ULYSSES TO EURYCLEA

Ulysses and his son remove the weapons out of the armoury. Ulysses, in conversation with Penelope,
gives a fictitious account of his adventures; then assures her he had formerly entertained her husband in
Crete; and describes exactly his person and dress; affirms to have heard of him in Phaeacia and
Thesprotia, and that his return is certain, and within a month. He then goes to bathe, and is attended by
Euryclea, who discovers him to be Ulysses by the scar upon his leg, which he formerly received in

hunting the wild boar on Parnassus. The poet inserts a digression relating that accident, with all its particulars.

Consulting secret with the blue-eyed maid,
Still in the dome divine Ulysses stay'd:
Revenge mature for act inflamed his breast;
And thus the son the fervent sire address'd:

"Instant convey those steely stores of war
To distant rooms, disposed with secret care:
The cause demanded by the suitor-train,
To soothe their fears, a specious reason feign:
Say, since Ulysses left his natal coast,
Obscene with smoke, their beamy lustre lost,
His arms deform the roof they wont adorn:
From the glad walls inglorious lumber torn.
Suggest, that Jove the peaceful thought inspired,
Lest they, by sight of swords to fury fired,
Dishonest wounds, or violence of soul,
Defame the bridal feast and friendly bowl."

The prince, obedient to the sage command,
To Euryclea thus: "The female band
In their apartments keep; secure the doors;
These swarthy arms among the covert stores
Are seemlier hid; my thoughtless youth they blame,
Imbrown'd with vapour of the smouldering flame."

"In happier hour (pleased Euryclea cries),
Tutour'd by early woes, grow early wise;
Inspect with sharpen'd sight, and frugal care,
Your patrimonial wealth, a prudent heir.
But who the lighted taper will provide
(The female train retired) your toils to guide?"

"Without infringing hospitable right,
This guest (he cried) shall bear the guiding light:
I cheer no lazy vagrants with repast;
They share the meal that earn it ere they taste."

He said: from female ken she straight secures
The purposed deed, and guards the bolted doors:
Auxiliar to his son, Ulysses bears
The plumy-crested helms and pointed spears,
With shields indented deep in glorious wars.
Minerva viewless on her charge attends,
And with her golden lamp his toil befriends.
Not such the sickly beams, which unsincere

Gild the gross vapour of this nether sphere!
A present deity the prince confess'd,
And wrapp'd with ecstasy the sire address'd:

"What miracle thus dazzles with surprise!
Distinct in rows the radiant columns rise;
The walls, where'er my wondering sight I turn,
And roofs, amidst a blaze of glory burn!
Some visitant of pure ethereal race
With his bright presence deigns the dome to grace."

"Be calm (replies the sire); to none impart,
But oft revolve the vision in thy heart:
Celestials, mantled in excess of light,
Can visit unapproach'd by mortal sight.
Seek thou repose: whilst here I sole remain,
To explore the conduct of the female train:
The pensive queen, perchance, desires to know
The series of my toils, to soothe her woe."

With tapers flaming day his train attends,
His bright alcove the obsequious youth ascends:
Soft slumberous shades his drooping eyelids close,
Till on her eastern throne Aurora glows.

Whilst, forming plans of death, Ulysses stay'd,
In counsel secret with the martial maid,
Attendant nymphs in beauteous order wait
The queen, descending from her bower of state.
Her cheeks the warmer blush of Venus wear,
Chasten'd with coy Diana's pensive air.
An ivory seat with silver ringlets graced,
By famed Icmalius wrought, the menials placed:
With ivory silver'd thick the footstool shone,
O'er which the panther's various hide was thrown.
The sovereign seat with graceful air she press'd;
To different tasks their toil the nymphs address'd:
The golden goblets some, and some restored
From stains of luxury the polish'd board:
These to remove the expiring embers came,
While those with unctuous fir foment the flame.

'Twas then Melantho with imperious mien
Renew'd the attack, incontinent of spleen:
"Avaunt (she cried), offensive to my sight!
Deem not in ambush here to lurk by night,
Into the woman-state asquint to pry;
A day-devourer, and an evening spy!

Vagrant, begone! before this blazing brand
Shall urge"—and waved it hissing in her hand.

The insulted hero rolls his wrathful eyes
And "Why so turbulent of soul? (he cries;)
Can these lean shrivell'd limbs, unnerved with age,
These poor but honest rags, enkindle rage?
In crowds, we wear the badge of hungry fate:
And beg, degraded from superior state!
Constrain'd a rent-charge on the rich I live;
Reduced to crave the good I once could give:
A palace, wealth, and slaves, I late possess'd,
And all that makes the great be call'd the bless'd:
My gate, an emblem of my open soul,
Embraced the poor, and dealt a bounteous dole.
Scorn not the sad reverse, injurious maid!
'Tis Jove's high will, and be his will obey'd!
Nor think thyself exempt: that rosy prime
Must share the general doom of withering time:
To some new channel soon the changeful tide
Of royal grace the offended queen may guide;
And her loved lord unplume thy towering pride.
Or, were he dead, 'tis wisdom to beware:
Sweet blooms the prince beneath Apollo's care;
Your deeds with quick impartial eye surveys,
Potent to punish what he cannot praise."

Her keen reproach had reach'd the sovereign's ear:
"Loquacious insolent! (she cries,) forbear;
To thee the purpose of my soul I told;
Venial discourse, unblamed, with him to hold;
The storied labours of my wandering lord,
To soothe my grief he haply may record:
Yet him, my guest, thy venom'd rage hath stung;
Thy head shall pay the forfeit of thy tongue!
But thou on whom my palace cares depend,
Eurynome, regard the stranger-friend:
A seat, soft spread with furry spoils, prepare;
Due-distant for us both to speak, and hear."

The menial fair obeys with duteous haste:
A seat adorn'd with furry spoils she placed:
Due-distant for discourse the hero sate;
When thus the sovereign from her chair of state:

"Reveal, obsequious to my first demand,
Thy name, thy lineage, and thy natal land."

He thus: "O queen! whose far-resounding fame
Is bounded only by the starry frame,
Consummate pattern of imperial sway,
Whose pious rule a warlike race obey!
In wavy gold thy summer vales are dress'd;
Thy autumns bind with copious fruit oppress'd:
With flocks and herds each grassy plain is stored;
And fish of every fin thy seas afford:
Their affluent joys the grateful realms confess;
And bless the power that still delights to bless,
Gracious permit this prayer, imperial dame!
Forbear to know my lineage, or my name:
Urge not this breast to heave, these eyes to weep;
In sweet oblivion let my sorrows sleep!
My woes awaked, will violate your ear,
And to this gay censorious train appear
A whiny vapour melting in a tear."

"Their gifts the gods resumed (the queen rejoin'd),
Exterior grace, and energy of mind,
When the dear partner of my nuptial joy,
Auxiliar troops combined, to conquer Troy.
My lord's protecting hand alone would raise
My drooping verdure, and extend my praise!
Peers from the distant Samian shore resort:
Here with Dulichians join'd, besiege the court:
Zacynthus, green with ever-shady groves,
And Ithaca, presumptuous, boast their loves:
Obtruding on my choice a second lord,
They press the Hymenaean rite abhorr'd.
Misrule thus mingling with domestic cares,
I live regardless of my state affairs;
Receive no stranger-guest, no poor relieve;
But ever for my lord in secret grieve!—
This art, instinct by some celestial power,
I tried, elusive of the bridal hour:

"'Ye peers, (I cry,) who press to gain a heart,
Where dead Ulysses claims no future part;
Rebate your loves, each rival suit suspend,
Till this funeral web my labours end:
Cease, till to good Laertes I bequeath
A pall of state, the ornament of death.
For when to fate he bows, each Grecian dame
With just reproach were licensed to defame,
Should he, long honour'd in supreme command,
Want the last duties of a daughter's hand.'
The fiction pleased; their loves I long elude;

The night still ravell'd what the day renew'd:
Three years successful in my heart conceal'd,
My ineffectual fraud the fourth reveal'd:
Befriended by my own domestic spies,
The woof unwrought the suitor-train surprise.
From nuptial rites they now no more recede,
And fear forbids to falsify the brede.
My anxious parents urge a speedy choice,
And to their suffrage gain the filial voice.
For rule mature, Telemachus deplores
His dome dishonour'd, and exhausted stores—
But, stranger! as thy days seem full of fate,
Divide discourse, in turn thy birth relate:
Thy port asserts thee of distinguish'd race;
No poor unfather'd product of disgrace."

"Princess! (he cries,) renew'd by your command,
The dear remembrance of my native land
Of secret grief unseals the fruitful source;
Fond tears repeat their long-forgotten course!
So pays the wretch whom fate constrains to roam,
The dues of nature to his natal home!—
But inward on my soul let sorrow prey,
Your sovereign will my duty bids obey.

"Crete awes the circling waves, a fruitful soil!
And ninety cities crown the sea-born isle:
Mix'd with her genuine sons, adopted names
In various tongues avow their various claims:
Cydonians, dreadful with the bended yew,
And bold Pelasgi boast a native's due:
The Dorians, plumed amid the files of war,
Her foodful glebe with fierce Achaians share;
Cnossus, her capital of high command;
Where sceptred Minos with impartial hand
Divided right: each ninth revolving year,
By Jove received in council to confer.
His son Deucalion bore successive sway:
His son, who gave me first to view the day!
The royal bed an elder issue bless'd,
Idomeneus whom Ilion fields attest
Of matchless deeds: untrain'd to martial toil,
I lived inglorious in my native isle.
Studious of peace, and Aethon is my name.
'Twas then to Crete the great Ulysses came.
For elemental war, and wintry Jove,
From Malea's gusty cape his navy drove
To bright Lucina's fane; the shelfy coast

Where loud Amnisus in the deep is lost.
His vessel's moor'd (an incommodious port!)
The hero speeded to the Cnossian court:
Ardent the partner of his arms to find,
In leagues of long commutual friendship join'd.
Vain hope! ten suns had warm'd the western strand
Since my brave brother, with his Cretan band,
Had sail'd for Troy: but to the genial feast
My honour'd roof received the royal guest:
Beeves for his train the Cnossian peers assign,
A public treat, with jars of generous wine.
Twelve days while Boreas vex'd the aerial space,
My hospitable dome he deign'd to grace:
And when the north had ceased the stormy roar,
He wing'd his voyage to the Phrygian shore."

Thus the fam'd hero, perfected in wiles,
With fair similitude of truth beguiles
The queen's attentive ear: dissolved in woe,
From her bright eyes the tears unbounded flow,
As snows collected on the mountain freeze;
When milder regions breathe a vernal breeze,
The fleecy pile obeys the whispering gales,
Ends in a stream, and murmurs through the vales:
So, melting with the pleasing tale he told,
Down her fair cheek the copious torrent roll'd:
She to her present lord laments him lost,
And views that object which she wants the most,
Withering at heart to see the weeping fair,
His eyes look stern, and cast a gloomy stare;
Of horn the stiff relentless balls appear,
Or globes of iron fix'd in either sphere;
Firm wisdom interdicts the softening tear.
A speechless interval of grief ensues,
Till thus the queen the tender theme renews.

"Stranger! that e'er thy hospitable roof
Ulysses graced, confirm by faithful proof;
Delineate to my view my warlike lord,
His form, his habit, and his train record."

"'Tis hard (he cries,) to bring to sudden sight
Ideas that have wing'd their distant flight;
Rare on the mind those images are traced,
Whose footsteps twenty winters have defaced:
But what I can, receive.—In ample mode,
A robe of military purple flow'd
O'er all his frame: illustrious on his breast,

The double-clasping gold the king confess'd.
In the rich woof a hound, mosaic drawn,
Bore on full stretch, and seized a dappled fawn;
Deep in the neck his fangs indent their hold;
They pant and struggle in the moving gold.
Fine as a filmy web beneath it shone
A vest, that dazzled like a cloudless sun:
The female train who round him throng'd to gaze,
In silent wonder sigh'd unwilling praise.
A sabre, when the warrior press'd to part,
I gave, enamell'd with Vulcanian art:
A mantle purple-tinged, and radiant vest,
Dimension'd equal to his size, express'd
Affection grateful to my honour'd guest.
A favourite herald in his train I knew,
His visage solemn, sad of sable hue:
Short woolly curls o'erfleeced his bending head,
O'er which a promontory shoulder spread;
Eurybates; in whose large soul alone
Ulysses view'd an image of his own."

His speech the tempest of her grief restored;
In all he told she recognized her lord:
But when the storm was spent in plenteous showers,
A pause inspiriting her languish'd powers,
"O thou, (she cried,) whom first inclement Fate
Made welcome to my hospitable gate;
With all thy wants the name of poor shall end:
Henceforth live honour'd, my domestic friend!
The vest much envied on your native coast,
And regal robe with figured gold emboss'd,
In happier hours my artful hand employ'd,
When my loved lord this blissful bower enjoy'd:
The fall of Troy erroneous and forlorn
Doom'd to survive, and never to return!"

Then he, with pity touch'd: "O royal dame!
Your ever-anxious mind, and beauteous frame,
From the devouring rage of grief reclaim.
I not the fondness of your soul reprove
For such a lord! who crown'd your virgin love
With the dear blessing of a fair increase;
Himself adorn'd with more than mortal grace:
Yet while I speak the mighty woe suspend;
Truth forms my tale; to pleasing truth attend.
The royal object of your dearest care
Breathes in no distant clime the vital air:
In rich Thesprotia, and the nearer bound

Of Thessaly, his name I heard renown'd:
Without retinue, to that friendly shore
Welcomed with gifts of price, a sumless store!
His sacrilegious train, who dared to prey
On herds devoted to the god of day,
Were doom'd by Jove, and Phoebus' just decree,
To perish in the rough Trinacrian sea.
To better fate the blameless chief ordain'd,
A floating fragment of the wreck regain'd,
And rode the storm; till, by the billows toss'd,
He landed on the fair Phaeacian coast.
That race who emulate the life of gods,
Receive him joyous to their bless'd abodes;
Large gifts confer, a ready sail command,
To speed his voyage to the Grecian strand.
But your wise lord (in whose capacious soul
High schemes of power in just succession roll)
His Ithaca refused from favouring Fate,
Till copious wealth might guard his regal state.
Phedon the fact affirm'd, whose sovereign sway
Thesprotian tribes, a duteous race, obey;
And bade the gods this added truth attest
(While pure libations crown'd the genial feast),
That anchor'd in his port the vessels stand,
To waft the hero to his natal land.
I for Dulichium urge the watery way,
But first the Ulyssean wealth survey:
So rich the value of a store so vast
Demands the pomp of centuries to waste!
The darling object of your royal love
Was journey'd thence to Dodonean Jove;
By the sure precept of the sylvan shrine,
To form the conduct of his great design;
Irresolute of soul, his state to shroud
In dark disguise, or come, a king avow'd!
Thus lives your lord; nor longer doom'd to roam;
Soon will he grace this dear paternal dome.
By Jove, the source of good, supreme in power!
By the bless'd genius of this friendly bower!
I ratify my speech, before the sun
His annual longitude of heaven shall run;
When the pale empress of yon starry train
In the next month renews her faded wane,
Ulysses will assert his rightful reign."

"What thanks! what boon! (replied the queen), are due,
When time shall prove the storied blessing true!
My lord's return should fate no more retard,

Envy shall sicken at thy vast reward.
But my prophetic fears, alas! presage
The wounds of Destiny's relentless rage.
I long must weep, nor will Ulysses come,
With royal gifts to send you honour'd home!—
Your other task, ye menial train forbear:
Now wash the stranger, and the bed prepare:
With splendid palls the downy fleece adorn:
Uprising early with the purple morn.
His sinews, shrunk with age, and stiff with toil,
In the warm bath foment with fragrant oil.
Then with Telemachus the social feast
Partaking free, my soul invited guest;
Whoe'er neglects to pay distinction due,
The breach of hospitable right may rue.
The vulgar of my sex I most exceed
In real fame, when most humane my deed;
And vainly to the praise of queen aspire,
If, stranger! I permit that mean attire
Beneath the feastful bower. A narrow space
Confines the circle of our destin'd race;
'Tis ours with good the scanty round to grace.
Those who to cruel wrong their state abuse,
Dreaded in life the mutter'd curse pursues;
By death disrobed of all their savage powers,
Then, licensed rage her hateful prey devours.
But he whose inborn worth his acts commend,
Of gentle soul, to human race a friend;
The wretched he relieves diffuse his fame,
And distant tongues extol the patron-name."

"Princess? (he cried) in vain your bounties flow
On me, confirm'd and obstinate in woe.
When my loved Crete received my final view,
And from my weeping eyes her cliffs withdrew;
These tatter'd weeds (my decent robes resign'd)
I chose, the livery of a woful mind!
Nor will my heart-corroding care abate
With splendid palls, and canopies of state:
Low-couch'd on earth, the gift of sleep I scorn,
And catch the glances of the waking morn.
The delicacy of your courtly train
To wash a wretched wanderer would disdain;
But if, in tract of long experience tried,
And sad similitude of woes allied,
Some wretch reluctant views aerial light,
To her mean hand assign the friendly rite."

Pleased with his wise reply, the queen rejoin'd:
"Such gentle manners, and so sage a mind,
In all who graced this hospitable bower
I ne'er discerned, before this social hour.
Such servant as your humble choice requires,
To light received the lord of my desires,
New from the birth; and with a mother's hand
His tender bloom to manly growth sustain'd:
Of matchless prudence, and a duteous mind;
Though now to life's extremest verge declined,
Of strength superior to the toil design'd—
Rise, Euryclea! with officious care
For the poor friend the cleansing bath prepare:
This debt his correspondent fortunes claim,
Too like Ulysses, and perhaps the same!
Thus old with woes my fancy paints him now!
For age untimely marks the careful brow."

Instant, obsequious to the mild command,
Sad Euryclea rose: with trembling hand
She veils the torrent of her tearful eyes;
And thus impassion'd to herself replies:

"Son of my love, and monarch of my cares,
What pangs for thee this wretched bosom bears!
Are thus by Jove who constant beg his aid
With pious deed, and pure devotion, paid?
He never dared defraud the sacred fane
Of perfect hecatombs in order slain:
There oft implored his tutelary power,
Long to protract the sad sepulchral hour;
That, form'd for empire with paternal care,
His realm might recognize an equal heir.
O destined head! The pious vows are lost;
His God forgets him on a foreign coast!—
Perhaps, like thee, poor guest! in wanton pride
The rich insult him, and the young deride!
Conscious of worth reviled, thy generous mind
The friendly rite of purity declined;
My will concurring with my queen's command,
Accept the bath from this obsequious hand.
A strong emotion shakes my anguish'd breast:
In thy whole form Ulysses seems express'd;
Of all the wretched harboured on our coast,
None imaged e'er like thee my master lost."

Thus half-discover'd through the dark disguise,
With cool composure feign'd, the chief replies:

"You join your suffrage to the public vote;
The same you think have all beholders thought."

He said: replenish'd from the purest springs,
The laver straight with busy care she brings:
In the deep vase, that shone like burnish'd gold,
The boiling fluid temperates the cold.
Meantime revolving in his thoughtful mind
The scar, with which his manly knee was sign'd;
His face averting from the crackling blaze,
His shoulders intercept the unfriendly rays:
Thus cautious in the obscure he hoped to fly
The curious search of Euryclea's eye.
Cautious in vain! nor ceased the dame to find
This scar with which his manly knee was sign'd.

This on Parnassus (combating the boar)
With glancing rage the tusky savage tore.
Attended by his brave maternal race,
His grandsire sent him to the sylvan chase,
Autolycus the bold (a mighty name
For spotless faith and deeds of martial fame:
Hermes, his patron god, those gifts bestow'd,
Whose shrine with weanling lambs he wont to load).
His course to Ithaca this hero sped,
When the first product of Laertes' bed
Was now disclosed to birth: the banquet ends,
When Euryclea from the queen descends,
And to his fond embrace the babe commends:
"Receive (she cries) your royal daughter's son;
And name the blessing that your prayers have won."
Then thus the hoary chief: "My victor arms
Have awed the realms around with dire alarms:
A sure memorial of my dreaded fame
The boy shall bear; Ulysses be his name!
And when with filial love the youth shall come
To view his mother's soil, my Delphic dome
With gifts of price shall send him joyous home."
Lured with the promised boon, when youthful prime
Ended in man, his mother's natal clime
Ulysses sought; with fond affection dear
Amphitea's arms received the royal heir:
Her ancient lord an equal joy possess'd;
Instant he bade prepare the genial feast:
A steer to form the sumptuous banquet bled,
Whose stately growth five flowery summers fed:
His sons divide, and roast with artful care
The limbs; then all the tasteful viands share.

Nor ceased discourse (the banquet of the soul),
Till Phoebus wheeling to the western goal
Resign'd the skies, and night involved the pole.
Their drooping eyes the slumberous shade oppress'd,
Sated they rose, and all retired to rest.

Soon as the morn, new-robed in purple light,
Pierced with her golden shafts the rear of night,
Ulysses, and his brave maternal race,
The young Autolyci, essay the chase.
Parnassus, thick perplex'd with horrid shades,
With deep-mouth'd hounds the hunter-troop invades;
What time the sun, from ocean's peaceful stream,
Darts o'er the lawn his horizontal beam.
The pack impatient snuff the tainted gale;
The thorny wilds the woodmen fierce assail:
And, foremost of the train, his cornel spear
Ulysses waved, to rouse the savage war.
Deep in the rough recesses of the wood,
A lofty copse, the growth of ages, stood;
Nor winter's boreal blast, nor thunderous shower,
Nor solar ray, could pierce the shady bower.
With wither'd foliage strew'd, a heapy store!
The warm pavilion of a dreadful boar.
Roused by the hounds' and hunters' mingling cries,
The savage from his leafy shelter flies;
With fiery glare his sanguine eye-balls shine,
And bristles high impale his horrid chine.
Young Ithacus advanced, defies the foe,
Poising his lifted lance in act to throw;
The savage renders vain the wound decreed,
And springs impetuous with opponent speed!
His tusks oblique he aim'd, the knee to gore;
Aslope they glanced, the sinewy fibres tore,
And bared the bone; Ulysses undismay'd,
Soon with redoubled force the wound repaid;
To the right shoulder-joint the spear applied,
His further flank with streaming purple dyed:
On earth he rushed with agonizing pain;
With joy and vast surprise, the applauding train
View'd his enormous bulk extended on the plain.
With bandage firm Ulysses' knee they bound;
Then, chanting mystic lays, the closing wound
Of sacred melody confess'd the force;
The tides of life regain'd their azure course.
Then back they led the youth with loud acclaim;
Autolycus, enamoured with his fame,
Confirm'd the cure; and from the Delphic dome

With added gifts return'd him glorious home.
He safe at Ithaca with joy received,
Relates the chase, and early praise achieved.

Deep o'er his knee inseam'd remain'd the scar;
Which noted token of the woodland war
When Euryclea found, the ablution ceased:
Down dropp'd the leg, from her slack hand released;
The mingled fluids from the base redound;
The vase reclining floats the floor around!
Smiles dew'd with tears the pleasing strife express'd
Of grief and joy, alternate in her breast.
Her fluttering words in melting murmurs died;
At length abrupt—"My son!—my king!"—she cried.
His neck with fond embrace infolding fast,
Full on the queen her raptured eye she cast
Ardent to speak the monarch safe restored:
But, studious to conceal her royal lord,
Minerva fix'd her mind on views remote,
And from the present bliss abstracts her thought.
His hand to Euryclea's mouth applied,
"Art thou foredoom'd my pest? (the hero cried:)
Thy milky founts my infant lips have drain'd;
And have the Fates thy babbling age ordain'd
To violate the life thy youth sustain'd?
An exile have I told, with weeping eyes,
Full twenty annual suns in distant skies;
At length return'd, some god inspires thy breast
To know thy king, and here I stand confess'd.
This heaven-discover'd truth to thee consign'd,
Reserve the treasure of thy inmost mind:
Else, if the gods my vengeful arm sustain,
And prostrate to my sword the suitor-train;
With their lewd mates, thy undistinguish'd age
Shall bleed a victim to vindictive rage."

Then thus rejoin'd the dame, devoid of fear:
"What words, my son, have passed thy lips severe?
Deep in my soul the trust shall lodge secured;
With ribs of steel, and marble heart, immured.
When Heaven, auspicious to thy right avow'd,
Shall prostrate to thy sword the suitor-crowd,
The deeds I'll blazon of the menial fair;
The lewd to death devote, the virtuous spare."

"Thy aid avails me not (the chief replied);
My own experience shall their doom decide:
A witness-judge precludes a long appeal:

Suffice it then thy monarch to conceal."

He said: obsequious, with redoubled pace,
She to the fount conveys the exhausted vase:
The bath renew'd, she ends the pleasing toil
With plenteous unction of ambrosial oil.
Adjusting to his limbs the tatter'd vest,
His former seat received the stranger guest;
Whom thus with pensive air the queen addressed:

"Though night, dissolving grief in grateful ease,
Your drooping eyes with soft impression seize;
Awhile, reluctant to her pleasing force,
Suspend the restful hour with sweet discourse.
The day (ne'er brighten'd with a beam of joy!)
My menials, and domestic cares employ;
And, unattended by sincere repose,
The night assists my ever-wakeful woes;
When nature's hush'd beneath her brooding shade,
My echoing griefs the starry vault invade.
As when the months are clad in flowery green,
Sad Philomel, in bowery shades unseen,
To vernal airs attunes her varied strains;
And Itylus sounds warbling o'er the plains;
Young Itylus, his parents' darling joy!
Whom chance misled the mother to destroy;
Now doom'd a wakeful bird to wail the beauteous boy.
So in nocturnal solitude forlorn,
A sad variety of woes I mourn!
My mind, reflective, in a thorny maze
Devious from care to care incessant strays.
Now, wavering doubt succeeds to long despair;
Shall I my virgin nuptial vow revere;
And, joining to my son's my menial train,
Partake his counsels, and assist his reign?
Or, since, mature in manhood, he deplores
His dome dishonour'd, and exhausted stores;
Shall I, reluctant! to his will accord;
And from the peers select the noblest lord;
So by my choice avow'd, at length decide
These wasteful love-debates, a mourning bride!
A visionary thought I'll now relate;
Illustrate, if you know, the shadow'd fate:

"A team of twenty geese (a snow-white train!)
Fed near the limpid lake with golden grain,
Amuse my pensive hours. The bird of Jove
Fierce from his mountain-eyrie downward drove;

Each favourite fowl he pounced with deathful sway,
And back triumphant wing'd his airy way.
My pitying eyes effused a plenteous stream,
To view their death thus imaged in a dream;
With tender sympathy to soothe my soul,
A troop of matrons, fancy-form'd, condole.
But whilst with grief and rage my bosom burn'd,
Sudden the tyrant of the skies returned;
Perch'd on the battlements he thus began
(In form an eagle, but in voice a man):
`O queen! no vulgar vision of the sky
I come, prophetic of approaching joy;
View in this plumy form thy victor-lord;
The geese (a glutton race) by thee deplored,
Portend the suitors fated to my sword.'
This said, the pleasing feather'd omen ceased.
When from the downy bands of sleep released,
Fast by the limpid lake my swan-like train
I found, insatiate of the golden grain."

"The vision self-explain'd (the chief replies)
Sincere reveals the sanction of the skies;
Ulysses speaks his own return decreed;
And by his sword the suitors sure to bleed."

"Hard is the task, and rare," (the queen rejoin'd,)
Impending destinies in dreams to find;
Immured within the silent bower of sleep,
Two portals firm the various phantoms keep;
Of ivory one; whence flit, to mock the brain,
Of winged lies a light fantastic train;
The gate opposed pellucid valves adorn,
And columns fair incased with polish'd horn;
Where images of truth for passage wait,
With visions manifest of future fate.
Not to this troop, I fear, that phantom soar'd,
Which spoke Ulysses to this realm restored;
Delusive semblance!-but my remnant life
Heaven shall determine in a gameful strife;
With that famed bow Ulysses taught to bend,
For me the rival archers shall contend.
As on the listed field he used to place
Six beams, opposed to six in equal space;
Elanced afar by his unerring art,
Sure through six circlets flew the whizzing dart.
So, when the sun restores the purple day,
Their strength and skill the suitors shall assay;
To him the spousal honour is decreed,

Who through the rings directs the feather'd reed.
Torn from these walls (where long the kinder powers
With joy and pomp have wing'd my youthful hours!)
On this poor breast no dawn of bliss shall beam;
The pleasure past supplies a copious theme
For many a dreary thought, and many a doleful dream!"

"Propose the sportive lot (the chief replies),
Nor dread to name yourself the bowyer's prize;
Ulysses will surprise the unfinish'd game,
Avow'd, and falsify the suitors' claim."

To whom with grace serene the queen rejoin'd:
"In all thy speech what pleasing force I find!
O'er my suspended woe thy words prevail;
I part reluctant from the pleasing tale,
But Heaven, that knows what all terrestrials need,
Repose to night, and toil to day decreed;
Grateful vicissitudes! yet me withdrawn,
Wakeful to weep and watch the tardy dawn
Establish'd use enjoins; to rest and joy
Estranged, since dear Ulysses sail'd to Troy!
Meantime instructed is the menial tribe
Your couch to fashion as yourself prescribe."

Thus affable, her bower the queen ascends;
The sovereign step a beauteous train attends;
There imaged to her soul Ulysses rose;
Down her pale cheek new-streaming sorrow flows;
Till soft oblivious shade Minerva spread,
And o'er her eyes ambrosial slumber shed.

BOOK XX

ARGUMENT

While Ulysses lies in the vestibule of the palace, he is witness to the disorders of the women. Minerva comforts him, and casts him asleep. At his waking he desires a favourable sign from Jupiter, which is granted. The feast of Apollo is celebrated by the people, and the suitors banquet in the palace. Telemachus exerts his authority amongst them; notwithstanding which, Ulysses is insulted by Caesippus, and the rest continue in their excesses. Strange prodigies are seen by Theoclymenus, the augur, who explains them to the destruction of the wooers.

An ample hide devine Ulysses spread.
And form'd of fleecy skins his humble bed
(The remnants of the spoil the suitor-crowd

In festival devour'd, and victims vow'd).
Then o'er the chief, Eurynome the chaste
With duteous care a downy carpet cast:
With dire revenge his thoughtful bosom glows,
And, ruminating wrath, he scorns repose.

As thus pavilion'd in the porch he lay,
Scenes of lewd loves his wakeful eyes survey,
Whilst to nocturnal joys impure repair,
With wanton glee, the prostituted fair.
His heart with rage this new dishonour stung,
Wavering his thoughts in dubious balance hung:
Or instant should he quench the guilty flame
With their own blood, and intercept the shame:
Or to their lust indulge a last embrace,
And let the peers consummate the disgrace
Round his swoln heart the murmurous fury rolls,
As o'er her young the mother-mastiff growls,
And bays the stranger groom: so wrath compress'd,
Recoiling, mutter'd thunder in his breast.
"Poor suffering heart! (he cried,) support the pain
Of wounded honour, and thy rage restrain.
Not fiercer woes thy fortitude could foil,
When the brave partners of thy ten years' toil
Dire Polypheme devour'd; I then was freed
By patient prudence from the death decreed."

Thus anchor'd safe on reason's peaceful coast,
Tempests of wrath his soul no longer toss'd;
Restless his body rolls, to rage resign'd
As one who long with pale-eyed famine pined,
The savoury cates on glowing embers cast
Incessant turns, impatient for repast
Ulysses so, from side to side-devolved,
In self-debate the suitor's doom resolved
When in the form of mortal nymph array'd,
From heaven descends the Jove-born martial maid;
And'hovering o'er his head in view confess'd,
The goddess thus her favourite care address'd:

"O thou, of mortals most inured to woes!
Why roll those eyes unfriended of repose?
Beneath thy palace-roof forget thy care;
Bless'd in thy queen! bless'd in thy blooming heir!
Whom, to the gods when suppliant fathers bow
They name the standard of their dearest vow."

"Just is thy kind reproach (the chief rejoin'd),

Deeds full of fate distract my various mind,
In contemplation wrapp'd. This hostile crew
What single arm hath prowess to subdue?
Or if, by Jove's and thy auxiliar aid,
They're doom'd to bleed; O say, celestial maid!
Where shall Ulysses shun, or how sustain
Nations embattled to revenge the slain?"

"Oh impotence of faith! (Minerva cries,)
If man on frail unknowing man relies,
Doubt you the gods? Lo, Pallas' self descends,
Inspires thy counsels, and thy toils attends.
In me affianced, fortify thy breast,
Though myriads leagued thy rightful claim contest
My sure divinity shall bear the shield,
And edge thy sword to reap the glorious field.
Now, pay the debt to craving nature due,
Her faded powers with balmy rest renew."
She ceased, ambrosial slumbers seal his eyes;
Her care dissolves in visionary joys
The goddess, pleased, regains her natal skies.

Not so the queen; the downy bands of sleep
By grief relax'd she waked again to weep:
A gloomy pause ensued of dumb despair;
Then thus her fate invoked, with fervent prayer

"Diana! speed thy deathful ebon dart,
And cure the pangs of this convulsive heart.
Snatch me, ye whirlwinds! far from human race,
Toss'd through the void illimitable space
Or if dismounted from the rapid cloud,
Me with his whelming wave let Ocean shroud!
So, Pandarus, thy hopes, three orphan fair;
Were doom'd to wander through the devious air;
Thyself untimely, and thy consort died,
But four celestials both your cares supplied.
Venus in tender delicacy rears
With honey, milk, and wine their infant years;
Imperial Juno to their youth assigned
A form majestic, and sagacious mind;
With shapely growth Diana graced their bloom;
And Pallas taught the texture of the loom.
But whilst, to learn their lots in nuptial love,
Bright Cytherea sought the bower of Jove
(The God supreme, to whose eternal eye
The registers of fate expanded lie;
Wing'd Harpies snatch the unguarded charge away,

And to the Furies bore a grateful prey.
Be such my lot! Or thou, Diana, speed
Thy shaft, and send me joyful to the dead;
To seek my lord among the warrior train,
Ere second vows my bridal faith profane.
When woes the waking sense alone assail,
Whilst Night extends her soft oblivious veil,
Of other wretches' care the torture ends;
No truce the warfare of my heart suspends!
The night renews the day distracting theme,
And airy terrors sable every dream.
The last alone a kind illusion wrought,
And to my bed my loved Ulysses brought,
In manly bloom, and each majestic grace,
As when for Troy he left my fond embrace;
Such raptures in my beating bosom rise,
I deem it sure a vision of the skies."

Thus, whilst Aurora mounts her purple throne,
In audible laments she breathes her moan;
The sounds assault Ulysses' wakeful ear;
Misjudging of the cause, a sudden fear
Of his arrival known, the chief alarms;
He thinks the queen is rushing to his arms.
Upspringing from his couch, with active haste
The fleece and carpet in the dome he placed
(The hide, without, imbibed the morning air);
And thus the gods invoked with ardent prayer:

"Jove, and eternal thrones! with heaven to friend,
If the long series of my woes shall end;
Of human race now rising from repose,
Let one a blissful omen here disclose;
And, to confirm my faith, propitious Jove!
Vouchsafe the sanction of a sign above."

Whilst lowly thus the chief adoring bows,
The pitying god his guardian aid avows.
Loud from a sapphire sky his thunder sounds;
With springing hope the hero's heart rebounds.
Soon, with consummate joy to crown his prayer,
An omen'd voice invades his ravish'd ear.
Beneath a pile that close the dome adjoin'd,
Twelve female slaves the gift of Ceres grind;
Task'd for the royal board to bolt the bran
From the pure flour (the growth and strength of man)
Discharging to the day the labour due,
Now early to repose the rest withdrew;

One maid unequal to the task assign'd,
Still turn'd the toilsome mill with anxious mind;
And thus in bitterness of soul divined:

"Father of gods and men, whose thunders roll
O'er the cerulean vault, and shake the pole:
Whoe'er from Heaven has gain'd this rare ostent
(Of granted vows a certain signal sent),
In this blest moment of accepted prayer,
Piteous, regard a wretch consumed with care!
Instant, O Jove! confound the suitor-train,
For whom o'ertoil'd I grind the golden grain:
Far from this dome the lewd devourers cast,
And be this festival decreed their last!"

Big with their doom denounced in earth and sky,
Ulysses' heart dilates with secret joy.
Meantime the menial train with unctious wood
Heap'd high the genial hearth, Vulcanian food:
When, early dress'd, advanced the royal heir;
With manly grasp he waved a martial spear;
A radiant sabre graced his purple zone,
And on his foot the golden sandal shone.
His steps impetuous to the portal press'd;
And Euryclea thus he there address'd:

"Say thou to whom my youth its nurture owes,
Was care for due refection and repose
Bestow'd the stranger-guest? Or waits he grieved,
His age not honour'd, nor his wants relieved?
Promiscuous grace on all the queen confers
(In woes bewilder'd, oft the wisest errs).
The wordy vagrant to the dole aspires,
And modest worth with noble scorn retires."

She thus: "O cease that ever-honour'd name
To blemish now: it ill deserves your blame,
A bowl of generous wine sufficed the guest;
In vain the queen the night refection press'd;
Nor would he court repose in downy state,
Unbless'd, abandon'd to the rage of Fate!
A hide beneath the portico was spread,
And fleecy skins composed an humble bed;
A downy carpet cast with duteous care,
Secured him from the keen nocturnal air."

His cornel javelin poised with regal port,
To the sage Greeks convened in Themis' court,

Forth-issuing from the dome the prince repair'd;
Two dogs of chase, a lion-hearted guard,
Behind him sourly stalked. Without delay
The dame divides the labour of the day;
Thus urging to the toil the menial train;

"What marks of luxury the marble stain
Its wonted lustre let the floor regain;
The seats with purple clothe in order due;
And let the abstersive sponge the board renew;
Let some refresh the vase's sullied mould;
Some bid the goblets boast their native gold;
Some to the spring, with each a jar, repair,
And copious waters pure for bathing bear;
Dispatch! for soon the suitors will essay
The lunar feast-rites to the god of day."

She said: with duteous haste a bevy fair
Of twenty virgins to the spring repair;
With varied toils the rest adorn the dome.
Magnificent, and blithe, the suitors come.
Some wield the sounding axe; the dodder'd oaks
Divide, obedient to the forceful strokes.
Soon from the fount, with each a brimming urn
(Eumaeus in their train), the maids return.
Three porkers for the feast, all brawny-chined,
He brought; the choicest of the tusky-kind;
In lodgments first secure his care he viewed,
Then to the king this friendly speech renew'd:
"Now say sincere, my guest! the suitor-train
Still treat thy worth with lordly dull disdain;
Or speaks their deed a bounteous mind humane?"

"Some pitying god (Ulysses sad replied)
With vollied vengeance blast their towering pride!
No conscious blush, no sense of right, restrains
The tides of lust that swell the boiling veins;
From vice to vice their appetites are toss'd,
All cheaply sated at another's cost!"

While thus the chief his woes indignant told,
Melanthius, master of the bearded fold,
The goodliest goats of all the royal herd
Spontaneous to the suitors' feast preferr'd;
Two grooms assistant bore the victims bound;
With quavering cries the vaulted roofs resound;
And to the chief austere aloud began
The wretch unfriendly to the race of man:

"Here vagrant, still? offensive to my lords!
Blows have more energy than airy words;
These arguments I'll use: nor conscious shame,
Nor threats, thy bold intrusion will reclaim.
On this high feast the meanest vulgar boast
A plenteous board! Hence! seek another host!"

Rejoinder to the churl the king disdain'd,
But shook his head, and rising wrath restrain'd.

From Cephanelia 'cross the surgy main
Philaetius late arrived, a faithful swain.
A steer ungrateful to the bull's embrace.
And goats he brought, the pride of all their race;
Imported in a shallop not his own;
The dome re-echoed to the mingl'd moan.
Straight to the guardian of the bristly kind
He thus began, benevolent of mind:

"What guest is he, of such majestic air?
His lineage and paternal clime declare:
Dim through the eclipse of fate, the rays divine
Of sovereign state with faded splendour shine.
If monarchs by the gods are plunged in woe,
To what abyss are we foredoom'd to go!"
Then affable he thus the chief address'd,
Whilst with pathetic warmth his hand he press'd:

"Stranger, may fate a milder aspect show,
And spin thy future with a whiter clue!
O Jove! for ever death to human cries;
The tyrant, not the father of the skies!
Unpiteous of the race thy will began!
The fool of fate, thy manufacture, man,
With penury, contempt, repulse, and care,
The galling load of life is doom'd to bear.
Ulysses from his state a wanderer still,
Upbraids thy power, thy wisdom, or thy will!
O monarch ever dear!-O man of woe!
Fresh flow my tears, and shall for ever flow!
Like thee, poor stranger guest, denied his home,
Like thee: in rags obscene decreed to roam!
Or, haply perish'd on some distant coast,
In stygian gloom he glides, a pensive ghost!
Oh, grateful for the good his bounty gave,
I'll grieve, till sorrow sink me to the grave!
His kind protecting hand my youth preferr'd,

The regent of his Cephalenian herd;
With vast increase beneath my care it spreads:
A stately breed! and blackens far the meads.
Constrain'd, the choicest beeves I thence import,
To cram these cormorants that crowd his court:
Who in partition seek his realm to share;
Nor human right nor wrath divine revere,
Since here resolved oppressive these reside,
Contending doubts my anxious heart divide:
Now to some foreign clime inclined to fly,
And with the royal herd protection buy;
Then, happier thoughts return the nodding scale,
Light mounts despair, alternate hopes prevail:
In opening prospects of ideal joy,
My king returns; the proud usurpers die."

To whom the chief: "In thy capacious mind
Since daring zeal with cool debate is join'd,
Attend a deed already ripe in fate:
Attest, O Jove! the truth I now relate!
This sacred truth attest, each genial power,
Who bless the board, and guard this friendly bower!
Before thou quit the dome (nor long delay)
Thy wish produced in act, with pleased survey,
Thy wondering eyes shall view: his rightful reign
By arms avow'd Ulysses shall regain,
And to the shades devote the suitor-train."

"O Jove supreme! (the raptured swain replies,)
With deeds consummate soon the promised joys!
These aged nerves, with new-born vigour strung,
In that blest cause should emulate the young."
Assents Eumaeus to the prayer address'd;
And equal ardours fire his loyal breast.

Meantime the suitors urge the prince's fate,
And deathful arts employ the dire debate:
When in his airy tour, the bird of Jove
Truss'd with his sinewy pounce a trembling dove;
Sinister to their hope! This omen eyed
Amphinomus, who thus presaging cried:

"The gods from force and fraud the prince defend;
O peers! the sanguinary scheme suspend:
Your future thought let sable fate employ;
And give the present hour to genial joy."

From council straight the assenting peerage ceased,

And in the dome prepared the genial feast.
Disrobed, their vests apart in order lay,
Then all with speed succinct the victims slay:
With sheep and shaggy goats the porkers bled,
And the proud steer was on the marble spread.
With fire prepared, they deal the morsels round,
Wine, rosy-bright, the brimming goblets crown'd,
By sage Eumaeus borne; the purple tide
Melanthius from an ample jar supplied:
High canisters of bread Philaetius placed;
And eager all devour the rich repast.
Disposed apart, Ulysses shares the treat;
A trivet table, and ignobler seat,
The prince appoints; but to his sire assigns
The tasteful inwards, and nectareous wines.
"Partake, my guest (he cried), without control
The social feast, and drain the cheering bowl:
Dread not the railer's laugh, nor ruffian's rage;
No vulgar roof protects thy honour'd age;
This dome a refuge to thy wrongs shall be,
From my great sire too soon devolved to me!
Your violence and scorn, ye suitors, cease,
Lest arms avenge the violated peace."

Awed by the prince, so haughty, brave, and young,
Rage gnaw'd the lip, amazement chain'd the tongue.
"Be patient, peers! (at length Antinous cries,)
The threats of vain imperious youth despise:
Would Jove permit the meditated blow,
That stream of eloquence should cease to flow."

Without reply vouchsafed, Antinous ceased:
Meanwhile the pomp of festival increased:
By heralds rank'd; in marshall'd order move
The city tribes, to pleased Apollo's grove:
Beneath the verdure of which awful shade,
The lunar hecatomb they grateful laid;
Partook the sacred feast, and ritual honours paid.
But the rich banquet, in the dome prepared
(An humble sideboard set) Ulysses shared.
Observant of the prince's high behest,
His menial train attend the stranger-guest;
Whom Pallas with unpardoning fury fired,
By lordly pride and keen reproach inspired.
A Samian peer, more studious than the rest
Of vice, who teem'd with many a dead-born jest;
And urged, for title to a consort queen,
Unnumber'd acres arable and green

(Otesippus named); this lord Ulysses eyed,
And thus burst out the imposthumate with pride:

"The sentence I propose, ye peers, attend:
Since due regard must wait the prince's friend,
Let each a token of esteem bestow:
This gift acquits the dear respect I owe;
With which he nobly may discharge his seat,
And pay the menials for a master's treat."

He said: and of the steer before him placed,
That sinewy fragment at Ulysses cast,
Where to the pastern-bone, by nerves combined,
The well-horn'd foot indissolubly join'd;
Which whizzing high, the wall unseemly sign'd.
The chief indignant grins a ghastly smile;
Revenge and scorn within his bosom boil:
When thus the prince with pious rage inflamed:
"Had not the inglorious wound thy malice aim'd
Fall'n guiltless of the mark, my certain spear
Had made thee buy the brutal triumph dear:
Nor should thy sire a queen his daughter boast;
The suitor, now, had vanish'd in a ghost:
No more, ye lewd compeers, with lawless power
Invade my dome, my herds and flocks devour:
For genuine worth, of age mature to know,
My grape shall redden, and my harvest grow
Or, if each other's wrongs ye still support,
With rapes and riot to profane my court;
What single arm with numbers can contend?
On me let all your lifted swords descend,
And with my life such vile dishonours end."

A long cessation of discourse ensued,
By gentler Agelaus thus renew'd:

"A just reproof, ye peers! your rage restrain
From the protected guest, and menial train:
And, prince! to stop the source of future ill,
Assent yourself, and gain the royal will.
Whilst hope prevail'd to see your sire restored,
Of right the queen refused a second lord:
But who so vain of faith, so blind to fate,
To think he still survives to claim the state?
Now press the sovereign dame with warm desire
To wed, as wealth or worth her choice inspire:
The lord selected to the nuptial joys
Far hence will lead the long-contested prize:

Whilst in paternal pomp with plenty bless'd,
You reign, of this imperial dome possess'd."

Sage and serene Telemachus replies:
"By him at whose behest the thunder flies,
And by the name on earth I most revere,
By great Ulysses and his woes I swear!
(Who never must review his dear domain;
Enroll'd, perhaps, in Pluto's dreary train),
Whene'er her choice the royal dame avows,
My bridal gifts shall load the future spouse:
But from this dome my parent queen to chase!
From me, ye gods! avert such dire disgrace."

But Pallas clouds with intellectual gloom
The suitors' souls, insensate of their doom!
A mirthful frenzy seized the fated crowd;
The roofs resound with causeless laughter loud;
Floating in gore, portentous to survey!
In each discolour'd vase the viands lay;
Then down each cheek the tears spontaneous flow
And sudden sighs precede approaching woe.
In vision wrapp'd, the Hyperesian seer
Uprose, and thus divined the vengeance near:

"O race to death devote! with Stygian shade
Each destin'd peer impending fates invade;
With tears your wan distorted cheeks are drown'd;
With sanguine drops the walls are rubied round:
Thick swarms the spacious hall with howling ghosts,
To people Orcus, and the burning coasts!
Nor gives the sun his golden orb to roll,
But universal night usurps the pole!"

Yet warn'd in vain, with laughter loud elate
The peers reproach the sure divine of Fate;
And thus Eurymachus: "The dotard's mind
To every sense is lost, to reason blind;
Swift from the dome conduct the slave away;
Let him in open air behold the day."

"Tax not (the heaven-illumined seer rejoin'd)
Of rage, or folly, my prophetic mind,
No clouds of error dim the ethereal rays,
Her equal power each faithful sense obeys.
Unguided hence my trembling steps I bend,
Far hence, before yon hovering deaths descend;
Lest the ripe harvest of revenge begun,

I share the doom ye suitors cannot shun."

This said, to sage Piraeus sped the seer,
His honour'd host, a welcome inmate there.
O'er the protracted feast the suitors sit,
And aim to wound the prince with pointless wit:
Cries one, with scornful leer and mimic voice,
"Thy charity we praise, but not thy choice;
Why such profusion of indulgence shown
To this poor, timorous, toil-detesting drone?
That others feeds on planetary schemes,
And pays his host with hideous noon-day dreams.
But, prince! for once at least believe a friend;
To some Sicilian mart these courtiers send,
Where, if they yield their freight across the main,
Dear sell the slaves! demand no greater gain."

Thus jovial they; but nought the prince replies;
Full on his sire he roll'd his ardent eyes:
Impatient straight to flesh his virgin-sword;
From the wise chief he waits the deathful word.
Nigh in her bright alcove, the pensive queen
To see the circle sate, of all unseen.
Sated at length they rise, and bid prepare
An eve-repast, with equal cost and care:
But vengeful Pallas, with preventing speed,
A feast proportion'd to their crimes decreed;
A feast of death, the feasters doom'd to bleed!

BOOK XXI

ARGUMENT

THE BENDING OF ULYSSES' BOW

Penelope, to put an end to the solicitation of the suitors, proposes to marry the person who shall first bend the bow of Ulysses, and shoot through the ringlets. After their attempts have proved ineffectual, Ulysses, taking Eumaeus and Philaetius apart, discovers himself to them; then returning, desires leave to try his strength at the bow, which, though refused with indignation by the suitors, Penelope and Telemachus cause it to be delivered to his hands. He bends it immediately, and shoots through all the rings. Jupiter at the same instant thunders from heaven; Ulysses accepts the omen, and gives a sign to Telemachus, who stands ready armed at his side.

And Pallas now, to raise the rivals' fires,
With her own art Penelope inspires
Who now can bend Ulysses' bow, and wing

The well-aim'd arrow through the distant ring,
Shall end the strife, and win the imperial dame:
But discord and black death await the game!

The prudent queen the lofty stair ascends:
At distance due a virgin-train attends;
A brazen key she held, the handle turn'd,
With steel and polish'd elephant adorn'd:
Swift to the inmost room she bent her way,
Where, safe reposed, the royal treasures lay:
There shone high heap'd the labour'd brass and ore,
And there the bow which great Ulysses bore;
And there the quiver, where now guiltless slept
Those winged deaths that many a matron wept.

This gift, long since when Sparta's shore he trod,
On young Ulysses Iphitus bestowed:
Beneath Orsilochus' roof they met;
One loss was private, one a public debt;
Messena's state from Ithaca detains
Three hundred sheep, and all the shepherd swains;
And to the youthful prince to urge the laws,
The king and elders trust their common cause.
But Iphitus, employed on other cares,
Search'd the wide country for his wandering mares,
And mules, the strongest of the labouring kind;
Hapless to search; more hapless still to find!
For journeying on to Hercules, at length
That lawless wretch, that man of brutal strength,
Deaf to Heaven's voice, the social rites transgress'd;
And for the beauteous mares destroy'd his guest.
He gave the bow; and on Ulysses' part
Received a pointed sword, and missile dart:
Of luckless friendship on a foreign shore
Their first, last pledges! for they met no more.
The bow, bequeath'd by this unhappy hand,
Ulysses bore not from his native land;
Nor in the front of battle taught to bend,
But kept in dear memorial of his friend.

Now gently winding up the fair ascent,
By many an easy step the matron went;
Then o'er the pavement glides with grace divine
(With polish'd oak the level pavements shine);
The folding gates a dazzling light display'd,
With pomp of various architrave o'erlaid.
The bolt, obedient to the silken string,
Forsakes the staple as she pulls the ring;

The wards respondent to the key turn round;
The bars fall back; the flying valves resound;
Loud as a bull makes hill and valley ring,
So roar'd the lock when it released the spring.
She moves majestic through the wealthy room,
Where treasured garments cast a rich perfume;
There from the column where aloft it hung,
Reach'd in its splendid case, the bow unstrung;
Across her knees she laid the well-known bow,
And pensive sate, and tears began to flow.
To full satiety of grief she mourns,
Then silent to the joyous hall returns,
To the proud suitors bears in pensive state
The unbended bow, and arrows winged with fate.

Behind, her train the polish'd coffer brings,
Which held the alternate brass and silver rings.
Full in the portal the chaste queen appears,
And with her veil conceals the coming tears:
On either side awaits a virgin fair;
While thus the matron, with majestic air:

"Say you, when these forbidden walls inclose,
For whom my victims bleed, my vintage flows:
If these neglected, faded charms can move?
Or is it but a vain pretence, you love?
If I the prize, if me you seek to wife,
Hear the conditions, and commence the strife.
Who first Ulysses' wondrous bow shall bend,
And through twelve ringlets the fleet arrow send;
Him will I follow, and forsake my home,
For him forsake this loved, this wealthy dome,
Long, long the scene of all my past delight,
And still to last, the vision of my night!"

Graceful she said, and bade Eumaeus show
The rival peers the ringlets and the bow.
From his full eyes the tears unbidden spring,
Touch'd at the dear memorials of his king.
Philaetius too relents, but secret shed
The tender drops. Antinous saw, and said:

"Hence to your fields, ye rustics! hence away,
Nor stain with grief the pleasures of the day;
Nor to the royal heart recall in vain
The sad remembrance of a perish'd man.
Enough her precious tears already flow—
Or share the feast with due respect; or go

To weep abroad, and leave to us the bow,
No vulgar task! Ill suits this courtly crew
That stubborn horn which brave Ulysses drew.
I well remember (for I gazed him o'er
While yet a child), what majesty he bore!
And still (all infant as I was) retain
The port, the strength, the grandeur of the man."

He said, but in his soul fond joys arise,
And his proud hopes already win the prize.
To speed the flying shaft through every ring,
Wretch! is not thine: the arrows of the king
Shall end those hopes, and fate is on the wing!

Then thus Telemachus: "Some god I find
With pleasing frenzy has possess'd my mind;
When a loved mother threatens to depart,
Why with this ill-timed gladness leaps my heart?
Come then, ye suitors! and dispute a prize
Richer than all the Achaian state supplies,
Than all proud Argos, or Mycaena knows,
Than all our isles or continents inclose;
A woman matchless, and almost divine,
Fit for the praise of every tongue but mine.
No more excuses then, no more delay;
Haste to the trial—Lo! I lead the way.

"I too may try, and if this arm can wing
The feather'd arrow through the destined ring,
Then if no happier night the conquest boast,
I shall not sorrow for a mother lost;
But, bless'd in her, possess those arms alone,
Heir of my father's strength, as well as throne."

He spoke; then rising, his broad sword unbound,
And cast his purple garment on the ground.
A trench he open'd: in a line he placed.
The level axes, and the points made fast
(His perfect skill the wondering gazers eyed,
The game as yet unseen, as yet untried).
Then, with a manly pace, he took his stand:
And grasp'd the bow, and twang'd it in his hand.
Three times, with beating heart, he made essay:
Three times, unequal to the task, gave way;
A modest boldness on his cheek appear'd:
And thrice he hoped, and thrice again he fear'd.
The fourth had drawn it. The great sire with joy
Beheld, but with a sign forbade the boy.

His ardour straight the obedient prince suppress'd,
And, artful, thus the suitor-train address'd:

"O lay the cause on youth yet immature!
(For heaven forbid such weakness should endure!)
How shall this arm, unequal to the bow,
Retort an insult, or repel a foe?
But you! whom Heaven with better nerves has bless'd,
Accept the trial, and the prize contest."

He cast the bow before him, and apart
Against the polish'd quiver propp'd the dart.
Resuming then his seat, Eupithes' son,
The bold Antinous, to the rest begun:
"From where the goblet first begins to flow,
From right to left in order take the bow;
And prove your several strengths." The princes heard
And first Leiodes, blameless priest'd, appear'd:
The eldest born of Oenops' noble race,
Who next the goblet held his holy place:
He, only he, of all the suitor throng,
Their deeds detested, and abjured the wrong.
With tender hands the stubborn horn he strains,
The stubborn horn resisted all his pains!
Already in despair he gives it o'er:
"Take it who will (he cries), I strive no more,
What numerous deaths attend this fatal bow!
What souls and spirits shall it send below!
Better, indeed, to die, and fairly give
Nature her debt, than disappointed live,
With each new sun to some new hope a prey,
Yet still to-morrow falser than to-day.
How long in vain Penelope we sought!
This bow shall ease us of that idle thought,
And send us with some humbler wife to live,
Whom gold shall gain, or destiny shall give."

Thus speaking, on the floor the bow he placed
(With rich inlay the various floor was graced):
At distance far the feather'd shaft he throws,
And to the seat returns from whence he rose.

To him Antinous thus with fury said:
"What words ill-omen'd from thy lips have fled?
Thy coward-function ever is in fear!
Those arms are dreadful which thou canst not bear,
Why should this bow be fatal to the brave?
Because the priest is born a peaceful slave.

Mark then what others can." He ended there,
And bade Melanthius a vast pile prepare;
He gives it instant flame, then fast beside
Spreads o'er an ample board a bullock's hide.
With melted lard they soak the weapon o'er,
Chafe every knot, and supple every pore.
Vain all their art, and all their strength as vain;
The bow inflexible resists their pain.
The force of great Eurymachus alone
And bold Antinous, yet untired, unknown:
Those only now remain'd; but those confess'd
Of all the train the mightiest and the best.

Then from the hall, and from the noisy crew,
The masters of the herd and flock withdrew.
The king observes them, he the hall forsakes,
And, past the limits of the court, o'ertakes.
Then thus with accent mild Ulysses spoke:
"Ye faithful guardians of the herd and flock!
Shall I the secret of my breast conceal,
Or (as my soul now dictates) shall I tell?
Say, should some favouring god restore again
The lost Ulysses to his native reign,
How beat your hearts? what aid would you afford
To the proud suitors, or your ancient lord?"

Philaetius thus: "O were thy word not vain!
Would mighty Jove restore that man again!
These aged sinews, with new vigour strung,
In his blest cause should emulate the young."
With equal vows Eumaeus too implored
Each power above, with wishes for his lord.

He saw their secret souls, and thus began:
"Those vows the gods accord; behold the man!
Your own Ulysses! twice ten years detain'd
By woes and wanderings from this hapless land:
At length he comes; but comes despised, unknown,
And finding faithful you, and you alone.
All else have cast him from their very thought,
E'en in their wishes and their prayers forgot!
Hear then, my friends: If Jove this arm succeed,
And give yon impious revellers to bleed,
My care shall be to bless your future lives
With large possessions and with faithful wives;
Fast by my palace shall your domes ascend,
And each on young Telemachus attend,
And each be call'd his brother and my friend.

To give you firmer faith, now trust your eye;
Lo! the broad scar indented on my thigh,
When with Autolycus' sons, of yore,
On Parnass' top I chased the tusky boar."
His ragged vest then drawn aside disclosed
The sign conspicuous, and the scar exposed:
Eager they view'd, with joy they stood amazed
With tearful eyes o'er all their master gazed:
Around his neck their longing arms they cast,
His head, his shoulders, and his knees embraced;
Tears followed tears; no word was in their power;
In solemn silence fell the kindly shower.
The king too weeps, the king too grasps their hands;
And moveless, as a marble fountain, stands.

Thus had their joy wept down the setting sun,
But first the wise man ceased, and thus begun:
"Enough—on other cares your thought employ,
For danger waits on all untimely joy.
Full many foes and fierce, observe us near;
Some may betray, and yonder walls may hear.
Re-enter then, not all at once, but stay
Some moments you, and let me lead the way.
To me, neglected as I am I know
The haughty suitors will deny the bow;
But thou, Eumaeus, as 'tis borne away,
Thy master's weapon to his hand convey.
At every portal let some matron wait,
And each lock fast the well-compacted gate:
Close let them keep, whate'er invades their ear;
Though arms, or shouts, or dying groans they hear.
To thy strict charge, Philaetius, we consign
The court's main gate: to guard that pass be thine."

This said, he first return'd; the faithful swains
At distance follow, as their king ordains.
Before the flame Eurymachus now stands,
And turns the bow, and chafes it with his hands
Still the tough bow unmoved. The lofty man
Sigh'd from his mighty soul, and thus began:

"I mourn the common cause: for, oh, my friends,
On me, on all, what grief, what shame attends!
Not the lost nuptials can affect me more
(For Greece has beauteous dames on every shore),
But baffled thus! confess'd so far below
Ulysses' strength, as not to bend his bow!
How shall all ages our attempt deride!

Our weakness scorn!" Antinous thus replied:

"Not so, Eurymachus: that no man draws
The wondrous bow, attend another cause.
Sacred to Phoebus is the solemn day,
Which thoughtless we in games would waste away:
Till the next dawn this ill-timed strife forego,
And here leave fixed the ringlets in a row.
Now bid the sewer approach, and let us join
In due libations, and in rites divine,
So end our night: before the day shall spring,
The choicest offerings let Melanthius bring:
Let then to Phoebus' name the fatted thighs
Feed the rich smokes high curling to the skies.
So shall the patron of these arts bestow
(For his the gift) the skill to bend the bow."

They heard well pleased: the ready heralds bring
The cleansing waters from the limpid spring:
The goblet high with rosy wine they crown'd,
In order circling to the peers around.
That rite complete, uprose the thoughtful man,
And thus his meditated scheme began:

"If what I ask your noble minds approve,
Ye peers and rivals in the royal love!
Chief, if it hurt not great Antinous' ear
(Whose sage decision I with wonder hear),
And if Eurymachus the motion please:
Give Heaven this day and rest the bow in peace.
To-morrow let your arms dispute the prize,
And take it he, the favour'd of the skies!
But, since till then this trial you delay,
Trust it one moment to my hands to-day:
Fain would I prove, before your judging eyes,
What once I was, whom wretched you despise:
If yet this arm its ancient force retain;
Or if my woes (a long-continued train)
And wants and insults, make me less than man."

Rage flash'd in lightning from the suitors' eyes,
Yet mixed with terror at the bold emprise.
Antinous then: "O miserable guest!
Is common sense quite banish'd from thy breast?
Sufficed it not, within the palace placed,
To sit distinguish'd, with our presence graced,
Admitted here with princes to confer,
A man unknown, a needy wanderer?

To copious wine this insolence we owe,
And much thy betters wine can overthrow:
The great Eurytian when this frenzy stung,
Pirithous' roofs with frantic riot rung;
Boundless the Centaur raged; till one and all
The heroes rose, and dragg'd him from the hall;
His nose they shorten'd, and his ears they slit,
And sent him sober'd home, with better wit.
Hence with long war the double race was cursed,
Fatal to all, but to the aggressor first.
Such fate I prophesy our guest attends,
If here this interdicted bow he bends:
Nor shall these walls such insolence contain:
The first fair wind transports him o'er the main,
Where Echetus to death the guilty brings
(The worst of mortals, e'en the worst of kings).
Better than that, if thou approve our cheer;
Cease the mad strife and share our bounty here."

To this the queen her just dislike express'd:

"'Tis impious, prince, to harm the stranger-guest,
Base to insult who bears a suppliant's name,
And some respect Telemachus may claim.
What if the immortals on the man bestow
Sufficient strength to draw the mighty bow?
Shall I, a queen, by rival chiefs adored,
Accept a wandering stranger for my lord?
A hope so idle never touch'd his brain:
Then ease your bosoms of a fear so vain.
Far be he banish'd from this stately scene
Who wrongs his princess with a thought so mean."

"O fair! and wisest of so fair a kind!
(Respectful thus Eurymachus rejoin'd,)
Moved by no weak surmise, but sense of shame,
We dread the all-arraigning voice of Fame:
We dread the censure of the meanest slave,
The weakest woman: all can wrong the brave.
'Behold what wretches to the bed pretend
Of that brave chief whose bow they could not bend!
In came a beggar of the strolling crew,
And did what all those princes could not do.'
Thus will the common voice our deed defame,
And thus posterity upbraid our name."

To whom the queen: "If fame engage your views,
Forbear those acts which infamy pursues;

Wrong and oppression no renown can raise;
Know, friend! that virtue is the path to praise.
The stature of our guest, his port, his face,
Speak him descended from no vulgar race.
To him the bow, as he desires, convey;
And to his hand if Phoebus give the day,
Hence, to reward his merit, be shall bear
A two-edged falchion and a shining spear,
Embroider'd sandals, a rich cloak and vest,
A safe conveyance to his port of rest."

"O royal mother! ever-honour'd name!
Permit me (cries Telemachus) to claim
A son's just right. No Grecian prince but I
Has power this bow to grant or to deny.
Of all that Ithaca's rough hills contain,
And all wide Elis' courser-breeding plain,
To me alone my father's arms descend;
And mine alone they are, to give or lend.
Retire, O queen! thy household task resume,
Tend, with thy maids, the labours of thy loom;
The bow, the darts, and arms of chivalry,
These cares to man belong, and most to me."

Mature beyond his years, the queen admired
His sage reply, and with her train retired;
There in her chamber as she sate apart,
Revolved his words, and placed them in her heart.
On her Ulysses then she fix'd her soul;
Down her fair cheek the tears abundant roll,
Till gentle Pallas, piteous of her cries,
In slumber closed her silver-streaming eyes.

Now through the press the bow Eumaeus bore,
And all was riot, noise, and wild uproar.
"Hold! lawless rustic! whither wilt thou go?
To whom, insensate, dost thou bear the bow?
Exiled for this to some sequester'd den,
Far from the sweet society of men,
To thy own dogs a prey thou shalt be made;
If Heaven and Phoebus lend the suitors aid."
Thus they. Aghast he laid the weapon down,
But bold Telemachus thus urged him on:
"Proceed, false slave, and slight their empty words:
What! hopes the fool to please so many lords?
Young as I am, thy prince's vengeful hand
Stretch'd forth in wrath shall drive thee from the land.
Oh! could the vigour of this arm as well

The oppressive suitors from my walls expel!
Then what a shoal of lawless men should go
To fill with tumult the dark courts below!"

The suitors with a scornful smile survey
The youth, indulging in the genial day.
Eumaeus, thus encouraged, hastes to bring
The strifeful bow and gives it to the king.
Old Euryclea calling them aside,
"Hear what Telemachus enjoins (he cried):
At every portal let some matron wait,
And each lock fast the well-compacted gate;
And if unusual sounds invade their ear,
If arms, or shouts, or dying groans they hear,
Let none to call or issue forth presume,
But close attend the labours of the loom."

Her prompt obedience on his order waits;
Closed in an instant were the palace gates.
In the same moment forth Philaetius flies,
Secures the court, and with a cable ties
The utmost gate (the cable strongly wrought
Of Byblos' reed, a ship from Egypt brought);
Then unperceived and silent at the board
His seat he takes, his eyes upon his lord.

And now his well-known bow the master bore,
Turn'd on all sides, and view'd it o'er and o'er;
Lest time or worms had done the weapon wrong,
Its owner absent, and untried so long.
While some deriding—"How he turns the bow!
Some other like it sure the man must know,
Or else would copy; or in bows he deals;
Perhaps he makes them, or perhaps he steals."
"Heaven to this wretch (another cried) be kind!
And bless, in all to which he stands inclined.
With such good fortune as he now shall find."

Heedless he heard them: but disdain'd reply;
The bow perusing with exactest eye.
Then, as some heavenly minstrel, taught to sing
High notes responsive to the trembling string,
To some new strain when he adapts the lyre,
Or the dumb lute refits with vocal wire,
Relaxes, strains, and draws them to and fro;
So the great master drew the mighty bow,
And drew with ease. One hand aloft display'd
The bending horns, and one the string essay'd.

From his essaying hand the string, let fly,
Twang'd short and sharp like the shrill swallow's cry.
A general horror ran through all the race,
Sunk was each heart, and pale was every face,
Signs from above ensued: the unfolding sky
In lightning burst; Jove thunder'd from on high.
Fired at the call of heaven's almighty Lord,
He snatch'd the shaft that glitter'd on the board
(Fast by, the rest lay sleeping in the sheath,
But soon to fly the messengers of death).

Now sitting as he was, the cord he drew,
Through every ringlet levelling his view:
Then notch'd the shaft, released, and gave it wing;
The whizzing arrow vanished from the string,
Sung on direct, and threaded every ring.
The solid gate its fury scarcely bounds;
Pierced through and through the solid gate resounds,
Then to the prince: "Nor have I wrought thee shame;
Nor err'd this hand unfaithful to its aim;
Nor prov'd the toil too hard; nor have I lost
That ancient vigour, once my pride and boast.
Ill I deserved these haughty peers' disdain;
Now let them comfort their dejected train,
In sweet repast their present hour employ,
Nor wait till evening for the genial joy:
Then to the lute's soft voice prolong the night;
Music, the banquet's most refined delight."

He said, then gave a nod; and at the word
Telemachus girds on his shining sword.
Fast by his father's side he takes his stand:
The beamy javelin lightens in his hand.

BOOK XXII

ARGUMENT

THE DEATH OF THE SUITORS

Ulysses begins the slaughter of the suitors by the death of Antinous. He declares himself, and lets fly his arrows at the rest. Telemachus assists and brings arms for his father, himself, Eumaeus, and Philaetius. Melanthius does the same for the wooers. Minerva encourages Ulysses in the shape of Mentor. The suitors are all slain, only Medon and Phemius are spared. Melanthius and the unfaithful servants are executed. The rest acknowledge their master with all demonstrations of joy.

Then fierce the hero o'er the threshold strode;
Stripp'd of his rags, he blazed out like a god.
Full in their face the lifted bow he bore,
And quiver'd deaths, a formidable store;
Before his feet the rattling shower he threw,
And thus, terrific, to the suitor-crew:

"One venturous game this hand hath won to-day,
Another, princes! yet remains to play;
Another mark our arrow must attain.
Phoebus, assist! nor be the labour vain."
Swift as the word the parting arrow sings,
And bears thy fate, Antinous, on its wings:
Wretch that he was, of unprophetic soul!
High in his hands he rear'd the golden bowl!
E'en then to drain it lengthen'd out his breath;
Changed to the deep, the bitter draught of death:
For fate who fear'd amidst a feastful band?
And fate to numbers, by a single hand?
Full through his throat Ulysses' weapon pass'd,
And pierced his neck. He falls, and breathes his last.
The tumbling goblet the wide floor o'erflows,
A stream of gore burst spouting from his nose;
Grim in convulsive agonies be sprawls:
Before him spurn'd the loaded table falls,
And spreads the pavement with a mingled flood
Of floating meats, and wine, and human blood.
Amazed, confounded, as they saw him fall,
Up rose he throngs tumultuous round the hall:
O'er all the dome they cast a haggard eye,
Each look'd for arms—in vain; no arms were nigh:
"Aim'st thou at princes? (all amazed they said;)
Thy last of games unhappy hast thou play'd;
Thy erring shaft has made our bravest bleed,
And death, unlucky guest, attends thy deed.
Vultures shall tear thee." Thus incensed they spoke,
While each to chance ascribed the wondrous stroke:
Blind as they were: for death e'en now invades
His destined prey, and wraps them all in shades.
Then, grimly frowning, with a dreadful look,
That wither'd all their hearts, Ulysses spoke:

"Dogs, ye have had your day! ye fear'd no more
Ulysses vengeful from the Trojan shore;
While, to your lust and spoil a guardless prey,
Our house, our wealth, our helpless handmaids lay:
Not so content, with bolder frenzy fired,
E'en to our bed presumptuous you aspired:

Laws or divine or human fail'd to move,
Or shame of men, or dread of gods above;
Heedless alike of infamy or praise,
Or Fame's eternal voice in future days;
The hour of vengeance, wretches, now is come;
Impending fate is yours, and instant doom."

Thus dreadful he. Confused the suitors stood,
From their pale cheeks recedes the flying blood:
Trembling they sought their guilty heads to hide.
Alone the bold Eurymachus replied:

"If, as thy words import (he thus began),
Ulysses lives, and thou the mighty man,
Great are thy wrongs, and much hast thou sustain'd
In thy spoil'd palace, and exhausted land;
The cause and author of those guilty deeds,
Lo! at thy feet unjust Antinous bleeds
Not love, but wild ambition was his guide;
To slay thy son, thy kingdom to divide,
These were his aims; but juster Jove denied.
Since cold in death the offender lies, oh spare
Thy suppliant people, and receive their prayer!
Brass, gold, and treasures, shall the spoil defray,
Two hundred oxen every prince shall pay:
The waste of years refunded in a day.
Till then thy wrath is just." Ulysses burn'd
With high disdain, and sternly thus return'd:

"All, all the treasure that enrich'd our throne
Before your rapines, join'd with all your own,
If offer'd, vainly should for mercy call;
'Tis you that offer, and I scorn them all;
Your blood is my demand, your lives the prize,
Till pale as yonder wretch each suitor lies.
Hence with those coward terms; or fight or fly;
This choice is left you, to resist or die:
And die I trust ye shall." He sternly spoke:
With guilty fears the pale assembly shook.
Alone Eurymachus exhorts the train:
"Yon archer, comrades, will not shoot in vain;
But from the threshold shall his darts be sped,
(Whoe'er he be), till every prince lie dead?
Be mindful of yourselves, draw forth your swords,
And to his shafts obtend these ample boards
(So need compels). Then, all united, strive
The bold invader from his post to drive:
The city roused shall to our rescue haste,

And this mad archer soon have shot his last."
Swift as he spoke, he drew his traitor sword,
And like a lion rush'd against his lord:
The wary chief the rushing foe repress'd,
Who met the point and forced it in his breast:
His falling hand deserts the lifted sword,
And prone he falls extended o'er the board!
Before him wide, in mix'd effusion roll
The untasted viands, and the jovial bowl.
Full through his liver pass'd the mortal wound,
With dying rage his forehead beats the ground;
He spurn'd the seat with fury as he fell,
And the fierce soul to darkness dived, and hell.
Next bold Amphinomus his arm extends
To force the pass; the godlike man defends.
Thy spear, Telemachus, prevents the attack,
The brazen weapon driving through his back.
Thence through his breast its bloody passage tore;
Flat falls he thundering on the marble floor,
And his crush'd forehead marks the stone with gore.
He left his javelin in the dead, for fear
The long encumbrance of the weighty spear
To the fierce foe advantage might afford,
To rash between and use the shorten'd sword.
With speedy ardour to his sire he flies,
And, "Arm, great father! arm (in haste he cries).
Lo, hence I run for other arms to wield,
For missive javelins, and for helm and shield;
Fast by our side let either faithful swain
In arms attend us, and their part sustain."

"Haste, and return (Ulysses made reply)
While yet the auxiliar shafts this hand supply;
Lest thus alone, encounter'd by an host,
Driven from the gate, the important past be lost."

With speed Telemachus obeys, and flies
Where piled in heaps the royal armour lies;
Four brazen helmets, eight refulgent spears,
And four broad bucklers to his sire he bears:
At once in brazen panoply they shone.
At once each servant braced his armour on;
Around their king a faithful guard they stand.
While yet each shaft flew deathful from his hand:
Chief after chief expired at every wound,
And swell'd the bleeding mountain on the ground.
Soon as his store of flying fates was spent.
Against the wall he set the bow unbent;

And now his shoulders bear the massy shield,
And now his hands two beamy javelins wield:
He frowns beneath his nodding plume, that play'd
O'er the high crest, and cast a dreadful shade.

There stood a window near, whence looking down
From o'er the porch appear'd the subject town.
A double strength of valves secured the place,
A high and narrow; but the only pass:
The cautious king, with all-preventing care,
To guard that outlet, placed Eumaeus there;
When Agelaus thus: "Has none the sense
To mount yon window, and alarm from thence
The neighbour-town? the town shall force the door,
And this bold archer soon shall shoot no more."
Melanthius then: "That outlet to the gate
So near adjoins, that one may guard the strait.
But other methods of defence remain;
Myself with arms can furnish all the train;
Stores from the royal magazine I bring,
And their own darts shall pierce the prince and king."

He said; and mounting up the lofty stairs,
Twelve shields, twelve lances, and twelve helmets bears:
All arm, and sudden round the hall appears
A blaze of bucklers, and a wood of spears.

The hero stands oppress'd with mighty woe,
On every side he sees the labour grow;
"Oh cursed event! and oh unlook'd for aid!
Melanthius or the women have betray'd—
Oh my dear son!"—The father with a sigh
Then ceased; the filial virtue made reply;

"Falsehood is folly, and 'tis just to own
The fault committed: this was mine alone;
My haste neglected yonder door to bar,
And hence the villain has supplied their war.
Run, good Eumaeus, then, and (what before
I thoughtless err'd in) well secure that door:
Learn, if by female fraud this deed were done,
Or (as my thought misgives) by Dolius' son."

While yet they spoke, in quest of arms again
To the high chamber stole the faithless swain,
Not unobserved. Eumaeus watchful eyed,
And thus address'd Ulysses near his side:

"The miscreant we suspected takes that way;
Him, if this arm be powerful, shall I slay?
Or drive him hither, to receive the meed
From thy own hand, of this detested deed?"

"Not so (replied Ulysses); leave him there,
For us sufficient is another care;
Within the structure of this palace wall
To keep enclosed his masters till they fall.
Go you, and seize the felon; backward bind
His arms and legs, and fix a plank behind:
On this his body by strong cords extend,
And on a column near the roof suspend:
So studied tortures his vile days shall end."

The ready swains obey'd with joyful haste,
Behind the felon unperceived they pass'd,
As round the room in quest of arms he goes
(The half-shut door conceal'd his lurking foes):
One hand sustain'd a helm, and one the shield
Which old Laertes wont in youth to wield,
Cover'd with dust, with dryness chapp'd and worn,
The brass corroded, and the leather torn.
Thus laden, o'er the threshold as he stepp'd,
Fierce on the villain from each side they leap'd,
Back by the hair the trembling dastard drew,
And down reluctant on the pavement threw.
Active and pleased the zealous swains fulfil
At every point their master's rigid will;
First, fast behind, his hands and feet they bound,
Then straighten'd cords involved his body round;
So drawn aloft, athwart the column tied,
The howling felon swung from side to side.

Eumaeus scoffing then with keen disdain:
"There pass thy pleasing night, O gentle swain!
On that soft pillow, from that envied height,
First may'st thou see the springing dawn of light;
So timely rise, when morning streaks the east,
To drive thy victims to the suitors' feast."

This said, they, left him, tortured as he lay,
Secured the door, and hasty strode away:
Each, breathing death, resumed his dangerous post
Near great Ulysses; four against an host,
When lo! descending to her hero's aid,
Jove's daughter, Pallas, War's triumphant maid:
In Mentor's friendly form she join'd his side:

Ulysses saw, and thus with transport cried:

"Come, ever welcome, and thy succour lend;
O every sacred name in one, my friend!
Early we loved, and long our loves have grown;
Whate'er through life's whole series I have done,
Or good, or grateful, now to mind recall,
And, aiding this one hour, repay it all."

Thus he; but pleasing hopes his bosom warm
Of Pallas latent in the friendly form.
The adverse host the phantom-warrior eyed,
And first, loud-threatening, Agelaus cried:

"Mentor, beware, nor let that tongue persuade
Thy frantic arm to lend Ulysses aid;
Our force successful shall our threat make good,
And with the sire and son commix thy blood.
What hopest thou here? Thee first the sword shall slay,
Then lop thy whole posterity away;
Far hence thy banish'd consort shall we send;
With his thy forfeit lands and treasures blend;
Thus, and thus only, shalt thou join thy friend."

His barbarous insult even the goddess fires,
Who thus the warrior to revenge inspires:

"Art thou Ulysses? where then shall we find
The patient body and the constant mind?
That courage, once the Trojans' daily dread,
Known nine long years, and felt by heroes dead?
And where that conduct, which revenged the lust
Of Priam's race, and laid proud Troy in dust?
If this, when Helen was the cause, were done;
What for thy country now, thy queen, thy son?
Rise then in combat, at my side attend;
Observe what vigour gratitude can lend,
And foes how weak, opposed against a friend!"

She spoke; but willing longer to survey
The sire and son's great acts withheld the day!
By farther toils decreed the brave to try,
And level poised the wings of victory;
Then with a change of form eludes their sight,
Perch'd like a swallow on a rafter's height,
And unperceived enjoys the rising fight.

Damastor's son, bold Agelaus, leads,

The guilty war, Eurynomus succeeds;
With these, Pisander, great Polyctor's son,
Sage Polybus, and stern Amphimedon,
With Demoptolemus: these six survive:
The best of all the shafts had left alive.
Amidst the carnage, desperate as they stand,
Thus Agelaus roused the lagging band:

"The hour has come, when yon fierce man no more
With bleeding princes shall bestrew the floor;
Lo! Mentor leaves him with an empty boast;
The four remain, but four against an host.
Let each at once discharge the deadly dart,
One sure of six shall reach Ulysses' heart:
The rest must perish, their great leader slain:
Thus shall one stroke the glory lost regain."

Then all at once their mingled lances threw,
And thirsty all of one man's blood they flew;
In vain! Minerva turned them with her breath,
And scattered short, or wide, the points of death!
With deaden'd sound one on the threshold falls,
One strikes the gate, one rings against the walls:
The storm passed innocent. The godlike man
Now loftier trod, and dreadful thus began:
"'Tis now (brave friends) our turn, at once to throw,
(So speed them Heaven) our javelins at the foe.
That impious race to all their past misdeeds
Would add our blood, injustice still proceeds."

He spoke: at once their fiery lances flew:
Great Demoptolemus Ulysses slew;
Euryades received the prince's dart;
The goatherd's quiver'd in Pisander's heart;
Fierce Elatus by thine, Eumaeus, falls;
Their fall in thunder echoes round the walls.
The rest retreat: the victors now advance,
Each from the dead resumes his bloody lance.
Again the foe discharge the steely shower;
Again made frustrate by the virgin-power.
Some, turn'd by Pallas, on the threshold fall,
Some wound the gate, some ring against the wall;
Some weak, or ponderous with the brazen head,
Drop harmless on the pavement, sounding dead.

Then bold Amphimedon his javelin cast:
Thy hand, Telemachus, it lightly razed:
And from Ctesippus' arm the spear elanced:

On good Eumaeus' shield and shoulder glanced;
Not lessened of their force (so light the wound)
Each sung along and dropped upon the ground.
Fate doom'd thee next, Eurydamus, to bear,
Thy death ennobled by Ulysses' spear.
By the bold son Amphimedon was slain,
And Polybus renown'd, the faithful swain.
Pierced through the breast the rude Ctesippus bled,
And thus Philaetius gloried o'er the dead:

"There end thy pompous vaunts and high disdain;
O sharp in scandal, voluble and vain!
How weak is mortal pride! To Heaven alone
The event of actions and our fates are known:
Scoffer, behold what gratitude we bear:
The victim's heel is answered with this spear."

Ulysses brandish'd high his vengeful steel,
And Damastorides that instant fell:
Fast by Leocritus expiring lay,
The prince's javelin tore its bloody way
Through all his bowels: down he tumbled prone,
His batter'd front and brains besmear the stone.

Now Pallas shines confess'd; aloft she spreads
The arm of vengeance o'er their guilty heads:
The dreadful aegis blazes in their eye:
Amazed they see, they tremble, and they fly:
Confused, distracted, through he rooms they fling:
Like oxen madden'd by the breeze's sting,
When sultry days, and long, succeed the gentle spring,
Not half so keen fierce vultures of the chase
Stoop from the mountains on the feather'd race,
When, the wide field extended snares beset,
With conscious dread they shun the quivering net:
No help, no flight; but wounded every way,
Headlong they drop; the fowlers seize their prey.
On all sides thus they double wound on wound,
In prostrate heaps the wretches beat the ground,
Unmanly shrieks precede each dying groan,
And a red deluge floats the reaking stone.

Leiodes first before the victor falls:
The wretched augur thus for mercy calls:
"Oh gracious hear, nor let thy suppliant bleed;
Still undishonoured, or by word or deed,
Thy house, for me remains; by me repress'd
Full oft was check'd the injustice of the rest:

Averse they heard me when I counselled well,
Their hearts were harden'd, and they justly fell.
O spare an augur's consecrated head,
Nor add the blameless to the guilty dead."

"Priest as thou art! for that detested band
Thy lying prophecies deceived the land;
Against Ulysses have thy vows been made,
For them thy daily orisons were paid:
Yet more, e'en to our bed thy pride aspires:
One common crime one common fate requires."

Thus speaking, from the ground the sword he took
Which Agelaus' dying hand forsook:
Full through his neck the weighty falchion sped;
Along the pavement roll'd the muttering head.

Phemius alone the hand of vengeance spared,
Phemius the sweet, the heaven-instructed bard.
Beside the gate the reverend minstrel stands;
The lyre now silent trembling in his hands;
Dubious to supplicate the chief, or fly
To Jove's inviolable altar nigh,
Where oft Laertes holy vows had paid,
And oft Ulysses smoking victims laid.
His honour'd harp with care he first set down,
Between the laver and the silver throne;
Then prostrate stretch'd before the dreadful man,
Persuasive thus, with accent soft began:

"O king! to mercy be thy soul inclined,
And spare the poet's ever-gentle kind.
A deed like this thy future fame would wrong,
For dear to gods and men is sacred song.
Self-taught I sing; by Heaven, and Heaven alone,
The genuine seeds of poesy are sown:
And (what the gods bestow) the lofty lay
To gods alone and godlike worth we pay.
Save then the poet, and thyself reward!
'Tis thine to merit, mine is to record.
That here I sung, was force, and not desire;
This hand reluctant touch'd the warbling wire;
And let thy son attest, nor sordid pay,
Nor servile flattery, stain'd the moral lay."

The moving words Telemachus attends,
His sire approaches, and the bard defends.
"O mix not, father, with those impious dead

The man divine! forbear that sacred head;
Medon, the herald, too, our arms may spare,
Medon, who made my infancy his care;
If yet he breathes, permit thy son to give
Thus much to gratitude, and bid him live."

Beneath a table, trembling with dismay,
Couch'd close to earth, unhappy Medon lay,
Wrapp'd in a new-slain ox's ample hide;
Swift at the word he cast his screen aside,
Sprung to the prince, embraced his knee with tears,
And thus with grateful voice address'd his ears

"O prince! O friend! lo, here thy Medon stands
Ah stop the hero's unresisted hands,
Incensed too justly by that impious brood,
Whose guilty glories now are set in blood."
To whom Ulysses with a pleasing eye:

"Be bold, on friendship and my son rely;
Live, an example for the world to read,
How much more safe the good than evil deed:
Thou, with the heaven-taught bard, in peace resort
From blood and carnage to yon open court:
Me other work requires." With timorous awe
From the dire scene the exempted two withdraw,
Scarce sure of life, look round, and trembling move
To the bright altars of Protector Jove.

Meanwhile Ulysses search'd the dome, to find
If yet there live of all the offending kind.
Not one! complete the bloody tale he found,
All steep'd in blood, all gasping on the ground.
So, when by hollow shores the fisher-train
Sweep with their arching nets the roaring main,
And scarce the meshy toils the copious draught contain,
All naked of their element, and bare,
The fishes pant, and gasp in thinner air;
Wide o'er the sands are spread the stiffening prey,
Till the warm sun exhales their soul away.

And now the king commands his son to call
Old Euryclea to the deathful hall:
The son observant not a moment stays;
The aged governess with speed obeys;
The sounding portals instant they display;
The matron moves, the prince directs the way.
On heaps of death the stern Ulysses stood,

All black with dust, and cover'd thick with blood.
So the grim lion from the slaughter comes,
Dreadful lie glares, and terribly he foams,
His breast with marks of carnage painted o'er,
His jaws all dropping with the bull's black gore.

Soon as her eyes the welcome object met,
The guilty fall'n, the mighty deed complete;
A scream of joy her feeble voice essay'd;
The hero check'd her, and composedly said.

"Woman, experienced as thou art, control
Indecent joy, and feast thy secret soul.
To insult the dead is cruel and unjust;
Fate and their crime have sunk them to the dust.
Nor heeded these the censure of mankind,
The good and bad were equal in their mind
Justly the price of worthlessness they paid,
And each now wails an unlamented shade.
But thou sincere! O Euryclea, say,
What maids dishonour us, and what obey?"

Then she: "In these thy kingly walls remain
(My son) full fifty of the handmaid train,
Taught by my care to cull the fleece or weave,
And servitude with pleasing tasks deceive;
Of these, twice six pursue their wicked way,
Nor me, nor chaste Penelope obey;
Nor fits it that Telemachus command
(Young as he is) his mother's female band.
Hence to the upper chambers let me fly
Where slumbers soft now close the royal eye;
There wake her with the news"—the matron cried
"Not so (Ulysses, more sedate, replied),
Bring first the crew who wrought these guilty deeds."
In haste the matron parts: the king proceeds;
"Now to dispose the dead, the care remains
To you, my son, and you, my faithfull swains;
The offending females to that task we doom,
To wash, to scent, and purify the room;
These (every table cleansed, and every throne,
And all the melancholy labour done)
Drive to yon court, without the palace wall,
There the revenging sword shall smite them all;
So with the suitors let them mix in dust,
Stretch'd in a long oblivion of their lust."
He said: the lamentable train appear,
Each vents a groan, and drops a tender tear;

Each heaved her mournful burden, and beneath
The porch deposed the ghastly heap of death.
The chief severe, compelling each to move,
Urged the dire task imperious from above;
With thirsty sponge they rub the tables o'er
(The swains unite their toil); the walls, the floor,
Wash'd with the effusive wave, are purged of gore.
Once more the palace set in fair array,
To the base court the females take their way;
There compass'd close between the dome and wall
(Their life's last scene) they trembling wait their fall.

Then thus the prince: "To these shall we afford
A fate so pure as by the martial sword?
To these, the nightly prostitutes to shame,
And base revilers of our house and name?"

Thus speaking, on the circling wall he strung
A ship's tough cable from a column hung;
Near the high top he strain'd it strongly round,
Whence no contending foot could reach the ground.
Their heads above connected in a row,
They beat the air with quivering feet below:
Thus on some tree hung struggling in the snare,
The doves or thrushes flap their wings in air.
Soon fled the soul impure, and left behind
The empty corse to waver with the wind.

Then forth they led Melanthius, and began
Their bloody work; they lopp'd away the man,
Morsel for dogs! then trimm'd with brazen shears
The wretch, and shorten'd of his nose and ears;
His hands and feet last felt the cruel steel:
He roar'd, and torments gave his soul to hell.
They wash, and to Ulysses take their way:
So ends the bloody business of the day.

To Euryclea then address'd the king:
("Bring hither fire, and hither sulphur bring,
To purge the palace: then the queen attend,
And let her with her matron-train descend;
The matron-train, with all the virgin-band,
Assemble here, to learn their lord's command."

Then Euryclea: "Joyful I obey,
But cast those mean dishonest rags away;
Permit me first the royal robes to bring:
Ill suits this garb the shoulders of a king."

"Bring sulphur straight, and fire" (the monarch cries).
She hears, and at the word obedient flies.
With fire and sulphur, cure of noxious fumes,
He purged the walls, and blood-polluted rooms.
Again the matron springs with eager pace,
And spreads her lord's return from place to place.
They hear, rush forth, and instant round him stand,
A gazing throng, a torch in every hand.
They saw, they knew him, and with fond embrace
Each humbly kiss'd his knee, or hand, or face;
He knows them all, in all such truth appears,
E'en he indulges the sweet joy of tears.

BOOK XXIII

ARGUMENT

Euryclea awakens Penelope with the news of Ulysses' return, and the death of the suitors. Penelope scarcely credits her; but supposes some god has punished them, and descends from her department in doubt. At the first interview of Ulysses and Penelope, she is quite unsatisfied. Minerva restores him to the beauty of his youth; but the queen continues incredulous, till by some circumstances she is convinced, and falls into all the transports of passion and tenderness. They recount to each other all that has passed during their long separation. The next morning Ulysses, arming himself and his friends, goes from the city to visit his father.

Then to the queen, as in repose she lay,
The nurse with eager rapture speeds her way:
The transports of her faithful heart supply
A sudden youth, and give her wings to fly.

"And sleeps my child? (the reverend matron cries)
Ulysses lives! arise, my child, arise!
At length appears the long-expected hour!
Ulysses comes! the suitors are no more!
No more they view the golden light of day!
Arise, and bless thee with the glad survey?"

Touch'd at her words, the mournful queen rejoin'd:
"Ah! whither wanders thy distemper'd mind?
The righteous powers, who tread the starry skies,
The weak enlighten, and confound the wise,
And human thought, with unresisted sway,
Depress or raise, enlarge or take away:
Truth, by their high decree, thy voice forsakes,
And folly with the tongue of wisdom speaks.
Unkind, the fond illusion to impose!

Was it to flatter or deride my woes?
Never did I sleep so sweet enjoy,
Since my dear lord left Ithaca for Troy.
Why must I wake to grieve, and curse thy shore,
O Troy?—may never tongue pronounce thee more!
Begone! another might have felt our rage,
But age is sacred, and we spare thy age."

To whom with warmth: "My soul a lie disdains;
Ulysses lives, thy own Ulysses reigns:
That stranger, patient of the suitors' wrongs,
And the rude license of ungovern'd tongues!
He, he is thine! Thy son his latent guest
Long knew, but lock'd the secret in his breast:
With well concerted art to end his woes,
And burst at once in vengeance on the foes."

While yet she spoke, the queen in transport sprung
Swift from the couch, and round the matron hung;
Fast from her eye descends the rolling tear:
"Say, once more say, is my Ulysses here?
How could that numerous and outrageous band
By one be slain, though by a hero's hand?"

"I saw it not (she cries), but heard alone,
When death was busy, a loud dying groan;
The damsel-train turn'd pale at every wound,
Immured we sate, and catch'd each passing sound;
When death had seized her prey, thy son attends,
And at his nod the damsel-train descends;
There terrible in arms Ulysses stood,
And the dead suitors almost swam in blood:
Thy heart had leap'd the hero to survey,
Stern as the surly lion o'er his prey,
Glorious in gore, now with sulphereous fire
The dome he purges, now the flame aspires;
Heap'd lie the dead without the palace walls—
Haste, daughter, haste, thy own Ulysses calls!
Thy every wish the bounteous gods bestow;
Enjoy the present good, and former woe.
Ulysses lives, his vanquish'd foes to see;
He lives to thy Telemachus and thee!"

"Ah, no! (with sighs Penelope rejoin'd,)
Excess of joy disturbs thy wandering mind;
How blest this happy hour, should he appear,
Dear to us all, to me supremely dear;
Ah, no! some god the suitors death decreed,

Some god descends, and by his hand they bleed;
Blind! to contemn the stranger's righteous cause,
And violate all hospitable laws!
The good they hated, and the powers defied!
But heaven is just, and by a god they died.
For never must Ulysses view this shore;
Never! the loved Ulysses is no more!"

"What words (the matron cries) have reach'd my ears?
Doubt we his presence, when he now appears!
Then hear conviction: Ere the fatal day
That forced Ulysses o'er the watery way,
A boar, fierce rushing in the sylvan war,
Plough'd half his thigh; I saw, I saw the scar,
And wild with transport had reveal'd the wound;
But ere I spoke, he rose, and check'd the sound.
Then, daughter, haste away! and if a lie
Flow from this tongue, then let thy servant die!"
To whom with dubious joy the queen replies:
"Wise is thy soul, but errors seize the wise;
The works of gods what mortal can survey?
Who knows their motives, who shall trace their way?
But learn we instant how the suitors trod
The paths of death, by man, or by a god."
Thus speaks the queen, and no reply attends,
But with alternate joy and fear descends;
At every step debates her lord to prove;
Or, rushing to his arms, confess her love!
Then gliding through the marble valves, in state
Opposed, before the shining sire she sate.
The monarch, by a column high enthroned,
His eye withdrew, and fix'd it on the ground;
Curious to hear his queen the silence break:
Amazed she sate, and impotent to speak;
O'er all the man her eyes she rolls in vain,
Now hopes, now fears, now knows, then doubts again.
At length Telemachus: "Oh, who can find
A woman like Penelope unkind?
Why thus in silence? why with winning charms
Thus slow to fly with rapture to his arms?
Stubborn the breast that with no transport glows,
When twice ten years are pass'd of mighty woes;
To softness lost, to spousal love unknown,
The gods have formed that rigid heart of stone!"
"O my Telemachus! (the queen rejoin'd,)
Distracting fears confound my labouring mind;
Powerless to speak. I scarce uplift my eyes,
Nor dare to question; doubts on doubts arise.

Oh deign he, if Ulysses, to remove
These boding thoughts, and what he is, to prove!"
Pleased with her virtuous fears, the king replies:
"Indulge, my son, the cautions of the wise;
Time shall the truth to sure remembrance bring:
This garb of poverty belies the king:
No more. This day our deepest care requires,
Cautious to act what thought mature inspires.
If one man's blood, though mean, distain our hands,
The homicide retreats to foreign lands;
By us, in heaps the illustrious peerage falls,
The important deed our whole attention calls."

"Be that thy care (Telemachus replies)
The world conspires to speak Ulysses wise;
For wisdom all is thine! lo, I obey,
And dauntless follow where you led the way;
Nor shalt thou in the day of danger find
Thy coward son degenerate lag behind."

"Then instant to the bath (the monarch cries),
Bid the gay youth and sprightly virgins rise,
Thence all descend in pomp and proud array,
And bid the dome resound the mirthful lay;
While the sweet lyrist airs of rapture sings,
And forms the dance responsive to the strings,
That hence the eluded passengers may say,
'Lo! the queen weds! we hear the spousal lay!'
The suitor's death, unknown, till we remove
Far from the court, and act inspired by Jove."

Thus spoke the king: the observant train obey,
At once they bathe, and dress in proud array:
The lyrist strikes the string; gay youths advance,
And fair-zoned damsels form the sprightly dance.
The voice, attuned to instrumental sounds,
Ascends the roof, the vaulted roof rebounds;
Not unobserved: the Greeks eluded say,
"Lo! the queen weds, we hear the spousal lay!
Inconstant! to admit the bridal hour."
Thus they—but nobly chaste she weds no more.

Meanwhile the wearied king the bath ascends;
With faithful cares Eurynome attends,
O'er every limb a shower of fragrance sheds;
Then, dress'd in pomp, magnificent he treads.
The warrior-goddess gives his frame to shine
With majesty enlarged, and grace divine.

Back from his brows in wavy ringlets fly
His thick large locks of hyacinthine dye.
As by some artist to whom Vulcan gives
His heavenly skill, a breathing image lives;
By Pallas taught, he frames the wondrous mould,
And the pale silver glows with fusile gold:
So Pallas his heroic form improves
With bloom divine, and like a god he moves!
More high he treads, and issuing forth in state,
Radiant before his gazing consort sate.
"And, O my queen! (he cries) what power above
Has steel'd that heart, averse to spousal love?
Canst thou, Penelope, when heaven restores
Thy lost Ulysses to his native shores,
Canst thou, O cruel! unconcern'd survey
Thy lost Ulysses, on this signal day?
Haste, Euryclea, and despatchful spread
For me, and me alone, the imperial bed,
My weary nature craves the balm of rest.
But Heaven with adamant has arm'd her breast."

"Ah no! (she cries) a tender heart I bear,
A foe to pride: no adamant is there;
And now, e'en now it melts! for sure I see
Once more Ulysses my beloved in thee!
Fix'd in my soul, as when he sailed to Troy,
His image dwells: then haste the bed of joy,
Haste, from the bridal bower the bed translate,
Fram'd by his hand, and be it dress'd in state!"

Thus speaks the queen, still dubious, with disguise
Touch'd at her words, the king with warmth replies
"Alas for this! what mortal strength can move
The enormous burden, who but Heaven above?
It mocks the weak attempts of human hands!
But the whole earth must move if Heaven commands
Then hear sure evidence, while we display
Words seal'd with sacred truth and truth obey:
This hand the wonder framed; an olive spread
Full in the court its ever verdant head.
Vast as some mighty column's bulk, on high
The huge trunk rose, and heaved into the sky;
Around the tree I raised a nuptial bower,
And roof'd defensive of the storm and shower;
The spacious valve, with art inwrought conjoins;
And the fair dome with polished marble shines.
I lopp'd the branchy head: aloft in twain
Sever'd the bole, and smoothed the shining grain;

Then posts, capacious of the frame, I raise,
And bore it, regular, from space to space:
Athwart the frame, at equal distance lie
Thongs of tough hides, that boast a purple dye;
Then polishing the whole, the finished mould
With silver shone, with elephant, and gold.
But if o'erturn'd by rude, ungovern'd hands,
Or still inviolate the olive stands,
'Tis thine, O queen, to say, and now impart,
If fears remain, or doubts distract thy heart."

While yet he speaks, her powers of life decay;
She sickens, trembles, falls, and faints away.
At length recovering, to his arms she flew,
And strain'd him close, as to his breast she grew.
The tears pour'd down amain, and "O (she cries)
Let not against thy spouse thine anger rise!
O versed in every, turn of human art,
Forgive the weakness of a woman's heart!
The righteous powers, that mortal lot dispose,
Decree us to sustain a length of woes.
And from the flower of life the bliss deny
To bloom together, fade away, and die.
O let me, let me not thine anger move,
That I forbore, thus, thus to speak my love:
Thus in fond kisses, while the transport warms
Pour out my soul and die within thine arms!
I dreaded fraud! Men, faithless men, betray
Our easy faith, and make our sex their prey:
Against the fondness of my heart I strove:
'Twas caution, O my lord! not want of love.
Like me had Helen fear'd, with wanton charms
Ere the fair mischief set two worlds in arms;
Ere Greece rose dreadful in the avenging day;
Thus had she fear'd, she had not gone astray.
But Heaven, averse to Greece, in wrath decreed
That she should wander, and that Greece should bleed:
Blind to the ills that from injustice flow,
She colour'd all our wretched lives with woe.
But why these sorrows when my lord arrives?
I yield, I yield! my own Ulysses lives!
The secrets of the bridal bed are known
To thee, to me, to Actoris alone
(My father's present in the spousal hour,
The sole attendant on our genial bower).
Since what no eye hath seen thy tongue reveal'd,
Hard and distrustful as I am, I yield."

Touch'd to the soul, the king with rapture hears,
Hangs round her neck, and speaks his joy in tears.
As to the shipwreck'd mariner, the shores
Delightful rise, when angry Neptune roars:
Then, when the surge in thunder mounts the sky,
And gulf'd in crowds at once the sailors die;
If one, more happy, while the tempest raves,
Outlives the tumult of conflicting waves,
All pale, with ooze deform'd, he views the strand,
And plunging forth with transport grasps the land:
The ravish'd queen with equal rapture glows,
Clasps her loved lord, and to his bosom grows.
Nor had they ended till the morning ray,
But Pallas backward held the rising day,
The wheels of night retarding, to detain
The gay Aurora in the wavy main;
Whose flaming steeds, emerging through the night.
Beam o'er the eastern hills with streaming light.

At length Ulysses with a sigh replies:
"Yet Fate, yet cruel Fate repose denies;
A labour long, and hard, remains behind;
By heaven above, by hell beneath enjoin'd:
For to Tiresias through the eternal gates
Of hell I trode, to learn my future fates.
But end we here—the night demands repose,
Be deck'd the couch! and peace awhile, my woes!"

To whom the queen: "Thy word we shall obey,
And deck the couch; far hence be woes away:
Since the just gods, who tread the starry plains,
Restore thee safe, since my Ulysses reigns.
But what those perils heaven decrees, impart;
Knowledge may grieve, but fear distracts the heart."

To this the king: "Ah, why must I disclose
A dreadful story of approaching woes?
Why in this hour of transport wound thy ears,
When thou must learn what I must speak with tears?
Heaven, by the Theban ghost, thy spouse decrees,
Torn from thy arms, to sail a length of seas;
From realm to realm, a nation to explore
Who ne'er knew salt, or heard the billows roar,
Nor saw gay vessel storm the surgy plain,
A painted wonder, flying on the main:
An oar my hand must bear; a shepherd eyes
The unknown instrument with strange surprise,
And calls a corn-van; this upon the plain

I fix, and hail the monarch of the main;
Then bathe his altars with the mingled gore
Of victims vow'd, a ram, a bull, a boar;
Thence swift re-sailing to my native shores,
Due victims slay to all the ethereal powers.
Then Heaven decrees, in peace to end my days
And steal myself from life by slow decays!
Unknown to pain, in age resign my breath,
When late stern Neptune points the shaft of death;
To the dark grave retiring as to rest;
My people blessing, by my people bless'd.
Such future scenes the all-righteous powers display
By their dread seer, and such my future day."

To whom thus firm of soul: "If ripe for death,
And full of days, thou gently yield thy breath;
While Heaven a kind release from ills foreshows,
Triumph, thou happy victor of thy woes?"

But Euryclea, with dispatchful care,
And sage Eurynome, the couch prepare;
Instant they bid the blazing torch display
Around the dome and artificial day;
Then to repose her steps the matron bends,
And to the queen Eurynome descends;
A torch she bears, to light with guiding fires
The royal pair; she guides them, and retires
The instant his fair spouse Ulysses led
To the chaste love-rites of the nuptial bed.

And now the blooming youths and sprightly fair
Cease the gay dance, and to their rest repair;
But in discourse the king and consort lay,
While the soft hours stole unperceived away;
Intent he hears Penelope disclose
A mournful story of domestic woes,
His servants' insults, his invaded bed,
How his whole flocks and herds exhausted bled,
His generous wines dishonour'd shed in vain,
And the wild riots of the suitor-train.
The king alternate a dire tale relates,
Of wars, of triumphs, and disastrous fates;
All he unfolds; his listening spouse turns pale
With pleasing horror at the dreadful tale;
Sleepless devours each word; and hears how slain
Cicons on Cicons swell the ensanguined plain;
How to the land of Lote unbless'd he sails;
And images the rills and flowery vales!

How dash'd like dogs, his friends the Cyclops tore
(Not unrevenged), and quaff'd the spouting gore;
How the loud storms in prison bound, he sails
From friendly Aeolus with prosperous gales:
Yet fate withstands! a sudden tempest roars,
And whirls him groaning from his native shores:
How on the barbarous Laestrigonian coast,
By savage hands his fleet and friends lie lost;
How scarce himself survived: he paints the bower,
The spells of Circe, and her magic power;
His dreadful journey to the realms beneath,
To seek Tiresias in the vales of death;
How in the doleful mansions lie survey'd
His royal mother, pale Anticlea's shade;
And friends in battle slain, heroic ghosts!
Then how, unharm'd, he pass'd the Syren-coasts,
The justling rocks where fierce Charybdis raves,
And howling Scylla whirls her thunderous waves,
The cave of death! How his companions slay
The oxen sacred to the god of day.
Till Jove in wrath the rattling tempest guides,
And whelms the offenders in the roaring tides:
How struggling through the surge lie reach'd the shores
Of fair Ogygia and Calypso's bowers;
Where the bay blooming nymph constrain'd his stay,
With sweet, reluctant, amorous delay;
And promised, vainly promised, to bestow
Immortal life, exempt from age and woe:
How saved from storms Phaeacia's coast he trod,
By great Alcinous honour'd as a god,
Who gave him last his country to behold,
With change of raiment, brass, and heaps of gold

He ended, sinking into sleep, and shares
A sweet forgetfulness of all his cares.

Soon as soft slumber eased the toils of day,
Minerva rushes through the aerial way,
And bids Aurora with her golden wheels
Flame from the ocean o'er the eastern hills;
Uprose Ulysses from the genial bed,
And thus with thought mature the monarch said:

"My queen, my consort! through a length of years
We drank the cup of sorrow mix'd with tears;
Thou, for thy lord; while me the immortal powers
Detain'd reluctant from my native shores.
Now, bless'd again by Heaven, the queen display,

And rule our palace with an equal sway.
Be it my care, by loans, or martial toils,
To throng my empty folds with gifts or spoils.
But now I haste to bless Laertes' eyes
With sight of his Ulysses ere he dies;
The good old man, to wasting woes a prey,
Weeps a sad life in solitude away.
But hear, though wise! This morning shall unfold
The deathful scene, on heroes heroes roll'd.
Thou with thy maids within the palace stay,
From all the scene of tumult far away!"

He spoke, and sheathed in arms incessant flies
To wake his son, and bid his friends arise.
"To arms!" aloud he cries; his friends obey,
With glittering arms their manly limbs array,
And pass the city gate; Ulysses leads the way.
Now flames the rosy dawn, but Pallas shrouds
The latent warriors in a veil of clouds.

BOOK XXIV

ARGUMENT

The souls of the suitors are conducted by Mercury to the infernal shades. Ulysses in the country goes to the retirement of his father, Laertes; he finds him busied in his garden all alone; the manner of his discovery to him is beautifully described. They return together to his lodge, and the king is acknowledged by Dolius and the servants. The Ithacensians, led by Eupithes, the father of Antinous, rise against Ulysses, who gives them battle in which Eupithes is killed by Laertes: and the goddess Pallas makes a lasting peace between Ulysses and his subjects, which concludes the Odyssey.

Cylenius now to Pluto's dreary reign
Conveys the dead, a lamentable train!
The golden wand, that causes sleep to fly,
Or in soft slumber seals the wakeful eye,
That drives the ghosts to realms of night or day,
Points out the long uncomfortable way.
Trembling the spectres glide, and plaintive vent
Thin, hollow screams, along the deep descent.
As in the cavern of some rifted den,
Where flock nocturnal bats, and birds obscene;
Cluster'd they hang, till at some sudden shock
They move, and murmurs run through all the rock!
So cowering fled the sable heaps of ghosts,
And such a scream fill'd all the dismal coasts.
And now they reach'd the earth's remotest ends,

And now the gates where evening Sol descends,
And Leucas' rock, and Ocean's utmost streams,
And now pervade the dusky land of dreams,
And rest at last, where souls unbodied dwell
In ever-flowing meads of asphodel.
The empty forms of men inhabit there,
Impassive semblance, images of air!
Naught else are all that shined on earth before:
Ajax and great Achilles are no more!
Yet still a master ghost, the rest he awed,
The rest adored him, towering as he trod;
Still at his side is Nestor's son survey'd,
And loved Patroclus still attends his shade.

New as they were to that infernal shore,
The suitors stopp'd, and gazed the hero o'er.
When, moving slow, the regal form they view'd
Of great Atrides: him in pomp pursued
And solemn sadness through the gloom of hell,
The train of those who by AEgysthus fell:

"O mighty chief! (Pelides thus began)
Honour'd by Jove above the lot of man!
King of a hundred kings! to whom resign'd
The strongest, bravest, greatest of mankind
Comest thou the first, to view this dreary state?
And was the noblest, the first mark of Fate,
Condemn'd to pay the great arrear so soon,
The lot, which all lament, and none can shun!
Oh! better hadst thou sunk in Trojan ground,
With all thy full-blown honours cover'd round;
Then grateful Greece with streaming eyes might raise
Historic marbles to record thy praise:
Thy praise eternal on the faithful stone
Had with transmissive glories graced thy son.
But heavier fates were destined to attend:
What man is happy, till he knows his end?"

"O son of Peleus! greater than mankind!
(Thus Agamemnon's kingly shade rejoin'd)
Thrice happy thou, to press the martial plain
'Midst heaps of heroes in thy quarrel slain:
In clouds of smoke raised by the noble fray,
Great and terrific e'en in death you lay,
And deluges of blood flow'd round you every way.
Nor ceased the strife till Jove himself opposed,
And all in Tempests the dire evening closed.
Then to the fleet we bore thy honour'd load,

And decent on the funeral bed bestow'd;
Then unguents sweet and tepid streams we shed;
Tears flow'd from every eye, and o'er the dead
Each clipp'd the curling honours of his head.
Struck at the news, thy azure mother came,
The sea-green sisters waited on the dame:
A voice of loud lament through all the main
Was heard; and terror seized the Grecian train:
Back to their ships the frighted host had fled;
But Nestor spoke, they listen'd and obey'd
(From old experience Nestor's counsel springs,
And long vicissitudes of human things):
'Forbear your flight: fair Thetis from the main
To mourn Achilles leads her azure train.'
Around thee stand the daughters of the deep,
Robe thee in heavenly vests, and round thee weep:
Round thee, the Muses, with alternate strain,
In ever-consecrating verse, complain.
Each warlike Greek the moving music hears,
And iron-hearted heroes melt in tears.
Till seventeen nights and seventeen days return'd
All that was mortal or immortal mourn'd,
To flames we gave thee, the succeeding day,
And fatted sheep and sable oxen slay;
With oils and honey blazed the augmented fires,
And, like a god adorn'd, thy earthly part expires.
Unnumber'd warriors round the burning pile
Urge the fleet coursers or the racer's toil;
Thick clouds of dust o'er all the circle rise,
And the mix'd clamour thunders in the skies.
Soon as absorb'd in all-embracing flame
Sunk what was mortal of thy mighty name,
We then collect thy snowy bones, and place
With wines and unguents in a golden vase
(The vase to Thetis Bacchus gave of old,
And Vulcan's art enrich'd the sculptured gold).
There, we thy relics, great Achilles! blend
With dear Patroclus, thy departed friend:
In the same urn a separate space contains
Thy next beloved, Antilochus' remains.
Now all the sons of warlike Greece surround
Thy destined tomb and cast a mighty mound;
High on the shore the growing hill we raise,
That wide the extended Hellespont surveys;
Where all, from age to age, who pass the coast,
May point Achilles' tomb, and hail the mighty ghost.
Thetis herself to all our peers proclaims
Heroic prizes and exequial games;

The gods assented; and around thee lay
Rich spoils and gifts that blazed against the day.
Oft have I seen with solemn funeral games
Heroes and kings committed to the flames;
But strength of youth, or valour of the brave,
With nobler contest ne'er renown'd a grave.
Such were the games by azure Thetis given,
And such thy honours, O beloved of Heaven!
Dear to mankind thy fame survives, nor fades
Its bloom eternal in the Stygian shades.
But what to me avail my honours gone,
Successful toils, and battles bravely won?
Doom'd by stern Jove at home to end my life,
By cursed Aegysthus, and a faithless wife!"
Thus they: while Hermes o'er the dreary plain
Led the sad numbers by Ulysses slain.
On each majestic form they cast a view,
And timorous pass'd, and awfully withdrew.
But Agamemnon, through the gloomy shade,
His ancient host Amphimedon survey'd:
"Son of Melanthius! (he began) O say!
What cause compell'd so many, and so gay,
To tread the downward, melancholy way?
Say, could one city yield a troop so fair?
Were all these partners of one native air?
Or did the rage of stormy Neptune sweep
Your lives at once, and whelm beneath the deep?
Did nightly thieves, or pirates' cruel bands,
Drench with your blood your pillaged country's sands?
Or well-defending some beleaguer'd wall,
Say,—for the public did ye greatly fall?
Inform thy guest: for such I was of yore
When our triumphant navies touch'd your shore;
Forced a long month the wintry seas to bear,
To move the great Ulysses to the war."

"O king of men! I faithful shall relate
(Replied Amphimedon) our hapless fate.
Ulysses absent, our ambitious aim
With rival loves pursued his royal dame;
Her coy reserve, and prudence mix'd with pride,
Our common suit nor granted, nor denied;
But close with inward hate our deaths design'd;
Versed in all arts of wily womankind.
Her hand, laborious, in delusion spread
A spacious loom, and mix'd the various thread.
'Ye peers (she cried) who press to gain my heart,
Where dead Ulysses claims no more a part,

Yet a short space your rival suit suspend,
Till this funereal web my labours end:
Cease, till to good Laertes I bequeath
A task of grief, his ornaments of death:
Lest when the Fates his royal ashes claim,
The Grecian matrons taint my spotless fame;
Should he, long honour'd with supreme command,
Want the last duties of a daughter's hand.'

"The fiction pleased, our generous train complies,
Nor fraud mistrusts in virtue's fair disguise.
The work she plied, but studious of delay,
Each following night reversed the toils of day.
Unheard, unseen, three years her arts prevail;
The fourth, her maid reveal'd the amazing tale,
And show'd as unperceived we took our stand,
The backward labours of her faithless hand.
Forced she completes it; and before us lay
The mingled web, whose gold and silver ray
Display'd the radiance of the night and day.

"Just as she finished her illustrious toil,
Ill fortune led Ulysses to our isle.
Far in a lonely nook, beside the sea,
At an old swineherd's rural lodge he lay:
Thither his son from sandy Pyle repairs,
And speedy lands, and secretly confers.
They plan our future ruin, and resort
Confederate to the city and the court.
First came the son; the father nest succeeds,
Clad like a beggar, whom Eumaeus leads;
Propp'd on a staff, deform'd with age and care,
And hung with rags that flutter'd in the air.
Who could Ulysses in that form behold?
Scorn'd by the young, forgotten by the old,
Ill-used by all! to every wrong resigned,
Patient he suffered with a constant mind.
But when, arising in his wrath to obey
The will of Jove, he gave the vengeance way:
The scattered arms that hung around the dome
Careful he treasured in a private room;
Then to her suitors bade his queen propose
The archer's strife, the source of future woes,
And omen of our death! In vain we drew
The twanging string, and tried the stubborn yew:
To none it yields but great Ulysses' hands;
In vain we threat; Telemachus commands:
The bow he snatch'd, and in an instant bent;

Through every ring the victor arrow went.
Fierce on the threshold then in arms he stood;
Poured forth the darts that thirsted for our blood,
And frown'd before us, dreadful as a god!
First bleeds Antinous: thick the shafts resound,
And heaps on heaps the wretches strew the ground;
This way, and that, we turn, we fly, we fall;
Some god assisted, and unmann'd us all;
Ignoble cries precede the dying groans;
And battered brains and blood besmear the stones.

"Thus, great Atrides, thus Ulysses drove
The shades thou seest from yon fair realms above;
Our mangled bodies now deformed with gore,
Cold and neglected, spread the marble floor.
No friend to bathe our wounds, or tears to shed
O'er the pale corse! the honours of the dead."

"Oh bless'd Ulysses! (thus the king express'd
His sudden rapture) in thy consort bless'd!
Not more thy wisdom than her virtue shined;
Not more thy patience than her constant mind.
Icarius' daughter, glory of the past,
And model to the future age, shall last:
The gods, to honour her fair fame, shall rise
(Their great reward) a poet in her praise.
Not such, O Tyndarus! thy daughter's deed,
By whose dire hand her king and husband bled;
Her shall the Muse to infamy prolong,
Example dread, and theme of tragic song!
The general sex shall suffer in her shame,
And e'en the best that bears a woman's name."

Thus in the regions of eternal shade
Conferr'd the mournful phantoms of the dead;
While from the town, Ulysses and his band
Pass'd to Laertes' cultivated land.
The ground himself had purchased with his pain,
And labour made the rugged soil a plain,
There stood his mansion of the rural sort,
With useful buildings round the lowly court;
Where the few servants that divide his care
Took their laborious rest, and homely fare;
And one Sicilian matron, old and sage,
With constant duty tends his drooping age.

Here now arriving, to his rustic band
And martial son, Ulysses gave command:

"Enter the house, and of the bristly swine
Select the largest to the powers divine.
Alone, and unattended, let me try
If yet I share the old man's memory:
If those dim eyes can yet Ulysses know
(Their light and dearest object long ago),
Now changed with time, with absence and with woe."
Then to his train he gives his spear and shield;
The house they enter; and he seeks the field,
Through rows of shade, with various fruitage crown'd,
And labour'd scenes of richest verdure round.
Nor aged Dolius; nor his sons, were there,
Nor servants, absent on another care;
To search the woods for sets of flowery thorn,
Their orchard bounds to strengthen and adorn.

But all alone the hoary king he found;
His habit course, but warmly wrapp'd around;
His head, that bow'd with many a pensive care,
Fenced with a double cap of goatskin hair:
His buskins old, in former service torn,
But swell repair'd; and gloves against the thorn.
In this array the kingly gardener stood,
And clear'd a plant, encumber'd with its wood.

Beneath a neighbouring tree, the chief divine
Gazed o'er his sire, retracing every line,
The ruins of himself, now worn away
With age, yet still majestic in decay!
Sudden his eyes released their watery store;
The much-enduring man could bear no more.
Doubtful he stood, if instant to embrace
His aged limbs, to kiss his reverend face,
With eager transport to disclose the whole,
And pour at once the torrent of his soul.—
Not so: his judgment takes the winding way
Of question distant, and of soft essay;
More gentle methods on weak age employs:
And moves the sorrows to enhance the joys.
Then, to his sire with beating heart he moves,
And with a tender pleasantry reproves;
Who digging round the plant still hangs his bead,
Nor aught remits the work, while thus he said:

"Great is thy skill, O father! great thy toil,
Thy careful hand is stamp'd on all the soil,
Thy squadron'd vineyards well thy art declare,
The olive green, blue fig, and pendent pear;

And not one empty spot escapes thy care.
On every plant and tree thy cares are shown,
Nothing neglected, but thyself alone.
Forgive me, father, if this fault I blame;
Age so advanced, may some indulgence claim.
Not for thy sloth, I deem thy lord unkind:
Nor speaks thy form a mean or servile mind;
I read a monarch in that princely air,
The same thy aspect, if the same thy care;
Soft sleep, fair garments, and the joys of wine,
These are the rights of age, and should be thine.
Who then thy master, say? and whose the land
So dress'd and managed by thy skilful hand?
But chief, oh tell me! (what I question most)
Is this the far-famed Ithacensian coast?
For so reported the first man I view'd
(Some surly islander, of manners rude),
Nor farther conference vouchsafed to stay;
Heedless he whistled, and pursued his way.
But thou whom years have taught to understand,
Humanely hear, and answer my demand:
A friend I seek, a wise one and a brave:
Say, lives he yet, or moulders in the grave?
Time was (my fortunes then were at the best)
When at my house I lodged this foreign guest;
He said, from Ithaca's fair isle he came,
And old Laertes was his father's name.
To him, whatever to a guest is owed
I paid, and hospitable gifts bestow'd:
To him seven talents of pure ore I told,
Twelve cloaks, twelve vests, twelve tunics stiff with gold:
A bowl, that rich with polish'd silver flames,
And skill'd in female works, four lovely dames."

At this the father, with a father's fears
(His venerable eyes bedimm'd with tears):
"This is the land; but ah! thy gifts are lost,
For godless men, and rude possess the coast:
Sunk is the glory of this once-famed shore!
Thy ancient friend, O stranger, is no more!
Full recompense thy bounty else had borne:
For every good man yields a just return:
So civil rights demand; and who begins
The track of friendship, not pursuing, sins.
But tell me, stranger, be the truth confess'd,
What years have circled since thou saw'st that guest?
That hapless guest, alas! for ever gone!
Wretch that he was! and that I am! my son!

If ever man to misery was born,
'Twas his to suffer, and 'tis mine to mourn!
Far from his friends, and from his native reign,
He lies a prey to monsters of the main;
Or savage beasts his mangled relics tear,
Or screaming vultures scatter through the air:
Nor could his mother funeral unguents shed;
Nor wail'd his father o'er the untimely dead:
Nor his sad consort, on the mournful bier,
Seal'd his cold eyes, or dropp'd a tender tear!

"But, tell me who thou art? and what thy race?
Thy town, thy parents, and thy native place?
Or, if a merchant in pursuit of gain,
What port received thy vessel from the main?
Or comest thou single, or attend thy train?"

Then thus the son: "From Alybas I came,
My palace there; Eperitus my name
Not vulgar born: from Aphidas, the king
Of Polyphemon's royal line, I spring.
Some adverse demon from Sicania bore
Our wandering course, and drove us on your shore;
Far from the town, an unfrequented bay
Relieved our wearied vessel from the sea.
Five years have circled since these eyes pursued
Ulysses parting through the sable flood:
Prosperous he sail'd, with dexter auguries,
And all the wing'd good omens of the skies.
Well hoped we then to meet on this fair shore,
Whom Heaven, alas! decreed to meet no more."

Quick through the father's heart these accents ran;
Grief seized at once, and wrapp'd up all the man:
Deep from his soul he sigh'd, and sorrowing spread
A cloud of ashes on his hoary head.
Trembling with agonies of strong delight
Stood the great son, heart-wounded with the sight:
He ran, he seized him with a strict embrace,
With thousand kisses wander'd o'er his face:
"I, I am he; O father, rise! behold
Thy son, with twenty winters now grown old;
Thy son, so long desired, so long detain'd,
Restored, and breathing in his native land:
These floods of sorrow, O my sire, restrain!
The vengeance is complete; the suitor train,
Stretch'd in our palace, by these hands lie slain."

Amazed, Laertes: "Give some certain sign
(If such thou art) to manifest thee mine."

"Lo here the wound (he cries) received of yore,
The scar indented by the tusky boar,
When, by thyself, and by Anticlea sent,
To old Autolycus' realms I went.
Yet by another sign thy offspring know;
The several trees you gave me long ago,
While yet a child, these fields I loved to trace,
And trod thy footsteps with unequal pace;
To every plant in order as we came,
Well-pleased, you told its nature and its name,
Whate'er my childish fancy ask'd, bestow'd:
Twelve pear-trees, bowing with their pendent load,
And ten, that red with blushing apples glow'd;
Full fifty purple figs; and many a row
Of various vines that then began to blow,
A future vintage! when the Hours produce
Their latent buds, and Sol exalts the juice."

Smit with the signs which all his doubts explain,
His heart within him melt; his knees sustain
Their feeble weight no more: his arms alone
Support him, round the loved Ulysses thrown;
He faints, he sinks, with mighty joys oppress'd:
Ulysses clasps him to his eager breast.
Soon as returning life regains its seat,
And his breath lengthens, and his pulses beat:
"Yes, I believe (he cries) almighty Jove!
Heaven rules us yet, and gods there are above.
'Tis so—the suitors for their wrongs have paid—
But what shall guard us, if the town invade?
If, while the news through every city flies,
All Ithaca and Cephalenia rise?"
To this Ulysses: "As the gods shall please
Be all the rest: and set thy soul at ease.
Haste to the cottage by this orchard's side,
And take the banquet which our cares provide;
There wait thy faithful band of rural friends,
And there the young Telemachus attends."

Thus, having said, they traced the garden o'er
And stooping entered at the lowly door.
The swains and young Telemachus they found.
The victim portion'd and the goblet crown'd.
The hoary king, his old Sicilian maid
Perfum'd and wash'd, and gorgeously arrayed.

Pallas attending gives his frame to shine
With awful port, and majesty divine;
His gazing son admires the godlike grace,
And air celestial dawning o'er his face.
"What god (he cried) my father's form improves!
How high he treads and how enlarged he moves!"

"Oh! would to all the deathless powers on high,
Pallas and Jove, and him who gilds the sky!
(Replied the king elated with his praise)
My strength were still, as once in better days:
When the bold Cephalens the leaguer form'd.
And proud Nericus trembled as I storm'd.
Such were I now, not absent from your deed
When the last sun beheld the suitors bleed,
This arm had aided yours, this hand bestrown
Our shores with death, and push'd the slaughter on;
Nor had the sire been separate from the son."

They communed thus; while homeward bent their way
The swains, fatigued with labours of the day:
Dolius, the first, the venerable man;
And next his sons, a long succeeding train.
For due refection to the bower they came,
Call'd by the careful old Sicilian dame,
Who nursed the children, and now tends the sire,
They see their lord, they gaze, and they admire.
On chairs and beds in order seated round,
They share the gladsome board; the roofs resound,
While thus Ulysses to his ancient friend:
"Forbear your wonder, and the feast attend:
The rites have waited long." The chief commands
Their love in vain; old Dolius spreads his hands,
Springs to his master with a warm embrace,
And fastens kisses on his hands and face;
Then thus broke out: "O long, O daily mourn'd!
Beyond our hopes, and to our wish return'd!
Conducted sure by Heaven! for Heaven alone
Could work this wonder: welcome to thy own!
And joys and happiness attend thy throne!
Who knows thy bless'd, thy wish'd return? oh say,
To the chaste queen shall we the news convey?
Or hears she, and with blessings loads the day?"

"Dismiss that care, for to the royal bride
Already is it known" (the king replied,
And straight resumed his seat); while round him bows
Each faithful youth, and breathes out ardent vows:

Then all beneath their father take their place,
Rank'd by their ages, and the banquet grace.

Now flying Fame the swift report had spread
Through all the city, of the suitors dead,
In throngs they rise, and to the palace crowd;
Their sighs were many and the tumult loud.
Weeping they bear the mangled heaps of slain;
Inhume the natives in their native plain,
The rest in ships are wafted o'er the main.
Then sad in council all the seniors sate,
Frequent and full, assembled to debate:
Amid the circle first Eupithes rose,
Big was his eye with tears, his heart with woes:
The bold Antinous was his age's pride,
The first who by Ulysses' arrow died.
Down his wan cheek the trickling torrent ran,
As mixing words with sighs he thus began:

"Great deeds, O friends! this wondrous man has wrought,
And mighty blessings to his country brought!
With ships he parted, and a numerous train,
Those, and their ships, he buried in the main.
Now he returns, and first essays his hand
In the best blood of all his native land.
Haste, then, and ere to neighbouring Pyle he flies,
Or sacred Elis, to procure supplies;
Arise (or ye for ever fall), arise!
Shame to this age, and all that shall succeed!
If unrevenged your sons and brothers bleed.
Prove that we live, by vengeance on his head,
Or sink at once forgotten with the dead."
Here ceased he, but indignant tears let fall
Spoke when he ceased: dumb sorrow touch'd them all.
When from the palace to the wondering throng
Sage Medon came, and Phemius came along
(Restless and early sleep's soft bands they broke);
And Medon first the assembled chiefs bespoke;

"Hear me, ye peers and elders of the land,
Who deem this act the work of mortal hand;
As o'er the heaps of death Ulysses strode,
These eyes, these eyes beheld a present god,
Who now before him, now beside him stood,
Fought as he fought, and mark'd his way with blood:
In vain old Mentor's form the god belied;
'Twas Heaven that struck, and Heaven was on his side."

A sudden horror all the assembly shook,
When slowly rising, Halitherses spoke
(Reverend and wise, whose comprehensive view
At once the present and the future knew):
"Me too, ye fathers, hear! from you proceed
The ills ye mourn; your own the guilty deed.
Ye gave your sons, your lawless sons, the rein
(Oft warn'd by Mentor and myself in vain);
An absent hero's bed they sought to soil,
An absent hero's wealth they made their spoil;
Immoderate riot, and intemperate lust!
The offence was great, the punishment was just.
Weigh then my counsels in an equal scale,
Nor rush to ruin. Justice will prevail."

His moderate words some better minds persuade:
They part, and join him: but the number stay'd.
They storm, they shout, with hasty frenzy fired,
And second all Eupithes' rage inspired.
They case their limbs in brass; to arms they run;
The broad effulgence blazes in the sun.
Before the city, and in ample plain,
They meet: Eupithes heads the frantic train.
Fierce for his son, he breathes his threats in air;
Fate bears them not, and Death attends him there.

This pass'd on earth, while in the realms above
Minerva thus to cloud-compelling Jove!
"May I presume to search thy secret soul?
O Power Supreme, O Ruler of the whole!
Say, hast thou doom'd to this divided state
Or peaceful amity or stern debate?
Declare thy purpose, for thy will is fate."

"Is not thy thought my own? (the god replies
Who rolls the thunder o'er the vaulted skies;)
Hath not long since thy knowing soul decreed
The chief's return should make the guilty bleed.
'Tis done, and at thy will the Fates succeed.
Yet hear the issue: Since Ulysses' hand
Has slain the suitors, Heaven shall bless the land.
None now the kindred of the unjust shall own;
Forgot the slaughter'd brother and the son:
Each future day increase of wealth shall bring,
And o'er the past Oblivion stretch her wing.
Long shall Ulysses in his empire rest,
His people blessing, by his people bless'd.
Let all be peace."—He said, and gave the nod

That binds the Fates; the sanction of the god
And prompt to execute the eternal will,
Descended Pallas from the Olympian hill.

Now sat Ulysses at the rural feast
The rage of hunger and of thirst repress'd:
To watch the foe a trusty spy he sent:
A son of Dolius on the message went,
Stood in the way, and at a glance beheld
The foe approach, embattled on the field.
With backward step he hastens to the bower,
And tells the news. They arm with all their power.
Four friends alone Ulysses' cause embrace,
And six were all the sons of Dolius' race:
Old Dolius too his rusted arms put on;
And, still more old, in arms Laertes shone.
Trembling with warmth, the hoary heroes stand,
And brazen panoply invests the band.
The opening gates at once their war display:
Fierce they rush forth: Ulysses leads the way.
That moment joins them with celestial aid,
In Mentor's form, the Jove-descended maid:
The suffering hero felt his patient breast
Swell with new joy, and thus his son address'd:

"Behold, Telemachus! (nor fear the sight,)
The brave embattled, the grim front of fight!
The valiant with the valiant must contend.
Shame not the line whence glorious you descend.
Wide o'er the world their martial fame was spread;
Regard thyself, the living and the dead."

"Thy eyes, great father! on this battle cast,
Shall learn from me Penelope was chaste."

So spoke Telemachus: the gallant boy
Good old Laertes heard with panting joy.
"And bless'd! thrice bless'd this happy day! (he cries,)
The day that shows me, ere I close my eyes,
A son and grandson of the Arcesian name
Strive for fair virtue, and contest for fame!"

Then thus Minerva in Laertes' ear:
"Son of Arcesius, reverend warrior, hear!
Jove and Jove's daughter first implore in prayer,
Then, whirling high, discharge thy lance in air."
She said, infusing courage with the word.
Jove and Jove's daughter then the chief implored,

And, whirling high, dismiss'd the lance in air.
Full at Eupithes drove the deathful spear:
The brass-cheek'd helmet opens to the wound;
He falls, earth thunders, and his arms resound.
Before the father and the conquering son
Heaps rush on heaps, they fight, they drop, they run
Now by the sword, and now the javelin, fall
The rebel race, and death had swallow'd all;
But from on high the blue-eyed virgin cried;
Her awful voice detain'd the headlong tide:
"Forbear, ye nations, your mad hands forbear
From mutual slaughter; Peace descends to spare."
Fear shook the nations: at the voice divine
They drop their javelins, and their rage resign.
All scatter'd round their glittering weapons lie;
Some fall to earth, and some confusedly fly.
With dreadful shouts Ulysses pour'd along,
Swift as an eagle, as an eagle strong.
But Jove's red arm the burning thunder aims:
Before Minerva shot the livid flames;
Blazing they fell, and at her feet expired;
Then stopped the goddess, trembled and retired.

"Descended from the gods! Ulysses, cease;
Offend not Jove: obey, and give the peace."

So Pallas spoke: the mandate from above
The king obey'd. The virgin-seed of Jove,
In Mentor's form, confirm'd the full accord,
And willing nations knew their lawful lord.

Alexander Pope – A Short Biography

Alexander Pope was born in Lombard Street, London, on the 21st of May 1688—the year of the Revolution. His father was a linen-merchant, in thriving circumstances, and said to have noble blood in his veins. His mother was Edith or Editha Turner, daughter of William Turner, Esq., of York. Mr Carruthers, in his excellent Life of the Poet, mentions that there was an Alexander Pope, a clergyman, in the remote parish of Reay, in Caithness, who rode all the way to Twickenham to pay his great namesake a visit, and was presented by him with a copy of the subscription edition of the "Odyssey," in five volumes quarto, which is still preserved by his descendants. Pope's father had made about £10,000 by trade; but being a Roman Catholic, and fond of a country life, he retired from business shortly after the Revolution, at the early age of forty-six. He resided first at Kensington, and then in Binfield, in the neighbourhood of Windsor Forest. He is said to have put his money in a strong box, and to have lived on the principal. His great delight was in his garden; and both he and his wife seem to have cherished the warmest interest in their son, who was very delicate in health, and their only child. Pope's study is still preserved in Binfield; and on the lawn, a cypress-tree which he is said to have planted, is pointed out.

Pope was a premature and precocious child. His figure was deformed—his back humped—his stature short (four feet six inches)—his legs and arms disproportionably long. He was sometimes compared to a spider, and sometimes to a windmill. The only mark of genius lay in his bright and piercing eye. He was sickly in constitution, and required and received great tenderness and care. Once, when three years old, he narrowly escaped from an angry cow, but was wounded in the throat. He was remarkable as a child for his amiable temper; and from the sweetness of his voice, received the name of the Little Nightingale. His aunt gave him his first lessons in reading, and he soon became an enthusiastic lover of books; and by copying printed characters, taught himself to write. When eight years old, he was placed under the care of the family priest, one Bannister, who taught him the Latin and Greek grammars together. He was next removed to a Catholic seminary at Twyford, near Winchester; and while there, read Ogilby's "Homer" and Sandys's "Ovid" with great delight. He had not been long at this school till he wrote a severe lampoon, of two hundred lines' length, on his master—so truly was the "boy the father of the man"—for which demi-Dunciad he was severely flogged. His father, offended at this, removed him to a London school, kept by a Mr Deane. This man taught the poet nothing; but his residence in London gave him the opportunity of attending the theatres. With these he was so captivated, that he wrote a kind of play, which was acted by his schoolfellows, consisting of speeches from Ogilby's "Iliad," tacked together with verses of his own. He became acquainted with Dryden's works, and went to Wills's coffee-house to see him. He says, "Virgilium tantum vidi." Such transient meetings of literary orbs are among the most interesting passages in biography. Thus met Galileo with Milton, Milton with Dryden, Dryden with Pope, and Burns with Scott. Carruthers strikingly remarks, "Considering the perils and uncertainties of a literary life—its precarious rewards, feverish anxieties, mortifications, and disappointments, joined to the tyranny of the Tonsons and Lintots, and the malice and envy of dunces, all of which Dryden had long and bitterly experienced—the aged poet could hardly have looked at the delicate and deformed boy, whose preternatural acuteness and sensibility were seen in his dark eyes, without a feeling approaching to grief, had he known that he was to fight a battle like that under which he was himself then sinking, even though the Temple of Fame should at length open to receive him." At twelve, he wrote the "Ode to Solitude;" and shortly after, his satirical piece on Elkanah Settle, and some of his translations and imitations. His next period, he says, was in Windsor Forest, where for several years he did nothing but read the classics and indite poetry. He wrote a tragedy, a comedy, and four books of an Epic called "Alexander," all of which afterwards he committed to the flames. He translated also a portion of Statius, and Cicero "De Senectute," and "thought himself the greatest genius that ever was." His father encouraged him in his studies, and when his verses did not please him, sent him back to "new turn" them, saying, "These are not good rhymes." His principal favourites were Virgil's "Eclogues," in Latin; and in English, Spencer, Waller, and Dryden—admiring Spencer, we presume, for his luxuriant fancy, Waller for his smooth versification, and Dryden for his vigorous sense and vivid sarcasm. In the Forest, he became acquainted with Sir William Trumbull, the retired secretary of state, a man of general accomplishments, who read, rode, conversed with the youthful poet; introduced him to old Wycherley, the dramatist; and was of material service to his views. With Wycherley, who was old, doted, and excessively vain, Pope did not continue long intimate. A coldness, springing from some criticisms which the youth ventured to make on the veteran's poetry, crept in between them. Walsh of Abberley, in Worcestershire, a man of good sense and taste, became, after a perusal of the "Pastorals" in MS., a warm friend and kind adviser of Pope's, who has immortalised him in more than one of his poems. Walsh told Pope that there had never hitherto appeared in Britain a poet who was at once great and correct, and exhorted him to aim at accuracy and elegance.

When fifteen, he visited London, in order to acquire a more thorough knowledge of French and Italian. At sixteen, he wrote the "Pastorals," and a portion of "Windsor Forest," although they were not published for some time afterwards. By his incessant exertions, he now began to feel his constitution injured. He imagined himself dying, and sent farewell letters to all his friends, including the Abbé Southcot. This gentleman communicated Pope's case to Dr Ratcliffe, who gave him some medical directions; by following which, the poet recovered. He was advised to relax in his studies, and to ride daily; and he prudently followed the advice. Many years afterwards, he repaid the benevolent Abbé by procuring for him, through Sir Robert Walpole, the nomination to an abbey in Avignon. This is only one of many proofs that, notwithstanding his waspish temper, and his no small share of malice as well as vanity, there was a warm heart in our poet.

In 1707, Pope became acquainted with Michael Blount of Maple, Durham, near Reading; whose two sisters, Martha and Teresa, he has commemorated in various verses. On his connexion with these ladies, some mystery rests. Bowles has strongly and plausibly urged that it was not of the purest or most creditable order. Others have contended that it did not go further than the manners of the age sanctioned; and they say, "a much greater license in conversation and in epistolary correspondence was permitted between the sexes than in our decorous age!" We are not careful to try and settle such a delicate question—only we are inclined to suspect, that when common decency quits the words of male and female parties in their mutual communications, it is a very ample charity that can suppose it to adhere to their actions. And nowhere do we find grosser language than in some of Pope's prose epistles to the Blounts.

His "Pastorals," after having been handed about in MS., and shewn to such reputed judges as Lord Halifax, Lord Somers, Garth, Congreve, &c., were at last, in 1709, printed in the sixth volume of Tonson's "Miscellanies." Like all well-finished commonplaces, they were received with instant and universal applause. It is humiliating to contrast the reception of these empty echoes of inspiration, these agreeable centos, with that of such genuine, although faulty poems, as Keat's "Endymion," Shelley's "Queen Mab," and Wordsworth's "Lyrical Ballads." Two years later, (in 1711), a far better and more characteristic production from his pen was ushered anonymously into the world. This was the "Essay on Criticism," a work which he had first written in prose, and which discovers a ripeness of judgment, a clearness of thought, a condensation of style, and a command over the information he possesses, worthy of any age in life, and almost of any mind in time. It serves, indeed, to shew what Pope's true forte was. That lay not so much in poetry, as in the knowledge of its principles and laws, not so much in creation, as in criticism. He was no Homer or Shakspeare; but he might have been nearly as acute a judge of poetry as Aristotle, and nearly as eloquent an expounder of the rules of art and the glories of genius as Longinus.

In the same year, Pope printed "The Rape of the Lock," in a volume of Miscellanies. Lord Petre had, much in the way described by the poet, stolen a lock of Miss Belle Fermor's hair, a feat which led to an estrangement between the families. Pope set himself to reconcile them by this beautiful poem, a poem which has embalmed at once the quarrel and the reconciliation to all future time. In its first version, the machinery was awanting, the "lock" was a desert, the "rape" a natural event, the small infantry of sylphs and gnomes were slumbering uncreated in the poet's mind; but in the next edition he contrived to introduce them in a manner so easy and so exquisite, as to remind you of the variations which occur in dreams, where one wonder seems softly to slide into the bosom of another, and where beautiful and fantastic fancies grow suddenly out of realities, like the bud from the bough, or the fairy-seeming wing of the summer-cloud from the stern azure of the heavens.

A little after this, Pope became acquainted with a far greater, better, and truer man than himself, Joseph Addison. Warburton, and others, have sadly misrepresented the connexion between these two famous wits, as well as their relative intellectual positions. Addison was a more amiable and childlike person than Pope. He had much more, too, of the Christian. He was not so elaborately polished and furbished as the author of "The Rape of the Lock;" but he had, naturally, a finer and richer genius. Pope found early occasion for imagining Addison his disguised enemy. He gave him a hint of his intention to introduce the machinery into "The Rape of the Lock." Of this, Addison disapproved, and said it was a delicious little thing already—merum sal. This, Pope, and some of his friends, have attributed to jealousy; but it is obvious that Addison could not foresee the success with which the machinery was to be managed, and did foresee the difficulties connected with tinkering such an exquisite production. We may allude here to the circumstances which, at a later date, produced an estrangement between these celebrated men. When Tickell, Addison's friend, published the first book of the "Iliad," in opposition to Pope's version, Addison gave it the preference. This moved Pope's indignation, and led him to assert that it was Addison's own composition. In this conjecture he was supported by Edward Young, who had known Tickell long and intimately, and had never heard of him having written at college, as was averred, this translation. It is now, however, we believe, certain, from the MS. which still exists, that Tickell was the real author. A coldness, from this date, began between Pope and Addison. An attempt to reconcile them only made matters worse; and at last the breach was rendered irremediable by Pope's writing the famous character of his rival, afterwards inserted in the Prologue to the Satires, a portrait drawn with the perfection of polished malice and bitter sarcasm, but which seems more a caricature than a likeness. Whatever Addison's faults, his conduct to Pope did not deserve such a return. The whole passage is only one of those painful incidents which disgrace the history of letters, and prove how much spleen, ingratitude, and baseness often co-exist with the highest parts. The words of Pope are as true now as ever they were—"the life of a wit is a warfare upon earth;" and a warfare in which poisoned missiles and every variety of falsehood are still common. We may also here mention, that while the friendship of Pope and Addison lasted, the former contributed the well-known prologue to the latter's "Cato."

One of Pope's most intimate friends in his early days was Henry Cromwell—a distant relative of the great Oliver—a gentleman of fortune, gallantry, and literary taste, who became his agreeable and fascinating, but somewhat dangerous, companion. He is supposed to have initiated Pope into some of the fashionable follies of the town. At this time, Pope's popularity roused one of his most formidable foes against him. This was that Cobbett of criticism, old John Dennis, a man of strong natural powers, much learning, and a rich, coarse vein of humour; but irascible, vindictive, vain, and capricious. Pope had provoked him by an attack in his "Essay on Criticism," and the savage old man revenged himself by a running fire of fierce diatribes against that "Essay" and "The Rape of the Lock." Pope waited till Dennis had committed himself by a powerful but furious assault on Addison's "Cato" (most of which Johnson has preserved in his Life of Pope); and then, partly to court Addison, and partly to indulge his spleen at the critic, wrote a prose satire, entitled, "The Narrative of Dr Robert Norris on the Frenzy of J.D." In this, however, he overshot the mark; and Addison signified to him that he was displeased with the spirit of his narrative, an intimation which Pope keenly resented. This scornful dog would not eat the dirty pudding that was graciously flung to him; and Pope found that, without having conciliated Addison, he had made Dennis's furnace of hate against himself seven times hotter than before.

In 1712 appeared "The Messiah," "The Dying Christian to his Soul," "The Temple of Fame," and the "Elegy on the Memory of an Unfortunate Lady." Her story is still involved in mystery. Her name is said to have been Wainsbury. She was attached to a lover above her degree, some say to the Duke of Berry, whom she had met in her early youth in France. In despair of obtaining her desire, she hanged herself. It is curious, if true, that she was as deformed in person as Pope himself. Her family seems to have been noble. In 1713, he published "Windsor Forest," an "Ode on St Cecilia's Day," and several papers in the Guardian—one of them being an exquisitely ironical paper, comparing Phillip's pastorals with his own, and affecting to give them the preference—the extracts being so selected as to damage his rival's claims. This year, also, he wrote, although he did not publish, his fine epistle to Jervas, the painter. Pope was passionately fond of the art of painting, and practised it a good deal under Jervas's instructions, although he did not reach great proficiency. The prodigy has yet to be born who combines the characters of a great painter and a great poet.

About this time, Pope commenced preparations for the great work of translating Homer; and subscription-papers, accordingly, were issued. Dean Swift was now in England, and took a deep interest in the success of this undertaking, recommending it in coffee-houses, and introducing the subject and Pope's name to the leading Tories. Pope met the Dean for the first time in Berkshire, where, in one of his fits of savage disgust at the conflicting parties of the period, he had retired to the house of a clergyman, and an intimacy commenced which was only terminated by death. We have often regretted that Pope had not selected some author more suitable to his genius than Homer. Horace or Lucretius, or even Ovid, would have been more congenial. His imitations of Horace shew us what he might have made of a complete translation. What a brilliant thing a version of Lucretius, in the style of the "Essay on Man," would have been! And his "Rape of the Lock" proves that he had considerable sympathy with the elaborate fancy, although not with the meretricious graces of Ovid. But with Homer, the severely grand, the simple, the warlike, the lover and painter of all Nature's old original forms—the ocean, the mountains, and the stars—what thorough sympathy could a man have who never saw a real mountain or a battle, and whose enthusiasm for scenery was confined to purling brooks, trim gardens, artificial grottos, and the shades of Windsor Forest? Accordingly, his Homer, although a beautiful and sparkling poem, is not a satisfactory translation of the "Iliad," and still less of the "Odyssey." He has trailed along the naked lances of the Homeric lines so many flowers and leaves that you can hardly recognise them, and feel that their point is deadened and their power gone. This at least is our opinion; although many to this day continue to admire these translations, and have even said that if they are not Homer, they are something better.

The "Iliad" took him six years, and was a work which cost him much anxiety as well as labour, the more as his scholarship was far from profound. He was assisted in the undertaking by Parnell (who wrote the Life of Homer), by Broome, Jortin, and others. The first volume appeared in June 1715, and the other volumes followed at irregular intervals. He began it in 1712, his twenty-fifth year, and finished it in 1718, his thirtieth year. Previous to its appearance, his remuneration for his poems had been small, and his circumstances were embarrassed; but the result of the subscription, which amounted to £5320, 4s., rendered him independent for life.

While at Binfield, he had often visited London; and there, in the society of Howe, Garth, Parnell, and the rest, used to indulge in occasional excesses, which did his feeble constitution no good; and once, according to Colley Cibber, he narrowly escaped a serious scrape in a house of a certain description, Colley, by his own account, "helping out the tomtit for the sake of Homer!" This statement, indeed, Pope has denied; but his veracity was by no means his strongest point. After writing a "Farewell to London," he retired, in 1715, to Twickenham, along with his parents; and remained there, cultivating his garden, digging his grottos, and diversifying his walks, till the end of his days.

Some years before, he had become acquainted with Lady Mary Wortley Montague, the most brilliant woman of her age—witty, fascinating, beautiful, and accomplished—full of enterprise and spirit, too, although decidedly French in her tastes, manners, and character. Pope fell violently in love with her, and had her undoubtedly in his eye when writing "Eloisa and Abelard," which he did at Oxford in 1716, shortly after her going abroad, and which appeared the next year. His passion was not requited, nay, was treated with contempt and ridicule; and he became in after years a bitter enemy and foul-mouthed detractor of the lady, although after her return, in 1718, she resided near him at Twickenham, and they seemed outwardly on good terms.

In 1717, and the succeeding year, Pope lost successively his father, Parnell, Garth, and Rowe, and bitterly felt their loss. He finished, as we have seen, the "Iliad" in 1718; but the fifth and sixth volumes, which were the last, did not appear till 1720. Its success, which at the time was triumphant, roused against him the whole host of envy and detraction. Dennis, and all Grub Street with him, were moved to assail him. Pamphlets after pamphlets were published, all of which, after reading with writhing anguish, Pope had the resolution to bind up into volumes—a great collection of calumny, which he preserved, probably, for purposes of future revenge. His own friends, on the other hand, hailed his work with applause, Gay writing a most graceful and elegant poem, in ottava rima, entitled, "Mr Pope's Welcome Home from Greece," in which his different friends are pictured as receiving him home on the shores of Britain, after an absence of six years. Bentley, that stern old Grecian, avoided the extremes of a howling Grub Street on the one hand, and a flattering aristocracy on the other, and expressed what is, we think, the just opinion when he said, "It is a pretty poem, but it is not Homer."

In 1721, he issued a selection from the poems of Parnell, and prefixed a very beautiful dedication to the Earl of Oxford, commencing with—

"Such were the notes thy once-loved poet sung,
Till death untimely stopp'd his tuneful tongue.
Oh, just beheld and lost, admired and mourn'd,
With softest manners, gentlest arts adorn'd!"

In 1722, he engaged to translate the "Odyssey." He employed Broome and Fenton as his assistants in the work; and the portions translated by them were thought as good as his. He remunerated them very handsomely. Of this work, the first three quarto volumes appeared in 1725; and the fourth and fifth, which completed the work, the following year. Pope sold the copyright to Lintot for £600.

He was busy at this time, too, with an edition of Shakspeare, not quite worthy of either poet. It appeared in six volumes, quarto, in 1725. His preface was good, but he was deficient in antiquarian lore; and his mortification was extreme when Theobald, destined to figure in "The Dunciad," a mere plodding hack, not only in his "Shakspeare Restored," exposed many blunders in Pope's edition; but issued, some years afterwards, an edition of his own, which was much better received by the public.

In 1726, there was a great gathering of the Tory wits at Twickenham. Swift had come from Ireland, and resided for some time with Pope. Bolingbroke came over occasionally from Dawley; and Gay was often there to laugh with, and be laughed at by, the rest. Swift had "Gulliver's Travels"—the most ingenious and elaborate libel against man and God ever written—in his pocket, nearly ready for publication; and we may conceive the grim, sardonic smile with which he read it to his friends, and their tumultuous mirth. Gay was projecting his "Beggars' Opera," and Pope preparing some of his witty "Miscellanies." At the end of two months, the Dean was hurried home by the tidings of Stella's illness. He left the "Travels" behind him, for the copyright of which Pope procured £300, a sum counted then very large, and which Swift generously handed over to Pope.

In September this year, when returning in Lord Bolingbroke's coach from Dawley, the poet was overturned in a little rivulet near Twickenhan, and nearly drowned. The unfortunate little man! One is reminded of Gulliver's accident in the Brobdignagian cream-pot. In trying to break the glasses of the coach, which were down, he severely cut his right hand, and lost the use of two of his fingers, an addition to his other deformities not very desirable; and we suspect that Pope thought Voltaire (who had met him at Bolingbroke's) but a miserable comforter, when, in a letter of pretended condolence, he asked—"Is it possible that those fingers which have written 'The Rape of the Lock,' and dressed Homer so becomingly in an English coat, should have been so barbarously treated? Let the hand of Dennis or of your poetasters be cut off; yours is sacred." It was perhaps in keeping that those mutilated fingers were soon to be employed in attacking Dennis, and that the embittered poet was about, with the half of his hand, but with the whole of his heart, to write "The Dunciad."

In the end of April 1727, we find Swift again in Twickenham, where his irritation at the continued ascendancy of Sir Robert Walpole served to infuse more venom into the "Miscellanies" concocted between him and Pope, two volumes of which appeared in June this year. Gay, also, and the ingenious and admirable Dr Arbuthnot, contributed their quota to these volumes. Swift speedily fell ill with that giddiness and deafness which were the avant-couriers of his final malady; and in August he left Twickenham, and in October, London and England, for ever.

In these "Miscellanies" there appeared the famous "Memoirs of Martinus Scriblerus," written chiefly by Pope, in which he lashed the various proficients in the bathos, under the names of flying fishes, swallows, parrots, frogs, eels, &c., and appended the initials of well-known authors to each head. This roused Grub Street, whose malice had nearly fallen asleep, into fresh fury, and he was bitterly assailed in every possible form. Like Hyder Ali, he now—to travesty Burke—"in the recesses of a mind capacious of such things, determined to leave all Duncedom an everlasting monument of vengeance, and became at length so confident of his force, so collected in his might, that he made no secret whatever of his dreadful resolution, but, compounding all the materials of fun, sarcasm, irony, and invective, into one black cloud, he hung for a while on the declivities of Richmond Hill; and whilst the authors were idly and stupidly gazing on this menacing meteor which blackened all their horizon, it suddenly burst and poured down the whole of its contents on the garrets of Grub Street. Then issued a scene of (ludicrous) woe, the like of which no eye had seen, no heart conceived, and which no tongue can adequately tell. All the horrors of literary war before known or heard of—(MacFlecknoe, the Rehearsal, &c.)—were mercy to the new tempest of havoc which burst from the brain of this remorseless poet. A storm of universal laughter filled every bookseller's shop, and penetrated into the remotest attics. The miserable dunces, in part, were stricken mad with rage—in part, dumb with consternation. Some fled for refuge to ale, and others to ink; while not a few fell, or feared to fall, into the 'jaws of famine.'" This singular poem was written in 1727. It was first printed surreptitiously (i.e., with the connivance of the author) in Dublin, and then reprinted in London. The first perfect edition, however, did not appear in London till 1729. On the day of its publication, according to Pope, a crowd of authors besieged the publisher's shop; and by entreaties, threats, nay, cries of treason, tried to hinder its appearance. What a scene it must have been—of teeth gnashing above ragged coats, and eyes glaring through old periwigs—of faces livid with famine and ferocity; while, to complete the confusion, hawkers, booksellers, and even lords, were mixed with the crowd, clamouring for its issue! And as, says Pope, "there is no stopping a torrent with a finger, out it came." The consequence he had foreseen. A universal howl of rage and pain burst from the aggrieved dunces, on whose naked sides the hot pitch had fallen. They pushed their rejoinders beyond the limits of civilised literary warfare; and although Pope had been coarse in his language, they were coarser far, and their blackguardism was not redeemed by wit or genius. Pope felt, or seemed to feel, entire indifference as to these assaults. On some of them, indeed, he could afford to look down with contempt, on account of their obvious animus and gross language. Others, again, were neutralised by the fact, that their authors had provoked reprisals by their previous insults or ingratitude to Pope. Many, however, were too obscure for his notice; and some, such as Aaron Hill and Bentley, did not deserve to be classed with the Theobalds and Ralphs. To Hill, he, after some finessing, was compelled to make an apology. Altogether, although this production increased Pope's fame, and the conception of his power, it did not tend to shew him in the most amiable light, or perhaps to promote his own comfort or peace of mind. After having emptied out his bile in "The Dunciad," he ought to have become mellower in temper, and resigned satire for ever. He continued, on the contrary, as ill-natured as before; and although he afterwards flew at higher game, the iron had entered into his soul, and he remained a satirist, and therefore an unhappy man, for life.

In 1731 appeared an "Epistle on Taste," which was very favourably received; only his enemies accused him of having satirised the Duke of Chandos in it, a man who had befriended Pope, and had lent him money. Pope denied the charge, although it is very possible, both from his own temperament, and from the frequent occurrence of similar cases of baseness in literary life, that it may have been true. Nothing is more common than for those who have been most liberally helped, to become first the secret, and then the open, enemies of their benefactors. In 1732 appeared his epistle on "The Use of Riches," addressed to Lord Bathurst. These two epistles were afterwards incorporated in his "Moral Essays."

As far back as 1725, Pope had been revolving the subject of the "Essay on Man;" and, indeed, some of its couplets remind you of "pebbles which had long been rolled over and polished in the ocean of his mind." It has been asserted, but not proved, that Lord Bolingbroke gave him the outline of this essay in prose. It is unquestionable, indeed, that Bolingbroke exercised influence over Pope's mind, and may have suggested some of the thoughts in the Essay; but it is not probable that a man like Pope would have set himself on such a subject simply to translate from another's mind. He published the first epistle of the Essay, in 1732, anonymously, as an experiment, and had the satisfaction to see it successful. It was received with rapture, and passed through several editions ere the author was known; although we must say that the value of this reception is considerably lessened, when we remember that the critics could not have been very acute who did not detect Pope's "fine Roman hand" in every sentence of this brilliant but most unsatisfactory and shallow performance.

In the same year died dear, simple-minded Gay, who found in Pope a sincere mourner, and an elegant elegiast; and on the 7th of June 1733, expired good old Mrs Pope, at the age of ninety-four. Pope, who had always been a dutiful son, erected an obelisk in his own grounds to her memory, with a simple but striking inscription in Latin. During this year, he published the third part of the "Essay on Man," an epistle to Lord Cobham, On the Knowledge and Characters of Man, and an Imitation of the First Satire of the Second Book of Horace. In this last, he attacks, in the most brutal style, his former love Lady Mary W. Montague, who replied in a piece of coarse cleverness, entitled, "Verses to the Imitator of the First Satire of the Second Book of Horace,"—verses in which she was assisted by Lord Harvey, another of Pope's victims. He wrote, but was prudent enough to suppress, an ironical reply.

In 1734 appeared his very clever and highly-finished epistle to Dr Arbuthnot (now entitled the "Prologue to the Satires"), who was then languishing toward death. Arbuthnot, from his deathbed, solemnly advised Pope to regulate his satire, and seems to have been afraid of his personal safety from his numerous foes. Pope replied in a manly but self-defensive style. He is said about this time to have in his walks carried arms, and had a large dog as his protector; but none of the dunces had courage enough to assail him. Dennis, who was no dunce, might have ventured on it—but he had become miserably infirm, poor, and blind; and Pope had heaped coals of fire on his head, by contributing a Prologue to a play which was acted for his behoof.

Our author's life becomes now little else than a record of multiplying labours and increasing infirmities. In 1734 appeared the fourth part of the "Essay on Man," and the Second Satire of the Second Book of Horace. In 1735 were issued his "Characters of Women: An Epistle to a Lady" (Martha Blount). In this appears his famous character of Atossa—the Duchess of Marlborough. It is said—we fear too truly—that these lines being shewn to her Grace, as a character of the Duchess of Buckingham, she recognised in them her own likeness, and bribed Pope with a thousand pounds to suppress it. He did so religiously—as long as she was alive—and then published it! In the same year he printed a second volume of his "Miscellaneous Works," in folio and quarto, uniform with the "Iliad" and "Odyssey," including a versification of the Satires of Donne; also, anonymously, a production disgraceful to his memory, entitled, "Sober Advice from Horace to the Young Gentlemen about Town," in which he commits many gross indecorums of language, and annexes the name of the great Bentley to several indecent notes. It is said that Bentley, when he read the pamphlet, cried, "'Tis an impudent dog, but I talked against his Homer, and the portentous cub never forgives."

The "Essay on Man" and the "Moral Epistles" were designed to be parts of a great system of ethics, which Pope had long revolved in his mind, and wished to incarnate in poetry. At this time occurred the strange, mysterious circumstances connected with the publication of his letters. It seems that, in 1729, Pope had recalled from his correspondents the letters he had written them, of many of which he had kept no copies. He was induced to this by the fact, that after Henry Cromwell's death, his mistress, Mrs Thomas, who was in indigent circumstances, had sold the letters which had passed between Pope and her keeper, to Curll the bookseller, who had published them without scruple. When Pope obtained his correspondence, he, according to his own statement, burned a great many and laid past the others, after having had a copy of them taken, and deposited in Lord Oxford's library. And his charge against Curll was, that he obtained surreptitiously some of these letters, and published them without Pope's consent. But, ere we come to the circumstances of the publication, several other things require to be noticed. In 1733, Curll, anxious to publish a Life of Pope, advertised for information; and, in consequence, one P.T., who professed to be an old friend of Pope's and his father's, wrote Curll a letter, giving an account of Pope's ancestry, which tallied exactly with what Pope himself, in a note to one of his poems, furnished the following year. P.T., in a second letter, offered to the publisher a large collection of Pope's letters, and inclosed a copy of an advertisement he had drawn out to be published by Curll. Strange as it seems, Curll took no notice of the proposal till 1735, when, having accidentally turned up a copy of P.T.'s advertisement, he sent it to Pope, with a letter requesting an interview, and mentioning that he had some papers of P.T.'s in reference to his family history, which he would shew him. Pope replied by three advertisements in the papers, denying all knowledge of P.T. or his collection of letters or MSS. P.T. then wrote Curll that he had printed the letters at his own expense, seeking a sum of money for them, and appointing an interview at a tavern to shew him the sheets. This was countermanded the next day, P.T. professing to be afraid of Pope and his "bravoes," although how Pope was to know of this meeting was, according to Curll, "the cream of the jest."

Soon after, a round, fat man, with a clergyman's gown and a barrister's band, called on Curll, at ten o'clock at night. He said his name was Smith, that he was a cousin of P.T.'s, and shewed the book in sheets, along with about a dozen of the original letters. After a good deal of negotiation with this personage, Curll obtained fifty copies of P.T.'s printed copies, and issued a flaming advertisement announcing the publication of Pope's letters for thirty years, and stating that the original MSS. were lying at his shop, and might be seen by any who chose, although not a single MS. seems to have been delivered. Smith, the day that the advertisement appeared, handed over, for a sum of money, about three hundred volumes to Curll. But as in the advertisement it was stated that various letters of lords were included, and as there is a law amongst regulations of the Upper House that no peer's letters can be published without his consent, at the instance of the Earl of Jersey, and in consequence, too, of an advertisement of Pope's, the books were seized, and Curll, and the printer of the paper where the advertisement appeared, were ordered to appear at the bar for breach of privilege. P.T. wrote Curll to tell him to conceal all that passed between him and the publisher, and promising him more valuable letters still. Curll, however, told the whole story; and as, when the books were examined, not a single lord's letter was found among them, Curll was acquitted, his books restored to him, the lords saying that they had been made the tools of Pope; and he proceeded to advertise the correspondence, in terms most insulting to Pope, who now felt himself compelled (!) to print, by subscription, his genuine letters, which, when printed, turned out, strange to tell, to be identical with those published by the rapacious bookseller! On viewing the whole transaction, we incline with Johnson, Warton, Bowles, Macaulay, and Carruthers, to look upon it as one of Pope's ape-like stratagems—to believe that P.T. was himself, Smith his agent, and that his objects were partly to outwit Curll, to mystify the public, to gratify that strange love of manoeuvring which dwelt as strongly in him as in any match-making mamma, and to attract interest and attention to the genuine correspondence when it should appear. Pope, it was said, could not "drink tea without a stratagem," and far less publish his correspondence without a series of contemptible tricks—tricks, however, in which he was true to his nature—that being a curious compound of the woman and the wit, the monkey and the genius.

In 1737, four of his Imitations of Horace were published, and in the next year appeared two Dialogues, each entitled "1738," which now form the Epilogue to the Satires. One of them was issued on the same day with Johnson's "London." In that year, too, he published his "Universal Prayer,"—a singular specimen of latitudinarian thought, expressed in a loose simplicity of language, quite unusual with its author. The next year he had intended to signalise by a third Dialogue, which he commenced in a vigorous style, but which he did not finish, owing to the dread of a prosecution before the Lords; and with the exception of letters (one of them interesting, as his last to Swift), his pen was altogether idle. In 1740, he did nothing but edit an edition of select Italian Poets. This year, Crousaz, a Swiss professor of note, having attacked (we think most justly) the "Essay on Man" as a mere Pagan prolusion—a thin philosophical smile cast on the Gordian knot of the mystery of the universe, instead of a sword cutting, or trying to cut, it in sunder—Warburton, a man of much talent and learning, but of more astuteness and anxiety to exalt himself, came forward to the rescue, and, with a mixture of casuistical cunning and real ingenuity, tried, as some one has it, "to make Pope a Christian," although, even in Warburton's hands, like the dying Donald Bane in "Waverley," he "makes but a queer Christian after all;" and his system, essentially Pantheistic, contrives to ignore the grand Scripture principles of a Fall, of a Divine Redeemer, of a Future World, and the glorious light or darkness which these and other Christian doctrines cast upon the Mystery of Man. If, however, Warburton, with all his scholastic subtlety, failed to make Pope a Christian, he made him a warm friend; Allen, Pope's acquaintance, a rich father-in-law; and himself, by and by, the Bishop of Gloucester. Sophistry has seldom, although sometimes, been thus richly rewarded.

The last scene of Pope's tiny and tortured existence was now at hand. But ere it closed, it must close like Dryden's, characteristically, with an author's quarrel. Colley Cibber had long been a favourite of Pope's ire, and had as often retorted scorn, till at last, by laughing upon the stage at Pope's play (partly Gay's), entitled, "Three Hours After Marriage," he roused the bard almost to frenzy; and Pope set to work to remodel "The Dunciad;" and, dethroning Theobald, set up Cibber as the lawful King of the Dull, a most unfortunate substitution, since, while Theobald was the ideal of stolid, solemn stupidity, Cibber was gay, light, pert, and clever; full of pluck, too, and who overflowed in reply, with pamphlets which gave Pope both a headache and a heartache whenever he perused them.

Pope had never been strong, and for many years the variety and multitude of his frailties had been increasing. He had habitually all his life been tormented with headaches, for which he found the steam of strong coffee the chief remedy. He had hurt his stomach, too, by indulging in excess of stimulating viands, such as potted lampreys, and in copious and frequent drams. He was assailed at last by dropsy and asthma; and on the 30th of May 1744, he breathed his last, fifty-six years of age. He had long, he said, "been tired of the world," and died with philosophic composure and serenity. He took the sacrament according to the form of the Roman Catholic Church; but merely, he said, because it "looked right." A little before his death, he called for his desk, and began an essay on the immortality of the soul, and on those material things which tend to weaken or to strengthen it for immortality, enumerating generous wines as among the latter influences, and spirituous liquors among the former! His last words were, "There is nothing that is meritorious but virtue and friendship; and, indeed, friendship itself is only a part of virtue." Thus, "motionless and moanless," without a word about Christ—the slightest syllable of repentance—and with a scrap of heathen morality in his mouth, died the brilliant Alexander Pope. Who is ready to say, "May my last end be like his"? His favourite Martha Blount behaved, according to some accounts, with disgusting unconcern on the occasion. So true it is, "there is no friendship among the wicked," even although the heartless Bolingbroke, too, was by, and seems to have succeeded in squeezing out some crocodile tears, as he bent over the dying poet, and said, "O God! what is man?" His remains were, according to his wish, deposited in Twickenham church, near his parents, where the single letter P on the stone alone distinguishes the spot.

Pope's character, apart from his poetry, which we intend criticising in our next volume, was not specially interesting or elevated. He was a spoiled child, a small self-tormentor, full to bursting with petty spites, mean animosities, and unfounded jealousies. While he sought, with the fury of a pampered slave, to trample on those authors that were beneath him in rank or in popularity, he could on all occasions fawn with the sycophancy of a eunuch upon the noble, the rich, and the powerful. Hazlitt speaks of Moore as a "pug-dog barking from the lap of a lady of quality at inferior passengers." The description is far more applicable to Pope. We have much allowance to make for the influence exerted on his mind by his singularly crooked frame and sickly habit of body, by his position as belonging to a proscribed faith, and by his want of training in a public school; but after all these deductions, we cannot but deplore the spectacle of one of the finest, clearest, and sharpest minds that England ever produced, so frequently reminding you of a bright sting set in the body, and steeped in the venom, of a wasp. And yet, withal, he possessed many virtues, which endeared him to a multitude of friends. He was a kind son. He was a faithful and devoted friend. He loved, if not man, yet many men with deep tenderness. A keen politician he was not; but, so far as he went along with his party, he was true to the common cause. In morals, he was greatly superior, in point of external decorum, to most of the wits of the time; but in falsehood, finesse, treachery, and envy, he stood at the bottom of the list, without that plea of poverty, or wretchedness, or despair, which so many of them might have urged. Uneasy, indeed, he always, and unhappy he often, was; but very much of his uneasiness and unhappiness sprung from his own fault. He attacked others, and could not bear to be attacked in return. He was a bully and a coward. He threw himself into a thorn-hedge, and was amazed that he came out covered with scratches and blood. While he shone in satirising many kinds of vice, he laid himself open to retort by his own want of delicacy. He, as well as Swift, was fond of alluding in his verse to polluted and forbidden things. There, and there alone, his taste deserted him; and there is something disgusting and unnatural in the combination of the elegant and the obscene—the coarse in sentiment and the polished in style. And whatever may be said for many of the amiable traits of the Man, there is very little to be said for the general tendency—so far as healthy morality and Christian principle are concerned—of the writings of the Poet.

Alexander Pope – A Concise Bibliography

The Major works
Pastorals (1709)
An Essay on Criticism (1711)
Messiah (1712)
The Rape of the Lock (1712 and enlarged in 1714)
Windsor Forest (1713)
Translation of the Iliad (1715-1720)
Eloisa to Abelard (1717)
Three Hours After Marriage, with others (1717)
Elegy to the Memory of an Unfortunate Lady (1717)
The Works of Shakespear, in Six Volumes (1723-1725)
Translation of the Odyssey (1725-1726)
Peri Bathous, Or the Art of Sinking in Poetry (1727)
The Dunciad (1728)
Essay on Man (1733-1734)
The Prologue to the Satires (1735)

www.ingramcontent.com/pod-product-compliance
Lightning Source LLC
Chambersburg PA
CBHW062148080426
42734CB00010B/1602